Bust to Boom?
The Irish Experience of Growth and Inequality

BUST TO BOOM?
THE IRISH EXPERIENCE OF
GROWTH AND INEQUALITY

Edited by
Brian Nolan, Philip J. O'Connell
and Christopher T. Whelan

IPA
INSTITUTE OF PUBLIC
ADMINISTRATION

First published 2000
Institute of Public Administration
57–61 Lansdowne Road
Dublin 4
Ireland

ISBN   HB: 1 902448 49 9
           PB: 1 902448 48 0

British Library Cataloguing-in-Publication Data
A catalogue record for this book is available from the British Library.

Cover design by Creative Inputs
Typeset in 10/12.5 Times Roman by Carole Lynch, Dublin
Printed by Johnswood Press

Contents

Acknowledgements   vii
Notes on authors   viii
Foreword   xii

1 Introduction
Brian Nolan, Philip J. O'Connell and Christopher T. Whelan   1

2 The Irish economy in comparative perspective
John Bradley   4

3 The story of Ireland's failure – and belated success
John Fitz Gerald   27

4 The dynamics of the Irish labour market in comparative perspective
Philip J. O'Connell   58

5 The rising tide and equality of opportunity: the changing class structure
Richard Layte and Christopher T. Whelan   90

6 Education and inequality
Emer Smyth and Damian F. Hannan   109

7 Earnings inequality, returns to education and low pay
Alan Barrett, John Fitz Gerald and Brian Nolan   127

8 Income inequality
Brian Nolan and Bertrand Maître   147

9 Trends in Poverty
Richard Layte, Brian Nolan and Christopher T. Whelan   163

10 Taxation and social welfare
Tim Callan and Brian Nolan   179

11 Cumulative disadvantage and polarisation
Richard Layte, Brian Nolan and Christopher T. Whelan   204

12 The spatial distribution of disadvantage in Ireland
Tony Fahey and James Williams   223

13 Gender equality, fertility decline and labour market patterns
    among women in Ireland
    Tony Fahey, Helen Russell and Emer Smyth   244

14 Political culture, growth and the conditions for success in the Irish
    economy
    Rona Fitzgerald and Brian Girvin   268

15 Social partnership, wage bargaining, and growth
    Niamh Hardiman   286

16 The role of the state in growth and welfare
    Seán Ó Riain and Philip J. O'Connell   310

17 Conclusion: the Irish experience of growth and inequality
    Brian Nolan, Philip J. O'Connell and Christopher T. Whelan 340

    Bibliography   354

Acknowledgements

Many debts have been accumulated in bringing this book to publication, which we wish to acknowledge on behalf of the contributors as well as the editors. We received unfailing encouragement and support from the Director of The Economic and Social Research Institute, Brendan Whelan. Colleagues at the ESRI have contributed a great deal to the formulations of the ideas presented, through comments on draft material, at seminars and informal discussion; Dorothy Watson has also played a central role in producing the survey data from the Living in Ireland Surveys, carried out by the ESRI, on which many of the authors rely. Frank Barry of the Department of Economics, University College Dublin has been extremely generous in helping us develop the book and debate the issues. We are grateful to the Institute of Public Administration, to Jim Power and Eleanor Ashe, and in particular to Tony McNamara for his assistance throughout in the production of the book. Finally, we wish to thank Merike Darmody for the efficiency and good humour with which she turned typescript from multiple authors into a seamless whole and provided support to the editors throughout.

Notes on Authors

JOHN BRADLEY is a Research Professor at the ESRI. He has published widely in the areas of domestic and EU policy analysis, having specialised in the development of formal economic models and their application to medium-term forecasting, the causes of unemployment, the impact of fiscal restructuring, and the impact of major EU policy initiatives. Among his recent publications are *Single Market Review 1996: Aggregate and regional impacts: the cases of Greece, Ireland, Portugal and Spain* (1997), *Regional Economic and Policy Impacts of EMU: The Case of Northern Ireland* (1998).

ALAN BARRETT is a Senior Research Officer at the ESRI. His areas of interest are Labour Economics and Environmental Economics. Dr Barrett is currently continuing his work on migration and in particular is looking at return migration into Ireland. He is also involved in a study on male-female wage differentials. He has published recently *The Impact of Agricultural and Forestry Subsidies on Land Prices and Land Uses in Ireland* with W. Trace (1999), and is co-author of *Exploring the Returns to Continuing Vocational Training in Enterprises* (1998).

TIM CALLAN is a Research Professor at the ESRI where he works on tax and social welfare policy, poverty and labour market issues. He has carried out a range of studies of labour supply behaviour, incentives to work, the incentive and distributional effects of tax and social welfare, and the economics of child care. Professor Callan's recent joint publications include *Income Tax and Social Welfare Policies* (1999), *Monitoring Poverty Trends, National Anti-Poverty Strategy* (1999), *Tax and Welfare Changes, Poverty and Work Incentives in Ireland, 1987-1994* (1999) and many others.

TONY FAHEY is a Senior Research Officer at the ESRI. He has published extensively on a range of topics, particularly the family, demography, the elderly, housing and various aspects of social policy. His most recent book, co-authored with John Fitz Gerald, is *Welfare Implications of Demographic Trends* (1997).

JOHN FITZ GERALD is a Research Professor at the ESRI. He specialises in applied macro-economic research, macro-economic modelling, and policy evaluation, and has also worked on the analysis of demographic patterns and educational participation and on the economics of energy use and its taxation. He is joint author of the ESRI's *Medium Term Review.*

RONA FITZGERALD is a Research Fellow at the European Policies Research Centre, University of Strathclyde. She is a political scientist by training and her recent work has focused on regional policy and the structural funds and the integration process in Europe.

BRIAN GIRVIN is a Professor in the Department of Politics, University of Glasgow, Scotland. His current research interests are concentrated on nationalism in comparative context, Irish nationalism and political culture and on conservative politics in the United States since the 1960s. His publications include *Between two Worlds: Politics and Economy in Independent Ireland* (1989), joint editorship of *Small States and the International System: Denmark, Ireland and the Integration Process in Europe* (forthcoming).

NIAMH HARDIMAN currently lectures in the Politics Department in University College Dublin. Her research interests are in political culture and comparative political economy, particularly labour movements and welfare states. Author of a number of articles on the politics of economic policy and organised interests in Ireland. She is currently working on a book examining institutional and policy-making features of the Irish state.

DAMIAN HANNAN is a Research Professor at the ESRI. He has published a number of studies of second-level schooling in Ireland, including *Co-education and Gender Equality, The Quality of Their Education, Schooling and Sex Roles.* More recently he has published *Trading Qualifications for Jobs.*

RICHARD LAYTE is a Research Officer at the ESRI. His main areas of interest are economic sociology, the methodology of health measurement and the implications of unemployment and insecure work for mental and physical health. He has recently published *Income, Deprivation and Well-Being among Older Irish People* with T. Fahey and C. Whelan (2000) and is the author of *Divided Time: Gender, Paid Employment and Domestic Labour* (1999).

BERTRAND MAÎTRE is a Statistical Analyst at the ESRI. He carries out analysis of the Living in Ireland and European Community Household Panel data across a range of projects. His current research focuses on poverty and income distribution. He is co-author of *Monitoring Poverty Trends* (1999), and other publications.

BRIAN NOLAN is a Research Professor at the ESRI. He has published extensively in the areas of poverty, income inequality, tax and social welfare policy, and the labour market. His most recent publication is *Child Poverty* (2000). He is joint editor of *Poverty and Policy in Ireland* (1994), and co-author of *Resources, Deprivation and Poverty* (1996), *Poverty in the 1990s* (1996), and many others. He is currently working on a programme of research on poverty and income inequality based on the European Community Household Panel Survey, and on a number of collaborative cross-country research projects on low pay, earnings inequality, and unemployment.

PHILIP J. O'CONNELL is a Senior Research Officer at the ESRI. He has published widely on training and labour market issues and is joint author of *Working Schemes? Active Labour Market Policy in Ireland* (1997) and editor of *Labour Market Studies: Ireland* (1996), and *Astonishing Success: Economic Growth and the Labour Market in Ireland* (1999). He is currently co-editing a new volume, *Education, Training and Employment Dynamics: Transitional Labour Markets in the European Union*, for publication in 2000. He is an associate editor of the *Economic and Social Review* and a member of the editorial board of *Work, Employment and Society.*

SEÁN Ó RIAIN is Assistant Professor of Sociology at the University of California, Davis. His research investigates the political institutions of economic globalisation, and in particular the role of the state in economic development and a recent article on this topic was published in *Politics and Society.* He also carries out research on work, inequality and economic democracy.

HELEN RUSSELL is a Research Officer at the ESRI. Her main areas of interest are gender, labour market disadvantage, work attitudes and social inequality. She has researched and published comparative studies of life satisfaction among the unemployed *(European Journal of Sociology)*, work values and work commitment (*British and European Social Attitudes,* 1998), and gender, welfare regimes and the experience of unemployment. She is currently working on issues of disadvantage in the Irish labour market.

EMER SMYTH is a Senior Research Officer at the ESRI. Her research interests centre on education, school to work transitions and women's employment. She has worked on a large-scale national study of the impact of co-education on pupil outcomes, published as *Co-education and Gender Equality.* More recently she has published an extensive study of school effectiveness in Ireland, *Do Schools Differ?*

CHRISTOPHER T. WHELAN is a Research Professor at the ESRI. He is joint author of *Understanding Contemporary Ireland* (1990), *Social Mobility and Social Class in Ireland* (1994) and *Resources, Deprivation and Poverty* (1996). He is a joint editor of *Values and Social Change in Ireland* and *Ireland North and South* (1999). He is an associate editor of the *European Sociological Review* and has published on a variety of topics in international journals.

JAMES WILLIAMS is a Senior Research Officer at the ESRI. His main research interests include survey techniques and methodology, regional development, poverty and geographic information systems. His most recent publications have been on a range of topics including income distribution, poverty and survey techniques. His main research interests include survey methodology and sample design poverty and income distribution, Geographic Information Systems (GIS) and regional development.

Foreword

This year the Economic and Social Research Institute celebrates the fortieth anniversary of its foundation. During that time the Institute has produced hundreds of papers, reports and books analysing every aspect of Ireland's economy and society. The themes of this work have varied in response to national and international developments. In the early 1960s, the focus was primarily on the management of the economy and on economic development. In the 1970s, the ESRI's perspective broadened to include social issues, reflecting the growing national consciousness of these questions. The main preoccupations of the 1980s were with spiralling unemployment and fiscal imbalances and the search for an enduring solution. In the 1990s, our work concentrated on the development of the economy especially in the context of EU developments such as the Single Market, the Structural Funds and Economic and Monetary Union, as well as on a variety of social themes such as poverty, healthcare and education. Throughout its forty years, ESRI research has formed an important component of the national debate on economic and social topics and continues to figure prominently in the media and in discussions of policy and planning.

The present book exemplifies many of the qualities to which we aspire in carrying out our work. It is thoroughly grounded in the current international literature of the various disciplines. Thus, the reader will find in it new insights into some of the key debates in modern social science such as the nature of economic convergence, the effect of globalisation on a small open economy, the functioning of the modern welfare state and the processes which determine poverty and inequality. The discussion is clear and accessible and the authors systematically address issues relevant to policy and its effectiveness.

A characteristic of Institute work in recent years of which we are particularly proud is the level of interdisciplinary collaboration which we have managed to attain. The present volume contains contributions from economists, sociologists, statisticians and political scientists. Their collaboration goes far beyond mere juxtaposition; there is genuine cross-disciplinary transfer of insights and ideas from one field to another. The participation by researchers from outside the Institute, and from outside Ireland, is to be welcomed, and has also been a feature of our recent work.

A final aspect of the book to which I would like to direct attention is the extent to which it draws on an established body of work in the form of models, databases and previous research. The painstaking accumulation of facts and meticulous checking of proposed explanations are at the heart of good research. A fundamental objective of the Institute is to provide the continuity needed for in-depth, strategic work of this kind. The book is an excellent example of the returns which such long-term investment can yield.

I would like to congratulate the authors and the editors on the quality of the book which will, I am sure, be read with keen interest both in Ireland and abroad.

Brendan J. Whelan
Director

1

Introduction

BRIAN NOLAN, PHILIP J. O'CONNELL AND CHRISTOPHER T. WHELAN

The performance of the Irish economy over the past decade has been the source of considerable international attention. The 'Celtic Tiger' label has been applied with what is now monotonous regularity despite providing an entirely misleading indication of the nature of the beast. In this volume we seek to take a longer-term perspective on the Irish growth experience and its social consequences. This requires that we understand Ireland's past failures as well as its current success. In this context we will consider the argument that the current boom is best seen as involving belated catching up. However, if this longer-term perspective provides an antidote to accounts of Irish success that place undue emphasis on the specific details of more recent policy initiatives, it is important that the latter emphasis is not replaced by notions of inexorable convergence, whatever their ideological flavour.

In order to understand the interest that has been generated by the Irish case it is necessary to locate it in the context of the recent debate on globalisation. While globalisation affects all states in the international economy its implications are particularly profound for small open economies. Irish success is seen as dependent on achieving competitiveness in internationally traded sectors and thus holds out the prospect of prescriptions that go beyond the Irish case. What is interesting about the Irish case is not spectacular growth rates as such but the evidence it provides that sustained development can be achieved by a combination of factors that, in principle, are available to other countries.

Over the past four decades Ireland has pursued an uninterrupted strategy of increasing integration into the world economy. Policy-making autonomy, as in the case of other small nations wishing to be part of the international economy, is now heavily circumscribed. However, the Irish growth experience and its distributional consequences is not a simple story of globalisation, forced withdrawal of the state and the promotion of neo-liberalism. The strategy of economic development pursued in Ireland since the 1960s has involved the opening up of the goods and capital markets as part of the long-term process of EU integration. However, there was a great deal more to Ireland's success than liberalisation of markets. The state has been deeply implicated in the entire process, managing both economic development and the welfare state. The most dramatic changes have taken place under the guidance of neo-corporatist arrangements.

There remain a variety of ways of connecting to the global economy with significantly different implications. Globalisation is not an entirely new phenomenon and while states have always been confronted by international constraints they have retained sufficient autonomy and capacity to pursue national agendas. Indeed extreme vulnerability to international forces was precisely what led small European nations to develop distinctive strategies in the post World War Two period. The openness and vulnerability of their economies has required the development of strategies that are flexible, reactive and developmental.

The achievement of Irish economists in locating the Irish growth experience in the context of wider models of small open economies is an essential building block in any more ambitious socio-economic interpretation of Irish society. Any such explanation must acknowledge the reality of external constraints. However, portraits of Irish society that see recent change as simply an acceleration of the movement from insularity to openness tend to be based on the assumption of convergence rather than any systematic testing of the hypothesis. A more adequate understanding can be achieved by an approach that views social and economic change in Ireland in the context of a contingent set of interactions between internal objectives and strategies and the international context. A historical perspective shows this to be as true for 'traditional' as for 'modern' Ireland.

An analysis of the Irish case in the context of recent theoretical ideas relating to globalisation requires that we move beyond notions of convergence or inexorable accommodation to external influences. Thus the changes set in motion in Ireland in the late 1950s involved an admission that an experiment in self-sufficiency had failed. The palpable sense of failure and the deepening malaise led to a new strategy. The adoption of this strategy was based on a particular understanding of the opportunities and constraints associated with an increasing openness to the international economic environment. However, it was at all stages influenced by the balance of domestic interests – economic, cultural and political. Similarly, the social partnership arrangement that emerged from the fiscal crisis of the late 1980s reflected the weakened position of the trade unions and their observation of developments in the United Kingdom, but also a new understanding on their part of the nature of the economic crisis and the appropriate response to it. The development of a shared understanding of key economic mechanisms and relationships is arguably the most crucial output from the partnership process.

Recently attention has been focused in the international literature, by authors who seek to formulate a 'third path solution' to accumulation/legitimacy problems, on the need to construct an alternative to the neo-liberal welfare state as reflected in terms such as 'progressive competition' and 'co-operative-regulation'. An enhancement of our understanding of such issues would benefit from in-depth analysis of the conflicts occurring in particular systems which draws on the insights of welfare regime theory but also takes into account the broader political economy of particular regimes. The Irish case would seem to provide just such an opportunity. The position we have adopted is one that argues that the state plays a central role in the shaping of developmental *and* distribution outcomes. However, we treat each of these state roles as largely referring to the relatively distinct and identifiable institutional realms of industrial and economic development policy and welfare state policy. Each may have a relatively autonomous logic but developments in one sphere may be crucial to the ability to pursue strategies. Such a perspective accepts that the role of the state is being transformed by processes of deregulation and capital mobility while continuing to argue that politics matter. However, the politics of welfare retrenchment have been of a different character to those of welfare growth. It is generally assumed that recent growth has been accompanied by a corresponding increase in inequality and the emergence of qualitatively different forms of marginalistion, exclusion and polarisation. Such arguments have generally not been accompanied by detailed empirical analysis and the reality, we will argue, is somewhat more complicated.

Attempts to interpret the Irish experience from neo liberal and statist extremes make politics and choice irrelevant and thus obscure the distinctive features of the Irish experience. In what follows we take up the challenge of providing an account of the Irish case that incorporates the complex mixture of successes and failures that, despite the small size of the Irish economy, make it such an interesting case.

2

The Irish Economy in Comparative Perspective

JOHN BRADLEY

It would be going too far to think of Ireland as if it were purely a regional economy, its growth driven by its export base. The kinds of macroeconomic issues that matter for bigger national economies also matter for Ireland. But by moving back and forth between thinking of Ireland as a productivity-driven national economy and as an export-driven regional economy we may be able to get a fuller picture (Krugman, 1997).

2.1 Introduction

Today Ireland enjoys the many economic advantages that come with membership of the European Union. Among the chief of these is that Irish policy makers – in both the public and private sectors – are able to plan in a more stable environment, with the co-operation as well as with the active financial support of other member states through the European Commission. However, in today's increasingly internationalised economy, policy-making autonomy has been progressively ceded by small states to supranational organisations. The policy-making autonomy of any small nation wishing to be part of this international economy is now heavily circumscribed; recognising this fact, and exploiting the consequences, is a wise exercise of national sovereignty.

In his controversial book *The End of History and the Last Man*, written in the immediate aftermath of the collapse of European Communism, Francis Fukuyama suggested that, however dramatic political, social and economic events may be in the future, there would be little by way of further progress in the development of basic underlying principles and institutions, because all the really big questions appear to have been settled (Fukuyama, 1992). Conventional (or neoclassical) economics had long asserted a special case of this wider thesis, which, in very simplified form, holds that market-based capitalism is a universal path towards development that is potentially available to all countries. Within the now universally dominant paradigm of liberal market economics, it is widely believed that no under-developed country is likely to remain permanently disadvantaged simply because it is late coming to the growth process. Nor can the established industrial powers block the development of a latecomer, provided that country plays by the rules of economic liberalism. Any remaining failure by a state to grow and prosper is likely to be self-inflicted.

Against this political and intellectual background we examine the Irish economy in an historical and comparative perspective. In doing so, there is a temptation to focus exclusively on the past decade of rapid growth and convergence, and indeed this is an interesting story that has attracted considerable international attention (Barry ed., 1999). Specific features and causes of recent growth performance are treated elsewhere in this volume. In this chapter we wish to place the recent Irish experience in context by comparisons that range across space, across time and across ideas. For example, the United Kingdom provided the encompassing economic context for Ireland until almost two decades after the end of the Second World War. However, during the decade and a half after Ireland joined the then EEC in 1973, the small, developed, core European states became an obvious touchstone, at a time when attempts were being made to diversify the economy away from excessive reliance on the United Kingdom towards wider European norms and standards. The so-called cohesion states (Greece, Ireland, Portugal and Spain) became standards of comparison during the late 1980s and the 1990s, a period when substantial development aid was forthcoming to these countries from the EU under the enlarged Structural Fund programmes. Today Ireland has many of the characteristics of a modern developed economy and its recent performance has itself become the object of international interest by less developed countries. The Irish developmental model is closely studied by the newly liberalised states of Central and Eastern Europe as they make their transition from Communist autarky and central planning to full integration into an enlarged EU.

The above series of different timeframes and countries provides the organising principle of this chapter. In section 2.2 we examine the historical perspective and briefly sketch some key economic features of a period when Ireland was constitutionally a region of the United Kingdom, and effectively continued to behave as an economic sub-region of the United Kingdom even after independence in 1922 until the early 1960s. In section 2.3 we examine the period from the early 1960s to the mid-1980s when the nature of Irish participation in the international economy changed, the missed opportunities of post-War European reconstruction became apparent, and the task of modernising the economy began to be addressed systemically for the first time. In section 2.4 we examine the period from the mid-1980s to the present day, when core-periphery issues and regional policy moved to the top of the EU policy agenda and the full forces of internationalisation swept over the country as it began to converge rapidly to EU average levels of development. In section 2.5 we look into the near future when the EU will be greatly enlarged to the East and where there will be many more small states on the periphery who will be seeking to emulate Irish economic policy initiatives and surpass its economic performance. Section 2.6 concludes the chapter.

2.2 The historical economic perspective

The 1960s represented a watershed in economic terms in Ireland. Policy actions taken from the late 1950s and early 1960s onwards launched the economy on a development path that differed radically from that pursued before and after independence. The core policy dilemma was not about whether the Irish economy should be open to trade and factor flows with the wider world economy, since Ireland already had a relatively open economy when compared to the other small European states in the late 1950s (Table 2.1). Rather, the issue was the nature of this involvement and whether there was to be a break with the heavy dependence on the UK market as the destination for exports of a very restricted variety of mainly agricultural products.

Table 2.1: Small EU economies: measures of openness in 1960 (1999)

Country	Exports of goods & services (% of GDP)	Imports of goods & services (% of GDP)
Luxembourg	85.6 (93.6)	72.4 (80.8)
The Netherlands	45.7 (56.6)	44.2 (49.8)
Belgium	39.0 (73.8)	39.2 (69.1)
Denmark	32.7 (34.6)	34.5 (31.8)
Ireland	30.4 (85.8)	35.5 (66.1)
Austria	23.7 (46.2)	24.4 (45.8)
Sweden	22.7 (46.0)	23.3 (40.1)
Finland	22.5 (41.1)	23.2 (32.2)
Portugal	16.0 (33.2)	21.3 (40.3)
Greece	7.1 (16.0)	14.2 (23.3)

Source: *European Economy*, No. 66, 1998

We touch on only three key factors that served to condition economic performance prior to 1960. The first concerns demographics, emigration and the openness of the Irish labour market. The second concerns economic geography and the emergence of a North-South divide in the economy, with the industrialising North achieving a much higher degree of prosperity than the mainly agricultural South. The third concerns the manner in which the economy of the island of Ireland, and later the separate economy of the Irish Free State, came to be almost totally dominated by trade and other policy links with Britain, the difficulty in breaking free from this embrace, and the consequences of the British link for Irish policy making.

Demographics, emigration and decline

Two unique features of Irish demographics stand out clearly. First, of the ten European comparison countries used by Lars Mjøset in his seminal NESC report (Mjøset, 1992), Ireland was unique in that it experienced a major decline in population between 1840 and 1960. Second, if a comparison is made with the three other European nations that displayed significant migration behaviour sometime during the period 1851-1960 (namely, Denmark, Norway and Sweden), only for a short period towards the end of the nineteenth century did emigration rates (i.e. emigration per thousand of the population) come anywhere near the persistently high Irish rates.

However, emigration was both a cause and an effect of slow growth originating from other wider failures in the economy. Causes and effects become circular, and the real challenge is to include emigration in a broader study of the Irish pattern of development. Mjøset introduces the notion of a *vicious circle* linking two key Irish characteristics: population decline via emigration, and a weak national system of innovation (Mjøset, 1992: 50-67). He suggests that in Ireland these two mechanisms reinforced each other negatively through the social structure: the pastoral bias of agrarian modernisation, paternalistic family structures, sluggish growth of the home market, and a further marginalisation through weak industrialisation. In a range of other small European states, *virtuous circles* tended to operate and promote development. Many of the elements in the weak national system of innovation arise in the context of the economic geography of nineteenth- and early twentieth-century Ireland.

Economic geography and the island's North-South divide

A striking feature of economic growth is that it not only occurs unpredictably and at different times, but it also occurs in forms that are highly concentrated spatially. The reasons behind the tendency towards concentration have been traditionally associated with the presence of increasing returns to scale and agglomeration economies that come from the more intense economic interactions that are encouraged by close proximity. Hence, it was not entirely surprising that when the Industrial Revolution came to Ireland in the latter half of the nineteenth century, it developed in a geographically concentrated form (Ó Gráda, 1994). However, Ireland's industrialisation did not emulate Britain's more generalised economic and technological leap forward. Rather, it came to involve a few specific sectors (brewing, linen, shipbuilding) and selected locations (mainly Dublin and Belfast), and by-passed much of the rest of the island. The spatial theory of economic growth provides suggestive insights into the process whereby Belfast developed rapidly as the only region in Ireland that fully participated in the latter phases of the Industrial Revolution (Krugman, 1995; Ó Gráda, 1994). In fact, the greater Belfast region took on all the attributes of an 'industrial district', a geographically-defined productive system characterised by a large number of firms that were involved, at various stages and in various inter-related ways, in the production of relatively homogeneous products.

Once under way, Northern growth became a virtuous circle of cumulative causation, bringing increased economic benefits (but not always widespread social benefits) to the north-east region of the island. Most strikingly, a decline in population of almost 55 per cent occurred between the years 1841 and 1951 in the area that was eventually to become the Republic of Ireland, compared with a decline of only 17 per cent in the area that was to become Northern Ireland (Mjøset, 1992: 222). Population actually grew in the area around Belfast, to the extent that by the year 1911 the population of the Belfast area (at 386,947) had outstripped that of Dublin (at 304,802). More generally, the north-east region eclipsed the rest of the island and established a clear edge in terms of industrial dynamism and economic strength.

Relations with the rest of the world

The political incorporation of Ireland into the United Kingdom in 1801 generated forces that led to comprehensive economic and trade integration as well. The full extent of this integration after more than one hundred years of Union is illustrated in Figure 2.1, which shows the UK-Irish trade position from just after partition to the year 1950. The proportion of Southern exports going to the UK showed a very small reduction from 98.6 per cent in 1924 to 92.7 per cent by 1950.

The failure of Ireland to diversify its economy away from an almost total dependence on the UK had serious consequences for its economic performance when compared to a range of other small European countries and has been the subject of research and comment.[1] The reluctance of the new Irish public administration to deviate too much from British policy norms has been well documented (Fanning, 1978). The nature of the difficulties faced by Irish policy makers in attempting to break free from the economic embrace of the UK reflected the wider behaviour of trade within the EU over the past thirty to forty years. Thomsen and Woolcock (1993) point out that the exports from individual countries to the rest of Europe are still highly concentrated in only a few markets. Export market proximity is a key factor, but market size, distance, common borders and similar languages strongly influence intra-industry trade and the pattern of overall trade in Europe.

Figure 2.1: Southern trade shares with Britain and the North

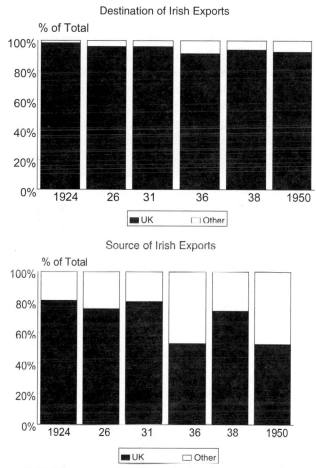

Wijkman (1990) has extended the analysis of geographical factors by looking at what he calls 'webs of dependency'. He suggests that there are three sub-regional trade blocs in Europe. The first is the *North* periphery, consisting of the UK, Ireland and Scandinavia. The second is the *South* periphery, comprising the Iberian peninsula, Greece and Turkey. The remaining countries are clustered around Germany and are called *Core Europe*. Comparing the trade pattern of 1958 with that in 1987, Wijkman found that in many cases these clusters have become more, rather than less, clearly defined as a result of greater EU integration. However, Ireland's relationship with Britain, which had been among the very strongest webs of dependency prior to 1960, weakened considerably thereafter for very specific reasons.

It was hardly surprising that Ireland and Britain formed a particularly strong web of dependency, continuing from independence well into the 1960s. While policies and policy makers in Ireland may have been less assertive and innovative than might have been desired, in the absence of a competitive and export-oriented industrial sector there is probably very little that could have been achieved to accelerate an earlier economic decoupling from the UK. The consequences followed inexorably. In the words of Mjøset: 'Ireland became a free rider on Britain's decline, while Austria and Switzerland were free riders on Germany's economic miracle' (Mjøset, 1992: 9).

The strong web of dependency between Ireland and the UK only began to weaken after the shift to foreign direct investment and export-led growth that followed the various *Programmes for Economic Expansion* in the late 1950s and during the 1960s. Figure 2.2 shows the behaviour of the shares of Irish exports going to the UK, and Irish imports originating in the UK, for the period 1960-92, after which shares tended to stabilise. The forces that brought about this changed pattern of behaviour – mainly export-oriented foreign direct investment – are examined in the next section.

Figure 2.2: Southern trade with the UK: export and import shares 1960-92

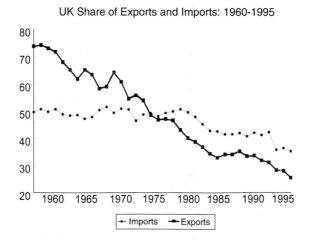

2.3 Internationalisation and foreign direct investment

The failure of the policy of industrialisation behind protective tariff barriers became apparent during the economic crises of the 1950s (O'Malley, 1989; Kennedy, Giblin and McHugh, 1988). A case can be made that union within the United Kingdom – at a time when Britain was the dominant world economic superpower – had been economically beneficial to Ireland during most of the nineteenth century, the main exception being the period of the Great Famine and its immediate aftermath (Ó Gráda, 1994). But the problems that beset the much weakened UK economy in the straitened circumstances that followed World War Two, the birth of the European Community with the signing of the Treaty of Rome in 1956, as well as the fact that the United States was the new hegemonic economic power, were factors that heavily influenced Irish strategic policy formulation.

To measure the extent to which Ireland lagged behind the other small European states in the late 1950s is a difficult task, since comparisons based on the simple conversion of domestic prices to a common currency are beset by problems. However, from the year 1960 we have standardised data that makes this comparison in terms of purchasing power parity (Table 2.2). Ignoring the special case of Luxembourg, the original six-member states of the then EEC formed a relatively homogeneous group, with Germany leading (at 122 relative to the average of 100) and Italy lagging (at 87). In the case of Italy, the low average concealed the fact that the Northern sub-regions were well above the European average, while the Southern (or *Mezzogiorno*) sub-region was well below. The other nine future members of what is now the EU consisted at that time of five wealthy countries (Denmark, Austria, Finland, Sweden and the UK, ranging from a high of 124 (UK) to a low of 88 (Finland)) and four much poorer countries (Greece, Spain, Ireland and Portugal, ranging from a high of 57 (Spain) to a low of 43 (Greece)).

At the time of the first enlargement in 1973, the Danish and Irish GDP per head figures had changed very little relative to the EU average, but the UK had declined in relative terms to about the EU average. Since Ireland was a heavily agricultural country even as late as 1973, debate on the wisdom of its entry into the then EEC focused attention on the likely benefits from higher prices of agricultural produce under the CAP rather than on regional policy. In the early years of its membership, the main benefits to Ireland came from the CAP in terms of greatly increased transfers under the price guarantee section (McAleese, 1975).

The aspect of modern Irish economic development that has attracted most attention internationally is the dynamic role played by foreign direct investment (FDI). Ireland is a case study of the effects on a small developing host economy of export-oriented FDI and this phenomenon has been the subject of much detailed research (O'Malley, 1989; Barry, Bradley and O'Malley, 1999). Ireland emerged in the late 1950s from a heavily protectionist regime and the switch to openness was more dramatic than in the other European states and was implemented in terms of a vigorous industrial incentive package consisting of a very low corporate tax regime and generous capital and training grants.

Table 2.2: GDP per head of population: (PPS), EU-15 = 100

Country	1960	1973	1986	1999
Belgium	98.6	104.5	104.2	112.5
Germany	122.1	114.5	116.8	109.1
France	105.3	110.5	109.8	103.7
Italy	87.3	94.0	102.5	101.2
Luxembourg	168.7	153.1	138.8	165.9
The Netherlands	112.1	107.1	102.2	105.3
Denmark (73)	119.9	114.4	117.9	114.6
Ireland (73)	60.8	58.9	63.7	111.0
United Kingdom (73)	123.9	104.4	101.9	98.4
Greece (82)	42.5	62.4	61.4	68.7
Portugal (86)	43.2	61.1	54.0	74.1
Spain (86)	56.9	74.8	69.7	80.2
Austria (95)	94.8	98.5	105.4	110.9
Finland (95)	87.8	94.3	100.6	101.8
Sweden (95)	122.7	115.0	112.5	96.5

Source: *European Economy*, 1998: 80–81

After a slow start in the 1960s, the foreign sector grew very rapidly during the 1980s and now accounts for about one half of Irish manufacturing employment and over two-thirds of gross manufacturing output (Barry and Bradley, 1997). Directly as well as indirectly, FDI has affected every corner of the Irish economy.

FDI inflows into Ireland did not go primarily into the more traditional sectors in which the economy had a comparative advantage (e.g. food processing, clothing, footwear) mainly because many indigenous manufacturing sectors are largely non-tradeable (i.e. directed mainly at serving the small local market), and the substantial high technology FDI inflows that came to Ireland turned out not to depend on local comparative advantage. Although the outward orientation occurred at a time when the concept of growth poles was universally popular as a spur to development (Buchanan, 1968), the normal processes of clustering and regional concentration in Ireland were impeded both by the branch-plant nature of the investment and by a public policy that encouraged geographical dispersal almost certainly at some expense to strict economic efficiency criteria. However, after more than three decades of exposure to foreign direct investment, Ireland eventually succeeded in attracting sufficient firms in the computer, instrument engineering, pharmaceutical and chemical sectors to merit a description of sectoral 'agglomerations' or 'clusters'.

The long overdue switch to an outward orientation from the 1960s was an enlightened response to changes in the world economy (Sachs, 1994). The engine of subsequent Irish growth was the manufacturing sector, and the engine of the manufacturing sector was the foreign-owned multinational sub-sector. Experience led to a better understanding of the role of small regions and small states in the increasingly integrated international economy, where:

> In Adam Smith's day, economic activity took place on a landscape largely defined – and circumscribed – by the political borders of nation states: Ireland with its wool, Portugal with its wines. Now, by contrast, economic activity is what defines the landscape on which all other institutions, including political institutions, must operate (Ohmae, 1995: 129).

On the global economic map, the lines that now mattered were rapidly becoming those defining 'natural economic zones', where the defining issue is that each such zone possesses, in one or other combination, the key ingredients for successful participation in the international economy. Thus, the rise of the EEC, the development of the Pacific Rim and the progressive liberalisation of world trade under successive GATT rounds, presented both opportunities and threats to Ireland. But the eventual dominance of the Irish manufacturing sector by foreign multinationals was unexpected and quite unique by OECD experience. With falling transportation and telecommunication costs, national economies were destined to become increasingly interdependent, and:

> the real economic challenge ... [of the nation] ... is to increase the potential value of what its citizens can add to the global economy, by enhancing their skills and capacities and by improving their means of linking those skills and capacities to the world market (Reich, 1993: 8).

This process of global competition is organised today mainly by multinational firms and not by governments. Production tends to be modularised, with individual modules spread across the globe so as to exploit the comparative advantages of different regions. Hence, individual small nations and regions have less power to influence their destinies than in previous periods of industrialisation, other than by refocusing their economic policies on location factors, especially those which are relatively immobile between regions: the quality of labour, infrastructure and economic governance, and the efficient functioning of labour markets.

Perhaps the most striking consequence of foreign investment inflows was that it hastened the de-coupling of the Irish economy from its almost total dependence on the United Kingdom. Ireland's development dilemma had always been that it could either stick closely to UK economic policy and institutional norms and be constrained by the erratic UK growth performance, with little prospect of rapid convergence to a higher standard of living; or implement a politically acceptable degree of local policy innovation that offered hope of a faster rate of growth than its dominant trading partner. The Irish economic policy-making environment during this period can be characterised as having shifted from one appropriate to a dependent state on the periphery of Europe to that of a region more fully integrated into an encompassing European economy. FDI renovated and boosted Irish productive capacity. The Single Market provided the primary source of demand. All that remained was for a big push on improvement in physical infrastructure, education and training, and this arrived in the form of a dramatic innovation in regional policy at the EU level.

2.4 Facilitating convergence: EU regional policy

The importance and emphasis given to regional policy within the EU has greatly increased since the late 1980s, a time when major policy reforms and extensions were introduced in the lead-up to the implementation of the Single Market and Economic and Monetary Union. This increased emphasis on the regional (or spatial) dimension of policy in the EU caught the mainstream economics profession somewhat off its guard. In the words of Paul Krugman, writing in 1995:

> Economic geography – the location of activity in space – is a subject of obvious practical importance and presumably of considerable intellectual interest. Yet it is almost completely absent from the standard corpus of economic theory (Krugman, 1995: viii).

Serious theoretical and technical issues lay behind this state of affairs and have only recently been partially resolved (Fujita, Krugman and Venables, 1999). In addition, after the turbulence of the 1970s and the 1980s, economic analysts tended to be more preoccupied with stabilisation (very much a national issue) rather than with growth (which usually has a regional dimension). It was not until the latter part of the 1980s, when inflation and unemployment disequilibria were brought more under control (nominal convergence), that a range of longer-term issues (such as real convergence and regional policy) moved towards the top of the EU agenda. It so happened that this coincided with a period when rapid progress was being made in the theoretical analysis of the determinants of growth, a field that had largely stagnated since the 1970s (Barro and Sala-i-Martin, 1995).

The rise of EU regional policy

In his 1975 paper examining the evidence for and against Ireland's membership of the EEC, McAleese concluded that:

> At this stage, more than ever before, attention will have to focus on regional policy. Ireland, as one of the least developed regions of the Community, has a particularly active interest in the evolution of such a policy. ... Paradoxically, therefore, the strongest long-run economic argument in favour of Ireland's joining the Community is based on a policy which does not yet exist (McAleese, 1975).

Four major driving forces of EU regional policy set the scene for public policy making in the lagging regional states of the EU.

(a) The progressive *enlargement* of the EU from its foundation in 1956 – when there had been a degree of homogeneity at the national level – brought about an ever increasing degree of socio-economic heterogeneity with the entry of Ireland, Greece, Portugal and Spain, the imminent entry of some low-income states from Central Europe, as well as a growing desire to address regional disparities within nation states and between states.

(b) In addition to the simple aspect of enlargement, the *internal and external socio-economic challenges* faced by the member states and regions became more complex and forced EU policy makers to address the task of preparing weaker states and regions to handle such initiatives as the Single Market (SEM), Economic and Monetary Union (EMU) and more recently the need to prepare for the transition of economies of Central and Eastern Europe to EU membership.

(c) While nation states have always operated internal regional policies of various types, what is different about EU regional policy is that significant *financial resources* were made available by the wealthier member states to fund regional policy initiatives in a limited number of the poorer member states. The available EU budget was initially dominated by the need to support the Common Agricultural Policy (CAP), but there were major expansions in resources to fund the reformed Community Support Frameworks of 1989-93, 1994-99 and 2000-06.

(d) The state of economic theory has a modest but significant influence on policy design and it is often the case that policy making is most vigorous where theory is most assertive. Another driving force of EU regional policy came from the insights and guidance provided by *theory*, in particular the 'new' trade and growth theory of the mid-1980s and advances made in economic geography (Helpman and Krugman, 1985; Barro and Sala-i-Martin, 1995; Fujita, Krugman and Venables, 1999).

If the original customs union of the Treaty of Rome had never deepened – in the sense of moving towards greater economic and monetary integration – the simple process of enlargement in itself would have required greater attention to be given to regional policy (see Table 2.2 above). After the entry of Ireland in 1973, the next two enlargements (Greece in 1982; Portugal and Spain in 1986) faced the EU with the danger of developing a two-tier community. In 1986, a very pronounced gap existed between four states (Greece, Ireland, Portugal and Spain) and the other eight. At that time, and using the measure of GDP per head, Spain was the wealthiest in relative terms (at 70) and Portugal lagged most (at 54). Ireland (at 64) and Greece (at 61) lay between these extremes.

If living standards are more accurately measured by private consumption per capita, as shown in Table 2.3, relative living standards are found to have improved only modestly in all four peripheral member states between 1973 and 1991. Ireland, on this measure, lay much closer to the lower levels of Portugal and Greece than to the relatively high level of Spain. With respect to unemployment rates, only in the 1990s did the Irish rate start to fall and converge towards the lower rates in Greece and Portugal, leaving Spain as the high unemployment outlier. The early convergence experience is therefore a little ambiguous.

Table 2.3: Economic indicators in the periphery

	Greece	Ireland	Portugal	Spain	EU-15
Unemployment Rate – Eurostat definition (%)					
1960	6.1	5.8	1.7	2.4	2.3
1973	2.0	6.2	2.6	2.6	2.6
1991	8.6	15.6	5.7	22.8	10.7
1999	9.1	7.4	5.1	17.2	10.2
Private Consumption/capita (PPS)					
1960	57	77	46	64	100
1973	70	65	62	81	100
1991	72	72	66	80	100
1999	78	83	74	79	100

Source: *European Economy*, No. 66, 1998

Internal and external challenges and EU regional policy

It is well known that economic disparities tend to increase during recessions and to lessen when growth is high and pervasive. The economies of the EU were hit by two major world recessions in the aftermath of the oil price crises of 1973 and 1979. Not only did national growth rates decline and diverge, but the fortunes of regions of nation states also diverged. Thus, in the UK the regions of the North (including Wales, Scotland and Northern Ireland) suffered badly relative to the more prosperous southern regions as traditional manufacturing declined precipitously. Although there was some response to the greater challenges faced by the EU, and regional policy was reformed and extended in various modest ways, the major reforms and extensions of EU regional policy were initiated only in the context of planning for the development of the Single Market that took place during the years 1985-88.

Progressive trade liberalisation within Europe was always likely to entail substantial industrial disruption in the periphery, either defined as the member states on the western and southern edge of the EU or as those sub-regions of member states that were located far from the centres of population and economic activity. Adjustment problems were therefore likely to be greater in the periphery. With respect to the Southern periphery's accession to the EU, Krugman suggested that:

> The trade expansion produced by EC enlargement is simply not likely to be as painless as the trade expansion produced by the formation of the Community and earlier enlargement. There will certainly be income distribution problems created by the changes, and also quite possibly some real costs in terms of unemployment (Krugman, 1987).

A massive shake-out of jobs in Irish and Spanish 'traditional' industry occurred as trade liberalisation progressed during the 1980s, even before the formal initiation of the Single Market. The low productivity sectors in Greece and Portugal also faced increasingly intense pressures. One of the potential difficulties faced by peripheral economies like Ireland in adjusting to EU membership was the possibility that as trade barriers fell, industries that had a high share of the plants that exhibit increasing returns to scale (i.e. plants where productivity increases with size) would be attracted away from the periphery towards the densely populated core markets. This process led to the decline of many traditional Irish indigenous industries. However, the influx of multinational companies more than offset this decline. Foreign firms locating in Ireland have tended to be in sectors where there are increasing returns to scale (IRS) at the industry level (computer equipment, pharmaceuticals, instrument engineering) but constant returns to scale (CRS) at the plant level; so the share of Irish employment in IRS sectors has increased substantially.

The reform of EU regional aid programmes into the so-called *Community Support Framework* (CSF) in the late 1980s presented EU as well as national policy makers and analysts in countries like Ireland with major challenges. The political rationale behind the CSF came from the fear that not all EU member states were likely to benefit equally from the Single Market, whose purpose was to dismantle all remaining non-tariff barriers within the Union. In particular, the less advanced economies of the Southern and Western periphery (mainly Greece, Portugal, Spain and Ireland) were felt to be particularly vulnerable unless they received development aid (Cecchini, 1988).

What was special about the reformed regional policies was their goals, i.e. to design and implement policies with the explicit aim of transforming the underlying structure of the beneficiary economies in order to prepare them for exposure to the competitive forces about to be unleashed by the Single Market. Thus, CSF policies moved far beyond a conventional demand-side stabilisation role, being directed at the promotion of structural change, faster long-term growth, and real convergence through mainly supply-side processes.

Regional policy and economic theory

Orthodox (or neo-classical) theory takes the view that all one has to do to promote real convergence between the regions of any state or between groupings of states is to put in place policies that facilitate the free movement of goods and the factors of production (i.e. labour and capital). So, tariff barriers were removed, as in the original Common Market initiative of the Treaty of Rome. Next, non-tariff barriers such as border controls, restrictive public procurement rules and regulations, national technical regulations in the design of goods, etc., must be dismantled, and this was what the Single Market carried out in the period 1986-92. Finally, all barriers to the free movement of workers (such as visa controls and recognition of qualifications) and of capital (exchange controls, etc.) must be removed. If all this is implemented, then orthodox theory says that factor incomes (wages as well as the returns on capital) will tend to converge to a common level across all regions. So, if all markets are competitive, any initial regional disparities will eventually vanish and there is no need for specific structural regional policies.

One of the interesting consequences of more recent advances in the study of spatial economic processes is that the conditions required for convergence to take place are increasingly seen as not holding in practice. Newer theoretical approaches have served to focus attention on the importance of such factors as the initial level of regional physical infrastructure, or local levels of human capital, or on the fact that regions which start off at a structural disadvantage may never converge in any reasonable time period. Such theories suggest that the removal of barriers to trade and factor movements may actually lead to a relative deterioration rather than an improvement of some regions (Fujita, Krugman and Venables, 1999).

As with much else in economics, there is no right or wrong answer here. The Irish experience had been that a crude erection of trade or other barriers in order to 'protect' weak regions was ultimately damaging to economic welfare. Equally, a blind belief in competition policy and the forces of market liberalisation can also be shown to be inadequate (Rodrik, 1999). A balance needed to be struck between these polar approaches, and the evolution of EU structural policy is a case where this balance has generally been maintained.

Thus, regional policies can be justified in many ways and every EU member state operates a wide range of such policies. Some of these operate automatically, such as the income support mechanisms of the unemployment transfer system in Ireland. Others are more discretionary and involve policies designed to address specific problems (e.g. regional de-industrialisation) and targeted at specific regions (e.g. Northern Ireland, the Italian *Mezzogiorno*, and East Germany). The question now arises: should such policies be the prerogative of the authorities of the individual member states, or should they be formulated and implemented at the EU level? Compelling reasons can be advanced as to why regional policy initiatives at the EU level are needed in order to augment purely national regional policies. For example,

(a) poor countries often have inadequate financial resources to address their developmental problems. If left to their own devices, such countries run the risk of drifting further away from the EU average level of income per head, thus threatening the cohesiveness of the EU

(b) if there is a desire among the member states to move towards deeper integration (e.g. the Single Market, EMU, etc.), then the benefits of the deepening may not be evenly spread and the fall-out needs to be addressed by regional policy at the EU level.

Was Ireland a case study of successful EU regional policy?

As part of the *Single Market Review* (Monti, 1996), research was carried out to analyse the likely combined effects of the Single Market and the Structural Funds on the countries of the EU periphery. Since these are very complex and systemic policies, macro-economic models of these economies were constructed which were then subjected to 'shocks' designed to capture the essential elements of the Single Market and CSF programmes (Barry et al, 1997).

The original Cecchini *ex ante* study of the impact of the Single Market had been based on analysis of the four largest EU economies plus Belgium and the

Netherlands, and the EU-wide results (including Ireland) were then derived by grossing up the results for these six economies (Cecchini, 1988). This presented an inaccurate picture of likely developments in the periphery, however, since developmental processes in the periphery tend to be quite different from those pertaining to the core.

A central element in the analysis of the impacts of the SEM and EMU on the Irish economy concerned its impact on manufacturing output, which consists of both tradable and non-(internationally)-tradable components, and is determined by a combination of cost-competitiveness and aggregate-demand factors. The greater the tradable component, the larger the impact on output of world demand relative to domestic demand. Among the peripheral economies, Ireland is the most open of the four economies in this regard, and Spain the least open.

For the four cohesion economies, the effects of the Single Market on manufacturing fall into different categories. For example, 'static' effects are those that arise as various sectors expand and others contract in each country in the wake of EU market integration. To determine which sectors are likely to expand and which contract, use was made of a detailed study of the competitiveness of industrial sectors in each EU country carried out by the European Commission (O'Malley, 1992a). The successful sectors expand through capturing increased foreign market share and the unsuccessful sectors decline through losing home-market share. Research suggested that the 'static' shock was positive for Ireland, marginally negative for Portugal, moderately negative for Spain and strongly negative for Greece. The reason for this was that Ireland and Portugal have the largest shares of employment and output in the sectors in which these individual countries were expected to benefit from the Single Market, relative to those in the country-specific sectors that were expected to be adversely affected.

For both Spain and Portugal, however, the adverse 'static' shocks were more than compensated for by beneficial 'locational' effects, by which is meant the increased FDI inflows that these economies had experienced in recent years. These increased inflows can be ascribed either to EU entry or to the Single Market programme. To the extent that the SEM is responsible, the net 'static' plus 'locational' effects for Ireland, Spain and Portugal are all positive. Finally, 'growth-dependent' effects arise since, with further trade liberalisation increasing the proportion of internationally tradable relative to non-tradable goods, the periphery economies will be more strongly affected by growth in the EU core than is the case at present. The converse is also the case, and economies like Ireland are now more affected by world recessions than when they were less open to the international economy.

Of course, one of the main reasons for the introduction of the *Community Support Framework*, consisting of the Delors-I (1989-93) and Delors-II (1994-99) packages, was the fear that gains to core countries from the Single Market would dominate the gains to the periphery. Barry et al (1997) also presented a separate analysis of the impacts of the CSF on the EU periphery countries. These programmes have effects on both the demand-side of the economy (in the sense of increasing aggregate spending) and on the supply-side (in the sense of increasing the productive capacity of the economy). The mechanisms underlying the first set of effects, being Keynesian in nature, are far simpler than those underlying the supply-side effects. There are three main channels through which the supply-side effects operate: the CSF improves the physical infrastructure of the economy, raises the level of human capital (through enhancing the skills and education of the labour force), and directly assists the private sector by subsidising investment.

Appropriately enough, since Greece was found to benefit least substantially from the Single Market, it, along with Portugal, benefited most substantially from the CSF. The benefits to Ireland and Spain were very much less. The relative size of these effects was due primarily to the relative size of the CSF funds allocated to each economy. For example, although Ireland did well in *per capita* terms from the CSF allocations, its relatively large GDP per head meant that the CSF allocations as a ratio of GDP were smaller than the equivalent ratios for Greece and Portugal.

After a full decade of Structural Funds and the Single Market, how have the cohesion countries performed? In Table 2.4 we show the convergence experience of these four countries, where it is seen that some quite rapid convergence has taken place in recent years.

Table 2.4: Relative GDP per capita in purchasing power parity terms (EU15 = 100)

	1991	1992	1993	1994	1995	1996	1997	1998	1999
Ireland	75.7	79.0	82.2	88.5	93.8	94.5	100.7	107.1	111.0
Spain	79.8	77.8	78.4	76.4	76.9	77.6	78.3	79.2	80.2
Greece	61.2	62.5	64.4	65.2	66.3	67.6	68.3	68.1	68.7
Portugal	64.7	65.4	68.3	70.0	70.7	70.3	71.3	72.7	74.1

Source: *European Economy*, No. 66, 1998

Adaptation to the competitive rigors of the Single Market and efficient use of Structural Funds underpin the dramatic convergence of Ireland that coincided with the implementation of the new EU regional policies. One is tempted to suggest that the combination of openness and the use of Structural Funds were the primary forces driving Irish convergence, but of course the full picture is more complex. The many other domestic issues associated with accelerated Irish growth (such as the growth of human capital, fiscal stabilisation, social partnership, etc.), are treated elsewhere in this volume. Nevertheless, it is the policy of openness and the use of Structural Funds that served to distinguish Ireland from, say, Greece, which had a similar distance to travel but which has only recently set its wider policy framework in the context of embracing internationalisation. Portugal, on the other hand, is in the process of repeating Irish success. It remains to be seen if these countries can sustain their convergent behaviour in times of recession as well as in times of growth. It also remains to be seen how they will compete with the transition economies of Eastern Europe, to which we now turn.

2.5 Ireland as a role model of development

The fall of the Berlin Wall in 1989 heralded the collapse of the Communist system in Europe and the disintegration of the COMECON grouping of Central and Eastern European (CEE) countries. These countries had traded mainly with each other under a form of central planning controlled by the former Soviet Union that had obstructed normal economic interactions with the countries of the EU. Prior to 1989 the EU had a poor periphery to the extreme west and south of Europe, of which Ireland was a small part. As the newly liberalised states of Central Europe grappled with the trauma of economic transformation and eventually sought membership of the EU, it became clear that the new poor periphery of the enlarged EU would be in the east. More seriously, the present relative standard of living in many of these countries relative to the EU average remained much lower than that of Greece in 1960 (Gros and Steinherr, 1995).

Why – one may ask – would the experience of Ireland and the other EU cohesion countries be relevant to a transitional economy? After all, the cohesion countries are faced with development needs and opportunities that appear to have very little in common with the pressing institutional and socio-economic challenges of transition from Central Planning to a market economy. Understandably, the attitudes and economic policy agendas of the large developed EU states as well as the United States and Japan tend to dominate dialogue within Europe since these are, and will remain, the main trading partners and sources of inward investment for smaller countries like Ireland. Turning away from the large developed countries, however, to the economic policy agendas of the EU cohesion countries, their processes of restructuring and convergence begin to look a bit more familiar to policy makers in the CEE transition economies as they plan supply-side reforms. As policy role models for a transition economy wishing to join the EU in the medium term, the experiences of the cohesion countries such as Ireland have become very relevant after the initial stages of transition are completed.

Transition and cohesion

The first phase of the transition of the former command economies of the CEE region has involved considerable disorganisation and a very basic overhauling of industrial and institutional capacity. Socio-economic mechanisms operating during this phase entail the creation of basic market-based institutional structures accompanied by substantial reallocation of labour between the public and private sectors as well as between manufacturing and market services. The initial impacts of restructuring generate the well-known U-shaped pattern of initial contraction followed by recovery for income and employment (Blanchard, 1997).

However, the second phase of CEE transition, the period during which economic processes operate in the context of a fairly stable institutional framework, is more likely to resemble the paths followed by the cohesion countries. As with cohesion, the driving forces behind the second phase will include:

- progressive trade integration
- foreign direct investment inflows
- technology transfer
- EU-aided investment programmes, mainly for the support of infrastructural and human-capital development.

Industrial strategy is likely to be at the centre of socio-economic renewal in the CEE regions. The required growth acceleration will come about through a complex of policy measures and changes with some common themes such as macro-economic stability and high investment. But otherwise, countries are likely to exercise a wide range of different choices, characterised by Dani Rodrik as follows:

> The rules of the international economy must be flexible enough to allow individual developing countries to develop their own 'styles' of capitalism. ... The fundamental dilemma of accountability in today's world economy is that it is domestic voters who choose national governments – and appropriately so – and not global markets (Rodrik, 1999).

Two broad stylised policy directions can be distinguished. The first direction might be characterised as the 'South Korean' model. Here, policy is directed mainly at selected segments of indigenous industry with the objective of gaining in efficiency and capturing greater export market share. Success from this strategic direction depends on the ability of domestic entrepreneurs to overcome entry barriers associated with the dominance of multinational firms from more highly developed market economies. This would entail the development of innovative and highly income-elastic products, efficient marketing and distribution systems, and substantial process and product innovation.

The second direction could be characterised as the 'Irish' model of convergence. Here, growth acceleration is sought from policies designed mainly to encourage export-oriented foreign direct investment inflows. Success from this strategic direction depends on the ability of policy makers to make the business and productive climate in their economies sufficiently attractive to capture a significant share of internationally mobile investment. Some of this attractiveness will be based on the efficiency of the domestic economy (in particular, the availability and quality of physical infrastructure and human resources). However, other crucial aspects are only partially subject to domestic policy influence, such as being located inside the EU with easy access to the benefits of the Single Market.

Drawing on the Irish experience, research indicates that the pursuit of a pure 'Korean' strategy by the smaller CEE economies is likely to run up against difficulties in breaking into dynamic export markets that are dominated by global firms with access to superior technology. Moreover, a 'Korean' strategy aimed at more traditional products (clothing, food, furniture, etc.) is unlikely to deliver fast growth since such products have low income elasticities of demand and the position of lowest cost producer may be in conflict with the target of income convergence with the EU. In this strategy, the domestic cost base is crucial and any breakdown in the appropriate evolution of wages quickly destroys a country's international competitiveness and puts a brake on convergence.

The 'Irish' strategy of FDI-led growth, on the other hand, appears to be superficially more attractive since it encompasses and facilitates a massive transfer of technology and brings with it ready-made access to global markets. However, a down-side is that the early stages of FDI-led growth tend to be associated with very high growth of labour productivity. Consequently, there is a serious risk of 'jobless' growth and this was indeed a difficulty in the early stages of the Irish convergence. Another characteristic of the 'Irish' strategy is that it gives rise to a dual economy: a high-technology, foreign-owned export-oriented modern sector and a more traditional, locally-owned sector that is oriented towards the domestic market or easy-to-enter adjoining markets. If wage growth in the modern sector is permitted to destabilise the continued competitiveness of the traditional sector, then the strategy becomes a zero-sum game. Wage-setting policy and social partnership is a crucial component of the strategy.

2.6 Conclusions

In a recent essay on Ireland's growth, Paul Krugman suggested that economies can be viewed in two different ways: as a national economy or as a regional economy (Krugman, 1997). The facts that one is examining may be the same, but the national or regional perspectives will make a big difference to what one believes is important. Regionality involves more than small size and dependence on trade. Krugman suggests that what makes Ireland like, say, Massachusetts, is that its labour market as well as its product and capital markets are very open. Here, it is in sharp contrast to other small EU and CEE states.

It is when he turns to examining the self-reinforcing nature of Irish success that Krugman comes close to the issues that will be central to the management of all small open EU economies in the future. Looking at the way poorer regions can seek to accelerate their growth rate in order to catch up, Krugman suggests that the Irish experience is essentially a working out of Marshallian externalities, i.e:

- An initial clustering of similar industries (often foreign owned and in the high technology areas such as computer equipment, software and pharmaceuticals) is supported by local suppliers of specialised inputs subject to economies of scale.
- These clusters generate a local labour market for skilled workers which further facilitates the growth of the cluster. At this stage, the training and human resource policies of the Structural Funds were a crucial aid in ensuring elastic labour supply.
- Spillovers of information further encourage growth in the high technology sectors and provide the basis for additional clustering effects, often in traditional areas that can benefit from new technologies in their supply chains (e.g. food processing). Here, the improvements in physical infrastructure and in the productive environment supported by the Structural Funds were crucial.
- Finally, a consensual process of social partnership needs to be put in place to ensure that there are as few losers as possible in the economic restructuring that accompanies such a virtuous circle, with the result that growth is less likely to be choked off by industrial unrest. Although there were valuable lessons to be learned in Ireland from wider EU experience in this area, the policies put in place tend to be country-specific.

Krugman draws attention to some of the risks to which a country like Ireland is exposed as it follows this growth process. First, the dynamic foreign manufacturing base is concentrated on a narrow range of technologies that can quickly move through maturity and into decline. Second, the policy initiatives that ensured that Ireland enjoyed an advantageous 'first mover' status in the early 1960s are unlikely to benefit other smaller economies to the same extent.

Using a business research perspective, Porter in his most recent work has returned to the sources of national and regional competitive advantage and places greater stress on the role of government policy than in his earlier work (Porter, 1990 and 1998). Porter examines national competitiveness analysis from a systematic integration of previous disaggregated analysis at the level of the individual firm and sector. In future national and regional planning, policy makers are going to have to think increasingly in this way rather than in aggregate macroeconomic terms. For example, cluster development in the Irish case was seeded and reinforced by foreign direct investment, mainly by an industrial policy that distorted competition in our favour. However, future clustering will need to focus on removing constraints to productivity growth in a far wider range of indigenous industries.

Almost without exception, the small European states have carved a path between liberalism and statism, and have evolved towards indirect forms of economic control (Katzenstein, 1985). What characterises the economic and political experience of small European states and sets them apart from the large industrial countries is the 'premise' of their planning efforts: namely, adaptation to external market forces and change. They have generally come to find detailed comprehensive sectoral planning efforts increasingly inapplicable, simply because of the openness and vulnerability of their economies. Their problem is one of selecting the devices of planning that are in harmony with their social objectives. Hence, the rationale for state intervention depends on the ability or otherwise of market forces to yield results consistent with these social objectives. Because of their lack of autonomy, their strategy must be flexible, reactive and incremental. They cannot oppose change by shifting its costs to others abroad. Neither can they ignore change if they wish to prosper. The Irish economy may be very small in size, but its policy experiences during the twentieth century provide a rich source of information and guidance for other small countries that seek to develop and prosper.

NOTES

1   Mjøset (1992) is a study of Irish economic under-performance that draws carefully from a wide European literature on social and economic development.

3

The Story of Ireland's Failure – and Belated Success

JOHN FITZ GERALD

3.1 Introduction

Ireland began its career as an independent state with many advantages. In particular, its standard of living in 1922 was higher than that of many other countries in Western Europe (Kennedy, Giblin and McHugh, 1988). In spite of these advantages, its ranking within Europe in terms of standard of living fell over the following 40 years. In the 15 years after World War Two its economic performance was dismal, and some of this failure must be attributed to the inappropriate policies of successive post-war governments, continuing the protectionist stance of the pre-war years (Ó Gráda, 1994). With this background, the story of the Irish economy in the twentieth century may be better considered as a case study in failure: the current boom is better seen as a belated catching up, consequent on the reversal of the ill-conceived policies of the immediate post-war years, rather than as an 'economic miracle'.

While the stance of domestic economic policy began to change in the late 1950s, over the following 30 years the process of catching up was delayed by bad luck and further bouts of inappropriate policy making. With the benefit of hindsight one might think that Ireland had worked hard at being a failure and that, of late, even that policy has thankfully failed!

Writing just over a decade ago, Lee (1989) sought to explain Ireland's relative economic failure since the beginning of the twentieth century. From the standpoint of the late 1980s that was a not unreasonable task. Now the question posed by outsiders looking at Ireland is, why is it such a success? To those living through the experience there is a certain sense of bemusement at this rapid reversal of fortunes. However, it is now becoming clear that, whatever the causes, the Irish economy is truly undergoing something of a renaissance. This chapter argues that it is not a temporary phenomenon, but rather represents the fruits of a strategy that has been pursued for a number of decades, with considerable consistency, by successive Irish governments.

The strategy of economic development adopted in Ireland since 1960 has involved the opening up of the goods and the capital markets as part of the long-term process of EU integration. However, there was more to Ireland's belated success than merely a liberalisation of markets. There was also active intervention by the state in investing in human capital and in encouraging foreign direct investment. This two-pronged approach has been pursued with consistency by all governments over the past 30 years. There were also 'enabling' factors that have facilitated the success of the past decade, as well as some policy mistakes that have rendered the convergence path unnecessarily bumpy.

The next section discusses this development strategy and it also considers some of the facilitating or enabling factors that have affected the path of economic development. Section 3.3 discusses the economic record of the past 40 years and it analyses the development strategy adopted in the context of a simple model of the labour market. The final section discusses some of the problems and challenges that the new, more successful, Ireland faces over the next decade, and it considers some of the lessons to be learned from the Irish experience.

3.2 Development strategy

Economics alone is not sufficient to explain the successful process of economic development in Ireland in recent years. The cultural and social environment in which an economy is set plays such a vital role in determining the relative success or failure of economic policy that to ignore the background is to miss the picture itself. In the case of Ireland, its economic successes and failures since independence have been chronicled and reflected in the social and cultural development of the past 75 years.

The Ireland of today has, in a sense, come of age, a process that is always difficult, and there may be some in the country who still hark back to the earlier days of the state in a protected environment. However, for most adults living in Ireland today their lifetime has seen profound changes in a number of different spheres:

- The opening up of Ireland to the outside world underlies the turnaround in economic fortunes since 1960. Central to the Irish consciousness over two centuries has been the continuing phenomenon of migration and this openness of the labour market has played an important role in changing the economy and society. More recently membership of the European Union has played a vital role as a force for change.
- In terms of domestic policy, the failure to develop the education system in the first 50 years of independence was probably the new nation's most

glaring mistake. A key element of the successful development strategy has been the accelerated investment in education in the past 25 years.

- The other key strand of development policy has been the active encouragement by the state of foreign direct investment. The background to this policy and its role in development has already been touched on in the previous chapter.
- The demographic structure of Ireland still sets it apart from many of its EU neighbours.
- Finally, mistakes in fiscal policy formation have made the path to convergence unnecessarily bumpy, while the partnership approach to policy formation since the late 1980s has made an important positive contribution in facilitating rapid growth.

Opening up

Ireland in the 1950s was a very closed and homogeneous society. Around 60 per cent of the population were blood group O, reflecting the limited influx of population over the last two or three millennia (Readers Digest, 1964). It was very homogeneous in terms of religion, with over 90 per cent of the population being Catholic. With the high cost of travel very few inhabitants had travelled in Europe or further afield. Compared to its European neighbours, it also had a very high proportion of its population living in rural areas. The size of the middle class in Ireland in 1951 was also exceptionally small (Breen et al, 1990). The business leaders of the time were drawn from a very small group in society (Kelleher, 1987). All this made for a rather claustrophobic environment in which to live and work.

While the censorship of publications probably had little significant impact on the flow of ideas from abroad, it was a sign of an inward-looking society. Symptomatic of this was the experience in the literary sphere where many writers sought freedom and inspiration outside Ireland in Britain, France, or further afield.

While Ireland in the period 1930 to 1960 had a very closed goods market, as a result of protection, it was unusual in the openness of the labour market. A very high proportion of the young population emigrated in the first six decades of the century and the bulk of them did not return. It was only for the post-war emigrants that a relatively frequent return on holidays was a realistic possibility. While this experience of emigration may have been taken for granted in earlier generations, by the 1950s, with the post-war recovery under way in Europe and with Ireland missing out on this process, the attitude of emigrants themselves began to change. Earlier generations showed more passive acceptance of the need to emigrate, while the post-war generation showed increasing feelings of anger and betrayal. This is reflected, to some extent, in literary work of the period, such as that of Brendan Behan or Edna O'Brien.

However, from the 1960s onwards this experience of emigration has gradually changed. By the 1970s a significant number of emigrants were beginning to return and this trend has gradually increased over the past twenty years. Today emigration is still part of the experience of up to a quarter of each generation (and of every family) but the difference is that the emigrants of today are seen more as 'homing pigeons'. The returning emigrants have brought with them the experience of business and culture outside Ireland; they carry new ideas, new contacts and even additional capital to Ireland. Across wide areas of Irish society, such as business and academic life, many of those in positions of authority are returned emigrants.

Set out below in Figures 3.1 and 3.2 is an analysis of net emigration classified by the educational attainment of the emigrants. The data show a fairly similar pattern in the late 1980s to the late 1960s, in terms of the proportion of the cohort of 15 to 29-year-olds emigrating (Figure 3.1). However, the second half of the 1980s saw a big change in the educational attainment of the emigrants. Up to the early 1980s the bulk of emigrants had limited educational attainment. Over the course of that decade the composition of emigration changed dramatically (Figure 3.2). Around a third of the emigrants had a third level education in the late 1980s, compared to under 20 per cent in the 1960s. In the late 1980s there was very little emigration by people with only a primary education, whereas they accounted for the bulk of emigrants in the 1960s. This latter change reflects the fact that the Irish welfare system, which was almost non-existent in 1960, grew to be more generous than that of the UK by the late 1980s.

Figure 3.1: Proportion of cohort emigrating

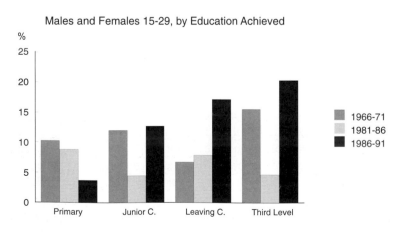

Source: Fahey, Fitz Gerald and Maître, 1998

Figure 3.2: Education of emigrants

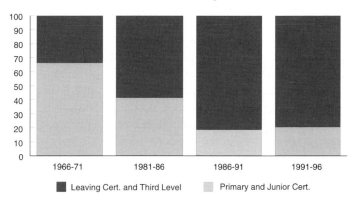

Males and Females, aged 15-29

Leaving Cert. and Third Level   Primary and Junior Cert.

Figure 3.3: Males who have resided abroad

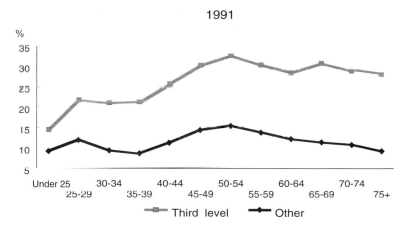

1991

Third level   Other

Source: CSO Census of Population

While those with a good education are now more likely to emigrate than those with only a primary education, they are also more likely to come back. As shown in Figure 3.3, in 1991 over a quarter of all those in the country (males and females) with a third level education had lived abroad for at least a year. For all other educational categories the proportion was 10 or 15 per cent. While the latter figure is exceptionally high by the standards of other EU countries, it still suggests a much lower return rate than for those with third level education. It means that, even in the face of continuing substantial gross outflows, the fact that individuals return with additional experience from working abroad may actually enhance the return from investment in education (Barrett and O'Connell, 2000).

Currently there is substantial net immigration. Over half of those coming to work in Ireland are returning emigrants, but in the past 3 or 4 years between 40 per cent and 50 per cent of them were not born in Ireland. In the case of new immigrants, whether or not they are Irish, the vast bulk of them have third level education (Barrett and Trace, 1998) and they have played an important role in helping the economy to grow at such a rapid pace. The high level of education of immigrants contrasts with the experience of other EU countries.

From an economic point of view this high degree of mobility, especially for skilled labour, greatly increases the elasticity of labour supply. As discussed later, this has tended to keep Irish skilled labour costs from rising rapidly. It makes the Irish labour market behave more like that of a US state than that of other EU national labour markets. What is also interesting is the extent to which the mobility now involves skilled individuals who are citizens of other EU countries – the UK, Germany, France, Sweden, Finland and the Netherlands. While a significant number of these immigrants are spouses or partners of returning Irish emigrants (Finneran and Punch, 1999), many of them have no traditional association with the country.

Immediately after independence there was a substantial outflow of Protestant citizens who found the new state unappealing, in spite of the well developed safeguards for their religious and civil rights. This loss of diversity was probably serious for the future development of the country, both culturally and economically. It is only today that returning emigrants, and some new immigrants, are beginning to provide a more diverse culture and a more exciting environment, suitable for rapid economic growth. Part of the recent transformation in society and the economy must be attributed to this influx of additional skilled labour with new ideas and skills, and new approaches to the many problems which Ireland faces.

The openness of the labour market is only one facet of a much wider process of European integration. A vital feature of this process has been the opening up of the economy and society as a whole to the wider European experience. In 1922 Ireland was the first of the British colonies to break away since the United States in 1776, and it had to write its own rules (Harkness, 1969). In the first years of independence there was a learning process when new patterns of behaviour, and new ways of thinking, had to be developed. In the world of the 1920s and 1930s Ireland took the road of protection and self-sufficiency, tending to close off the influence of the outside world. Its economic manifestation was the erection of very high tariff barriers to the outside world and its prime political manifestation was the decision to remain neutral in World War Two. This period of isolation left a serious economic and political legacy after the war ended.

The advent of free trade from the beginning of the 1960s was only one, and probably not the most important, aspect of the opening up of the country to outside influences and ideas. The influence of the media, principally television, played an important role in the process. News of a better world outside was no longer confined to intermittent letters from emigrant sisters or brothers. However, probably the most important force for change in the economy and domestic politics was entry into the then EEC, along with the UK, in 1973.

Ireland was not unique in twentieth-century Western Europe in experiencing independence from a much larger and dominant neighbour; Finland, Norway, and Latvia, for example, have also shared this experience. In the case of both Ireland and Finland, their experience of the first 25 years of independence has coloured their response to the European Union and European institutions. Public opinion in Ireland, and also in Finland, is much more favourable to the institutions of the EU than is the case, for example, in the old imperial powers of Sweden[1] or the United Kingdom. Ireland, and even more so Finland, suffered in their initial years of independence from the absence of a supranational framework of law to regulate their relations with their former Imperial power. In the case of Ireland, even in economic matters, the relative generosity of successive UK governments eased the problem (Fanning, 1978). However, until Ireland joined the European Union, its external economic relations were characterised by a dependent relationship on the UK. For Finland relations with the Soviet Union proved much more traumatic, culminating in the experience of World War Two. As a result, for Ireland and Finland membership of the European Union is, in a way, the culmination of a long path to independence.

This new liberating experience of EU membership took many different forms. It brought about huge changes in the way the civil service operated. All governments were opened up to new influences and many Irish policy makers suddenly found themselves playing on a European stage. A similar process affected many other Irish social and political institutions. Both the trade union movement and the business community greatly benefited from the stimulus provided by other European models of behaviour. The successful growth of the social partnership model owes an intellectual debt to the experiences of countries such as the Netherlands and Germany, rather than to the more traditional channel of influence from the UK (Sexton and O'Connell, eds, 1996). For all the major institutions of Irish society EU membership shifted the focus of attention to a new multilateral world where Ireland was both legally, and *de facto*, equal to all other members. It took some time to realise that the UK was not always the opposition, but often a friend and ally in furthering common interests.

The economic adjustment to the changing circumstances had costs as well as benefits. The costs were seen in the closure of many businesses as the economy adjusted, a process that Central Europe today understands very well. This process of adjustment continued into the 1980s but it is now largely complete for the manufacturing sector, and what problems remain affect the services sector. A corollary of this process of adjustment by existing industry was the introduction of new foreign-owned businesses across a wide range of sectors, but especially in certain key areas of manufacturing industry. The new multinational industry came to Ireland because it offered access to the EU market. Without such access Ireland would have been of little interest as a location for investment from the early 1970s onwards.

Membership of the EU was particularly important in the access it gave to the wider EU market for agricultural produce under the CAP. Even before membership in 1973, the impact of the impending CAP began changing Irish agriculture. While the CAP and the agricultural sector were crucial to the economy at the time of membership, their significance has steadily fallen. Nonetheless, the EU receipts as part of the CAP remain larger than all the receipts under the Structural Funds and the direction CAP reform will take over the decade will still be an important political issue for future Irish governments.[2]

In the long run, more important than any other economic feature of EU membership, is access to the single market. The single market reforms were expected to bring significantly greater benefits to Ireland than the related increase in Structural Funds (Bradley et al, 1992; Barry, Bradley et al, 1997). The extent of the integration of the Irish economy into the wider EU economy means that Ireland's economic interests are now inextricably tied up with those of its EU neighbours. For example, Ireland paid a small part of the price of German unification in the early 1990s, as high interest rates temporarily cost up to 3 or 4 per cent of total employment (Bradley, Fitz Gerald and McCoy, 1991). However, this was a small price to pay in terms of the wider benefits of EU membership.

While the structural fund payments from the EU have played a significant role in underpinning essential public investment in the 1990s, their overall role in promoting economic convergence has been limited (Fitz Gerald, 1998), though nonetheless welcome. At least as important as the actual investment has been the way the structural fund process has affected the administrative and political system. The increase under the first CSF encouraged the government to raise public investment from its extremely low level in the late 1980s. Without such a stimulus Ireland could have found itself suffering from even greater under-investment than is actually the case in the face of rapid growth in recent years. The CSF process has also forced the introduction of long-term planning. In addition, the need to satisfy the ghost of Mrs Thatcher, and the more substantial ghost of Chancellor Kohl, that their EU contributions were well spent resulted in the introduction of a fairly rigorous set of evaluation procedures. This has helped change the way the domestic administration approaches public expenditure.

Developing the economy

Two key areas where successive Irish governments had scope to influence economic development through domestic action were: investment in human capital – education and training – and industrial policy. In both cases, once policy was changed to a more developmental role, the new policies were pursued with consistency by all subsequent governments, providing considerable continuity in policy formation.

Figure 3.4: Educational attainment

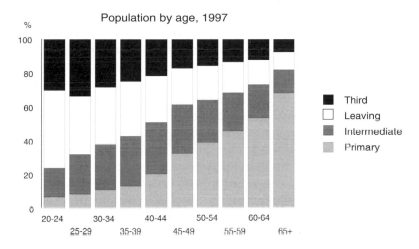

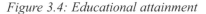

Source: Labour Force Survey micro data

In the immediate post-war years all of Northern Europe, with the exception of Ireland, began a major programme of public investment in human capital, greatly increasing participation in both second- and third-level education. In Ireland, by contrast, the immediate post-war years saw no recognition of the need for change in this area. It was not until after the publication in 1966 of an OECD report, *Investment in Education*,[3] that free second level education was introduced in 1967. Since then the strategy of investing in education has been pursued by successive governments.

Even in the 1980s, when many other sectors suffered severe financial cutbacks, the education system was largely protected, and participation rates continued to rise. In fact, the rise in participation rates since 1980 has been even greater than that which occurred under the first 15 years of the 'free education' policy. The effects of this policy can be seen in Figure 3.4, which shows the educational attainment of the population by age. Latest data indicate that throughout the 1990s participation in third level education has continued to rise, with around 80 per cent of the 1995 school-leaving cohort having a leaving certificate and over 50 per cent continuing on to some form of third level education.[4] On average women have been slightly better educated than men throughout the past two generations, but the gap has, until recently, been relatively small.

This change in policy has had a profound effect on the Irish economy and society and its full effects are far from complete. The impact on the labour market has been complex and this factor is vital in explaining the current rapid growth in employment. This issue is discussed later.

The long-tailed impact of the change in educational policy is not surprising. Many of the other countries of Northern Europe, which invested heavily in education in the immediate post-war years, saw rapid rates of growth up to and including the 1970s. Ireland began 20 years late and is seeing the benefits of the investment 20 years after its Northern European counterparts (Koman and Marin, 1997).

As discussed in Chapter 2, a key feature of the changing structure of the Irish economy from the end of the 1950s has been the growing importance of foreign direct investment (FDI), in particular in the manufacturing sector. In 1960 the Irish economy was heavily dependent on agriculture. The concentration on this sector was much greater than for other neighbouring countries. There was a need to shift attention to the industrial sector so that industrial growth would counterbalance the inevitable decline in the importance of agriculture. This was reflected in the change in industrial policy in the late 1950s to favour foreign investment in manufacturing. It is now clear that this process has played a very important role in transforming the economy. The strategy, which relied originally on tax breaks, now relies heavily on the availability of skilled labour to attract foreign firms. The concentration on certain sub-sectors of manufacturing, such as computers and electronics, also appears to have been beneficial.

It is important to recognise the consistency with which industrial policy has been pursued by all governments for 40 years (Ruane and Görg, 1997). Such a strategic approach to economic policy mirrors that of some Asian countries in more recent times, and it highlights the importance of creating an environment of certainty for foreign investors. While the extent of the concentration on developing the multinational sector at the expense of attention to existing domestic firms has frequently been called into question, some of the promised fruits of that policy are currently to be seen in the rapid growth in the manufacturing sector (Barry, Bradley and O'Malley, 1999).

While the low rate of corporation tax has long been the key incentive for locating investment in Ireland, since the late 1980s the availability of skilled labour at a reasonable cost has grown in importance as an attraction for foreign multinationals (Barry and Bradley, 1997). The location decision of multinational firms is a function of the relative cost of production in a range of different possible competing locations (Bradley and Fitz Gerald, 1988). The cost of production itself is affected by the tax regime, labour costs, the cost of capital and the cost of other services bought in locally.

As well as bringing a demand for skilled labour, the advent of multinational firms also brought new management skills and access to a range of technologies that were not available locally. In recent years there has been some sign of a transfer of these skills to local firms. In addition, the growth in the critical mass of firms operating in the high technology sectors has seen a rise in the local labour market's supply of necessary skills.

The high proportion of foreign direct investment in the Irish manufacturing sector and its export-oriented development makes the Irish economy quite unique among the EU peripheral members. At this stage foreign-owned firms account for over half of all output in manufacturing and almost half of all employment (Barry, Bradley and O'Malley, 1999). Foreign-owned manufacturing firms export almost 90 per cent of their output whereas Irish-owned manufacturing firms export around 36 per cent of output. Thus the influx of foreign-owned firms over four decades has played a vital role in opening up the economy.

The result of this outward-oriented strategy was that there was a significant restructuring of the manufacturing sector, especially in the 1970s and 1980s. Production in manufacturing shifted from dominance by a largely indigenous, low-technology group of 'traditional' industries, which had strong links to the domestic and UK market, to the current dominance by a group of 'high-technology' industries, concentrated in electronics and pharmaceuticals. This group is largely foreign-owned and export-oriented.

Figure 3.5: Manufacturing employment 1970-1996

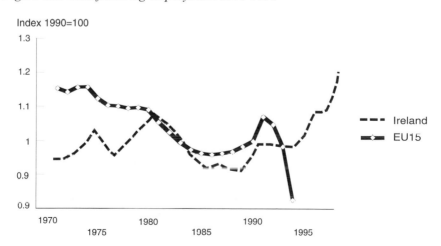

During the 1980s this restructuring resulted in a sharp decline in employment in manufacturing and led many commentators to question the wisdom of deliberately courting foreign firms. It was argued that the relatively low labour-intensity of production in the foreign-owned sector, and its low linkages with the domestic economy, signalled a danger that the indigenous sector was being crowded out and that the economy was becoming increasingly reliant on foot-loose foreign multinationals.

However, the restructuring within the traditional group of industries was an inevitable consequence of the progressive opening of the economy to international trade. External pressures from low-wage competing countries forced many inefficient industries out of production. Similar adjustments occurred in the manufacturing sector of most developed countries, albeit over a longer period.[5] Viewed in this context, the pro-active industrial strategy pursued by Irish policy makers was central to the long-term development of a strong industrial base. Indeed Irish employment in manufacturing between 1975 and 1991 grew more strongly than the EU average, despite its poor performance in absolute terms. The long-term downward trend in EU manufacturing employment can be seen in Figure 3.5.

Figure 3.6: Ireland's share of US FDI into the EU

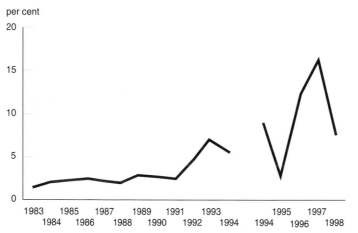

Source: US Survey of Current Business. Data 1983-1994 are Capital Expenditure by Foreign Affiliates of US Companies; Data post 1994 are Direct Investment Abroad

The success of this strategy of attracting foreign investment is illustrated in Figure 3.6. In particular in the 1990s, Ireland's share of all US foreign direct investment into the EU averaged well over 5 per cent, with even higher levels achieved in the most recent years. With the increasing concentration of these firms in high technology sectors, the new investment has significantly tightened the market for skilled labour.

Enabling factors

As well as the broadly favourable external environment and the pursuit of suitable development policies, a number of other factors have facilitated the rapid convergence of living standards to the EU average in the 1990s. Among the most important of these is the unusual demographic structure, the restoration to order of the public finances, and the development of a social partnership model suitable to the changed circumstances of the economy and society in the 1990s.

Figure 3.7: The birth rate

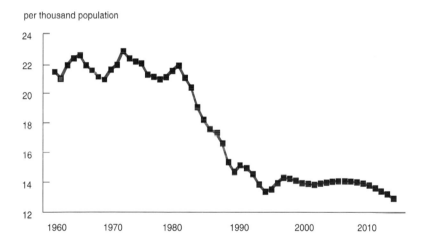

While the post-war baby boom petered out in most of the rest of Europe by 1960, Ireland continued to have a very high birth rate until 1980. Since then it has fallen fairly steadily (Figure 3.7). This delayed fall in fertility has meant that the supply of young people coming onto the labour market has, until now, continued to rise rapidly, long after it had fallen off elsewhere in the EU. It is only in the next five years that the inevitable consequence of the post-1980 decline in the birth rate will come to impact on the labour market.

The combination of this delayed pattern of fertility decline, and the lasting effects of the high emigration in the pre-1960 period, makes the Irish population structure very unusual by the standards of the EU. Figure 3.8 shows the age structure of the population in 1999.

Figure 3.8: Structure of the population, 1999

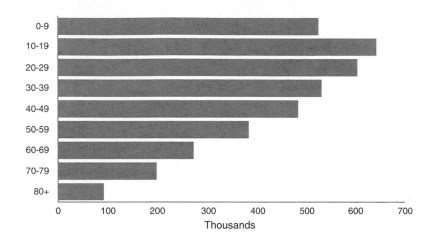

Figure 3.9: Economic dependency

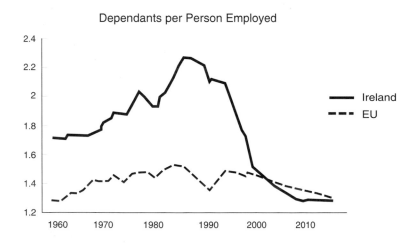

The effects of the 'baby boom' of the 1970s can be seen in today's cohort of teenagers that is larger than any cohort that went before, and also larger than the cohort of children aged under 10. The size of this cohort relative to all others will continue to influence the Irish population profile for decades to come. The very rapid fall off in the population aged over 60 reflects the continuing effects of the very high level of emigration in the 1950s. This means that the number of people in the retired age groups will remain relatively low for another 20 years.

Figure 3.9 shows the movement in the economic dependency ratio for Ireland relative to that of the EU. This ratio measures the proportion of the population not working relative to those working. A combination of many children and low labour force participation meant that Ireland had a much higher dependency ratio than the rest of the EU in the 1960s and the 1970s. In the 1980s rising unemployment further aggravated this situation. However, the changing demographic structure and the improving economic circumstances have been reinforcing one another since the late 1980s, so that Ireland is facing an exceptionally favourable demographic structure in the current period. It is only in the twenty years after 2015 that the rate of old-age dependency will begin to rise rapidly, as it is currently doing in EU countries such as Germany.

A second important factor that has affected the pattern of economic convergence, if not the convergence process itself, has been the course of fiscal policy. The serious policy mistakes of the 1970s laid up problems that dogged the economy in the 1980s. The failure to tackle these problems sufficiently rapidly aggravated the situation, increasing the ultimate cost of the necessary correction on output and employment. Of course, without the fiscal correction that took place over the course of the 1980s, the convergence in living standards would not have been possible.

While some outside observers have suggested that the nature of the adjustment process meant that the costs were small (Giavazzi and Pagano, 1990), the work of Whelan (1991) indicates that this was not, in fact, the case. The serious costs of the fiscal contraction were offset by the fortuitous effects of an acceleration in the rate of economic growth in the outside world.

Figure 3.10: Stance of fiscal policy

Difference Between Indexed and Actual EBR, % of GNP

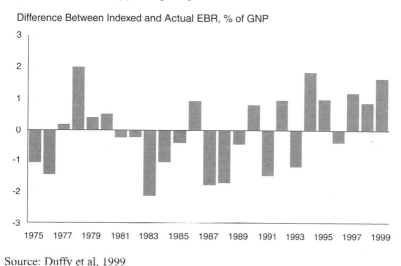

Source: Duffy et al, 1999

In Figure 3.10 we show the stance of fiscal policy on a year by year basis since 1974. Eight out of ten budgets over the course of the period 1980 to 1989 were deflationary. This was necessary to correct the huge imbalance in the public finances and it represented a strongly pro-cyclical fiscal stance at a time of very low growth. Over the 10 years, the cumulative deflationary impetus imparted by fiscal policy amounted to around 8 per cent of GNP. It is not surprising that the Irish economy did not shine over that period!

Figure 3.11: Effects of neutral fiscal policy – deviation from actual outturn

Using the ESRI HERMES model we simulated what might have happened if a neutral fiscal policy had been pursued from 1974 to 1999, compared to the more pro-cyclical stance adopted by successive governments in the 1970s and the 1980s. Figure 3.11 shows the deviation of GNP under the neutral policy stance assumption compared to the actual outturn. This suggests that a more orthodox fiscal stance would have resulted in lower growth in the late 1970s and early 1980s, but that the long-term effects would have been significantly positive. It suggests that even today the economy still has the scars from the painful adjustment process of the 1980s.

The development of a 'partnership' approach to wage formation and policy making from the late 1980s has received a lot of attention (Sweeney, 1997). Undoubtedly it has helped change the industrial relations environment, compared to the experience of the 1960s and the 1970s (Sexton and O'Connell, eds, 1996). While it is difficult to quantify the benefits of a substantial reduction in industrial disputes, this factor has played a significant role in enhancing the performance of the economy. The partnership approach has also contributed to a more coherent approach to economic policy making.

However, its impact on wage formation in the longer term has probably been quite limited. The evidence available suggests that there was a change in the pattern of wage settlements from the early 1980s, before the partnership approach was implemented (Fitz Gerald, 1999). While the agreements have probably served to validate the rate of increase in wage rates that market forces determined, this 'validation' was obtained with less industrial strife than in earlier periods – a significant benefit.

3.3 Policy or luck?

The performance of the Irish economy over the course of the 1990s, when seen in isolation from the experience of previous decades, appears spectacular. Here we first describe this progress. We then consider the key driving factors[6] that explain the current success (and also the past failure) within the framework of a simple model of the labour market: factors that have shifted the supply of labour and factors that have affected the demand for labour.

The record

In the late 1970s the then Irish government pursued a 'dash for growth' policy that involved a huge fiscal injection. Even at the time economists warned that this was unsustainable[7] and, in the early 1980s, when the storm of world recession hit, it almost wrecked the Irish economy. As shown in Figure 3.10, the result was a period of almost 10 years of fiscal retrenchment in the 1980s as successive governments tried to put the economy together again. The process was extremely painful, involving both major increases in taxation and a massive cut-back in state expenditure.

Figure 3.12: Growth in GNP

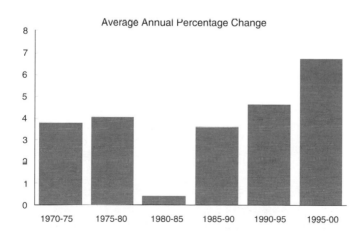

Source: Duffy et al, 1999

Figure 3.12 shows the growth rate for GNP for each of the five-year periods from 1960 to 2000. With the exception of the first half of the 1980s, when the fiscal retrenchment knocked the economy way off course, between 1960 and 1990 there was relatively little deviation from an apparent trend growth of 4 per cent a year. For the 1990s the growth rate picked up, so that the economy is currently growing at a rate well above its past trend.

Probably more remarkable than the apparent pick-up in the trend growth rate is the experience on employment growth (Figure 3.13). By contrast with a dismal performance in the 1980s, employment has grown at an unprecedented rate in the 1990s. The bulk of this employment growth is occurring in the private sector. The reduction in unemployment is equally remarkable (Figure 3.14), falling from a peak of over 15 per cent of the labour force in 1993 to under 5 per cent today, the lowest level seen since the early 1970s.

Figure 3.13: Growth in employment

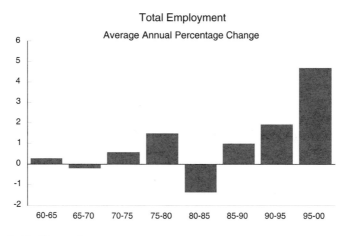

Figure 3.14: Unemployment

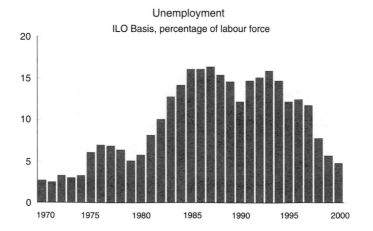

The labour market – supply

Over the past 30 years the Irish labour market has been profoundly affected by a number of different domestic policies that have altered the supply of labour: changes in the education system and changes in the social welfare system. In addition to these changes in domestic policy, two other special features of the economy affected labour supply: cultural changes, affecting the participation of women in the labour force (Fahey and Fitz Gerald, 1997) and the pattern of migration. These have had the effect of increasing the supply of skilled labour and gradually reducing the supply of unskilled labour – shifting outwards the supply curve for skilled labour and shifting inwards the supply curve for unskilled labour. They have also changed the shape of the supply curve, making the supply curve for skilled labour significantly more elastic to changes in wage rates in Ireland.

Figure 3.15: Female labour force participation by level of education

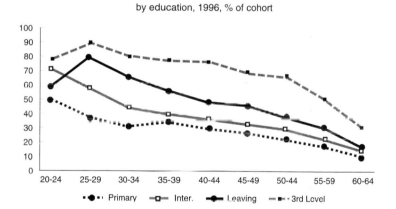

Source: CSO Labour Force Survey, micro data

The rising educational attainment of the population, due to the substantial investment in human capital, greatly increased the supply of skilled labour. This effect has been particularly important since 1980. Given the rise in educational participation in the 1990s, the effects of this upgrading in skills will continue to be felt for some considerable time. This rise in educational participation has been superimposed on the rapid rise in the supply of young labour market entrants stemming from the high birth rate up to 1980.

The rising investment in education has had a particular effect on the supply of female labour. Participation rates for women are highly correlated with level of education (Figure 3.15). As more and more young women have remained on in the educational system, this has increased the probability of them remaining on in the labour force when they have children, or of returning to it as their children grow up. Fahey and Fitz Gerald (1997) suggest that around a third of the very big rise in female participation rates since 1980 is attributable to the effects of investment in education. The factors affecting female labour supply are discussed in more detail in Chapter 5.

The elasticity of supply of skilled labour in Ireland has been greatly increased by migration. Until now, when the labour market tightens in Ireland, firms have been able to attract workers from abroad without any great difficulty. This reflects the big, though diminishing stock of Irish emigrants (Fahey and Fitz Gerald, 1998). When the labour market was weak in Ireland and unemployment tended upwards, Irish people sought better opportunities abroad (Kearney, 1998b). The converse has been seen in the 1990s, where improving labour market conditions have attracted increasing numbers of Irish emigrants home, and also significant numbers of skilled non-Irish workers. As outlined earlier, since the mid-1980s the vast bulk of this pool of mobile labour has been skilled. In increasing the elasticity of supply of skilled labour it has, until recently, allowed the economy to expand without undue pressures on skilled wage rates.

For unskilled labour the possibilities of migration have been greatly reduced compared to the period up to 1980. Hannan, Sexton and Walsh (1991), showed that the prospects for those with limited skills improving their labour market prospects through migration were low. The increased role of social welfare systems in providing income support in Ireland, and elsewhere, made migration difficult and unattractive. In addition, the declining labour market prospects for unskilled labour in the traditional alternative labour market, the UK, also rendered migration unattractive (Nickell and Bell, 1995).

The long-term policy of investment in education has clearly had a major impact on the supply of unskilled labour in Ireland over the past 20 years. The labour market prospects for those with limited education have been very poor since at least the early 1980s (Figure 3.16) and the reduction in supply effected a major improvement in the share of the population at risk of long-term unemployment. Breen and Shortall (1992) indicated that, in purely financial terms, the exchequer had much to gain from upgrading the educational attainment of those leaving school without qualifications.

Figure 3.16: Unemployment by level of education

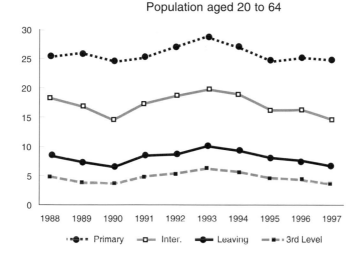

Source: CSO Labour Force Survey, micro data

The effects of the implementation of policy measures to tackle this phenomenon can be seen in the reduction in the supply of unskilled labour over the course of the 1990s – the inward shift in the supply curve for unskilled labour.

Figure 3.17: Replacement rate

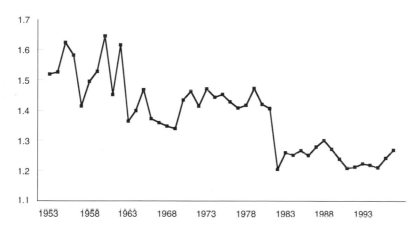

Note: Average hourly earnings in clothing relative to Unemployment Benefit for someone with an adult dependent and 2 children

In Ireland a big change in the replacement ratio occurred in the early 1980s, affecting unskilled labour supply. Figure 3.17 shows the ratio of average earnings in clothing (the least skilled sector of manufacturing) to unemployment benefit payments for a couple with two dependent children. It increased the reservation wage for unskilled labour in the early 1980s, at a time when the economy was facing a series of other shocks.

Figure 3.18: Unskilled labour market

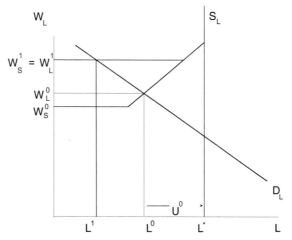

In the 1950s, at a time when the UK had developed a sophisticated social welfare safety net, no such protection was available in Ireland. As a result, unskilled labour in Ireland faced a choice between emigration to the UK, generally to take up employment there, or employment at any price in Ireland. Figure 3.18 illustrates this position for unskilled labour (L), where the supply curve is vertical at full employment and horizontal at the floor provided by social welfare payments. Initially the going wage rate in Ireland W_L^0 was above the rate of social welfare payments W_S^0 leaving unskilled employment at L^0. The shape of the supply curve for unskilled labour in the period up to 1980 was greatly influenced by the propensity of unskilled labour to emigrate to the UK. However, as discussed above, by the early 1980s the rate of social welfare payments W_S^1 effectively set a minimum wage, pulling up the market wage rate W_L^1 so that the supply curve for unskilled labour became horizontal at the rate of social welfare payments. The result was a fall in employment to L^1.

Labour market – demand

The Irish economy over the past 70 years has provided a very interesting test-bed of the effects of economic integration. Having been an integral part of the

United Kingdom until independence in 1922, a series of changes over the following ten years introduced major restrictions on trade.[8] In the early 1930s very high tariffs encouraged the development of local industry to supply the domestic market, resulting in a substantial growth in industrial employment. However, the new firms were very small with low productivity. As discussed above, with the progressive dismantling of tariffs from the late 1950s, the Irish economy, including the protected industrial sector, was opened to major new forces through the subsequent growth in trade.

Figure 3.19: Proportion of national output exported

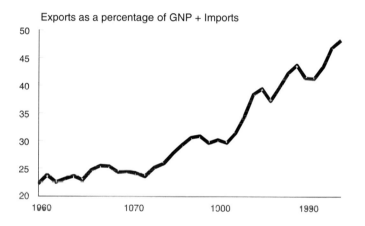

Exports as a percentage of GNP + Imports

The most obvious economic manifestation of the gradual opening up of the economy since 1960 was the growth in the importance of foreign trade and the diversification of the markets where that trade took place. As shown in Figure 3.19, since 1960 the proportion of Irish output that is exported has more than doubled. Initially the process of opening up the economy to free trade began with a unilateral dismantling of extremely high tariff barriers. The opening up of the economy to the rest of Europe also began in the 1960s and this is reflected in the diversification of trade which has taken place since that date. Entry into the EU, which took place at the beginning of 1973, was thus part of a longer-term process of integration.

Over the past 20 years the changing nature of technology and the changing structure of the world economy has seen a rapid rise in the demand for skilled labour in countries such as the US and the UK (Nickell and Bell, 1995). The impact of foreign direct investment has been to ensure that the Irish economy has also shared in this shift in labour demand.

As discussed above, the consistency with which a policy of attracting foreign direct investment was pursued has ensured that Ireland has shared in the globalisation of the world economy, attracting more than its share of new investment in capacity designed to supply the European or the world market. While the early FDI in the 1960s and the 1970s aimed to exploit lower labour costs and the tax advantages of locating in Ireland, more recently the investment has depended on the availability of a rapidly increasing supply of skilled labour. When taken together with the rapid growth in the private services sector in areas that also require skilled employees, the combined effect on the demand for skilled labour has been very substantial.

The opening up of the economy to competition over the past 40 years meant that those companies operating in the tradable sector that depended on unskilled labour faced increasing competition. Corcoran, Hughes and Sexton (1993) document the effect of this on employment of unskilled labour. Since the early 1970s the absolute number of unskilled labourers has been cut by over 50 per cent, with smaller declines in other categories of unskilled labour. The decline in demand accelerated in the early 1980s when a series of shocks affected the economy. These shocks meant that the more traditional firms in the tradable sector, employing relatively unskilled labour, found themselves very uncompetitive. The consequence was an even more rapid scaling down in demand for unskilled labour.

Since the early 1980s firms employing unskilled labour in the tradable sector have continued to experience pressures from manufacturers outside the EU. However, the demand for unskilled labour in certain parts of the services sector (retailing and catering) has risen rapidly in the 1990s in the face of the rapid growth in domestic demand. While the jobs on offer in the first half of the 1990s were still not attractive to some of those eligible for social welfare,[9] as the economy has expanded exceptionally rapidly in the past five years the demand for unskilled labour has also risen. With a continuing fall in supply of unskilled labour (a supply that is less elastic than that for skilled labour) this has bid up unskilled wage rates (Sexton, Nolan and McCormick, 1999). The consequence has been a rapid fall in unemployment rates over the past two years.

The labour market – equilibrium?

The implications of this analysis are that, when faced with a fixed downward sloping demand for skilled labour, any increase in supply will not be fully matched by an increase in employment – 'qualification inflation'. However, unless the supply of skilled labour is infinitely elastic there will be some increase in total employment in the economy, as in the second half of the 1980s. While the majority of the skilled workers will find employment in positions that require their skills, there will also be some increase in the number of skilled workers in jobs that do not require their full talents. In this case, an increase in the supply of skilled labour would tend to reduce wage rates (provided that the supply curve is not infinitely elastic). In the late 1980s skilled labour reacted to the fall in returns to education by emigrating.

The situation since 1990 has been rather different. While the supply of skilled labour has continued to shift outwards, the demand has also shifted outwards. This rapid increase in the demand for skilled labour is taking place throughout the developed world. In the UK and the US the effect since the beginning of the 1980s has been to increase the wage differential between skilled and unskilled workers (Nickell and Bell, 1995). This reflects the fact that the supply of skilled labour has not grown very rapidly in these countries. The big investment in education occurred much earlier there than in Ireland and the post-war baby boom generation in the US and the UK entered the labour force in the 1970s.

Figure 3.20: Returns to education – female

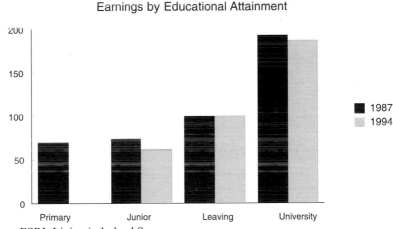

Earnings by Educational Attainment

Source: ESRI, Living in Ireland Survey

Figure 3.20 shows the average earnings of women employed in 1987 and 1994, classified by their level of education (Callan, 1993 and Callan and Wren, 1994).[10] (The figures for men are fairly similar). It shows that the premium in terms of wages which university education commanded in 1987[11] changed little over the following seven years. Later work by Barrett, Callan and Nolan (1999) indicates that, if anything, the returns to education actually increased over that period of rapidly increasing supply. In the face of a major outward shift in the supply curve for skilled labour, this can only be explained by a similar sizeable outward shift in the demand curve. The result has been that the investment in education, and the other policies aimed at increasing the supply of skilled labour, have shown a high rate of return.

For unskilled labour it is only very recently, with the sustained period of high growth, that demand has risen sufficiently to make a major impact on unemployment. With a fairly inelastic supply (compared to the supply of skilled labour) the tightening in the unskilled labour market is resulting in a more rapid increase in unskilled wage rates (Sexton, Nolan and McCormick, 1999). The implications of this for earnings inequality are dealt with later.

In addition to the direct effects on the supply of labour, investment in education has also had a significant impact on productivity in the economy. Durkan, Fitzgerald and Harmon (1999) estimate that between 1986 and 1996 the increase in educational attainment added around one per cent to the effective labour force.

Figure 3.21: Index of human capital

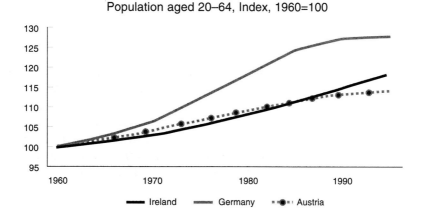

Source: Duffy et al, 1997

These results indicate that the benefits from investment in human capital are occurring later in Ireland than in other Northern European EU members. The movement in the index of human capital reflects the fact that, as each person retires, generally with only a primary education, he or she is replaced by a person with a good leaving certificate or a third level education. As a result of this switch, output will rise, as reflected in the increase in average earnings. The growth in the index was quite slow in the 1960s at around 0.3 percentage points a year. From 1970 onwards it averaged around 0.5 percentage points a year, and its growth reached a peak in the first half of the 1990s, suggesting that investment in human capital was contributing around one percentage point a year to the growth in that period. While the rate of growth in the index is expected to slow in the future, as the average educational attainment of the labour force rises, the index will still be rising at around a half of a percentage point a year at the end of the next decade. It would suggest that currently around one percentage point of the growth rate in GNP may be attributable to the rising educational attainment of the labour force (through the effects on raising productivity).

Table 3.1: Contributions to effective labour supply, percentage points

	1990s	1997-98
Natural increase	1.0	1.0
Female participation	1.0	1.0
Migration		1.0
Human capital	1.0	1.0
Total	3.0	4.0

Using the Durkan et al estimate of the impact of education on the effective labour supply, we show in Table 3.1 a decomposition of the impact of the different forces, discussed above, on the supply of labour in the 1990s. This contrasts with the situation in many other EU members where the labour force is growing quite slowly and where the major benefits of the post-war investment in human capital have already been reaped. Even if the Irish rate of productivity growth were the same as for the rest of the EU, these differences in the factors affecting labour supply go a long way towards explaining Ireland's rather different growth experience in the 1990s.

Figure 3.22: Relative standard of living

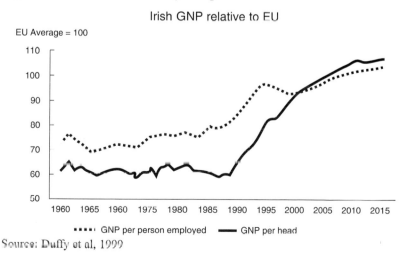

Irish GNP relative to EU

This difference in factors affecting labour supply, when taken together with the range of social and economic factors described earlier, explains why the Irish economy is growing more rapidly than those of other EU members. However, it is also clear that the benefits of the key supply side factors currently boosting growth will fall gradually over the next 15 years, bringing the Irish economic experience back into line with that of its neighbours. By then the task of bringing the Irish standard of living up to that of its neighbours will have been completed.

The result of the relatively rapid period of growth is that Ireland, which in 1990 had a GDP per head of around 74 per cent of the EU average, already exceeds the EU average. A more appropriate measure is GNP per head (which excludes profit repatriations by foreign multinationals). On this measure Ireland can also be seen to have narrowed the gap in living standards, with output per head compared to the EU as a whole rising from 66 per cent in 1990 to well over 90 per cent this year (Figure 3.22). On the basis of this forecast, using GNP, Ireland should achieve the average standard of living in the EU between 2000 and 2005.

The pattern of development discussed above suggests a marked change in gear around 1990; between 1960 and 1990 there was little change in Ireland's position within the EU, measured in terms of GNP per head. However, it now seems possible that over the next 15 years Ireland may achieve a standard of living among the highest within the EU.

While this may appear to be an exceptional rate of convergence in living standards, measured as GNP per head, the situation looks rather different when considered in terms of output per person employed – national productivity broadly defined. On this measure the Irish economy has been converging towards EU standards of productivity fairly steadily since the 1970s. While we are currently seeing some acceleration in the rate of convergence, this is not out of character with the past 30 years. The explanation for the contrast between the two measures, GNP per head and GNP per person employed, lies in the movement in the economic dependency ratio – the ratio of the population not in paid employment to those who are at work. As discussed earlier, while Ireland still has an economic dependency ratio well above the EU level in the 1980s, it will actually fall below the EU average some time in the next few years. This contrast, and its related effects on living standards represented by the movement in GNP per head, reflects the window of opportunity which Ireland faces over the next 20 years. The declining dependency ratio, at a time when the ratio is rising elsewhere in the EU, will make possible a rapid rise in living standards in Ireland.

3.4 Conclusions

The story of the Irish economic renaissance is not yet finished and, if it is to have a happy ending, there is much that still needs to be done. The falling dependency ratio represents a window of opportunity that will last for fifteen or twenty years; after that the ageing process will change the character of the economy and of society, just as it has changed Germany and Japan. From the middle of the next decade the driving factors behind the rapid growth will begin to slow and the rate of growth in output will gradually decelerate towards the EU average.

The first priority for future Irish governments must be to ensure that the potential for further growth is realised. There is then the issue of how best to use the fruits of success. Finally there is a range of long-term strategic issues arising from Ireland's changing economic and social structure.

Lessons for the periphery

Ireland achieved its independence in 1922 on foot of a Sinn Féin – ourselves alone[12] – programme. The relative failure of that strategy, especially in the post-war years, contributed to the depression of the 1950s, which permeated Irish society. The success of today owes much to the enthusiasm with which Ireland has subsequently approached the globalisation of its economy and the opening up of its society to outside influences. While along the way some scepticism was expressed about the benefits of globalisation for the Irish economy (e.g. Girvin, 1989a), the experience of the last decade indicates that it has proved a successful long-term strategy. In viewing EU membership as essentially liberating it has created a positive, outward-looking attitude that affects business, the educational system, and politics. In the past there was concern that Ireland might lose its identity either within the English-speaking world, or more recently within the EU. Such concerns are much less frequently expressed as a new self-confidence takes over.

- It is this cultural change that is probably the single most important factor underlying the current Irish economic renaissance. The factors that brought it about are clearly very specific to Irish society and they do not translate to other countries or regions. However, the benefit of actively embracing the outside world probably does have relevance for other Central European nations.
- A second feature of the Irish experience is the importance of following a consistent strategy over a long period of time. The broad social and political consensus behind the industrial and educational policies followed over the past 30 years has ensured a high level of continuity. This is one aspect of Ireland's experience which it is important to stress when considering the future for countries aspiring to EU membership. Ireland's current success is built on investment over 30 to 40 years, and also on the pain of a major

restructuring of the economy in the 1980s. There is no quick fix for problems of underdevelopment, though there is every reason to believe that the process can be accomplished more efficiently, with less pain, and in a shorter time scale than has been the Irish experience.

- The centrality of investment in education to the process of economic growth does have relevance for other countries. The changing nature of the world economy appears to be favouring those with very high levels of education over the least educated and those regions of Europe which ride the crest of this wave may reap the major benefits. Over the past 30 years the strength of the economies of countries such as that of Germany and the Netherlands owes much to this factor.

- The second strand of Irish development strategy that is relevant for other countries in transition is the area of industrial policy. Ireland has pursued a particular policy of attracting foreign direct investment consistently over 40 years. During that period there have been failures as well as successes. In the past, the concentration on tax incentives has probably unduly favoured foreign firms over domestic firms. The policy, begun in the late 1970s, of targeting particular sectors also carried significant risks. However, we are now seeing the benefits of critical mass in certain key sectors where the investment has succeeded. The presence of a very active labour market in people with information technology skills makes it possible to attract more and more investment in this area. A second aspect of industrial policy has been its focus on sectors which are in the ascendant and the very limited attention given to attracting investment or protecting existing firms in what are essentially declining sectors – don't throw good money after bad.

- The experience of the 1980s indicates the importance of sound financial policies. The slow adjustment of fiscal policy to the serious problems of the early 1980s cost Ireland dear. The experience of Finland in the 1990s suggests that a rapid fiscal response to serious shocks can greatly reduce the ultimate cost.

- Ireland has had two advantages that may not be available to all peripheral regions – the English language and the existence of a core of employment in sophisticated services sectors which are in the ascendant internationally and which require skilled labour. In the case of the English language, all Irish people find that when travelling abroad it is a great advantage to speak English but not to be English or American! It is no accident that the information technology (IT) sector, which is dominated by the English language, has been a sector in which Ireland has done well. In the case of tradable services, Ireland has the advantage of having a core of employment in sophisticated legal and financial services. Being a separate country, albeit small, confers certain advantages in this regard over regions of larger countries.[13] It has provided a foothold in an area of economic activity that is growing rapidly internationally.

- Diversity of experience and culture within the country can be a positive advantage. In the case of Ireland, past failures and current successes owe something to changing attitudes to investment in education. It is clear that an important ingredient of the current Irish success story is luck. In so far as countries make their own successes each country has to find its own path. It is this diversity of experience that is both a stimulus and a challenge.

NOTES

1 While the UK's 'heyday' was the late nineteenth century, the seventeenth century saw Sweden one of the great European powers.

2 Because of the greatly diminished size of the agricultural sector, the outcome of the process of reforming the CAP over the next decade will not have a major economic impact.

3 This study was undertaken with the help of the OECD. It was commissioned in 1962 and published in 1966. Among its authors were Professor P. Lynch of UCD and Professor M. O'Donoghue of TCD.

4 The figures for participation are significantly higher for women than for men.

5 In the 1990s many countries in Central Europe had to undergo such a transition in a much more extreme form over a shorter period than was the case for Ireland.

6 Referred to as long-term factors in Bradley et al, 1997.

7 P. Geary, 1978, 'How Fianna Fáil's economic policies cannot get this country moving again', *Magill*, April.

8 There was free movement of funds within the sterling area until Irish entry into the EMS in 1979. However, until the mid-1950s, there were extensive controls on direct foreign investment in Ireland.

9 Much of the supply of labour at these rates has come from women or students working part-time who may not be eligible for social welfare payments.

10 The picture for males is rather similar to that for females.

11 Roughly a doubling compared to wages of those with leaving certificates.

12 The literal English translation of Sinn Féin is 'ourselves alone'.

13 It also has additional costs as there are definitely increasing returns in the case of many of the services needed to run a modern state.

4

The Dynamics of the Irish Labour Market in Comparative Perspective

PHILIP J. O'CONNELL

4.1 Introduction

The Irish economy has been transformed over the past decade. In the late 1980s Ireland was an economy in crisis. In 1987, with mass unemployment, falling employment levels, a fiscal crisis of the state and living standards well below the European average, it was widely regarded as 'a sick man of Europe'. A decade or so later the economy was performing at exceptional levels. Gross national product grew at an astonishing rate of over 8 per cent in 1999, a continuation of more than a decade of rapid growth; unemployment had fallen to about 5 per cent, well below the European average – employment had been growing at over 5 per cent *per annum* for the previous five years; and, instead of incurring heavy deficits in order to keep the economy and society afloat, the government was able to report a public budget surplus for the first time in decades.

Tansey (1998: 249), reviewing the transformation, writes:

> The Irish economy has enjoyed a decade of unparalleled economic progress. Irish economic growth has been unmatched in the European Union. Material living standards have risen appreciably for the majority of Irish citizens. Social safety nets have been strengthened. The exodus of people from the country has ceased. The population is growing …

The decade of growth in Ireland compares well with the Netherlands, which was dubbed the 'Dutch Miracle' on the basis of annual growth rates of 2.2 per cent in GDP, and 1.5 per cent in employment between 1991-1996, and the reduction of unemployment to 6 per cent (Visser and Hemerijck, 1997). Ireland's rates of output and employment growth have been higher than those of the Dutch, the fall in unemployment has been greater, and its fiscal balance is healthier. Moreover, much unemployment in the Netherlands is hidden by exceptionally high proportions of the adult population in receipt of disability payments (and thus counted as outside the labour force) and in addition, large numbers of workers are in subsidised employment. The recent Irish labour market performance thus appears as a highly unusual success story, and one that sets Ireland apart from its European neighbours.

Critics of the globalisation of economic activity contend that late-comers to economic development confront barriers to development in the international division of labour, and that the progressive internationalisation of production and exchange undermines the steering capacity of the state, destroys jobs, increases earnings dispersion and increases the flexibility of the labour market to the detriment of workers. Advocates of free trade, on the other hand, argue that the free movement of goods, services and labour across national borders increases economic efficiency without lowering real wages or raising the level of unemployment. Ireland represents a particularly interesting case in which to examine processes of economic development and internationalisation. It underwent a delayed and very rapid process of industrialisation over the last four decades of the twentieth century. As Bradley (this volume) and Fitz Gerald (this volume) note, it is characterised by exceptionally high openness in both its economy and labour market. Following a period of fiscal crisis of the state and mass unemployment in the 1980s, its recent period of exceptional growth has taken place in the context of social partnership and against a backdrop of retrenchment in public expenditure.

Given the extent of change in the Irish labour market, this chapter seeks first to provide a description of the successes in the Irish labour market over the past decade and relate them to longer-run trends in the quantity and structure of employment. The chapter then addresses concerns about the quality of employment, seeking to investigate whether the rapid growth in output and employment has been associated with a deterioration in the quality of work.

4.2 Principal developments in the labour market

The labour force

Labour force trends over the past two decades have been erratic, alternating between periods of very rapid growth as at present, and periods of contraction, as during the 1980s. Trends in the labour force reflect not only underlying demographic trends in the adult population, but also changes in women's labour force participation, levels of participation in education, retirement patterns, and, particularly in the Irish case, migration. Table 4.1 shows adult population by principal economic status from 1981 to 1999, distinguishing between those in the labour force, in education, engaged in home duties and an 'other' residual category which mainly consists of those who have retired from the work force.

The numbers in the labour force grew slowly at an annual average of about 11,000 per annum between 1981 and 1991, and very rapidly by about 38,000 per annum between 1991 and 1999. These labour force trends can be attributed to four principal factors. First, there was strong underlying growth in the adult population over the entire period. Second, however, growth in both the labour force and the adult population was reduced by net emigration, which peaked in the latter half of the 1980s. The reversal of net migration since 1991 has meant that the adult population grew unhindered by 14 per cent between 1991-99.

Third, there has been a marked increase in women's labour force participation. Historically, women's labour force participation in Ireland has been low, and, it has been argued, lagged behind what might be expected from the rapid industrialisation of the economy since the 1960s (O'Connor and Shortall, 1999). The female labour force participation rate was less than 28 per cent in 1971, and it remained under 30 per cent a decade later (O'Connell, 1999a). The growth in female labour force participation continued to be sluggish through the mid-1980s (32 per cent in 1986), but it increased dramatically thereafter, to 35 per cent in 1991 and to 44 per cent in 1999.[1] Men's participation in the labour force has been moving in the opposite direction: the participation rate fell from 81 per cent of adult males in 1971 to 76 per cent in 1981 and it has hovered around 71 per cent throughout the 1990s. These countervailing trends in men's and women's labour force participation meant that the overall labour force participation rate remained virtually unchanged over the 1980s – 53 per cent in 1981 and 53.5 per cent in 1991 – although it increased to 57 per cent of the adult population in 1999.

A fourth underlying factor influencing labour market trends results from increased educational participation. The total numbers engaged in education increased from 200,000 in 1981 to 283,000 in 1991 and to 359,000 in 1999. Thus the numbers in education increased by 80 per cent over the 1981-99 period, and by 27 per cent from the beginning to the end of the 1990s. This had two countervailing effects: (1) It radically reduced the number of young people in the labour force (the labour force participation rate for the 15-24 year age group fell from 61 per cent in 1981 to about 45 per cent in 1996; and (2) as noted above, it led to increased labour force participation among women. Sexton and O'Connell (1996) note that increased participation in education among younger age groups, as well as increased retirement among older age groups, and the dramatic increase in women's labour force participation meant that the apparent near-stability in labour force participation rates over the past 15 years masked fundamental changes in the structure of the labour force entailing a much greater proportion of women and a burgeoning share accounted for by the 'middle age' group.

Table 4.1: The labour force and economically inactive population aged 15 and over, 1981-1999

	1981	1991	1996	1999
Men				
Total in labour force	912.5	911.2	960.3	1028.4
Student	97.3	140.1	166.9	172.4
Home duties	1.0	2.7	4.1	8.8
Other	183.1	216.6	227.4	239.0
Total aged 15 years and over	1193.9	1270.6	1358.8	1448.6
Labour Force Participation Rate	76.4	71.7	70.7	71.0
Women				
Total in labour force	358.6	471.7	573.7	658.9
Student	103.0	143.0	172.7	186.7
Home duties	661.5	592.8	549.1	563.5
Other	82.6	107.1	112.5	90.1
Total aged 15 years and over	1205.7	1314.6	1407.9	1499.2
Labour Force Participation Rate	29.7	35.9	40.7	44.0
All Persons				
Total in labour force	1271.1	1382.9	1534.0	1687.3
Student	200.3	283.1	339.6	359.1
Home duties	662.6	595.5	553.2	572.3
Other	265.7	323.7	339.9	329.1
Total aged 15 years and over	2399.7	2585.1	2766.7	2947.8
Labour Force Participation Rate	53.0	53.5	55.4	57.2

Sources: Central Statistics Office, various years, *Census of population,* and *Quarterly National Household Survey*, 1999,Q4

Employment and unemployment

The decade of the 1980s was particularly severe for the Irish economy. The numbers at work declined over the first half of the 1980s while the size of the labour force increased, due both to natural population growth and increasing labour force participation by women. Contraction in employment combined with labour force growth resulted in an increase in the unemployment rate from just under 10 per cent of the labour force in 1981 to a peak of almost 17 per cent in 1987. The decade from 1987-97 saw a remarkable turn-around in Irish economic fortunes, with growth in GDP amounting to 79 per cent over the decade, giving rise to substantial increases in employment, and in the 1990s, to a marked fall in unemployment.

Table 4.2: Numbers at work, unemployed, labour force and net migration, 1987-1999

Year	At Work	Unemployed	Labour Force	Unemployment Rate	Net Migration
	(1,000)	*(1,000)*	*(1,000)*	*per cent*	*(1,000)*
1987	1110	226	1336	16.9	-23
1988	1111	217	1328	16.3	-42
1989	1111	197	1308	15.1	-44
1990	1160	172	1332	12.9	-23
1991	1156	199	1355	14.7	-2
1992	1165	207	1372	15.1	7
1993	1183	220	1403	15.7	0
1994	1221	211	1432	14.7	-5
1995	1282	177	1459	12.1	-2
1996	1329	179	1508	11.9	8
1997	1380	159	1539	10.3	15
1998	1495	127	1622	7.8	22
1999	1591	97	1688	5.7	19

Sources: Central Statistics Office, various years, *Labour Force Survey*, and Central Statistics Office, various years, *Quarterly National Household Survey*

While impressive growth was achieved over the decade as a whole, the rate of growth was, in fact, uneven, and three sub-periods can be identified. Table 4.2 shows trends in numbers at work, unemployed, and the labour force, as well as net migration over the years 1987-99.[2]

- *Recovery, 1987-90.* A period of recovery from 1987-90, with strong growth in investment and exports and curtailment of public spending. In the labour market, these aggregate growth trends generated a brief employment boom between 1989-90, when total employment increased by 4 per cent and unemployment fell to 13 per cent.
- *Sluggish growth, 1991-93.* A downturn in international activity, initially in Britain in 1990 and throughout Europe in 1992 and 1993, which coincided with dramatic increases in interest rates and an exchange rate crisis, meant that growth faltered in Ireland. In Ireland sluggish growth led to employment declines in 1991 and 1992, and with burgeoning growth in the labour force, to increased unemployment, which reached almost 16 per cent in 1993.
- *Very rapid growth, 1993-99.* Since 1993 the Irish economy has expanded very rapidly, with annual rates of growth in excess of 8 per cent averaged

over the 1993-97 period, stimulated by both accelerated export growth and by increased domestic demand. These growth rates have given rise to a rapid and dramatic improvement in labour market conditions. Total employment grew by about 400,000 or about 33 per cent, in the six years from 1993 to 1999. The unemployment rate fell to 5.7 per cent in April 1999, and was down to 5 per cent by the end of that year. Most forecasts are for a continuation of strong growth for the foreseeable future, with a continuation of strong labour demand and low unemployment.

Emigration has fluctuated in accordance with demand in both domestic and external labour markets. It rose dramatically in the late 1980s and peaked in 1989, when net emigration (in-migration minus out-migration) rose to 44,000 individuals, representing almost 3.5 per cent of the labour force in that year. The tightening of the labour market and the emergence of skills shortages has attracted increasing numbers of Irish migrants to return as well as a substantial number of skilled non-Irish immigrants, with the result that in 1999 inward migration exceeded out-migration by about 19,000.

Employment and activity in comparative perspective

It is useful to consider Irish employment and activity rates in comparison with other European societies. Table 4.3 shows total employment, unemployment and economic inactivity, each expressed as a percentage of the working age population (aged 15-64).

Table 4.3: Employment, unemployment and inactivity rates, 1985 and 1998 (Percentage of the working age population)

	Employment			Unemployment			Inactivity		
	1985	1998	Change	1985	1998	Change	1985	1998	Change
Austria	67.3	70.1	2.8	2.4	3.3	0.9	30.3	26.6	-3.7
Belgium	53.1	57.5	4.4	6.2	6.0	-0.2	40.7	36.5	-4.2
Denmark	77.4	78.9	1.5	5.8	4.1	-1.7	16.8	17.0	0.2
Finland	75.2	65.1	-10.1	4.7	8.3	3.6	20.1	26.6	6.5
Greece	57.3	57.2	-0.1	4.3	7.4	3.1	38.4	35.4	-3.0
Ireland	51.4	60.5	9.1	10.5	5.2	-5.3	38.1	34.3	-3.8
Netherlands	57.7	68.3	10.6	4.8	2.8	-2.0	37.5	28.9	-8.6
Portugal	63.5	68.9	5.4	6.0	3.7	-2.3	30.5	27.4	-3.1
Spain	44.1	50.2	6.1	12.2	11.6	-0.6	43.7	38.2	-5.5
UK	66.5	71.4	4.9	8.2	4.8	-3.4	25.3	23.8	-1.5
EU	59.8	61.1	1.3	6.6	6.9	0.3	33.6	32.0	-1.6

Source: European Commission, 2000, *Employment in Europe 1999*

In 1985 the employment-population ratio in Ireland, 51.4, lagged well behind the EU average of 59.8. The rapid growth in employment over the 1990s meant that by 1998 the Irish ratio, at 60.5, had all but caught up with the European average. However, the Irish employment-population ratio continues to lag well behind the Nordic countries as well as the UK.

More than one in every ten adults was unemployed in Ireland in 1985, an unemployment-population ratio that was substantially higher than the European average of 6.6 and second only to the Spanish rate of 12.2. Between 1985-98 the ratio in Ireland halved. This was the most rapid decline in the EU, and the EU average ratio actually increased to 6.9 over the period. Inactivity rates have also declined in Ireland, from 38.1 in 1985 to 34.3 in 1998, and this rate of decline in the inactivity rate was faster than the EU average. Nevertheless, the Irish inactivity ratio remains comparatively high by northern European standards and is more similar to a southern European inactivity pattern. Combining the changes in the three ratios suggests that Ireland went through a substantial convergence with European patterns of economic activity during the 1990s.

There are substantial international differences in activity rates by gender. In general, men's employment and inactivity rates are higher than women's and there is less variation between countries. Table 4.4 shows that in 1998 the Irish male employment-population ratio was 73.5, somewhat higher than the EU average, while the unemployment ratio, at 6.4, was slightly lower than the average, as was the inactivity ratio. The employment rate among women, 47.4, was much lower than that for men, and also lower than the European average, this despite the rapid increase in women's employment in Ireland described below. The unemployment-population ratio among women in Ireland was also lower than the Irish male rate, and the EU average. Inactivity among Irish women, 48.6, was much higher than among Irish men and also higher than the EU average. These gender differences are reflected in the male-female employment ratio gap, which was over 26 in Ireland, compared to an EU average of 20. Table 4.4 shows that if the aggregate Irish employment and activity rates lag behind those elsewhere in Europe, most of that differential is due to the continuation of lower employment and activity rates among women in Ireland. It is likely therefore that if further growth in the employment ratio is to be achieved in Ireland in the future this will entail a further increase in labour force participation among women.

Table 4.4: Employment, unemployment and activity to population ratios, men and women, 1998

	Men			Women			Male-Female Employment Gap
	Employment	Unemployment	Inactivity	Employment	Unemployment	Inactivity	
Austria	80.1	3.2	16.7	60.1	3.6	36.3	20.0
Belgium	67.3	5.6	27.1	47.7	6.4	45.9	19.6
Denmark	84.4	3.3	12.3	73.3	4.9	21.8	11.1
Finland	68.2	8.4	23.4	62.0	8.4	29.6	6.2
Greece	73.9	6.2	19.9	41.3	8.5	50.2	32.6
Ireland	73.5	6.4	20.1	47.4	4.0	48.6	26.1
Netherlands	79.6	2.5	17.9	56.6	3.2	40.2	23.0
Portugal	78.3	3.4	18.3	59.9	4.1	36.0	18.4
Spain	65.6	10.5	23.9	35.2	12.7	52.1	30.4
UK	78.5	5.9	15.6	64.1	3.8	32.1	14.4
EU	71.1	6.8	22.1	51.2	6.9	41.9	19.9

Source: European Commission, 2000, *Employment in Europe 1999*

Table 4.5 shows employment by gender in Ireland for the years 1988, 1993 and 1999. Total employment increased by an average of almost 4 per cent per annum over the entire period, although this entailed slow growth in the 1988-93 period, followed by growth of 5.7 per cent per annum between 1993 and 1999. Employment trends have differed markedly between men and women, with total employment among men falling strongly in the first half of the 1980s (Sexton and O'Connell, 1996), and increasing only marginally between 1988-93. It was only in the 1990s that men's employment levels picked up – increasing by 4.4 per cent per annum in the 1993-99 period. As a consequence of these fluctuating trends, male employment in the late 1990s was only marginally above its level in 1981 although, as we shall see, the composition of that employment had shifted markedly in the intervening period.

Table 4.5: Total employment by gender, 1988, 1993 and 1999

	Total	Men	Women	Female Share
	(1,000)	*(1,000)*	*(1,000)*	*per cent*
1988	1111.8	747.0	364.7	32.8
1993	1183.1	749.4	433.7	36.7
1999	1591.1	947.3	643.9	40.5
Annual percentage change				
1988-93	1.3	0.1	3.8	2.4
1993-99	5.7	4.4	8.1	1.7
1988-99	3.9	2.4	7.0	2.1

Source: Central Statistics Office, various years, *Labour Force Survey*
Note: In order to render the 1998 data comparable with earlier years, annual percentage changes are estimated on adjusted data, which reduce the total number employed in 1998 by 20,000 (8,000 men and 12,000 women) to take account of changes in measurement (see footnote 2 above).

Total employment among women grew strongly – by an average of 7 per cent per annum over the 1988-99 period. Women's employment was also influenced by labour market conditions, with the result that in the early 1980s, while total employment did not fall, as it did among men, employment growth was negligible. Growth in women's employment increased to 3.8 per cent per annum from 1988 to 1993, and then took off, averaging an annual increase of 8.1 per cent between 1993 and 1999. By 1999 the total number of women at work was more than two-thirds higher than it had been in 1981. Because of these diverging trends between men and women, there was a marked change in the gender balance of employment, and women's share of total employment increased steadily from 29 per cent in 1981 (Sexton and O'Connell, 1996) to 33 per cent in 1988 and to over 40 per cent in 1998.

Employment by economic sector

Sectoral employment trends have been quite divergent over the period since 1981. Employment by sector is presented in Table 4.6. Employment in agriculture continued its long-established decline: total employment in the sector fell by 55,000 from 189,000 in 1981 to 134,000 in 1997. The share of agricultural in total employment accordingly fell from 17 per cent to 10 per cent.

Table 4.6: Employment by economic sector, 1981-97

	1981	1991	1997
Number		*(1,000s)*	
Agriculture	189	155	134
Manufacturing	264	245	289
Construction	102	78	97
Market services	376	427	527
Non-market services	206	229	291
Total	1137	1134	1338
Share		*per cent*	
Agriculture	16.6	13.7	10.0
Manufacturing	23.2	21.6	21.6
Construction	9.0	6.9	7.2
Market services	33.1	37.7	39.4
Non-market services	18.1	20.2	21.7
Total	100.0	100.0	100.0

Source: Hughes, McCormick and Sexton, 2000

Manufacturing employment went through a severe decline in the early 1980s, and even after some recovery in the late 1980s the numbers employed in the sector fell by 20,000 between 1981-91, and its share of total employment fell from 23 per cent to less than 22 per cent. Manufacturing employment has grown rapidly in the 1990s, by an annual average of 3 per cent, a similar rate of expansion to that of employment as a whole, with the result that manufacturing employment maintained its share of almost 22 per cent of the total between 1991-97. The expansion of employment in manufacturing marks Ireland as an exception to trends elsewhere in the developed world, where industrial employment is in decline (Sexton and O'Connell, 1996). The growth of manufacturing in Ireland is mainly due to the continued influx of foreign direct investment – prompted by a range of tax and grant concessions, a moderate cost structure, and the plentiful supply of young well-educated workers. In recent years the resurgence of growth in manufacturing has occurred in both indigenous as well as foreign-owned firms, and employment in the former grew by 8,400 between 1993-96.

The largest growth in employment took place in services. Employment increased across the broad range of service activities over the entire period from 1981-97: slowly during the 1980s and rapidly during the 1990s. Total services employment grew from 582,000 in 1981 to 818,000 in 1997, an expansion of over 40 per cent. Most of the employment expansion in services generally can be attributed to market services, which increased by 100,000 (or 23 per cent) from 427,000 in 1991 to 527,000 in 1997. Within the market services sector, employment trends in transport, communication and distribution have been erratic, and most of the growth in the sector has been concentrated in a range of professional, business and personal services (Sexton and O'Connell, 1996).

The highest rate of growth in the 1991-97 period occurred in non-market services (mainly public sector activities). Within non-market services, the bulk of the growth took place in education and health services (Duggan, Hughes and Sexton, 1997).

Unemployment

The aggregate trends in unemployment over the period from 1988 to 1999 have already been discussed above (see Table 4.2). This section provides a more detailed breakdown of unemployment by age, gender and duration.

Table 4.7: Unemployment by age group, 1999

	15-24	25-44	45+	Total
Number unemployed	*1,000s*	*1,000s*	*1,000s*	*1,000s*
Men	19.3	24.9	14.6	58.8
Women	18.7	16.7	6.8	42.2
All	38.1	41.6	21.4	101.1
Distribution by age group	*per cent*	*per cent*	*per cent*	*per cent*
Men	32.8	42.3	24.8	100.0
Women	44.3	39.6	16.1	100.0
All	37.7	41.1	21.2	100.0

Source: CSO, 1999, *Quarterly National Household Survey*, 3rd Quarter, 1999

Table 4.7 shows unemployment by age and gender in 1999. Total unemployment in the third quarter of 1999 was just over 100,000, consisting of almost 59,000 men and 42,000 women. The largest number unemployed are in the prime working-age-group, 25-44, which accounted for almost 42 per cent of total unemployment in 1999. However, the distribution of unemployment by age group is skewed towards younger people: almost 38 per cent of the unemployed are in the smaller 15-24 age group. Sexton and O'Connell (1996) show that unemployment among young people increased very dramatically over the course of the 1980s and 1990s. O'Connell (1999b) shows that the 15-24 year age group accounted for 30 per cent of total unemployment in 1997, so while the numbers unemployed have fallen since 1997 the proportion of young people among the unemployed has increased, and the number unemployed has fallen more rapidly among prime age workers than among young people. The skewed age distribution of unemployment is more pronounced among women: in 1999 44 per cent of all unemployed women were in the younger age group, compared to 33 per cent of unemployed men.

Figure 4.1: Unemployment rates by age-group and gender

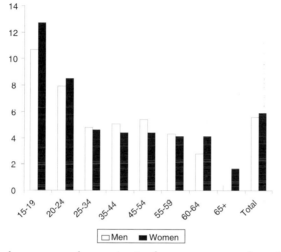

Figure 4.1 shows unemployment rates by age group and gender in 1999. The figure confirms the difficulties facing young people in the labour market. The unemployment rate was 11½ per cent among those aged 15-19 and 8 per cent among those aged 20-24, compared to less than 5 per cent among those aged over 25. Women showed slightly higher unemployment rates than men overall, but there is some variation by age group, with younger men showing lower rates of unemployment than young women.

Figure 4.2: Trends in total, long- and short-term unemployment, 1988-99

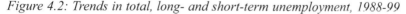
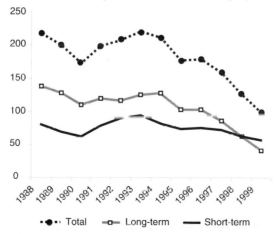

Long-term unemployment

Figure 4.2 shows the trends in total, short- and long-term unemployment from 1988-99. Total unemployment fell between 1988 and 1990, but increased again to about 220,000 in 1993. The rapid growth in the economy and in employment since 1993 has resulted in a steady decline in total unemployment – from just under 16 per cent of the labour force in 1993 to less than 6 per cent in 1999.

The trend in long-term unemployment has followed a slightly different path, increasing rather more slowly than total unemployment in the early to mid-1990s and falling more rapidly than the total since the mid-1999s. This reflects an unusual time-trend in 'short-term' unemployment (i.e. unemployment of less than one year's duration), which has fallen less since the mid 1990s than long-term unemployment. Thus, between 1995 and 1999, total unemployment fell by 45 per cent, long-term unemployment by 60 per cent and short-term unemployment by only 25 per cent. By 1999, the number of short-term unemployed exceeded the number of long-term unemployed for the first time in over a decade and a half.

Table 4.8: Unemployment by duration, 1988-99

	Total Unemployed	Unemployed less than 1 year	Long-term Unemployed	Total Unemployed	Long-term Unemployed Rate	Long-term share in total
	1,000s	*1,000s*	*1,000s*	*per cent*	*per cent*	*per cent*
1988	217.0	79.2	137.8	16.3	10.4	63.5
1989	196.8	68.8	128	15.0	9.8	65.0
1990	172.4	62.2	110.2	12.9	8.3	63.9
1991	198.5	78.8	119.7	14.7	8.8	60.3
1992	206.6	90.1	116.5	15.1	8.5	56.4
1993	220.1	94.7	125.4	15.7	8.9	57.0
1994	211.0	82.8	128.2	14.7	9.0	60.8
1995	177.4	74.1	103.3	12.2	7.1	58.2
1996	179.0	75.7	103.3	11.9	6.9	57.7
1997	159.0	72.7	86.3	10.3	5.6	54.3
1998	126.6	63.1	63.5	7.8	3.9	50.2
1999	96.9	55.3	41.6	5.7	2.5	42.9

Source: CSO, 1999, *Quarterly National Household Survey*, 3rd Quarter 1999

These trends in long-term unemployment are very encouraging, but they should be interpreted with some caution. Over the two years from 1996-98, long-term unemployment fell by 39,800 but the reduction in the number unemployed for less than one year fell by only 12,600. Between 1998-99, long-term unemployment fell by another 22,000; short-term unemployment fell by just under 8,000. These trends appear to confound our conventional understanding of the labour market. We would expect that during an employment boom the 'short-term' unemployed would be hired first both because the long-term unemployed are likely to be more disadvantaged in terms of skills and work experience than the 'short-term' unemployed, and because of the effects of 'state dependence' which suggests that the longer an individual has been unemployed the lower the probability that that individual will escape from unemployment and re-enter work (Heckman and Borjas, 1980).

In Ireland, however, most of the reduction in unemployment in recent years has occurred in respect of long-term unemployment. O'Connell (1998) argues that much of the reduction in long-term unemployment achieved in Ireland in the 1994-97 period may be attributable to participation in labour market training and temporary employment schemes. Quarterly National Household Survey data show that the numbers participating in the schemes at each survey in 1998-99 has been about 40,000. However, the 'throughput' from labour market schemes, which is a flow measure of the number of individuals completing schemes and re-entering the labour market, was about twice that number (O'Connell, 1998). This suggests that the ratio of the number of participants in active labour market programmes to measured unemployment, approaching unity, is very high in Ireland and that the very large scale of labour market programmes may have a very strong influence on our measurement of the balance between short- and long-term unemployment because participants who return to unemployment after leaving programmes are counted as new entrants to unemployment, even where they had been long-term unemployed prior to participation. This potential underestimate relates to the balance between short- and long-term unemployment, not to the total level of unemployment.

With unemployment falling to around 5 per cent at the turn of the century, Ireland approaches a situation of near full-employment with increasing evidence of skill and labour shortages (Williams and Hughes, 1999). Further reductions in unemployment are likely to take place slowly, both because much remaining unemployment is likely to be frictional in nature, related to labour market entry and mobility between jobs, and because in such a tight labour market those remaining unemployed, particularly the long-term unemployed, tend to suffer particularly severe disadvantages which reduce their capacity to compete for work (NESF, 2000).

4.3 The quality of employment

While many commentators have lauded the Irish employment performance of
recent years (see, for example, Tansey, 1998; NESC, 1999), concerns have also
been raised about the quality of jobs created in the booming economy.
Questioning the quality of new employment in the 1990s, O'Hearn (2000: 78-81)
argues that 'employment growth has been concentrated in routine low-paying
services', that 'women account for 70 per cent of new jobs', that there has been
an increase in 'atypical' workers in part-time work or on fixed-term contracts,
and that earnings became more unequal since the late 1980s. He attributes this
suspected deterioration in the quality in employment to the dependent nature of
economic development in Ireland in the 1990s. These are important issues that
warrant serious empirical investigation.

Class transformation

If the economic restructuring associated with the particular trajectory of
economic development in Ireland has resulted in a deterioration in the quality of
work in Ireland, then, arguably, the fist place to look for such a deterioration
would be in the structure of positions in the economy: the class structure of
those at work. Table 4.9 provides a summary of the long-run transformation of
class positions of both men and women at work from the start of the process of
rapid economic development in 1961, mid-way through the process in 1981,
and, more recently, in 1996.

Between 1961 and 1996 the total number at work increased by 235,000, and,
as we have seen above, most of this growth took place in the 1990s. As noted
already, there were very substantial gender differences. Male employment
increased by only 4 per cent between 1961 and 1996, and male employment in
1996 was actually lower than it had been in 1981. Women's employment, on the
other hand, increased by 75 per cent over the three-and-a-half decades, with
most of the growth taking place in the fifteen years after 1981. These differing
trends meant that women's share of total employment increased from 26 per
cent in 1961 to 29 per cent in 1981 and to almost 38 per cent in 1996.

Table 4.9: Men and women at work by class position, 1961, 1981 and 1996

	Men			Women			All		
	1961	1981	1996	1961	1981	1996	1961	1981	1996
Employers and Self-employed	43.9	29.0	28.1	22.6	8.4	9.4	38.3	23.0	21.0
Agriculture									
1 Employers	1.8	1.7	1.1	1.1	0.3	0.3	1.6	1.3	0.8
2 Self-employed	34.3	17.5	12.2	13.9	3.2	2.1	28.9	13.4	8.4
Non-Agriculture									
1 Employers	1.6	4.4	5.8	1.1	1.7	2.2	1.5	3.7	4.4
2 Self-employed	6.2	5.3	9.1	6.5	3.2	4.8	6.3	4.7	7.5
Employees	56.1	71.0	71.9	77.4	91.6	90.6	61.7	77.0	79.0
1 Upper middle class	7.6	16.0	20.4	14.8	24.3	28.9	9.5	18.4	23.6
Higher Professional	2.2	4.3	5.6	5.0	4.2	4.2	3.0	4.2	5.1
Lower Professional	1.7	3.7	5.3	8.9	17.6	18.8	3.6	7.7	10.4
Employers/Managers	2.0	5.6	7.3	0.8	2.0	4.4	1.7	4.6	6.2
Salaried Employees	1.6	2.4	2.3	0.0	0.5	1.5	1.2	1.9	2.0
2 Lower middle class	15.6	20.3	21.1	42.7	51.4	48.4	22.8	29.3	31.4
Inter. Non-manual	8.6	10.5	10.5	24.7	38.2	35.0	12.8	18.5	19.8
Other Non-manual	7.1	9.8	10.6	17.9	13.1	13.4	10.0	10.7	11.6
3 Skilled manual	12.0	20.6	18.1	5.8	3.9	3.2	10.3	15.8	12.5
4 Semi/Unskilled manual	20.9	14.2	12.3	14.1	12.0	10.1	19.1	13.5	11.5
Total	100.0	100.0	100.0	100.0	100.0	100.0	100.0	100.0	100.0
Total at work (1000s)	774.5	808.7	801.0	278.0	329.2	486.4	1052.5	1137.8	1287.4
Unemployment Rate	5.7	10.0	14.7	3.0	6.1	9.7	5.0	8.9	12.9

Sources: CSO, 1961 and 1981: *Census of Population;* 1996: Author's analysis of *Labour Force Survey* micro data

Perhaps the most marked change that can be observed over the 35-year period is the decline in the number of employers and self-employed individuals deriving their income from property ownership – from almost 40 per cent of the total in 1961 to 21 per cent in 1996 – and the consequent increase in the numbers of wage- and salary-dependent workers. This is, of course, one of the common effects of industrialisation, and what is most noticeable in the Irish context is the rapid pace of that transformation.

The most important source of the decline in the importance of property ownership is the decline in agriculture discussed above – from 30 per cent of class positions in 1961 to just over 9 per cent in 1996. Among men the decline in agricultural employment and self-employment was from 36 per cent to 13 per cent of all positions. By 1996 women had almost disappeared from agriculture.

Outside of agriculture there was some increase in the proportion of employers, from 1.5 per cent to 4 per cent. This was true also of self-employment, albeit to a lesser extent, entailing a decline from 6 per cent to 5 per cent of the total between 1961-81, and subsequent growth, to 7.5 per cent in 1996. Among men, there was a marked increase in the proportion of non-agricultural employers – from 1.6 per cent of the total in 1961 to almost 6 per cent in 1996, and self-employment also increased from 6 per cent to 9 per cent. Among women, however, there was a much smaller growth in the proportion of employers, from 1 per cent to 2 per cent, and both the number and proportion of self-employed women fell between 1961-81 but recovered somewhat between 1981 and 1996.

The number of employees increased from 62 per cent in 1961 to almost 80 per cent in 1996. Here, the most dramatic change was the growth in middle-class positions. Between 1961 and 1996, the proportion of upper middle-class employees – including professionals, managers, and salaried employees – increased by a factor of 2.5: from 9.5 per cent of total employment to 23.6 per cent. Within the upper middle class there were important gender differences. The proportion of men occupying higher professional positions more than doubled, from 2.2 per cent to 5.6 per cent, while the corresponding proportion of women in the higher professional category declined (although the number increased). Among women, however, there was a very substantial increase in the lower professional category – from less than 9 per cent of total women's employment in 1961 to 19 per cent in 1996. Most of the increase in this category can be attributed to the marked expansion over this period of lower professional employment in health and education in the public sector.

. The lower middle class also expanded, although less dramatically, from 23 per cent in 1961 to 31 per cent in 1996. Women predominate in this class category, which includes a rather diverse range of white-collar occupations, including clerical workers, shop assistants, and personal service workers. By 1996, lower middle class positions accounted for almost half of all women's employment but just over one-fifth of men's employment.

Skilled manual work increased slightly, from 10 per cent of total employment in 1961 to 12.5 per cent in 1996, but these aggregate figures also conceal offsetting trends between men and women. The proportion of skilled manual male employees increased from 12 per cent to almost 18 per cent while the proportion of women in skilled manual occupations declined from 6 per cent to

3 per cent over the 35-year period. There was a steady decline in semi- and unskilled manual work, from 19 per cent in 1961 to 12 per cent in 1996. That decline was particularly severe among men, with the share of unskilled manual work declining from 21 per cent to 12 per cent.

Finally, the table also shows that unemployment increased dramatically – from 5 per cent of the labour force in 1961 to almost 13 per cent in 1996, although as shown above, unemployment had subsequently fallen back to about 5 per cent in 1999. Unemployment among men increased from almost 6 per cent in 1961 to almost 15 per cent in 1996, while the increase among women was from 3 per cent to almost 10 per cent.

Table 4.9 suggests that the transformation of the structure of the labour market was more far-reaching than just a shift from agriculture to industrial and service sector employment, or from manual to non-manual activities, although both of these changes did take place. The new types of occupation required either qualifications or personal skills which had not been required by traditional employment, or which were unnecessary to inherit the family business in a class structure dominated by property ownership. Many of the changes in the structure of labour market positions coincided with the removal of at least some of the impediments to women's participation in the labour market, with the result that many of the newly created opportunities were taken by women, contributing to the substantial increase in women's employment over the three decades. Women, and those possessing educational qualifications, were the main beneficiaries of the transformation, and indeed, part of the reason for the dramatic increase in women's employment-population ratio is the increased educational attainment among women since the 1970s. Among the losers in the transformation were those who lost jobs in traditional industries, and, particularly older workers, lacking the qualifications and skills to compete for the newly created positions, became unemployed and, eventually long-term unemployed.

Previous work reviewing this long-run transformation of the class structure over the three decades from 1961-91. (O'Connell, 1999a), argues that five overarching trends could be observed:

- A secular contraction in agriculture, and more generally, a substantial decline in the importance of positions deriving income from property ownership, and consequently, an increase in the importance of wage- and salary-dependent employment
- A marked expansion in public sector employment
- A general upgrading of the quality of positions in the labour market, with well over half of all those at work occupying middle class positions by 1991
- A substantial increase in the number of women at work

- A marked increase in unemployment – itself entailing a further augmentation of the numbers dependent on the state for their income.

This characterisation of the transformation remains pertinent to the end of the century, with, fortunately, the exception of unemployment, which has fallen to a historically low level. This suggests that the more recent trends related to the booming economy of the 1990s represent a continuation of well-established trends over the past three or four decades. Overall the long-run trends in the class structure have entailed an up-grading of the quality of positions in the labour market and there is little in this long-run transformation of the class structure to suggest a deterioration in the quality of jobs.

Table 4.10 shows employment by main occupational group in 1991 and 1997, thus allowing us to focus more precisely on the more recent period. The two most substantial changes there relate to the increase in the share of professional employment, up from 17 per cent in 1991 to 18 per cent in 1997, and the decline in the share of unskilled manual workers, down from 4.2 per cent to 3.5 per cent. Of the net increase of 204,000 in employment, professionals accounted for almost 28 per cent, managers for 9 per cent, skilled workers for 20 per cent. Sales and service workers together accounted for about 27 per cent of the increased employment. The rate of growth between 1991-97 was about 30 per cent among production workers, professionals and service workers, and the number of sales workers also increased by 26 per cent over the period.

Table 4.10: Employment by main occupational group, 1991-1997

	1991		1997		1991-1997		
	Number	Share	Number	Share	Number	Share	Percent Change
	(1,000s)	*per cent*	*(1,000s)*	*per cent*	*(1,000s)*	*per cent*	*per cent*
Agricultural	144.0	12.7	131.2	9.8	-12.8	-6.3	-8.9
Managers	113.9	10.0	132.3	9.9	18.4	9.0	16.2
Professional	189.3	16.7	245.9	18.4	56.6	27.6	29.9
Clerical	158.0	13.9	178.2	13.3	20.2	9.9	12.8
Sales	82.8	7.3	104.3	7.8	21.5	10.5	26.0
Service workers	114.4	10.1	147.7	11.0	33.3	16.3	29.1
Skilled manual	195.8	17.3	236.6	17.7	40.8	19.9	20.8
Production workers	88.1	7.8	115.2	8.6	27.1	13.2	30.8
Unskilled manual	47.3	4.2	47.0	3.5	-0.3	-0.1	-0.6
Total	1133.6	100.0	1338.4	100.0	204.8	100.0	18.1

Source: Hughes, McCormick and Sexton, 2000

Thus, notwithstanding some increases in employment in sales and service occupations, these have been more than offset by increases in professional, managerial and skilled occupations. These trends in occupational structure provide more support for an occupational up-grading thesis than for a contention that most employment growth in the 1990s has been in routine poorly-paid occupations.

Atypical working

The extent of atypical working, including both part-time work and temporary fixed-term contracts, has increased in Ireland in the past decade or so. In this, Ireland participates in an international trend of increased flexibility of working hours and contractual relationships. The spread of part-time working in Europe has raised concerns about the quality of part-time jobs. Part-time work is female dominated, as we have seen above, and part-time jobs tend to be concentrated in low-paid low-status occupations (Smith, Fagan and Rubery, 1998). However, cross-national differences in the quality of part-time jobs are related to national labour market institutions and regulations. In Ireland employment protection legislation was extended in the early 1990s to cover both part-time employees as well as those on fixed-term contracts (Sexton and O'Connell, 1996).[4]

O'Connell (1999b) shows that the incidence of part-time working increased from 8 per cent of total employment in 1990 to almost 17 per cent in 1998, and that women account for over 70 per cent of part-time workers. Sexton and O'Connell (1996) show that part-time work accounted for all of the modest growth in employment that occurred in Ireland between 1983 and 1993 and that the numbers in full-time employment actually declined during that period. However, with the surge in employment since 1993, the balance between growth in part-time versus full-time work has shifted again. Since 1993 the increase in employment has consisted mainly of full-time jobs, although the rate of increase in part-time employment was higher, with the result that the share of part-time working in total employment continues to rise gradually (O'Connell, 1999b).

The increase in part-time work in Ireland is part of a widespread international trend. Table 4.11 shows the incidence of part-time working in EU countries in 1997. In 1997, part-time employment accounted for just over 12 per cent of total employment in Ireland, lower than the EU average of 17 per cent, and well behind the rates in the Netherlands (38 per cent), as well as Sweden, the United Kingdom and Denmark (all between 22 per cent and 25 per cent). The common pattern is for men to show relatively low rates of part-time working, and this is true of the Irish case. The main exception to this is the Netherlands, where 17 per cent of male employment was part-time. Women are far more likely to work part-time. Averaging across the EU, women working part-time account for about one-third of total female employment. In Ireland they account for about one-quarter of total female employment; in the Netherlands, about two-thirds. Thus notwithstanding the gradual rise in part-time working in Ireland in recent decades, Irish rates of part-time working are comparatively low by European standards.

Table 4.11: The share of part-time in total employment, 1997

	All	Men	Women
Belgium	14.7	3.2	31.4
Denmark	22.2	12.1	34.4
Germany	17.5	4.2	35.1
Greece	4.6	2.6	8.1
Spain	8.2	3.2	17.4
France	16.8	5.5	30.9
Ireland	12.3	5.4	23.2
Italy	7.1	3.3	13.7
Netherlands	37.9	17.0	67.6
Austria	14.9	4.0	29.0
Portugal	9.9	5.7	15.0
Finland	11.4	7.6	15.6
Sweden	23.8	9.2	39.9
United Kingdom	24.9	8.7	44.8
EU-15	16.9	5.8	32.3

Source: Eurostat, 1998, Labour Force Survey Results 1997

The voluntary nature of part-time working is also relevant to a consideration of the quality of jobs. Table 4.12 presents an analysis of part-time workers by gender and 'under-employment' for 1992 and 1997. Part-time workers are considered to be under-employed if they indicate in response to the Labour Force Survey that they were looking and available for another part-time job or a full-time job. The table suggests that most part-time working is a matter of preference: in both years well over 80 per cent of all part-time workers were not under-employed, i.e. they were not working part-time because of an inability to find a full-time job. The table also indicates that the incidence of under-employment among part-time workers fell. Between 1992 and 1997, while the absolute number of part-time workers increased dramatically, the proportion underemployed fell from 18 per cent to 13 per cent, reflecting the tightening of the Irish labour market.

Table 4.12: Part-time employment and under-employment by gender, 1992 and 1997

	Total part-time	Not under-employed		Under-employed	
	(1,000s)	*(1,000s)*	*per cent*	*(1,000s)*	*per cent*
1992					
Men	28.7	18.4	64.1	10.3	35.9
Women	75.7	66.9	88.4	8.8	11.6
All	104.4	85.3	81.7	19.1	18.3
1997					
Men	45.4	33.8	74.4	11.6	25.6
Women	124.6	114.4	91.8	10.2	8.2
All	169.9	148.1	87.2	21.8	12.8

Source: CSO, 1997b, *Labour Force Survey*

Table 4.12 also reveals interesting gender differences, with men working part-time far more likely than women to indicate that they were under-employed: in 1997 over one-quarter of men working part-time reported that they were under-employed, true of only 8 per cent of women working part-time. The large majority of part-time workers are women and the rapid increases in both employment and labour force participation in Ireland in recent years is partly due to an increase in the demand for part-time workers, an arrangement which allows women greater scope to combine working with child rearing and other domestic work – a particularly important factor in Ireland, given the absence of public provision of, or even support for, child-care services.

A second important dimension of atypical work is fixed-term temporary employment. In Ireland the numbers working on fixed-term contracts also increased somewhat, from 8.5 per cent in 1990 to 9.4 per cent in 1997, while over the same period, the average incidence of fixed-term contracts across the EU increased from 10 per cent to 12 per cent (European Commission, 2000). Table 4.13 shows the share of employees with a temporary job in total employment by gender for the EU countries in 1997. Averaging across the EU countries, employees in temporary jobs accounted for 10 per cent of total employment in 1997. The rate was just over 7 per cent in Ireland, and was highest in Spain at over 25 per cent. In general, women were somewhat more likely than men to be in temporary jobs (9.2 per cent versus 11.4 per cent on average in the EU). Gender differences were particularly marked in Ireland: only 5 per cent of men were in temporary employment, compared to 11 per cent of women.

Table 4.13: Temporary employment as a per cent of total employment, 1997

	All	Men	Women
Belgium	5.2	3.7	7.3
Denmark	10.1	9.3	10.9
Germany	10.3	9.9	10.9
Greece	6.0	5.4	6.9
Spain	25.5	24.1	28.1
France	11.4	10.2	12.8
Ireland	7.4	5.1	11.0
Italy	5.9	5.0	7.4
Netherlands	10.0	7.6	13.4
Austria	6.7	6.2	7.3
Portugal	8.6	8.0	9.2
Finland	14.4	12.0	17.1
Sweden	10.6	8.4	13.0
United Kingdom	6.3	5.3	7.6
EU-15	10.1	9.2	11.4

Source: Eurostat, 1998, Labour Force Survey Results 1997

With regard to both part-time working and temporary contracts, Ireland has participated in a common European trend towards increased flexibility. However, while Ireland has followed this trend, the rate of flexibilisation of employment in Ireland has been slower than the EU average, and the extent of both part-time and temporary working in the latter half of the 1990s remained lower than the EU average.

The question remains as to whether more than a decade of unprecedented growth in output and employment has contributed to improvements in living standards. This question centres on both trends in real earnings as well as their distribution. Barrett, Fitzgerald and Nolan (this volume) discuss the evolution of earnings inequality over the 1987-97 period in some depth. They show that there was a substantial increase in earnings dispersion over the decade from 1987-97. They argue that this dispersion was more pronounced in the 1987-94 period than in the period following 1994, suggesting that rapid economic growth was not associated with an acceleration in the trend. They also show that in the latter period the bottom decile and quartile each kept pace with the rate of increase in median income, and that increasing inequality mainly derived from incomes in the top decile increasing more rapidly than the median.

Sexton, Nolan and McCormick (1999) show that average hourly earnings increased by just over 5 per cent annually between 1987 and 1997. When adjusted for consumer price inflation this translated into an annual rise of 2.5 per cent per annum in real income over the decade. They also show that over the decade from 1987 to 1997 the more skilled and better qualified made the greatest gains.

But if average earnings in Ireland have increased in real terms over the past decade or so, they have done so from a comparatively low base. Duffy et al (1997) observe that skilled labour in Ireland is comparatively cheap. Figure 4.3, which shows average hourly total and direct labour costs in industry in ECUs from the Eurostat Labour Costs surveys for 1995, confirms that average wage costs in Ireland are substantially below those in most European countries. Total labour costs refer to the total expenditure borne by employers to employ workers; direct labour costs to total remuneration paid to employees, inclusive of bonuses and fringe benefits. The residual consists mainly of social security contributions, training costs borne by employers, and other social costs. Average total hourly labour costs in Ireland in 1995 were higher only than in Greece and Portugal. When adjusted for social security contributions, direct labour costs (i.e. wages and benefits) in Ireland remained ahead of Greece and Portugal, and were on a par with Spain and Italy. O'Connell (1999b), moreover, shows that between 1988 and 1995, while labour costs increased by an average of 40 per cent across the countries reported in Figure 4.3, the corresponding increase in Ireland was only 24 per cent, with the result that Irish labour costs fell relative to the average up to 1995.

Figure 4.3: Direct and total labour costs, 1995 (euro)

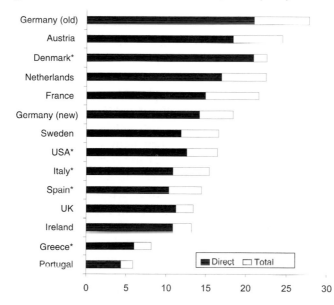

Source: Eurostat, 1997, Labour Costs Updating 1992 1995.
* Share of direct and total labour costs estimated from the ratio in earlier years.

Figure 4.4 shows trends in real compensation per employee, adjusted for inflation and indexed at 1985=100 for Ireland, the UK, the US and the European average. Over the period since 1985, real compensation per employee increased by 32 per cent in Ireland and 29 per cent in the UK, both substantially ahead of average increases in the European Union (18 per cent) or the US (11 per cent). But these increases notwithstanding, the Irish increases since 1995 were not sufficient to close the gap between average earnings in Ireland and other European countries revealed in Figure 4.5.

Figure 4.4: Trends in real compensation per employee (1985=100)

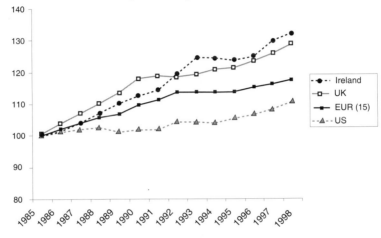

Source: European Economy, No. 65, 1998

Figure 4.5 provides a direct comparison of average earnings in manufacturing in Ireland, expressed as a ratio of the UK average, adjusted for inflation, exchange rate movements, and differences in purchasing power parities, from 1985 to 1999. This provides the most appropriate comparison between the real value of pre-tax earnings of manufacturing workers in both countries, and shows that Irish manufacturing earnings increased from 95 per cent of the corresponding UK earnings in 1985, and fluctuated around parity with the UK throughout the late 1980s and early 1990s. The purchasing power of the average pre-tax wage in Irish manufacturing increased to about 13 per cent above its UK equivalent in 1995 before declining to 5 per cent less in 1998 and 1999. This latter decline in the Irish:UK ratio was partly due to the strength of Sterling, but also resulted from the continued incomes restraint on the part of Irish workers achieved under social partnership since 1987.

Earnings increases in Ireland over the past decade can be regarded as moderate, given increases in output achieved over a similar period. Figure 4.6

shows trends in real unit labour costs, which adjust labour costs for productivity gains, between 1985 and 1998 for Ireland, the United Kingdom, the United States and the average for the fifteen European Union countries.

Figure 4.5: Average earnings in manufacturing in Ireland as a ratio of earnings in the UK (Adjusted for inflation, exchange rate changes and purchasing power parities)

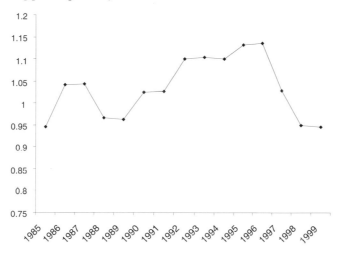

Figure 4.6: Real unit labour costs, total economy 1987-97 (1985=100)

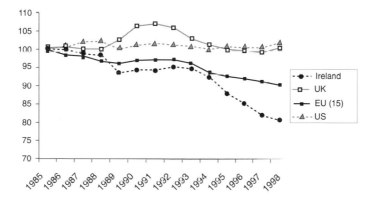

Source: European Economy, No. 65, 1998

For most years except 1991-93 changes in Irish unit labour costs have been negative and well below those in the rest of the EU and the United States. Over the entire period 1985-98 unit labour costs fell by about 20 per cent in Ireland, and by 10 per cent, on average, across the European Union. This suggests that wage increases have been sufficiently moderate to maintain and even enhance Ireland's international competitiveness.

Figure 4.8: Adjusted wage share in GDP, 1985-99

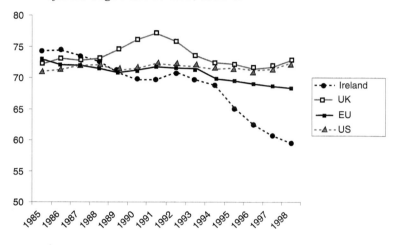

Source: European Economy, No. 65, 1998

An additional perspective on trends in Irish earnings can be gained by examining trends in the wage share of GDP over time. Figure 4.8 shows a dramatic decline in the share of wages in total output in Ireland over the period 1985 to 1999. In 1985 wages accounted for just under 75 per cent of GDP in Ireland, slightly higher than elsewhere in Europe and the United States. Over the course of the 1990s, however, while the wage share dropped somewhat to just under 70 per cent on average in Europe, and actually increased slightly in the United States, it fell to below 60 per cent in Ireland in 1998. Commenting on these trends Lane (1998: 24) observes: 'The decline in the labour income share is a remarkable feature of the economic resurgence in Ireland. The national strategy of wage moderation has been a major contributory factor in facilitating rapid economic growth but at the same time has limited the extent to which workers have shared in the fruits of rising prosperity.'

It must of course be acknowledged that the trends in average earnings underestimate the growth in after-tax income in Ireland since 1987. A central element of national collective bargaining has been a trade-off between wage restraint and tax reductions. O'Connell (1999b) argues that the combined effects of pay increases plus tax reductions between 1987-97 were to increase the real purchasing power of all household types – by between one-fifth and one-third. The distribution of these gains is discussed in greater detail in Callan and Nolan (this volume), but the greatest gains over the period were achieved by those who had paid the largest effective tax rates in 1987 and whose taxes were subsequently reduced – including those earning substantially more than the average industrial wage and single people at about the average.

Table 4.14: Indices of gross earnings, after-tax pay and take-home pay

Country	Year	Gross earnings	After-tax pay	Take-home pay	Consumer prices
		Index: 1991=100			
Ireland	1993	110	111	109	104
	1994	113	115	115	107
Austria	1993	106	106	106	103
	1994	114	114	113	106
Denmark	1993	106	106	105	103
	1994	109	121	112	105
Netherlands	1993	109	108	106	106
	1994	111	116	109	109

Source: OECD, 1995, Taxes and Benefits of Average Production Workers

Table 4.14 provides comparative data on movements in gross, after-tax and take-home pay for selected European countries between 1991-94. In Ireland, average gross earnings of the average production worker increased by 13 per cent between 1991-94, 1 percentage point behind Austria, and slightly ahead of the Netherlands. The effects of tax reductions over those years were that average take-home pay increased by 15 per cent in Ireland, compared to increases of about 9 per cent in the Netherlands, 12 per cent in Denmark and 13 per cent in Austria. This increase in average take-home pay was 8 percentage points higher than the rate of inflation, compared with a differential of 7 percentage points in Denmark and Austria, and no real change in the Netherlands. These data suggest that in comparative terms, Irish production workers may have made very slight gains in average take-home pay relative to their counterparts in other small European countries over the years 1991-94. But while fiscal policy, by reducing income taxes, has helped to improve the growth rate of post-tax earnings in Ireland, and mitigated the effects of moderation in market earnings, the weight of evidence suggests both that average earnings in Ireland are low compared to other prosperous European societies, and that the recent boom in the economy and the labour market has done little to close this earnings gap.

4.4 Conclusions

If we focus on the main trends in the Irish labour market over the past decade or so, a clear picture emerges. More than a decade of rapid economic growth has generated a dramatic increase in employment since about 1993. This has brought about a convergence with EU employment levels, although the employment-population ratio and labour force participation rates in Ireland still lag behind those in the core European societies. This is mainly due to comparatively low employment and activity rates among women in Ireland. However, women's labour force participation has increased very rapidly since the mid-1980s and women's employment has grown much faster than men's. In terms of class structure, the 1990s have seen a continuation of the long-run trends towards up-grading of the quality of positions in the labour market.

Perhaps the most outstanding aspect of Irish labour market performance has been the reduction in unemployment, from almost 17 per cent in 1987 to about 4 per cent in 2000. One of the more noteworthy features in that decline has been the very sharp fall in long-term unemployment, compared to a somewhat more gradual reduction in short-term unemployment. This chapter has argued that our measures of the balance between long- versus short-term unemployment probably underestimate the true level of long-term unemployment, because of the very large scale of active labour market programme provision in Ireland and because participants who return to unemployment after leaving programmes are counted as new entrants to unemployment. This potential underestimate relates to the balance between short- and long-term unemployment, not to the total level of unemployment.

The rapid increase in employment and decline in unemployment means that in the course of about a decade the Irish labour market moved from a position of labour surplus to labour shortage. The ESRI survey of vacancies in 1998 showed that a significant minority of firms (27 per cent) had current vacancies, and the national vacancy rate was estimated at 6 per cent (Williams and Hughes, 1999).

Reviewing the available evidence relating to the quality of employment suggests that the effect of rapid economic growth has been complex, certainly more complex than can be described by a simple deterioration thesis. The long-run upgrading of class positions referred to above suggests that more advantaged positions in the class structure, including professional and skilled occupations, accounted for a disproportionately large share of the employment growth. While other less privileged positions also expanded in the 1990s, this was not sufficient to offset the overall trend toward occupational up-grading.

We have also seen an increase in atypical working arrangements. Ireland has participated in a common European trend towards increased part-time working and greater use of temporary fixed-term contracts. However, in respect of both of these forms of atypical employment, the rate of flexibilisation has been slower in Ireland than the EU average, and in the late 1990s the extent of both part-time and temporary working was lower in Ireland than in the EU as a whole. In Ireland, moreover, the vast majority of part-time workers work part-time as a matter of choice and the extent of under-employment among part-timers fell substantially over the 1990s.

Barrett, Fitz Gerald and Nolan (this volume) show that earnings inequality increased over the 1987-97 period, but they also show that the increase in dispersion was greater during the 1987-94 period than since then, suggesting that rapid economic growth did not lead to an acceleration in earnings dispersion. It is also the case, however, that Irish wage costs and earnings were substantially lower than in the core European countries in the mid-1990s, and there is little to suggest that subsequent increases in earnings in Ireland have been sufficient to close that gap. Moreover, the marked decline in the wage share of national income during the 1990s suggests that the pursuit of international competitiveness has limited the extent to which workers in Ireland have shared in the fruits of prosperity. This raises the question of whether the national strategy of pursuing wage moderation through social partnership has excessively limited wage growth and generates increased pressure on the state to continue to reduce the tax burden on workers.

There is a danger that success on the scale achieved in the Irish case can carry with it the seeds of its own destruction. Ireland has moved from a position of severe labour surplus to one of shortage in a relatively short period of time. Labour shortages are not simply confined to high skill occupations, but extend also to less skilled workers. Labour shortages can be expected to lead to increased pressure on wages and there is clear evidence of growing dissatisfaction among workers, particularly the low paid, who do not see sufficient evidence of the fruits of growth in their wage packets. It is thus hardly surprising that with the surge in growth and employment over the past decade wage moderation has proven difficult to secure in recent national wage agreement negotiations, and many bargaining groups feel dissatisfied with, or have even opted out of, the most recent agreement, the Programme for Participation and Fairness (2000), as Hardiman (this volume), argues. The dilemma is that wage increases substantially ahead of those in other Euro currency countries could reduce Irish competitiveness and undermine long-term growth and employment prospects.

One strategy to reduce labour shortages is to seek to increase the supply of labour. The absence of state provision or financial support for child-care represents a barrier to mothers' participation in paid work; and state intervention to relieve the burden of child-care expenses on working mothers has the added advantage of helping to alleviate labour shortages.

Given that labour shortages are now emerging in low-skilled work, it is useful to consider the role of labour market policies in stimulating labour supply. Here, at least part of the problem is that many low-skill and low-paid jobs are not sufficiently financially rewarding. As Barrett, Fitz Gerald and Nolan (this volume) argue, the tightening of the labour market is likely to raise the wages of substantial numbers of low-paid workers, and should, therefore, contribute to the easing of labour shortages, although the demand-side impact of the minimum wage on low-paid employment is not yet known. Active labour market policies also have a role to play, and here labour shortages can be regarded as an opportunity to reintegrate the most disadvantaged in the labour market.

The decline in unemployment has left a residual group of increasingly hard to place long-term unemployed, unable to compete in the labour market without extensive state intervention. If the employability of the very poorly skilled is to be enhanced, this will require considerable investment in education and training specifically targeted on those experiencing the greatest disadvantages in the labour market. Empirical analysis of the impact of such active labour market programmes in Ireland suggests that well-targeted programmes with strong linkages to the market can improve the employment prospects of their participants (O'Connell and McGinnity, 1997a; O'Connell, 1999c). Nevertheless, the majority of participants in such active programmes in Ireland continue to participate in programmes with weak market linkages which have little impact on subsequent employment prospects (O'Connell, 1998). A successful strategy to reintegrate the long-term unemployed carries with it the advantage of increasing the effective supply of labour and easing skill shortages. Failure to intervene effectively at a time of rapid growth in employment and of labour shortages, would represent a missed opportunity to enable a sizeable segment of society to become more productive and independent, and both contribute to, and reap the benefits of, economic and social progress.

NOTES

1 Table 5.1 shows employment by principal economic status, which yields a lower estimate of total employment than the International Labour Office total, mainly because the ILO measure counts any employment of at least 1 hour in the week preceding the survey whereas the PES measure is based on usual activity. The main discrepancy between the two counts relates to those whose PES is education or home duties but who work part-time. The ILO measure shows a higher labour force participation rate – about 3 percentage points in the case of women in 1999.

2 The data from 1987-97 are drawn from the annual Labour Force Survey. From 1997, the Irish Central Statistics Office switched from its annual survey to a quarterly household survey. In so doing the CSO introduced some changes to the questions relating to employment, with the result that in the second quarter of 1998 an

additional 20,000 individuals were recorded as part of the labour force: an estimated 8,000 men and 12,000 women. The adjustment is confined almost exclusively to part-time workers in the services sector, with the result that data relating to part-time working in 1998 are not comparable with earlier years. In Table 4.2 we report the total number employed as recorded in 1998; however, in estimating percentage changes in total employment, we adjust the 1998 total downwards by 20,000 to render the 1998 data comparable with earlier years. This adjustment is consistent with the practice adopted by CSO (1998) in its reporting of change over time in total employment.

3 Over the 1985-98 period, the Irish growth in the employment-population ratio was exceeded only in the Netherlands, and in the latter, a substantial part of the growth was due to an increase in part-time working. Part-timers accounted for 12.3 per cent of total employment in Ireland in 1997 but 38 per cent in the Netherlands, with the result that, expressed in terms of full-time equivalents, the employment population ratio was 54.0 in Ireland and 52.8 in the Netherlands.

4 Relevant changes in legislation include: the Worker Protection (Regular Part-time Employees) Act, (1991), and the Unfair Dismissals (Amendment) Act, 1993.

5

The Rising Tide and Equality of Opportunity: The Changing Class Structure

RICHARD LAYTE AND
CHRISTOPHER T. WHELAN

5.1 Introduction

One of the central themes of social mobility research to date has been the validity of the 'industrialisation thesis'[1]. This held that economically advanced societies would share a high level of social mobility because this was necessary for these types of societies to function. Such uniformly high rates of mobility would come about they argued, first because these societies spawned a large number of higher managerial and professional positions, but also because these positions would be filled on the basis of meritocratic and 'universalistic' principles rather than social position and family connections. The former directs attention to changes in the occupational structure and thus the total amount of social mobility, known as the rate of *absolute mobility*. The latter directs our attention to changes in the standards of judgement and decision making that determine access to the newly created opportunities. The family firm gives way to the bureaucratic organisation with its formal methods of selection, with education becoming a more important determinant of occupational position than occupational inheritance. A focus on the trend towards universalism highlights the application of decision criteria that derive from considerations of rationality and efficiency and leads to a focus on changes in relative occupational success of people from different class origins, known as the rate of *relative mobility*. Critics have suggested that the liberal theory takes too simplistic a view of the extent to which the forces of competition lead to more meritocratic selection procedures. They draw attention to the ability of those in positions of power and privilege to maintain their position against encroachment, even in the face of the functional requirements of industrial or post-industrial society (Goldthorpe, 1985).

Although a variety of studies have presented evidence that challenge the liberal thesis, almost all have used data from countries that have already reached industrial maturity. It could be argued that these data do not permit a full test of the industrialisation thesis since they do not allow us to compare trends in mobility patterns that involve comparisons before and after the process of industrialisation. As Erikson and Jonsson (1996:46) note, perhaps the most appropriate test of the ascription-to-achievement hypothesis has involved studies of the Irish case.[2] However, even these studies have examined possible changes in social fluidity between cohorts, or within individual careers and have not compared fluidity between data sets collected at different points in time using individuals who would have experienced different structural conditions.

In this chapter we use data collected at three points in time – 1973, 1987 and 1994   to examine the relationship between social class origins and destination class, and the role that education plays in mediating this relationship. In the early 1970s, Ireland was still very much in transition from an agricultural to an industrial society; by 1987 the process of transition had largely been completed and by the mid-1990s arguably, Ireland had progressed further toward a 'post-industrial' society than many other European nations (Whelan, Breen and Whelan, 1992 ; O'Connell, 1999a and this volume). The availability of this data in the Irish case thus allows us to perform an appropriate test of what Jonsson (1993) has labelled the 'Increased Merit Selection' (IMS) hypothesis, which suggests that with industrialisation access to education becomes decreasingly determined by class origin and that class position is increasingly dependent on educational achievement, as the influence of characteristics associated with family background become irrelevant.

Figure 5.1: IMS hypothesis

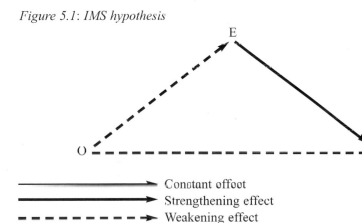

Constant effect
Strengthening effect
Weakening effect

Source: Golthorpe 1996:263

If we label class origin (O), educational qualifications (E) and class destination (D) then the IMS hypothesis suggests a pattern of change over time, as portrayed in Figure 5.1, whereby the links between O and E and O and D weaken over time while the association between E and D strengthens. Not only are individuals allocated to positions on the basis of achievement but the social inequalities that result can claim legitimacy, in a way that ascriptive inequalities cannot, because they contribute to the efficient functioning of society as a whole.

It should be acknowledged that the argument that inequality based on educational achievement is both legitimate and functional, is far from being unchallenged. Educational credentials are not the only factor relevant to economic success. In addition the extent to which merit can be defined in a sufficiently 'objective' fashion is contested. Needs and rights are among the alternative principles on which resources may be distributed.[3] We will return in our conclusion to issues of legitimation. However, the primary purpose of this chapter is to test how well the IMS thesis, whatever its conceptual and philosophical limitations, accords with the empirical evidence relating to the changing nature of intergenerational class transmission in Ireland.

In section 5.2 we outline the data on which we draw and describe the class and educational classifications we employ. In section 5.3 we deal with the broad pattern of class transformation and its consequences in terms of the inflow patterns from class origins into current class locations and absolute levels of mobility. In section 5.4 we deal with the relationship between class origins and educational qualifications and the extent to which this has changed over time. In section 5.5 we address the impact of such qualifications on class destination and whether this has become stronger at the later observation points. In section 5.6 we examine the overall origin destination relationship and the extent to which this is mediated through educational qualifications. By examining this pattern of relationships over time we will be able to assess the extent to which the process of class attainment conforms to the pattern predicted by the IMS hypothesis, as outlined in Figure 5.1.

It would be preferable to be able to examine jointly the patterning of both men and women's mobility, but unfortunately the data for the 1970s refer only to married women, at a point in time when labour market participation by such women was extremely low. Analysis of both 1987 and 1994 national surveys shows that, while gender differences in absolute mobility exist, patterns of social fluidity are largely unaffected (Breen and Whelan, 1996; Whelan and Hannan, 1999).[4]

5.2 Data and classifications

Unlike previous work on social mobility in Ireland, which has compared cohorts, or examined changing social mobility through the study of individual careers, here we are able to draw upon data collected at three points in time – 1973, 1987, 1994 – across almost a quarter of a century.[5] This allows us to examine the changing nature of social mobility in Ireland as it passed from largely pre-industrial to post-industrial society.

Our analysis involves a comparison of the mobility patterns of men aged 20-64 at the three points in time. Both the social class variables and education variables are coded using the classifications employed in the CASMIN study (Erikson et al, 1979). Thus the origin and destination class variables are seven category groupings of the original eleven classes in the following manner:

Professional and managerial class
Routine non-manual class
Self-employed farmers
Skilled manual workers, lower grade technicians and supervisors
Non-skilled workers not in agriculture
Agricultural labourers

The following educational categories are distinguished[7]:

Primary Certificate, or no qualifications
Group or Intermediate Certificate
Leaving Certificate or equivalent
Third Level

5.3 The transformation of the class structure

In discussing the industrialisation of the Republic of Ireland, it is hard to overstate the speed of the transition that occurred and the effects that this had, not only on the economy, but also on the social structure of Irish society. Whereas the country entered the 1960s as an agricultural society both economically and culturally, it found itself, by the late-1970s, as a society more reliant on industry than property for a living, where service workers already outnumbered manual employees and education was increasingly important. It has been argued that the dynamism of economic growth in itself leads to increased social mobility,[8] but it seems more plausible to see changes in absolute mobility as being due to changes in the overall 'shape' of the occupational structure within which mobility is being observed. Though these 'shift' effects may be contemporaneous with economic growth, there is no evidence that they will steadily increase with economic development or that their importance is closely correlated with prevailing rates of economic growth.[9] Our attention then is on the changing structural context within which mobility occurs rather than economic growth *per se*, although with the exception of certain phases of particular economic difficulty that period involved is one in which Ireland went through a catching-up phase relative to its Western European neighbours.

After the inception of the state in 1922 and prior to the 1960s there had actually been very little industrial development. The founding of the state in 1922 separated the industrial north-east of the country from the largely agricultural 26 counties in the south and there was little subsequent industrial development, in spite of government attempts to stimulate domestic industry through protectionist policies. Even as late as 1961, two-thirds of Irish exports were agricultural, mainly to Britain, and this was reflected in the proportion of males in agricultural work at 44 per cent. Agriculture itself was based on small, usually family-run farming enterprises with the consequence that 46 per cent of the labour force derived their living from property. This had particular implications for social mobility since: 'life chances centred on the prospects of inheriting the family business and the accompanying house and household goods. Realistically, education or training could secure a livelihood within Ireland for only a minority of those aspiring to the workforce' (O'Connell and Rottman, 1992: 69).

Even up until the early 1970s this meant that inheritance was a particularly strong feature of Irish society. After 1961, social and economic change occurred rapidly with profound effects on Irish society. Between 1961 and 1996, the proportion of males in agriculture as a percentage of the total labour force fell from 36 per cent to 13 per cent whilst the proportion of managers, professionals and administrators grew from 8 per cent to over 20 per cent. Similarly, the skilled manual workforce grew from 12 to 21 per cent by 1981, although this declined to 18 per cent by 1996 as recession hit the Irish economy in the mid-1980s. What effects did such changes in the occupational structure have on the shape of the class system?

Such large changes in the occupational structure away from agriculture are bound to lead to increased class mobility out of these locations and this is evident when we consider changes over time in the distributions of class origins and destinations. The proportion of those from farming backgrounds fell dramatically from 38 per cent in 1973 to 26 per cent in 1987, though remaining relatively stable thereafter. Similarly, those entering the farming class fell from 20 per cent in 1973 to half this at 10 per cent in 1987 and then remained relatively stable. This fall in the farming category is mirrored in the agricultural labourers class where the proportion with class origins in this group falls from around 7 per cent in 1973 to just 3 per cent by 1994. However, Ireland never developed the heavy industries or large factory system common to the 'golden period' of industrialisation in other countries and in many respects moved from an agricultural society into a post-industrial one without the intervening period. The restructuring that occurred among protected Irish industries in the 1980s as they were exposed to international competition in a global recession encouraged this process. This meant that unskilled manual workers actually formed a smaller proportion of employees in 1994 than they did in 1973 and skilled manual destinations, after an increase between 1973 and 1987, remained stable in the subsequent period. At the same time professional and managerial and routine non-manual classes[10] were expanding rapidly. As the industrial base expanded, professional and managerial occupations increased in number from 13 per cent of destinations in 1973 to 17 per cent in 1987 and to 19 per cent by 1994; routine non-manual work almost doubled during this period.

The pattern of change was rather different in our two observation periods. This is illustrated in Figure 5.2 where we show the increase in the percentage of individuals found in the professional and managerial class and the decrease in the percentage found in the manual and non-manual classes. Between 1973 and 1987 there was an increase of 6 per cent in the percentage in non-manual positions and an increase of 8 per cent in the number in manual work. Thus the structural context of changes in mobility patterns was one in which a decline in numbers in farming was being accommodated by increased opportunity at both ends of the class hierarchy. Between 1987 and 1994 the non-manual classes increased by 7 per cent while the number in manual work declined by 3 per cent. During this period the decline in farming was a good deal more modest.

These large changes in economic and occupational structures must inevitably have profound effects on the patterning of social mobility, in two particular ways. Firstly, we can expect to see some changes in the composition of classes. Secondly, we can anticipate significant increases in the absolute rate of mobility. Changes of the former kind between 1973 and 1994 can be summarised as follows:

- In the professional managerial class self-recruitment remained fairly constant, although it must be stressed that only a quarter of this class had been born into it. The number drawn from the propertied classes fell from approximately four out of ten to less than one in four. At the same time the numbers drawn from the routine non-manual class increased substantially and those from the manual classes increased modestly.

Figure 5.2: Change in % in non-manual and manual work

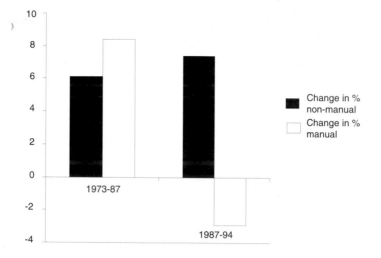

- The routine non-manual class remained an extremely heterogeneous class.
- The degree of self-recruitment among the self-employed fell gradually from just less than one-third to one-sixth. The inflow from farming remained constant at almost 30 per cent. This was complimented by an increase in the proportion drawn from the manual classes from one in five to four out of ten.
- Between 1973 and 1987 the degree of recruitment from the manual class into the non-skilled manual class rose from just less than one in two to two out of three and remained fairly stable subsequently. This in large part arose from a decline in the proportion drawn from the propertied classes from one in three to just over one in five.

The second set of changes to which we address our attention concerns the extent of absolute social mobility and the degree to which this can be characterised as upward and downward. Class societies are not caste societies. At all three of our observation points, more than half of the respondents had been mobile between the seven categories of the class schema. In 1973 just less than six out of ten exhibited such mobility and this rose to almost two out of three by 1994. Of course a good deal of such mobility may not involve hierarchical movement and a further portion will involve short-term movements. However, mobility is by no means restricted to such movement and there is a clear trend over time towards increased upward and long-range upward mobility. Figure 5.3 shows levels of absolute mobility in the three periods. In 1973 just less than 10 per cent had been mobile into the professional and managerial class. By 1987 this had increased to 12 per cent and by 1994 to 14 per cent. A 'rising tide' had indeed raised many boats. A similar trend was experienced in relation to long-range upward mobility. In 1973 less than 4 per cent had risen from the working class to the professional and managerial. By 1987 this was just less than 6 per cent and by 1994 it was close to 7 per cent. It is clear from Figure 5.4 that such enhanced prospects were not earned at the expense of deterioration in the mobility outcomes of others.

Figure 5.3: Trends in absolute mobility levels

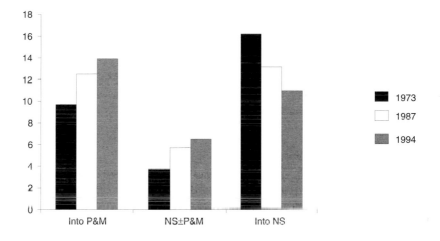

Over time, rather than observing a corresponding increase in long-range downward mobility, precisely the opposite outcome was observed. In 1973, 16 per cent had fallen from professional and managerial origins to a current position in the unskilled manual class. By 1987 this figure had declined slightly to 13 per cent and by 1994 it fell to 11 per cent. The profound changes in the class structure had created a situation where working-class respondents experienced significantly increased long-range upward mobility opportunities. At the same time groups more favourably located in the class structure were also able to substantially reduce their risks of falling into the non-skilled manual class. Since the benefits of the upgrading of the class structure were experienced across the continuum of class origins, what effect did this have on the pattern of relative mobility between classes? Returning to the hypothesis outlined in the introduction to this chapter, do we see increasing openness and 'fluidity' in Irish society in the period covered by our data, or are some classes more successful than others in gaining higher social class positions?

Industrialisation brought with it a decrease in recruitment into agricultural positions and an increase in service class and routine non-manual positions. Moreover, the structure of these classes has become more heterogeneous as those from other class origins are recruited into these classes. Yet these developments not only changed the shape of the class structure; they also changed the nature of social mobility itself in Ireland. There were two main effects. The importance of inheritance as a way of acquiring social position in Ireland declined after the 1960s. Whereas 50 per cent of men aged 15-19 in the 1920s who did not emigrate could depend upon family employment leading to inheritance, this figure had dropped to less than 15 per cent in the 1970s. In addition, educational qualifications became an increasingly important prerequisite of access to the expanding white-collar opportunities. In 1967 free secondary education was introduced and this increased the take up of education such that the proportion in full-time education up to Leaving Certificate rose from 14 per cent in 1964 to 40 per cent in 1985 and around 75 per cent by the early 1990s. As we have already seen, some have predicted that with increasing industrialisation educational credentials become the pre-eminent selection criterion in employer recruitment. Moreover, in Ireland the high level of 'standardisation' in the Irish educational system after 1967 would have facilitated this.[11] Were enhanced absolute mobility opportunities and the expansion of educational opportunities associated with greater equality of opportunity? Did Ireland become a more meritocratic society? It is to these issues that we now turn. We start by considering how the relationship between class origin and educational attainment has changed over time.

5.4 Trends in the influence of class origins on educational attainment

The chapter by Smyth and Hannan in this volume will deal with the nature of the Irish educational system and will provide a general account of educational inequalities.[12] Our purpose here is more limited – it is to provide an account of the relationship between class origins and educational achievement in the adult male population that can serve as a stepping stone in our attempt to provide an account of the overall mobility process. In Figure 5.4 we document class inequalities for men in 1994 in gaining third level qualification and in terminating without qualifications.

Figure 5.4: Educational attainment by class origins

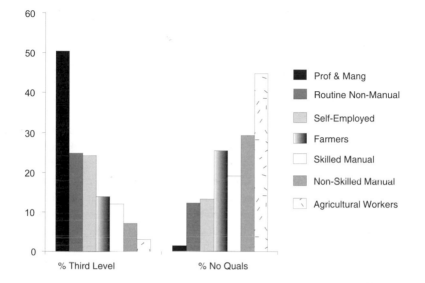

Over one in two from professional and managerial origins achieve a third level qualification. They are followed by the self-employed and the routine non-manual class where one in four are found at this level. The figure falls to one in seven for farmers, to one in nine for the skilled manual class and one in fourteen for the non-skilled manual. Finally those with agricultural worker origins, a very small group, display particularly low levels of achievement. Inequalities in educational failure are even greater than those for educational attainment. Almost one in two from agricultural origins and over one in four from the non-skilled manual group lack educational qualifications. This declines to one in four for farming and one in five for the skilled manual class and to one in eight for the self-employed and routine non-manual classes, and finally to one in seventy for the professional and managerial class.

In developing an index of inequality of outcome, between for instance the professional and managerial class and the non-skilled manual class, we may proceed as follows. First we assess the disparity in gaining third level qualifications which gives us a disparity ratio of 7:1 (50.4/7.2). Similarly we calculate the equality in ability to avoid having no qualifications, which gives us a disparity ratio of 20.9:1 (29.3/1.4). Multiplying these disparity ratios gives us what is known as an odds ratio with a value of 146.3:1. This figure summarises the degree of inequality in the competition between the professional and managerial and non-skilled manual classes to achieve third level qualifications and to avoid terminating without an educational qualification. We can calculate such an odds ratio for each pair of origins and destinations. These ratios capture the set of relativities implicit in a cross-tabulation of educational destinations by class origins and are unaffected by changes in the distributions of origins and destinations which influence absolute opportunities. We can make use of these odds ratios to apply formal statistical procedures to test whether the underlying pattern of relativities has changed over time.[13]

The result of applying such a procedure to the three education-by-class-origin tables for 1973, 1987 and 1994 is quite straightforward. A model that assumes that the underlying pattern of relativities stays constant over time succeeds in correctly classifying 96 per cent of the cases in the three tables. In order to improve this level to 98 per cent it is necessary that we take into account two kinds of changes over time. The most important of these is a substantial increase in the advantage enjoyed by the professional and managerial class in access to third-level qualifications. The second involves a decline in the advantage enjoyed by those from routine non-manual origins and to a lesser extent by the skilled manual class. Thus, rather than finding any general reduction in the scale of class advantage we observe, in one important respect, a significant increase.

5.5 Educational categories and class destination

In this section the question we address is – to what extent does educational attainment influence one's class position and how has this changed between 1973 and 1994? In this case, class is the outcome rather than the determining variable. In Figure 5.5 we show the percentage in the professional and managerial and non-skilled manual classes by educational qualification for men in 1994. Not surprisingly third-level education confers a substantial advantage in access to the former class. Seven out of ten with such a qualification are found in the professional and managerial class compared to one in five with a Leaving Certificate, one in twenty of those with an Inter Certificate and less than one in thirty of those with no qualifications. At the bottom of the class structure somewhat less differentiation is observed. Three out of ten of those with no qualifications are found in the unskilled manual class compared to one in four of those with an Intermediate Certificate, one in nine of those with a Leaving Certificate and one in forty of those with a third-level qualification.[14] Following a similar procedure to that used in the previous section we can calculate the advantage conferred by a third level qualification versus the absence of qualifications in facilitating entry to the professional and managerial class and averting entry to the non-skilled manual class.

Figure 5.5: Class destination by education

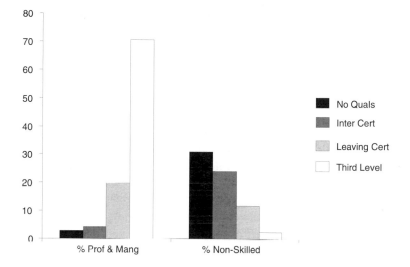

The disparity ratio for the former is 24.3 (70.6/2.9) and for the latter 12.9 (31/2.4), giving an odds ration of 313.5:1 which provides an indicator of competitive advantage. As before, the class destinations and educational qualifications table can be seen as reflecting the outcomes of a series of competitions involving pairs of origin and destination categories. Thus we can proceed to apply statistical models to test whether the underlying pattern of inequalities has changed over time.[15] A model that assumes that this pattern is uniform across time correctly classifies 96 per cent of the cases relating to the three education-qualification-class destination tables. It is possible to improve the success rate to 98 per cent by taking into account a process of qualification inflation over time whereby both Inter Cert and Leaving Cert confer less relative advantage in competition for professional and managerial positions and third level qualifications more often result in routine white-collar jobs. More broadly the relative advantage provided by superior education in promoting access to the white-collar classes rather than all other classes declines. Thus, rather than, as suggested by the IMS thesis, education becoming a more important determinant of class attainment it has actually become a less powerful predictor.

5.6 The relationship between class origin and destination

In this section we examine trends over time in the underlying patterns of social fluidity which shape the outflows from class origins to destinations. Our concern is thus not with opportunities for absolute mobility created by an upgrading in the class structure but with changes in the relative advantages enjoyed by different class origins. We expect such patterns to be shaped by three factors. The first is the relative desirability of different class destinations; the second, the resources available to individuals within each class origin which help them gain access to more desirable destinations; and thirdly, the barriers to movement between classes. Typically we think of resources as 'economic, cultural and social resources' (Erikson and Goldthorpe, 1987:64), while barriers to mobility would include the necessity to own the means of production or educational and other qualifications needed for entry to the occupations that comprise a class grouping. Thus, on the basis of earlier work, when we observe the outflow from class origins to destinations we expect the pattern of inequalities to be shaped by the following factors.[16]

- *Barriers to entry to agriculture*
- *Hierarchical barriers:* If we distinguish four levels of hierarchy, as below, we expect movements involving more levels to be less frequent than those requiring shorter range movements.
    - (i) The professional and managerial class
    - (ii) The routine non-manual class
    - (iii) The petty-bourgeoisie, farming and unskilled manual class
    - (iv) The non-skilled manual class.
- *Within-property movement:* We expect reciprocal movement between the farming and self-employed classes to be stronger than other moves.
- *Additional advantages associated with self-employment:* The self-employed also appear to apply their resources to achieve greater access to the professional managerial class than we would otherwise expect.
- *Inheritance:* A very specific resource for mobility is indicated by the tendency for class inheritance where origin in a given class improves one's relative chances of remaining in that class even when we control for other factors such as hierarchy. The reasons for this are diverse but include aspects such as direct inheritance of the means of production, family tradition and access to social networks. Levels of inheritance tend to be strongest for the property-owning classes, intermediate for the skilled manual class and weakest for other employee classes.

In Figure 5.6, for men in 1994, we show the relative chances of ending up in professional and managerial and non-skilled manual destinations for those originating in each of these origins.

Figure 5.6: Class destination by class origin

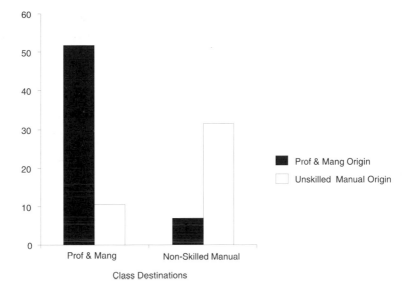

These outcomes are influenced both by the hierarchy and inheritance factors outlined earlier. Just over one in two of those from professional and managerial backgrounds were currently found in this class compared to just under one in ten of those drawn from the non-skilled manual class. Correspondingly over three out of ten of the latter were currently in the non-skilled manual class compared to less than one in fourteen of those with professional and managerial backgrounds. The respective disparity ratios are 4.9:1 and 4.5:1, giving us an odds ratio of 22:1 summarising the outcome of this competition. Each pair of origins and destinations can be seen as involving a competition which is influenced by a particular set of factors drawn from those outlined above. A model that assumes that the outcome of such competitions remains constant across time succeeds in correctly classifying 95 per cent of the cases from the three-origin-destination tables. We can bring about a modest improvement to 97 per cent by taking into account a number of changes over time. The first is a reduction by 1987 in the tendency towards inheritance among the skilled manual class. The second change involves a modest but statistically significant reduction in the relative barrier to long-range movement across the hierarchy of classes. Aside from this final trend, the expectations of the IMS thesis are confounded. Rather than observing a reduction in the association between origins and destination, our evidence broadly confirms a pattern of little change over time.

Further analysis which considers simultaneously the relationship between origins, education and destinations shows that controlling for educational qualifications accounts for half the effect of class hierarchy and produces a modest reduction in additional advantage enjoyed by the self-employed in access to the professional and managerial class. The advantages associated with the ownership of property are entirely independent of educational attainment and display no signs of becoming less so.

In Figure 5.7 we show the actual, as opposed to the hypothesised outcomes, relating to the IMS thesis. The relationship between class origins and educational qualifications, if anything, strengthens. The impact of educational qualifications on class destination weakens. Finally the direct impact of class origins on destination increases slightly as indicated by the improved access of those from farming origins to the professional and managerial class. There is no evidence to support the hypothesis of increasing meritocracy.

Figure 5.7: IMS – actual outcomes

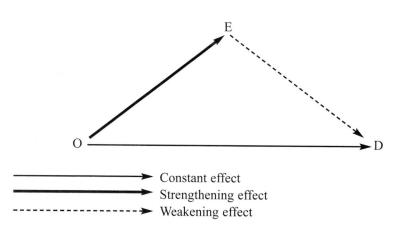

Source: Golthorpe 1996:263

Conclusions

In this chapter we have analysed trends in social mobility from the early 1970s to the mid-1990s. The changes in the class origins and destinations distributions that we have observed reflect the economic transformation from an agrarian and petty bourgeois society to a modern industrial, and indeed, post-industrial society. The three observation points available to us allow us to identify two rather different periods of this transformation. Between 1973 and 1994 a decline in farming was accompanied by a growth in employee groups, both manual and non-manual. Between 1987-94 growth was observed predominantly in the professional and managerial class with a corresponding decline in the manual sector. As a consequence it is among the latter that we observe a striking increase in upward mobility and a proportionate decline in downward mobility. The nature of the long-term transformation of the class structure in Ireland was such that extreme social closure at the top was not a possibility. While increased heterogeneity is the predominant pattern, the opposite is the case with the non-skilled manual class, which becomes largely recruited from the manual classes. The demise of the traditional small proprietor is reflected in the changing composition of the self-employed which increasingly recruits from the manual working class and is dominated by 'own account' skilled manual men. In most cases the decreased importance of the propertied classes results in greater heterogeneity, except at the bottom of the hierarchy where it leads to the emergence of a smaller but self-recruiting unskilled manual block that more closely resembles the 'mature' working class of countries who had industrialised in the last century or in the early twentieth century.

Between 1973 and 1994 in the Republic of Ireland transformation of the class structure was largely associated with increased heterogeneity in terms of class composition and increased levels of absolute mobility. Much of our attention has been focused on the question of whether such developments were associated with greater equality of opportunity and the emergence of a more meritocratic society. Our analysis provides little support for the IMS thesis. Over time there is no diminution in the impact of class origins on educational level. In fact the relative access of those from professional and managerial backgrounds to third level qualifications improves over time. While substantial numbers of working class children availed of increased educational opportunities, the underlying pattern of class relativities was accentuated by the increased advantage over time enjoyed by the professional and managerial class in access to third level education. The pattern that emerged has been described elsewhere as one of maximally maintained inequality where any change is a consequence of expansion in opportunities rather than their distribution.[17]

A comparison of Ireland North and South shows that substantially greater absolute educational opportunities for working-class children in the South is accompanied by significantly greater class inequalities.[18] While the origin-destination association strengthened slightly, the impact of education on class destination actually weakened.

No evidence was found of a significant weakening in either the gross or net relationship between class origins and destination. We found a tendency over time towards equalisation of inheritance tendencies within the employee classes and a modest reduction in relative barriers to long-range mobility. Education served to mediate about half of the effects associated with position in the class hierarchy. However, it played almost no role in accounting for the inheritance or property effects that also serve to determine class outcomes. Nor did it account for increased inequalities over time. These findings suggest that we need to take the advantages associated with property in advanced economies more seriously.

The Irish evidence on the trend over time in the relationship between class origins and educational achievement is very much in line with the international evidence.[19] In order to save the IMS thesis in its complete form it is necessary to resort to hereditarian theories or arguments couched in terms of class differences in educational tastes or aspirations.[20] However, the finding relating to the declining impact of educational qualifications is one that many will find counter-intuitive. Our results, however, are consistent with earlier findings by Breen and Whelan (1993) based on cohort analysis of the 1987 Irish data and focusing on first occupation. Our findings on the restricted role of education also mirror Breen's (1998) finding, based on the School Leavers Survey that class differences in employment status in the Republic of Ireland are only weakly mediated by education with the cumulative impact of other channels of class influence being significantly greater. Similar findings have been reported for Britain and Sweden.[21] Thus, as Goldthorpe (1996:268) notes, if it is accepted that in modern industrial societies the educational system plays the main role in discovering talent, and educational attainment is the prime indicator of merit, then results of the kind we have reported must seriously undermine the notion of increasing merit selection. Breen and Goldthorpe (forthcoming) point to a number of developments that may have contributed to this trend in Britain, including reduction in the size of the public sector, declining levels of trade unionism, deregulation of the labour market and educational expansion. All of these tendencies, except the final one, are significantly weaker in the Irish case, suggesting that the declining impact of education is not dependent on the emergence of a neo-liberal regime.

In absolute terms we would clearly expect to observe diminishing returns to educational qualifications as the numbers possessing them increase. Thus as Boudon (1974) observed, the rational decision of individuals to acquire more education has an unforeseen effect at the aggregate level. However, the findings we have referred to are net of the changes over time in the distribution of educational qualifications. Furthermore, there is no reason why educational expansion *per se* should lead to educational qualifications becoming less potent predictors of class destinations. There appears to be no strong evidence for absolute devaluation of qualifications arising from declining standards. It is interesting in this regard that the unchanging impact of class origin suggests that such qualifications have not been devalued in the eyes of the more advantaged classes. At any educational level the average level of ability may have declined over time but this could occur without changing relativities. In addition to finding a general weakening in the impact of education on class destination, we also found a particular decline in the ability of those with senior secondary level qualifications to obtain professional and managerial positions. However, even in a situation where educational expansion outpaces job opportunities, there is no reason why educational qualifications could not maintain or increase their role as 'rationing' devices. In fact the available Irish evidence suggests that where employers rely on indicators of educational achievement they are capable of quite fine discriminations (Breen et al, 1995).

It may be true though that, where an increasing number of people enjoy high levels of education, employers may come to judge that such qualifications provide a weaker signal of productivity. In that case high average levels of education, by ensuring that a substantial number of candidates come above a minimum threshold, may allow employers to make use of additional criteria without incurring significant costs and in some cases with considerable gain. The former would be the case where the additional criteria are of an ascribed type, as in the case of favouring members of particular social networks. The latter may be the outcome where merit-related criteria unrelated to education such as 'emotional intelligence' are applied.[22] In any event, whatever the balance which exists between the use of these different criteria, the continued strength of direct class origin effects indicates that they are no less class related than those applied in earlier periods. It is not unreasonable to express a certain scepticism relating to the fact that emotional intelligence turns out to be as strongly linked to class origins as cognitive ability.

Even if the meritocratic argument can be saved by developing the argument along the lines we have outlined it appears highly unlikely that this form of the argument can constitute as potent a legitimating ideology for inequalities of outcome as that founded on just deserts, based on functional importance to the economy, arising from educational achievement. In light of the emerging evidence which runs contrary to the IMS thesis, it is hardly surprising that the available survey evidence suggests that: 'in popular perception, failure is not "individualised" to the degree that a dominant meritocratic ideology would imply, nor is success taken to reflect so favourably on those who have attained it' (Goldthorpe, 1996: 282).[23]

NOTES

1 See Lipset and Bendix (1959) and Blau and Duncan (1967).
2 See Whelan, Breen and Whelan (1992); Breen and Whelan (1992); Halpin (1992); Breen and Whelan (1993); Breen and Whelan (1996).
3 For a sociological discussion of such issues see Erikson and Jonsson (1996), Goldthorpe (1996) and Marshal et al (1997) and for broader philosophical discussion Miller (1989,1992).

4 We will deal with male-female comparisons for the origin-education-destination relationships in a forthcoming paper.

5 See Hout (1989), Callan et al (1989, 1997) for sample details.

6 For convenience we will refer to non-agricultural self-employed as the 'self-employed'.

7 The 1973 Survey of the Determinants of Occupational Status and Mobility used a collapsed qualificational schema which we interpreted in the following manner: no education up to incomplete primary was coded as 'primary or less' in the CASMIN schema, incomplete secondary as 'lower secondary', complete secondary as 'higher secondary' and incomplete tertiary and above as 'tertiary'.

8 See Lipset and Bendix (1959).

9 See Goldthorpe (1980/1987: 558-559).

10 Agricultural workers have not been included in the manual classes.

11 For a discussion of standardisation see Allmendinger (1989) and for a development of its implications in the Irish situation see Breen et al (1995).

12 See also Whelan and Hannan (1999).

13 The modelling procedure we apply is known as a 'row effects model' (Breen, 1985; Hout, 1981).

14 Those with no qualifications are likely to experience much higher levels of unemployment (cf. Chapter 6).

15 This involves estimating a 'column-effects' model (Breen, 1984; Hout, 1981).

16 The underlying model here is the AHP model developed by Breen and Whelan (1992, 1994, 1996).

17 See Raftery and Hout (1993) and Whelan and Hannan (1999).

18 See Breen, Heath and Whelan (1999).

19 See Shavit and Blossfeld (1993).

20 For critiques of such approaches see Goldthorpe (1996) and Breen and Goldthorpe (1997,1999).

21 See Goldthorpe and Breen (forthcoming), Jonsson (1993), Heath et al (1993).

22 See Goldthorpe (1996) for a discussion of these issues.

23 See Miller (1992), Marshall et al (1997) and van Oorschot and Halman (2000).

6

Education and Inequality

EMER SMYTH AND DAMIAN F. HANNAN

The period since the 1980s has been one of rapid expansion in educational participation among young people in Ireland. It is commonly assumed that this expansion in educational participation has benefited most, if not all, young people. Given an already high level of participation among the middle classes, we might expect that rising educational participation levels would reduce relative differences in middle- and working-class participation. This chapter analyses whether increasing educational participation has, in fact, resulted in any reduction in inequalities in educational attainment and in the relationship between educational and labour market outcomes among young people. The main objectives of the paper are: (i) to describe the specific nature of the Irish educational system and its implications for inequality in educational participation and attainment; (ii) to analyse the nature and extent of gender and social class inequalities in educational outcomes since the early 1980s; and (iii), to explore changes in early labour market integration among young people in the context of rapid educational expansion.

6.1 The Irish educational system

The Irish educational system represents a specific combination of a highly centralised, standardised system with a significant degree of discretion in policy and practice at the school level. Within the second-level system, curricula and examinations at the Junior and Leaving Certificate levels are nationally standardised. Outside the core curriculum, schools have some discretion concerning which subjects they provide to pupils, but syllabi and standards within the selected subjects are nationally determined. The structure and content of national examinations are also centrally determined. The standardisation of the Irish second-level system contrasts sharply with other educational systems, such as that in the United States, where curricula and examinations vary from state to state and even within states themselves. Educational standardisation has important consequences for the recognition of qualifications for entry to further education and for access to employment.

The Irish second-level system is relatively undifferentiated, focusing on the provision of 'general' education rather than tailoring curricula to specific occupational niches (Hannan, Raffe and Smyth, 1996). In recent years, the introduction of Post-Leaving Certificate vocational courses, along with the new Leaving Certificate Vocational and Applied programmes, has resulted in a greater differentiation between vocational and academic routes within upper second-level education. In spite of these changes, the Irish system remains quite distinct from the highly differentiated systems of vocational education in Germany and the Netherlands (Hannan, Smyth et al, 1999). Educational outcomes are, however, highly differentiated hierarchically in terms of the stage at which young people leave school, the level of courses they take and the grades they receive. Educational attainment in terms of level and grades is highly predictive of access to further education and employment in the Irish context (Breen, Hannan and O'Leary, 1995).

Alongside this strongly centralised and standardised system, there exists a considerable degree of discretion in policy and practice at the school level. Some of this variation has its origins in the tripartite development of the second-level system. Secondary schools were mainly established on a voluntary basis by religious (mainly Catholic) denominations from the nineteenth century onwards. Most voluntary secondary schools became integrated into the Free Education Scheme in 1967. Secondary schools were primarily focused on providing an academic curriculum either as preparation for university entry or for direct access to white-collar occupations. The Vocational Education Act of 1930 resulted in the establishment of vocational schools, intended to provide vocationally-oriented education geared to the needs of local employers; the principal clientele of these schools were working-class males. Community/comprehensive schools were introduced in the 1960s in an attempt to bridge the gap between the academic secondary and vocational sectors, offering a broad curriculum to all pupils (Coolahan, 1981). It was not intended, however, to bring about a wholesale comprehensivisation of the schooling system and these schools continue to make up a very small proportion of all second-level schools in Ireland.

Formal differences between the secondary, vocational and community/comprehensive sectors have reduced somewhat in importance over time, although sectoral differences in ownership and funding structures persist. Educational reforms in the 1960s meant that all three sectors became integrated into a common curricular and examination framework. The consequence of such reforms was an overall weakening of vocational education and an increased emphasis on 'general' education within all school sectors (Breen et al, 1990). Informal differences have persisted between secondary, vocational and community/comprehensive schools, however. Vocational schools continue to attract a higher proportion of pupils from working-class and unemployed backgrounds while a disproportionate number of middle-class pupils attend secondary schools (Hannan, Smyth et al, 1996).

There has been a good deal of discussion of the 'market model' of education in the British context with increasing competition evident between schools for pupils. In contrast, the degree of competition between schools in the Irish context has been underestimated. A survey of Junior Certificate pupils indicated that almost half were not attending their nearest or most accessible school (Hannan, Smyth et al, 1996). In the context of relatively low population density with consequent dispersion of school provision in some parts of the country, this finding indicates quite a remarkable degree of active selection of schools on the part of parents and pupils. Parental choice of school is closely related to social class, with those from higher professional groups making more active selections than those from other groups. School selection processes, therefore, will accentuate differences between school sectors and among individual schools in their social class mix. The resulting social segregation between school sectors and among individual schools has important implications for the persistence of social class inequalities in educational outcomes. Pupils who attend schools with a high intake of pupils from disadvantaged backgrounds are more likely to drop out of school before the Leaving Certificate, and tend to under-perform in the Junior and Leaving Cert examinations, compared to those in other schools, an effect which operates over and above that of individual social background (Smyth, 1999b).

The degree of discretion in policy and practice at the school level may also result in very different educational experiences for young people. Schools vary significantly in their approach to ability grouping, degree of subject choice, level of pupil and parental involvement, disciplinary climate, nature of pupil-teacher interaction and academic climate (Smyth, 1999b). All of these aspects of school policy and practice have important consequences for educational participation and attainment and thus for potential inequalities in educational outcomes.

Policy relating to educational inequality: from 'opportunity' to 'disadvantage'?

There was no coherent policy on equality of educational opportunity until the 1960s (Ó Buachalla, 1988). However, the joint Department of Education/OECD *Investment in Education Report* (1966) highlighted significant social class and regional disparities in educational participation as well as detailing the limitations of the educational system in producing the trained workforce necessary for economic growth. The report prompted the introduction of the Free Education Scheme that resulted in free second-level education for all pupils in participating schools and provided school transport for pupils in rural areas. Interestingly, this reform ran counter to original proposals that suggested that substantial improvements in vocational and comprehensive schooling should occur before 'free education' was introduced for those attending secondary schools. In the absence of such reforms, the introduction of the scheme had the effect of reinforcing the influence of privately-owned secondary schools while effectively downgrading the effectiveness of vocational education.

In the period from the late 1960s until the mid-1980s, the main thrust of policy was concerned with the overall expansion of participation levels rather than with addressing social class inequalities in educational attainment. No serious attempts were made at fundamental institutional reform, at least partly because of the strong opposition of the private owners of secondary schools (primarily religious orders) to local communal and regional reorganisation. Later attempts through the White Paper on Education (Department of Education, 1995) to introduce regional education authorities, at least partly in an attempt to achieve greater equality of opportunity among schools in a particular area, were opposed by local politicians on county vocational educational committees and were not included in subsequent legislation. Perhaps because radical institutional reform was not treated as a serious option, in the 1980s and 1990s state policy became increasingly concerned with reducing educational 'disadvantage', focusing on those 'failing' or being 'failed' by the educational system. Initiatives targeted on 'disadvantaged schools' and 'disadvantaged areas' were primarily designed to reduce the scale of educational under-achievement among children and young people from the most disadvantaged family backgrounds. As such, these initiatives could be seen as drawing on an 'educational deficit' model, concerned only with tackling under-performance among particular groups of children rather than addressing broader educational inequalities. Recent initiatives have included the following:

- Provision of early childhood education for children in disadvantaged areas (the Early Start programme)
- Targeting of additional funding towards schools serving disadvantaged populations (Breaking the Cycle; Programme for Schools in Disadvantaged Areas)
- Introduction of new curricular programmes and approaches to certification to promote pupil retention (the Junior Cert Schools Programme; the Leaving Cert Applied Programme; the introduction of foundation levels in some exam subjects)
- Locally and/or institutionally-based initiatives to promote third-level participation among young people in disadvantaged areas (for example, the Trinity Access Programme).

Due to the highly centralised and standardised nature of the Irish educational system, many of the policy responses to educational disadvantage have originated at the national level. More recently, a number of locally-based measures have been initiated, either through individual universities or institutes of technology promoting links with schools or in conjunction with local area partnerships designed to tackle long-term unemployment and social exclusion (Smyth and McCabe, 1997).

In spite of the development of a number of programmes to tackle educational disadvantage, a substantial proportion of pupils from disadvantaged backgrounds are not covered by such schemes and the effectiveness of the interventions themselves is as yet unclear. While some programmes have indicated positive outcomes for disadvantaged children and young people, many programmes have not been systematically evaluated or are awaiting such evaluation. At present, the programmes fall under the jurisdiction of several government departments and state agencies, a situation that reduces the potential for the development of a co-ordinated approach to educational disadvantage. In addition, the target groups concerned can differ from programme to programme. It has been argued that there is much greater scope for a co-ordination of effort between the various schemes and that clear targets should be established in order to assess their impact (see ESF Programme Evaluation Unit, 1997; Smyth and McCabe, 1997; Technical Working Group, 1998).

There is a broader question concerning the persistence of social class inequalities in the face of educational interventions. Broadly speaking, educational choice can be regarded as the product of the relative costs and benefits of continued participation. The relative costs of schooling are likely to vary by social class, parents with higher levels of education will be better able to help their children negotiate their way through the schooling system, and the perceived benefits and probabilities of success may differ between social groups (Erikson and Jonsson, 1996). If social groups continue to differ in their financial and cultural resources, then differences in educational participation are likely to persist. For this reason, there is a remarkable similarity between countries with very different educational systems in the persistence of educational inequality among different social classes (Shavit and Blossfeld, 1993). Only in Sweden (and, to a lesser extent, the Netherlands) has there been any significant reduction in inequality of educational opportunity over time, a process that is attributable not only to educational reform but also to diminishing social class differences in income and living conditions (Erikson, 1996). Educational systems can serve to exacerbate or reduce existing social class inequalities. This section has highlighted specific aspects of the Irish educational system which are likely to contribute to the reproduction, if not the accentuation, of social class inequalities in educational participation and outcomes. The following section explores whether the rapid educational expansion of recent years and new policies to allay educational disadvantage have succeeded in reducing educational inequalities in Irish society.

6.2 Educational inequalities

The introduction of the Free Education Scheme was followed by a rapid increase in participation in second-level education. In 1966 only one in four of seventeen-year-olds was participating in full-time education compared with over three out of four of this group thirty years later. In comparative perspective, Ireland has experienced a much more rapid expansion of educational attainment among younger age cohorts than in many other European countries. In this respect, it is quite similar to the Mediterranean countries where educational qualifications expanded from a relatively low base (Müller and Wolbers, 1999). In terms of per capita public expenditure on education, however, Ireland remains below the OECD average for the primary and second-level sectors. In addition, educational expenditure is more regressive in Ireland than in most other countries, with considerably more being spent on the more select group in tertiary education than on those in the primary or second-level sectors (OECD, 1998b).

The period since the early 1980s has been one of rapid expansion in educational participation. Data from the regular surveys of school leavers carried out by the ESRI provide a useful way of assessing the nature of educational change as they allow us to link trends in participation with individual information on family background. There has been a rapid increase in the proportion of young people staying on to the end of upper second-level education in Ireland since the early 1980s. Figure 6.1 indicates that in 1979 60 per cent of school-leavers had taken the Leaving Certificate but by 1997 this had increased to 81 per cent. The increase was accompanied by a decline in the proportion of young people leaving school at the end of lower second-level education (Junior Certificate). There has also been some decline in the proportion leaving school without taking any formal examinations.

In addition to those who leave during their second-level schooling, it has been estimated that almost 1,000 young people do not transfer from primary to second-level education (Hannan, 1996). More recent figures indicate that approximately 700 pupils left primary school in 1996/7 without transferring to another school or had unknown destinations (Department of Education and Science, 1999). Much less is known about the characteristics of this group since they are not included in sources of information such as the annual surveys of second-level school leavers. However, many of this group are likely to come from Traveller families. It is estimated that eighty per cent of 12 to 15-year-old children from Traveller families do not attend second-level schools, and that the majority of those who attend second-level schools leave within their first two years (Task Force on the Travelling Community, 1995).

Figure 6.1: Patterns of school leaving 1979-1997

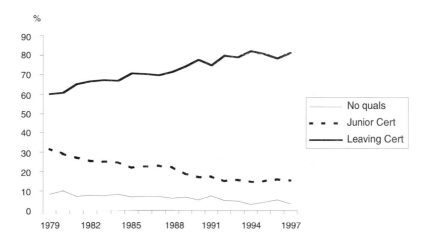

Source: Annual School Leavers' Survey, various years.

In addition to the growth in educational participation at second level, there has been a rapid growth in the numbers of young people entering full-time third-level education after completing their Leaving Certificate (see Figure 6.2). This proportion has almost doubled since 1979 with the rapid expansion of third-level provision, particularly in the non-university sector, an expansion that was primarily facilitated by EU funding.

Figure 6.2: Entry to full-time third-level education among Leaving Cert leavers

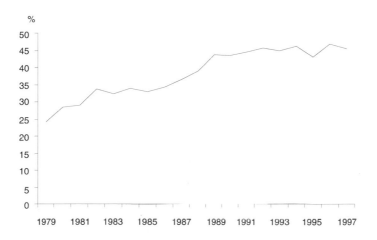

Source: Annual School Leavers' Survey, various years.

It has been argued that educational expansion can result in a reduction in inequalities on the basis of social background as demand for education is saturated among the higher social classes (Raftery and Hout, 1993). On this basis, we would expect a reduction in inequalities among those staying on to the Leaving Certificate. The following sections explore whether this is indeed the case.

Gender differences in educational participation

Female educational participation in Ireland has grown since the early twentieth century with females making up almost half of those passing the Leaving Certificate by the middle of the century. Second-level completion rates continued to increase among later cohorts of young women (Whelan and Hannan, 1999) and by the early 1980s young women were significantly more likely than their male counterparts to leave school at the Leaving Certificate level (see Figure 6.3). In addition, young women tend to achieve higher results in formal examinations, controlling for their initial ability/performance levels and social background (Smyth, 1999b).

Figure 6.3: Leaving Certificate completion by gender 1979-1997

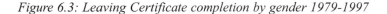
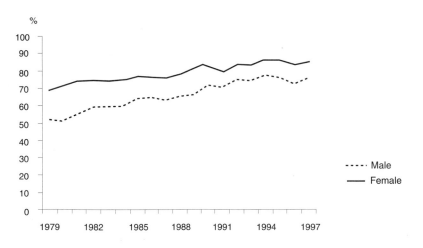

Source: Annual School Leavers' Survey, various years.

The most significant shift in educational differences by gender, however, has occurred in relation to third-level participation. In the early 1980s, a higher proportion of males than females went on to third-level education but this difference has reversed over time (see Figure 6.4). However, gender differences persist in the type of courses taken by young women and men at both second and third level (Smyth, 2000; Clancy, 1995), differences which are likely to have significant consequences for subsequent labour market segregation by gender (see below).

Figure 6.4: Third-level participation among Leaving Cert leavers by gender

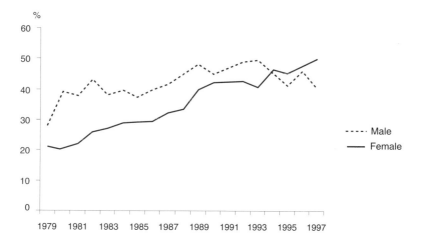

Social background differences in educational participation

In contrast to the changes in gender differences in educational participation, there has been a notable persistence in educational inequalities by social background (see Smyth, 1999a). The professional groups have almost reached saturation point in Leaving Certificate completion rates with 89-91 per cent of these groups reaching this level in 1998 compared with 62 per cent of those with parents from an unskilled manual background.[1] Figure 6.5 indicates that all social classes have experienced educational expansion since 1979. The position of young people from farming backgrounds has changed considerably over the period. In 1979 farm groups occupied an intermediate position between the non-manual and manual groups while by 1998 Leaving Cert completion rates among farm children were comparable to those from professional groups. The overall pattern over the period concerned is one of *absolute* growth in the numbers of young people from working-class backgrounds who complete the Leaving Certificate. However, analyses indicate that there has been no significant reduction in *relative* inequalities between the different social classes in upper second-level completion rates (see Smyth, 1999a).

Figure 6.5: Leaving Certificate completion by social class

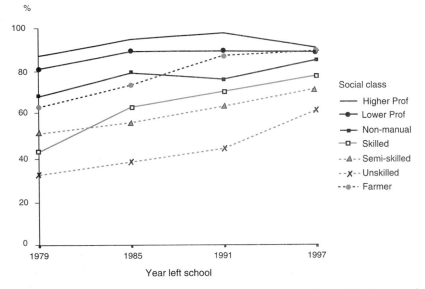

While social class is the most commonly used measure of social background, other aspects of family background are found to have significant relationships with educational participation. Participation tends to be higher among those whose parents themselves have higher levels of education and among those from smaller families. Educational level is also associated with parental employment status. Figure 6.6 indicates that those with one or both parents in employment are more likely to complete the Leaving Certificate than those whose parents are not employed.

Figure 6.6: Educational level by parental employment, 1997

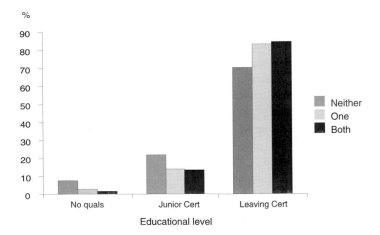

Examination performance is also significantly related to socio-economic background. Educational under-performance is more evident among pupils from working-class backgrounds, those with parents who are unemployed, those whose parents have lower levels of education and those who come from larger families (Smyth, 1999b; Hannan, Smyth et al, 1996). Most of the difference between schools in the average exam performance of their pupils is due to pupil composition factors, that is, to the gender, ability and social background mix of pupils. These differences in educational attainment are likely to have important consequences for access to employment and further education (see below).

The pattern of socio-economic inequalities in educational participation is also evident in relation to the third-level sector. Among those leaving school in 1997, 64 per cent of those from higher professional backgrounds went on to full-time higher education compared with 17 per cent of those from unskilled manual backgrounds. Previous research had indicated some decrease in socio-economic inequalities in third-level participation over the period 1980 to 1992 (Clancy, 1995). However, analyses of the school leavers' surveys indicate a persistence in social class inequalities in access over time.[2] While all social groups have increased their participation at third-level, if anything, a widening gap is evident over the whole period between the professional and unskilled manual groups in their access to full-time third-level education. As with Leaving Cert completion, rates of participation among young people (especially young women) from farming backgrounds have increased to levels approaching those of the professional groups.

Figure 6.7: Third-level entry by social class

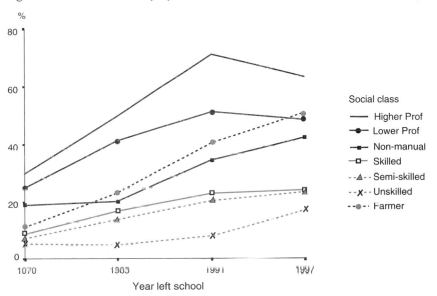

This section has indicated significant changes in educational participation by gender, changes that must be placed in the context of broader shifts in female labour force participation and access to employment. In contrast, there has been a remarkable persistence of social class inequalities in educational outcomes in the face of educational expansion and policies explicitly designed to reduce such inequalities. Indeed, there is some indication of a widening social gap in access to full-time third-level education since the early 1980s. The persistence of such inequality must be placed in the context of the specific institutional characteristics of the Irish educational system. In particular, the role of middle-class parents in school selection, the importance of hierarchical differentiation in terms of grades along with the comparative absence (at least until recently) of vocational routes designed to retain young people within the schooling system have inhibited the reduction of social class inequalities. Experience from other countries indicates that educational reform alone may not be sufficient to secure more equal educational outcomes and that greater equalisation of life-chances in general has an important influence (Erikson, 1996). From this perspective, continuing, if not increasing, inequality in income distribution (see Barrett, Fitz Gerald and Nolan, this volume) is likely to contribute to the persistence of educational inequalities.

This section has described the persistence of social inequalities in educational outcomes. The following section explores the extent to which these inequalities result in further disparities between young people in the transition from school to the labour market.

6.3 Education and early labour market integration

Previous research has indicated the significant consequences of education for access to employment, social mobility and pay levels (see, for example, Layte, Nolan and Whelan, this volume; Callan and Harmon, 1997). This section focuses on the relationship between education and the process of early labour market integration among young people and the extent to which this has changed over time in response to a rapid increase in educational participation. More specifically, we focus on: (i) the extent to which newer forms of post-school education and training compensate for initial educational disadvantage; (ii) whether there have been changes over time in the 'employment gap' between those with no qualifications and others; (iii) whether the nature of competition for jobs between young people with different levels of education has altered over time; and, (iv) whether an increase in educational participation and changing employment patterns have resulted in a reduction in social class and gender inequalities in early labour market integration.

Post-school education/training

The previous section examined the rapid increase in participation in third-level education since the early 1980s. However, it is also important to examine participation in education/training among young people who do not directly enter third-level education on leaving school. Research has indicated that the education system in Ireland tends to be one-way with little flexibility in terms of alternative routes within the system (Hannan, McCabe and McCoy, 1998). Part of the underlying reason for this rigidity has been the almost exclusive reliance on Leaving Certificate performance for competitive entry to third-level education coupled with a (until recently) growing cohort seeking entry.

One notable trend, however, has been the development and expansion of in-school vocational training for those who have completed general education, often benefiting from EU funding. Participation in these Post-Leaving Cert vocational programmes has increased from 10 per cent at the beginning of the 1980s to a situation where almost half of those with Leaving Certificates who do not proceed to third-level education take such courses (Hannan and Doyle, 2000). As well as increasing in coverage, provision has diversified in terms of the vocational skills covered and has become increasingly integrated into a standardised certification system. However, it should be noted that those taking PLC courses are predominantly those who have already been relatively successful within the educational system (that is, by taking the Leaving Certificate) and the expansion of within-school vocational provision has not benefited those without general educational qualifications to the same extent.

Since the early 1980s there has been significant improvement in the extent to which young people improve their qualifications by participating in post-school education and training outside the third level sector over their first six years in the labour market. Comparing three cohorts of school leavers over the period 1982 to 1998, participation in non-third level education/vocational courses increased from around 15 per cent of 1982 school-leavers to 36 per cent of those leaving school in 1992 (Hannan and Doyle, 2000). Almost one-third of the later cohort of school leavers with a Leaving Certificate qualification who did not go on immediately to third-level education subsequently upgraded their qualifications, a substantial improvement over the 5-6 per cent of those within the earlier cohort who did so. In contrast, however, those who left school without any formal educational qualifications achieved almost no improvement in their qualifications.

It is clear, therefore, that participation in further education and training tends to be more prevalent among those with initially higher levels of education, a process which reinforces, rather than compensates for, initial inequalities in educational outcomes. In other systems, apprenticeship and state training courses are often used to provide alternative routes to qualifications for those who have left school without general educational qualifications (Hannan, Raffe and Smyth, 1996). However, in the Irish case apprenticeship has moved away from being a route for those with junior cycle qualifications and has become increasingly dominated by those with Leaving Cert qualifications. In contrast, state training programmes (such as Youth Reach) are targeted towards less qualified young people but are less likely to yield marketable qualifications (Smyth and Hannan, 1995). Other research has also indicated that those without qualifications are less likely to participate in the kinds of training programmes which are likely to yield labour market success (O'Connell and McGinnity, 1997b).

Education and labour market entry

Figure 6.8: Unemployment rate by educational level

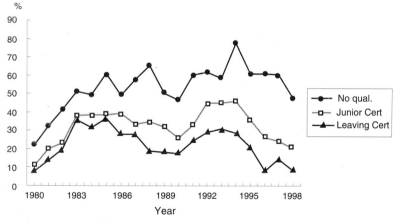

Source: McCoy et al, 1999

There are substantial differences by educational level in the rate of unemployment and in the time spent unemployed after leaving school. Those with higher levels of education have fewer and shorter unemployment spells. It also takes longer for those with lower educational levels to obtain their first job (Hannan, McCabe and McCoy, 1998; Hannan and Doyle, 2000). Figure 6.8 illustrates unemployment rates among school-leavers with different levels of education between 1980 and 1998. It shows clearly that the absolute gap in unemployment rates between those with a Leaving Certificate and those without any qualifications has increased steadily over time.

What is more surprising is that the relative gap widened even more dramatically from the mid-1990s onwards as employment grew rapidly. By

1998 unemployment rates still stood at over 40 per cent for those without qualifications and this group appears to be increasingly marginalised within the youth labour market (see Figure 6.9). Furthermore, the relative position of those without qualifications tends to further deteriorate over the first five to six years in the labour market (Smyth and Hannan, 1995; Breen, 1991).

Figure 6.9: Unemployment ratios – unqualified v. Leaving Cert

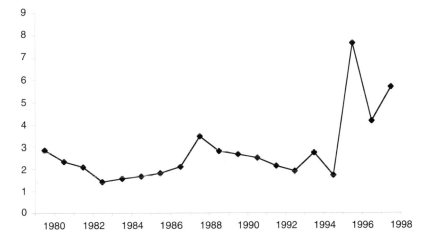

Young people with higher levels of exam performance are more likely to secure access to paid employment (Breen, Hannan and O'Leary, 1995) while higher levels, and longer spells, of unemployment occur among those who 'fail' their final examinations (McCoy, Doyle and Williams, 1999). Educational attainment is also predictive of the type of job obtained. Young people who complete upper second-level education are much more likely to enter managerial, professional or clerical jobs than their less qualified counterparts. Educational qualifications become more predictive of occupational attainment over the early career in the labour market (Hannan, McCabe and McCoy, 1998).

Job competition and 'overqualification'

Compared to other systems such as Germany and the Netherlands, there are few institutional linkages between education, training and the labour market in Ireland. However, educational attainment (in the form of levels and grades) does play an important 'signalling' role in securing access to paid employment (Hannan, Raffe and Smyth, 1996). Given the general nature of the Irish educational system, there are fewer linkages between the type of education and the type of occupation achieved. For these reasons, there is a higher degree of open competition between school leavers with different levels of education for the same jobs in Ireland. This situation is reinforced by the relatively low level of labour market regulation in Ireland compared with other countries (see OECD, 1999).

In Ireland, over 40 per cent of those entering the labour market for the first time take jobs that are mostly filled by people with lower levels of education than themselves (Hannan, McCabe and McCoy, 1998). Whether measured in terms of dissimilarity indices or other measures of 'over-qualification', a very high degree of occupational overlap occurs between people with different levels of education, especially for 'first jobs'. Over time in the labour market, however, there is evidence of some 'sorting', with those with higher levels of education gradually moving into higher status/paid jobs (Hannan, McCabe and McCoy, 1998). In spite of employment growth in the 1990s, there is no evidence that the extent of 'over-qualification' has changed over time (Hannan and Doyle, 2000).

Class and gender inequalities in early labour market integration

The previous sections have shown that educational attainment is strongly associated with social class and gender. Furthermore, education is highly predictive of labour market outcomes among young people. On this basis, one would expect young women and those from middle-class backgrounds to fare better on the labour market. However, the meritocracy hypothesis would indicate that over time social class background will have no independent effect on early labour market career and that any effect will be wholly mediated by education. This hypothesis is clearly rejected by the evidence (Hannan, McCabe and McCoy, 1998: 84-96). Controlling for the effects of educational level achieved and other relevant variables, social background continues to influence occupational status achieved; even with the same level of education, working-class young people are still disadvantaged in terms of the quality of first and subsequent jobs over their early years in the labour market. In addition, young people whose parents are unemployed and/or from unskilled manual groups tend to experience disproportionate levels of unemployment (Hannan and Ó Riain, 1993). While direct inheritance effects are still important (through employment in the family farm/firm, for example), they now account for a very small proportion of first jobs. Other factors, such as the role of informal networks in providing employment information and easing access to jobs, and 'social capital' (status-linked personal characteristics, such as self-confidence, self-presentation, accent, etc.) may explain the continuing influence of familial statuses on early employment. Irish research in this area is, however, almost non-existent.

The previous sections have indicated that young women tend to achieve higher levels of education than their male counterparts. However, take-up of particular subject areas remains sharply differentiated by gender at both second-

and third-level stages. Young women have some advantages on labour market entry in terms of access to paid employment and the occupational status of first jobs achieved. However, young women remain concentrated in a relatively narrow range of occupations (clerical and service jobs) and pay levels are somewhat lower among females than males, when their higher educational attainment is controlled for (Smyth, 2000). In addition, early withdrawal from the labour market is an almost exclusively female phenomenon, one which is closely linked both to poor educational and early labour-market histories. This pattern was clearly evident in the 1980s and early 1990s (Hannan and Ó Riain, 1993). However, there is some evidence of lower levels of labour market withdrawal among more recent cohorts of female school-leavers (Hannan and Doyle, 2000). Any female advantage in the labour market is not retained throughout the early period of labour market integration. Young men are more likely than young women to secure mobility out of secondary sector jobs during their first six years in the labour market (Hannan, Smyth and McCabe, 1997). In addition, controlling for educational level, males have higher net weekly pay than females six years after leaving school (Smyth and Hannan, 1995).

6.4 Conclusions

This chapter has explored inequalities in educational outcomes and in the relationship between education and labour market entry among young people. In spite of a rapid increase in educational participation since the early 1980s and recent initiatives to counter educational disadvantage, educational participation and attainment remain strongly differentiated in terms of social class background. Indeed, there is evidence of a widening gap between the social classes in third-level entry. In the absence of a fundamental reduction in inequalities in life-chances, it is difficult to see how these inequalities will diminish radically in the future. Such disparities in educational outcomes must be seen in the context of the specific characteristics of the Irish educational system, in particular the combination of a centralised system with a good deal of discretion at the school level in terms of policy and practice. Recent reforms have made some attempt to improve pupil retention through new curricular programmes and certification systems. Paradoxically, however, one of these reforms, the Leaving Certificate Applied programme, may facilitate continued disparities in access to third-level education since it is not recognised in terms of third-level entry criteria. Because of the strong association between education and labour market outcomes, young people in Ireland who do not achieve educational qualifications are disproportionately likely to experience labour market marginalisation in terms of unemployment, insecure jobs and/or low pay. If educational outcomes are associated with social class background, then labour market marginalisation will be more prevalent among working-class youth. Furthermore, there is evidence that family background factors have a direct effect on the early labour market career, even controlling for education, further disadvantaging young people without employment networks or 'social capital'.

In contrast to the persistence of social class inequalities, there has been a shift in the pattern of gender differences, with females now more likely than their male counterparts to enter third-level education. These educational differences translate, to some extent, into female advantage on early entry to the labour market, with higher employment rates and higher occupational statuses among young women. However, such labour market 'advantage' is ambiguous since pay levels among young women do not reflect the higher status of the jobs they enter. Furthermore, young women are much less likely than young men to achieve mobility out of unstable, lower paid jobs over their early years in the labour market. The persistence of these gender differences must be placed in the context of continuing gender differentiation in the type of education received and of the existence of occupational and industrial segregation by gender in the labour market.

NOTES

1 Interestingly, the professional groups appear to be further away from 'saturation point' in 1998 than in the early 1990s. This phenomenon appears to be, at least partly, related to a transfer among middle-class pupils to 'grind' schools for the senior cycle; as these schools are outside the recognised school system, they are counted as pre-Leaving Cert leavers for survey purposes. At least a quarter of those from higher professional backgrounds who left before the Leaving Cert in 1997 appeared to transfer to private 'grind' schools.

2 The difference between our analyses and those of Clancy are likely to relate to changes over time in the method of data collection used for the HEA survey (see Smyth, 1999a).

Earnings Inequality, Returns to Education and Low Pay

ALAN BARRETT, JOHN FITZ GERALD AND BRIAN NOLAN

7.1 Introduction

A central feature of the global environment against which recent Irish experience has to be set is increasing earnings inequality within some major industrialised countries, and a widespread concern about increasing inequality in household incomes driven by what has been happening to earnings. Some see this as a product of inexorable forces of globalisation and technological advance, which individual countries have little scope to affect but with potentially profound social and political implications. For others, it reflects both institutional factors and the way countries have chosen to react to changing patterns of trade and competition. Against that background, analysis of the distribution of earnings and income and their recent evolution has an essential part to play in understanding recent Irish experience and drawing lessons from it. Chapter 8 will deal with the household income distribution, but here we focus on the earnings distribution.

Increasing earnings dispersion has been pronounced in the United Kingdom and the United States, and has given rise to a great deal of research there. The common factor in this research is the emphasis placed on rising returns to education and skill.[1] There has been less agreement on why this has happened, some for example attributing it to a shift in demand towards more skilled labour due to factors such as skill-biased technical change (Katz and Murphy, 1992) and others highlighting globalisation and competition from developing countries (Wood, 1994).[2] Some industrialised countries have in fact experienced much smaller increases in inequality than the USA and the UK, while others again have maintained stability in their earnings distributions (OECD, 1993 and 1996). This has focused attention on the role of institutional factors. Countries such as Germany and the Netherlands which have seen little or no increase in earnings inequality have some form of centralised wage bargaining. This has led to the hypothesis that these wage setting institutions were the primary factor limiting the growth in inequality in those countries.[3] Labour market deregulation and declining union membership are widely seen to have played some role in widening dispersion in the UK, particularly the virtual elimination of minimum wages through the abolition of the Wages Councils (Gosling and Machin, 1995; Machin, 1997), the decline of unions, and changes in collective bargaining arrangements (Leslie and Pu, 1996). Declines in unionisation and in the real value of the minimum wage have also been advanced as important factors in rising US earnings dispersion by, for example, Freeman (1993), DiNardo, Fortin and Lemieux (1996), and DiNardo and Lemieux (1997).

Against this background Ireland offers a particularly interesting comparative case study. As a small and extremely open economy, external influences should be even more important than in for example the UK, much less the USA. Unlike those countries, however, the strength of labour market and associated institutions has been increasing rather than declining. As analysed in some detail in other chapters, over the period on which we concentrate Ireland has been characterised by highly centralised wage bargaining. In addition, minimum wage coverage has widened and welfare benefits have provided a floor for the unemployed. Finally, as already discussed in detail in earlier chapters, the supply of skilled labour has been increasing very rapidly but so has the demand, fuelled by inward direct investment. Our central focus in this chapter is to tease out what has happened to the earnings distribution when this complex mix of factors has been in operation.

The chapter is structured as follows. The next section examines trends in the earnings distribution in Ireland between 1987 and 1997. This shows that there was a marked increase in earnings dispersion over the period, and the following section analyses in some depth the role of returns to different levels of educational attainment in producing that increase. We then focus on the bottom of the distribution, examining the extent and nature of low pay in Ireland. A major institutional innovation, the introduction of a national minimum wage, is then discussed, followed by a summary of the main conclusions.

7.2 The distribution of earnings in Ireland

In analysing the distribution of earnings across individual earners, the accounting period adopted can make a considerable difference to the extent of dispersion one observes. Hourly earnings, weekly earnings, earnings over a full year, or indeed lifetime earnings are all distinct measures and may show different patterns. Weekly earnings will be affected both by the hourly rate of pay and by the number of hours worked, annual earnings by the number of weeks spent in work as well as the weekly rate, and lifetime earnings by how much time one spends in work as well as the evolution of the annual rate of pay over the lifecycle. Each of these provides valuable information, and the choice of measure will depend both on the issue at hand and the available data. In analysing the distribution of earnings, a focus on hourly earnings provides the most direct measure of differences in pay rates abstracting from variations in time spent working. It is also common practice in this context to examine the distribution of weekly earnings for full-time employees only, and that of annual earnings among full-time employees who have been working all year.

In charting how earnings dispersion has evolved in Ireland in recent years we rely on the data provided by the 1987 ESRI household survey and the 1994 and 1997 Living in Ireland surveys. These have also been employed in earlier chapters, and a detailed description of these surveys is provided elsewhere. Here however, since we are focusing on individual earners rather than households, it is worth noting that validation against external sources has shown the employees in the sample to be representative in terms of age, occupational group and industrial sector. While data are produced regularly by the Central Statistics Office on average earnings in specific sectors such as industry, building and construction and the public sector, the household surveys cover the whole economy and allow the overall distribution of earnings at individual level to be studied.

Given appropriate data on individual earnings, there are various ways of assessing or presenting the shape of the distribution and the degree of dispersion. Most often, various percentiles of the distribution are expressed as proportions of the median. The median of the distribution is the earnings level above and below which half the earners are found. Ranking all employees by earnings from lowest to highest, the bottom decile cut-off is the earnings level below which the lowest 10 per cent of all earners fall, and the top decile the cut-off above which the highest 10 per cent are found. Correspondingly, the bottom and top quintiles are the cut-offs below/above which the bottom/top quarter of the distribution is found. A conventional approach to presenting the dispersion in earnings is then to express the bottom decile, bottom quartile, top quartile and top decile as proportions of the median. While this gives a picture of a number of different points in the distribution, a single summary measure of dispersion may also be useful. It is conventional to use for this purpose the ratio of the top to the bottom decile, though it is worth mentioning that different summary measures may not always lead to the same conclusions in terms of comparisons over time or across countries.

We focus first on the hourly earnings of all employees, and Table 7.1 shows the distribution of gross hourly earnings in the 1987, 1994 and 1997 surveys as captured by these measures. The table shows that from 1987 to 1994 there was a marked widening in dispersion at the top of the distribution. The ratio of the top decile to the median rose from 1.96 to 2.24, while the top quartile also moved further away from the median. In the bottom half of the distribution, the bottom quartile fell away from the median but the bottom decile did not. The overall picture is thus of widening dispersion throughout the distribution except at the very bottom, with the ratio of the top to the bottom decile rising sharply from 4.2 to 4.8.

Table 7.1: Distribution of hourly earnings in 1987, 1994 and 1997, all employees

as proportion of median	1987	1994	1997
all employees, hourly earnings:			
Bottom decile	0.47	0.47	0.48
Bottom quartile	0.73	0.68	0.69
Top quartile	1.37	1.50	1.53
Top decile	1.96	2.24	2.33
Top decile/bottom decile	4.16	4.77	4.81

It is particularly interesting to see whether this trend continued from 1994 to 1997, as economic growth accelerated rapidly. We see that the top decile did continue to move away from the median, reaching 2.33 by 1997, with the top quartile also moving slightly further from the median. In the bottom half of the distribution, however, both the bottom decile and the bottom quartile now kept pace with the median, if anything increasing marginally faster. As a result, the ratio of the top to the bottom decile was essentially unchanged.

Over the whole period from 1987 to 1997, then, there was a substantial widening in earnings dispersion in terms of hourly wages among all employees. This was more pronounced in the 1987-94 period than from 1994 on, so rapid economic growth did not lead to acceleration in the trend. It was primarily driven by relatively rapid increases for those towards the top of the distribution, with no indication that the bottom has been falling behind the median. In the light of the relatively rapid increase in the top decile compared with the median it is of interest to look at what was happening towards the very top. The 95th percentile (cutting off the top 5 per cent) rose even more rapidly than the 90th percentile, going from 2.4 times the median in 1987 to 2.8 in 1994 and 3.0 in 1997. The 99th percentile (cutting off the top 1 per cent) went from 3.6 in 1987 to 3.8 in 1994 and 4.3 in 1997. So over the whole period top earnings rose very rapidly, but it is only at the very top that there is any suggestion that this might have accelerated from 1994 to 1997.

It is also of interest to look at the distribution of weekly gross earnings among full-time employees. Various definitions and measures of what constitutes 'full-time' are used in different countries or with different datasets, depending on custom and practice and the nature of the available data. In some cases survey respondents' own categorisation of their status as full versus part-time is taken, in others different hours cut-offs are applied to reported hours worked. Here we base the distinction on total hours of work reported by respondents, and count as full-time those reporting at least 30 hours usual work per week, the cut-off regarded as most suitable for comparative purposes by the OECD. About 10 per cent of employees worked less than this in 1987, but by 1994 the figure was up to 15 per cent and by 1997 it was 19 per cent. Table 7.2 shows the distribution of gross hourly and weekly earnings in 1987, 1994 and 1997 among full-time employees distinguished on this basis.

Once again we see that from 1987 to 1994 there was a consistent widening in dispersion at the top of the distribution. The top decile as a proportion of the median rose from 1.82 to 1.97, and the top quartile also moved further from the median. The bottom decile was just below half the median in 1987 and 1994 and just above it in 1997. The top half of the distribution showed little change between 1994 and 1997. Over the decade as a whole, then, the ratio of the top to the bottom decile increased markedly, but this was concentrated in the period from 1987 to 1994.

Table 7.2: Distribution of weekly earnings in 1987, 1994 and 1997, full-time employees

Weekly earnings as proportion of median	1987	1994	1997
Bottom decile	0.49	0.48	0.51
Bottom quartile	0.75	0.72	0.71
Top quartile	1.35	1.43	1.43
Top decile	1.82	1.97	2.02
Top decile/ bottom decile	3.68	4 .06	3.93

A comparative perspective on the Irish earnings distribution and the way it has been changing since 1987 can be obtained using measures of earnings dispersion for a range of developed countries brought together by the OECD. These figures generally refer to full-time employees and to weekly, monthly or annual rather than hourly gross earnings, so for Ireland we focus on the results for weekly earnings among full-time employees. Table 7.3 shows the ratio of the top to the bottom decile in 1987 and 1994 for Ireland and the other OECD countries for which figures are available for both these points in time, together with the more limited figures available for 1997. We see first that Ireland had a relatively high level of earnings inequality in 1987 compared with other OECD countries, only Canada and the USA having a higher ratio of top to bottom decile. We then see that the increase in earnings dispersion in Ireland between 1987 and 1994 was the greatest of any of the countries shown, although over the decade from 1987 the USA saw a more substantial increase in this measure. There are potentially important differences in definition and coverage across countries (including the period over which earnings are measured, how 'full-time' is defined and measured, and whether all sectors are covered), so these comparisons should be treated with considerable care, but they certainly suggest that earnings dispersion in Ireland rose relatively rapidly over this period.

Table 7.3: Trends in earnings dispersion, Ireland and other OECD countries, 1987-97

	top decile/bottom decile			Change	
	1987	1994	1997	1987-94	1987-97
Austria	3.47	3.65		0.18	
Australia	2.81	2.86	2.95	0.05	0.14
Belgium	2.45	2.24*		-0.19	
Canada	4.45*	4.18		-0.27	
Finland	2.51	2.35	2.33*	-0.16	-0.18
France	3.18	3.08	3.06*	-0.10	-0.12
Germany	2.83	2.80		-0.03	
Ireland	3.68	4.06	3.93	0.38	0.25
Italy	2.30	2.33	2.39*	0.03	0.09
Japan	3.15	3.01	3.01	-0.14	-0.14
Netherlands	2.53	2.58		0.05	
New Zealand	2.83*	3.03		0.20	
Sweden	2.10	2.18	2.27*	0.08	0.17
United Kingdom	3.31	3.39	3.41	0.08	0.10
USA	4.24	4.52	4.61	0.29	0.37

Source: OECD Earnings Database. * Figures refer to 1986 rather than 1987, 1993 rather than 1994, 1996 rather than 1997.

To explore in more depth the way the Irish earnings distribution has evolved, we focus once again on hourly earnings and distinguish men and women, part-time versus full-time employees, and different age groups. The increase in dispersion was in fact particularly marked among men, with the top decile as a proportion of the (male) median rising from 3.5 to 5.0 over the decade. This reflects the bottom decile lagging behind the median, falling from 0.53 to 0.47, but also the sharp increase in the top decile from 1.9 to 2.3 times the median. Although dispersion was greater among women than men employees in 1987 it rose by much less over the decade. With the ratio of the top to the bottom decile increasing for women from 4.4 in 1987 to 4.6 in 1997, dispersion was by then less than for men. The gap between average male and female earnings also narrowed a good deal over the decade.

Where in 1987 hourly earnings for women were 82 per cent of the corresponding average for men, by 1997 this figure had risen to 85 per cent. This represents a continuation of a longer-term trend, and the range of influences involved are analysed in detail in Barrett et al, 2000. For present purposes, in terms of overall earnings dispersion the continuing convergence of mean (and median) hourly earnings of men and women will have served to partially offset the increase in dispersion among women and more particularly among men.

Distinguishing part-time from full-time employees on the basis of a 30-hour per week cut-off, one finds that average hourly earnings are actually consistently higher for part-timers throughout the period. This reflects the fact that significant numbers in professional occupations, including in particular teachers, will be classed as part-timers on that basis. A comparison of median earnings for the two groups gives a rather different picture, with the median for part-timers below that for full-time employees, bringing out the different shapes of the two distributions. As already mentioned, the percentage working part-time had increased substantially over the period, from 10 per cent in 1987 to 19 per cent in 1997. The part-time/full-time distinction also sheds an interesting sidelight on male versus female earnings. A much higher proportion of women than men work part-time – in the 1997 sample about one-third of full-time employees versus three-quarters of part-time employees were women. Among full-timers, the average hourly wage for women went from 77 per cent of the male average in 1987 to 84 per cent in 1997.

When employees are categorised by age, the most striking feature over the decade from 1987 is the increase in dispersion within age ranges rather than across them. Within the 25 to 34 age range, for example, the ratio of the top to the bottom decile rose from 3 to 3.6, while within the 35 to 44 range it went from 3.7 to 4.4. There was also some increase in variation of median earnings across the age groups, however. The median for employees aged under 25 went from 70 per cent of the overall median in 1987 down to 66 per cent in 1997, while the 55-64 age group saw its median rise from 116 per cent to 126 per cent.

Bringing age and gender together, it is of interest to abstract for a moment from the impact of part-time working and to focus on full-time 'adult' wages. Table 7.4 shows the way the distribution has evolved for full-time men aged 21 or over, and we see that there has been a pronounced increase in dispersion among this group. The top decile has gone from 2.9 to 3.6 times the median over the decade, with most of this change occurring by 1994. Among full-time women aged 21 or over, by contrast, there was very little change in dispersion over the period.

Table 7.4: Distribution of hourly earnings in 1987, 1994 and 1997, full-time male employees aged 21 or over

as proportion of median	1987	1994	1997
Hourly earnings:			
Bottom decile	0.63	0.55	0.57
Bottom quartile	0.78	0.74	0.75
Top quartile	1.33	1.42	1.44
Top decile	1.79	2.04	2.07
Top decile/bottom decile	2.86	3.68	3.61

7.3 The returns to education

In the introduction to this chapter, we discussed how the increase in earnings inequality that has been observed in some countries has in turn been linked to increasing returns to skills, and in particular to education. We now explore the degree to which the trends in earnings inequality in Ireland described in the previous section are also linked to this factor. One would certainly expect the demand for educated and skilled workers to have increased in the Irish case given the pace and nature of economic growth during the 1990s. However, it is possible in the light of the rapid educational expansion in recent years, discussed in detail in Chapter 6, that increasing demand for skills was actually met with an increased supply on a similar scale. The return to those skills could then have remained unchanged, and the explanation for the increase in earnings inequality documented earlier would have to be sought elsewhere.

In order to provide a sense of the increase in the supply of skilled labour in the Irish labour market in recent years, Figure 7.1 shows estimates of skilled and unskilled labour supply[5] over the past 25 years. Skilled labour is defined as those members of the labour force who have at least a Leaving Certificate (high school graduation) and unskilled as those with lower levels of educational attainment. From the early 1980s onwards the supply of unskilled labour fell quite rapidly, as a result of increasing educational participation at second level.

There may also have been a 'discouraged worker' effect in the 1980s due to the prolonged recession. In the 1990s the fall in supply of unskilled labour has continued, albeit more slowly. It has been modified in recent years by rising labour force participation among women with limited educational attainment.

Over the whole period from 1971 to 1997 the supply of skilled labour has risen rapidly and fairly continuously. The one exception was the late 1980s, when emigration, predominantly of skilled people (see Chapter 4), peaked. Between 1971 and 1981 the supply of skilled labour rose by 95 per cent, between 1981 and 1991 it rose by over 72 per cent and between 1991 and 1997 there was a further increase of 35 per cent. In the 1990s immigration and rising female labour force participation have contributed to the increase in skilled labour.

As regards labour demand, rising demand for skilled labour occurred throughout the industrialised economies (Nickell and Bell, 1995) over the 1980s and the 1990s. However, the shift in demand in Ireland has been accentuated by the impact of foreign direct investment on the economy.

Figure 7.1: Labour supply by educational attainment

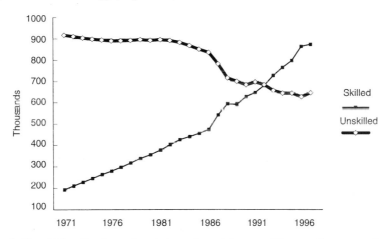

The bulk of the foreign direct investment has, until recently, gone to the manufacturing sector. By 1997 almost 50 per cent of all employment in manufacturing was in foreign-owned firms and a quarter of all employment was in US-owned firms (Table 7.5). The bulk of this employment in foreign-owned firms was in the high-technology sector, broadly defined.

In the 1960s the two sectors of the economy that employed the bulk of the skilled labour force were financial and professional services. They still are the major employers of skilled labour, but the gap in levels of human capital employed in these sectors and in the rest of the economy has narrowed considerably, with a general upgrading of the skill levels in high-technology manufacturing (engineering, including computers, and chemicals).

The high-technology manufacturing sector, driven by the inflow of foreign firms, now has an above-average level of human capital in its labour force.

Table 7.5: Share of total manufacturing employment by sector and by ownership

	Irish-owned	Foreign-owned	Of which: US-owned	Total
Other	40.1	17.3	7.1	57.4
High Tech.	12.1	30.5	18.2	42.6
Total	52.2	47.8	25.2	100.0

The most rapid increase in the demand for skilled labour in the 1990s has occurred in high-technology manufacturing and in financial services, both of which are affected by the inflow of new firms from abroad.

We now turn to our analysis of the relative impacts of increasing labour supply and labour demand on the returns to education. For this purpose, we have estimated earnings functions and examine the return to different levels of educational attainment in the years 1987, 1994 and 1997, once again drawing on the ESRI household survey data sets described earlier. We present the regression results elsewhere (Barrett, Fitz Gerald and Nolan, 2000), concentrating here on the pattern of results and their implications. The dependent variable in the estimated equations is the logarithm of hourly earnings,[6] and we include as independent variables a range of factors that influence earnings, including education, with a range of different specifications. While the coefficients on the educational categories turn out to vary across these specifications, a general picture does emerge as we shall see.

The education categories, based on the highest level of schooling attained, are as follows:

- 'Primary only': This includes those who left school at the end of primary level, or did some second-level schooling but obtained no qualification.
- Junior cycle: This includes the Group and Intermediate Certificates, as well as their recent replacement, the Junior Certificate. These are exams taken at the midway stage of second level education.
- Leaving Certificate: This is the qualification obtained by those successfully completing the senior cycle of second-level education, plus a small number with qualifications under the Post Leaving Certificate and Vocational Preparation and Training Programmes.
- Diploma or other third level: This includes non-degree qualifications from such institutions as regional technical colleges.
- University degree: This includes both primary and higher degrees.

The results show first that, as would be expected, earnings rise in each year with level of education. For example, in 1987 one of the specifications suggests that those with Junior cycle qualifications earned 17 per cent more per hour than those with only primary schooling; those with Leaving Certificates earned 37 per cent more and those with degrees earned 86 per cent more. Turning to the comparison of these returns over time, while there is some movement in the point estimates between 1987 and 1994 the only differences that are statistically significant are those for university degrees where all our specifications show the returns to the highest education increasing. This finding is consistent with the increase in earnings inequality between 1987 and 1994, documented earlier. It suggests that in spite of increased numbers of skilled employees and centralised wage bargaining, the increase in the demand for skilled labour was sufficiently strong for the price of that labour to be bid up.

Comparing the returns to education in 1994 and 1997, on the other hand, in some specifications the returns to university education in 1997 were statistically the same as in 1994, while in some they actually fell. A conservative summary of the result would thus be that the increase in returns to university education observed between 1987 and 1994 did not continue between 1994 and 1997. Again, this is consistent with the reduction in the growth of earnings inequality between 1994 and 1997.

It then proved productive to look at estimates of education returns distinguishing different age groups. The increases in returns to university-level attainment between 1987 and 1994 for the overall sample are now seen to have been concentrated among the middle or older age groups. This different trend in returns to university education across age groups calls for an explanation.

One possible explanation is based on the notion that the skilled labour market is not homogeneous but rather is differentiated by experience levels. By this we mean that inexperienced skilled workers are not perfect substitutes for experienced skilled workers. As the increase in supply of educated workers would have been made up of those leaving the education system, they would have been primarily in the younger age category. If the skilled labour market is indeed differentiated between the newly skilled and the more experienced skilled employees, the increase in supply of newly skilled employees would not have an impact in the market of experienced skilled workers. Hence, the increase in demand for skills was met with a supply increase in one part of the skilled market and so the price did not rise; in the other part of the market, i.e. the experienced skilled market, no supply increase was forthcoming and so prices did rise.

Turning to the 1994-97 period, age-differentiated specifications reveal that the returns to university-level attainment again appear to have stayed the same for younger employees, but now seem to have fallen for the middle-aged group.

For younger skilled workers this could once again reflect increasing supply from the education system, but we need to look elsewhere for an explanation of the decline in the return for older workers.

We suggest another supply explanation. The growth in the economy in recent years has brought with it the return to Ireland of former emigrants and the entry of immigrants. Two characteristics of the inflow are relevant to our findings. First, although there was a net inflow of 16,400 between 1994 and 1997, this aggregate figure hides large differences across age groups. For those aged 15-25, there was a net outflow of 44,100; for those aged 25-44, there was a net inflow of 27,400.[7] This inflow figure suggests that there was a significant addition to the labour force in the middle age group. The second relevant characteristic of the inflow relates to its educational composition. Barrett and Trace (1998) have shown that both returning migrants and immigrants in the years 1994 to 1996 had higher levels of educational attainment than the domestic population. For example, while 12.7 per cent of the domestic labour force aged 30 to 39 had university degrees, 28 per cent of returning migrants in that age group had degrees. The corresponding figure for immigrants was 43.2 per cent. The net result of these two factors, the size of the inflow in the middle age group and its educational level, is that there was a significant increase in the supply of middle-aged skilled labour between 1994 and 1997. This may explain the possible fall or stability in the return to university education for this group over that period.

We can test this immigration hypothesis following an approach used by Borjas, Freeman and Katz (1997). While many studies have looked at the labour market impact of immigration by relating changes in wages to inflows of migrants across regions, Borjas et al have criticised this approach. They argue that adjustments to immigration may take the form of native workers not moving to areas that have experienced large inflows of immigrants. If this does occur, immigrants may have effects on the national labour market that are not observed in inter-regional comparisons. For this reason, Borjas et al simulate the impact of immigrants on wages in a national framework. They do so by comparing the nation's supplies of skilled and unskilled labour under different immigration levels and then assessing the relative wage impacts.

Broadly following this approach, we develop a simple model of the Irish labour market that allows us to compare outcomes with and without an inflow of skilled immigrants. The model is based on a theoretical structure, the parameters of which are then estimated using data from 1971 to 1996.

More extensive details of the model can be found in Barrett, Fitz Gerald and Nolan (2000) but here we provide the essential features. The model consists of two kinds of labour – skilled and unskilled. Within the model, the wages of the skilled and employment levels of both the skilled and unskilled are determined, along with output.[8] Among the specific features are the following. While the supply of unskilled labour is assumed to be inelastic, the elasticity of supply of skilled labour is assumed to be greater. This reflects the fact that the skilled elasticity has been unusually high because of the ready movement of skilled labour in and out of the country and because of the elasticity of supply of skilled female labour. The elasticity of substitution between skilled and unskilled labour in Ireland has been found to be relatively low (Kearney, 1998a) and this is incorporated into the model by assuming that the elasticity of substitution is zero. Regarding output, an equation is used to reflect the fact that Irish output is quite sensitive to the relative cost (or profitability) of producing in Ireland compared to other countries (Bradley and Fitz Gerald, 1988; Bradley, Fitz Gerald and Kearney, 1993). At the level of the Irish economy skilled and unskilled labour are assumed to be complements – a rise in the cost of either factor will reduce Irish output and employment of both kinds of labour. Because of the assumed zero elasticity of substitution between the two kinds of labour within the economy the output (or scale) effect dominates any substitution effect (Bradley, Fitz Gerald and Kearney, 1993).

Within this model the effect of immigration of skilled labour is to reduce upward pressure on the skilled wage rate. In turn, this reduces the cost of producing in Ireland and increases output. Because Irish skilled and unskilled labour are complements, the increase in competitiveness due to falling skilled wage rates also increases the demand for unskilled labour. Thus the effect of skilled migration is to reduce the pressures for growing inequality in wage rates through reducing skilled wage rates and tightening the market for unskilled labour.

Over the four years 1996 to 1999 net immigration averaged 16,000 a year. As Barrett and Trace (1998) have shown, the bulk of these people, whether they were returning emigrants or foreigners, had a high level of education. As a result, they significantly increased the supply of skilled labour over that period. Applying an increase in skilled labour of this magnitude to the labour market model described above allows us to estimate the impact of immigration into Ireland.

The estimates of the effects are presented in Table 7.8. Four years after the shock, the impact of the immigration was to increase the supply of skilled labour by 3.2 per cent and to reduce skilled wage rates by 4.7 percentage points. (The model assumes that due to high levels of unskilled unemployment unskilled wage rates are unaffected by demand.)[9] As a result, the model would suggest that the impact of net immigration of skilled labour was to narrow the gap between skilled and unskilled wage rates by around 4.5 percentage points compared to the situation with no net migration.

This relaxation in the skilled labour supply constraint, and the resulting reduction in skilled wage rates, made Ireland more competitive on world markets. The model would suggest that this raised the level of GNP in the short run by 1.5

percentage points. The long-run impact would be substantially greater, due to the slow adjustment of productive capacity to changing economic circumstances. Ultimately the model would suggest that the impact of the improved competitiveness would be to raise the level of GNP by around 4 percentage points. With rapid adjustment of both skilled and unskilled employment (they are complements) to the changed circumstances, the unemployment rate is estimated to have fallen by around 0.7 percentage points, all of which is concentrated among those members of the labour force with limited education.

Table 7.8: Effects of net migration in the four years ended 1999

Skilled labour supply	per cent	3.2
Skilled wage rates	per cent	-4.7
GNP	per cent	1.5
Total employment	per cent	3.2
Unemployment rate	Percentage points	-0.7

Of course this analysis is only partial in nature as it does not take account of the wider impact of higher growth in putting increased pressure on existing infrastructure, in particular on housing. The model also incorporates some simplifying assumptions that are probably inappropriate under current circumstances. While the model assumption that unskilled wage rates are unaffected by labour market pressures was reasonably appropriate in the 1980s and early 1990s, it is clearly unrealistic under current circumstances. To the extent that the tightening of the unskilled labour market impacts on unskilled wage rates, the narrowing in wage dispersion arising from immigration will be even greater than shown in Table 7.8.

7.4 Low pay

The way the earnings distribution has been evolving in Ireland, as analysed in this chapter, has major implications across a whole range of areas, and many of these are taken up in subsequent chapters. Most obviously, the impact on the household income distribution is of central importance to the socio-economic effects of increasing earnings dispersion, and this relationship is shown in Chapter 8 to be rather more complex than might be immediately realised. In the rest of this chapter, though, we turn to the bottom of the earnings distribution, describing the extent of low pay and the minimum wage which has just been introduced to combat it.

There is no consensus on what constitutes 'low pay', in Ireland or elsewhere. As Fernie and Metcalf (1996: 5) put it, 'There are almost as many definitions of the low pay "threshold" as there are writers on the subject, so the benchmark chosen is wholly arbitrary.' However, the most common approach is to measure low pay *vis-à-vis* benchmarks derived from the distribution of earnings, such as half or two-thirds of the median. Substantial scope for divergence still arises depending on whether one uses the median for all employees or only a sub-set (males, adults, full-time workers), whether one focuses on hourly, weekly or annual earnings, and how earnings are defined and measured (e.g. whether overtime pay is included). We focus on the percentage of all employees with hourly gross pay below half and two-thirds of the median. The percentage below half the median was stable at 11 per cent in 1987, 1994 and 1997. While 20 per cent of employees were below two-thirds of the median in 1987, this had risen to 23 per cent by 1994. Between 1994 and 1997, this fell back marginally to 22 per cent.

International comparisons of the extent of low pay are problematic because of differences across countries and studies in methods, coverage, definitions, etc. The broadest cross-country comparisons can be made using figures produced by the OECD, which define low-paid workers as full-time workers who earn less than two-thirds of the median weekly earnings for full-time workers. On this basis Ireland in the mid-1990s had one of the highest levels of low pay of the countries covered by the OECD figures. Ireland and the UK had similar levels (about 20 per cent), only the USA with 25 per cent and Canada with 24 per cent were higher, while most of the other countries covered were below 15 per cent.

The characteristics distinguishing low-paid from other employees in Ireland are similar to elsewhere and have been quite stable over time. Part-time employees face a substantially higher risk of being low paid than full-time workers; employees aged under 25 face a much higher risk of being low paid than those aged 25 or over. There is no difference in risk between men and women aged under 25, but women over that age face a substantially higher risk of being low paid than men, with married women particularly heavily over-represented among the low paid. The risk of being low paid is closely related to the individual's level of educational attainment, though the pattern varies considerably with age. Almost half the low paid have attained a Leaving Certificate or higher level of qualification, but many of these relatively highly qualified employees are aged between 18 and 24. The risk of being low paid also varies a good deal across occupation and industry, being particularly high for those working in retailing and personal services.

It is important to note that the relationship between low pay and household poverty is weaker than often assumed. This is because earnings below conventional low pay thresholds are still generally above the social welfare support rates on which many households rely, and many of the low paid are not in any case the only earner in their household. As a result, only a small minority of the low paid are in households that would generally be identified as poor. A recent OECD study has demonstrated that this applies to many other industrialised countries. The USA had almost 40 per cent of its low paid employees in 'poor or near-poor' households, but for most of the other countries covered the figure was much lower. Most workers in poor households are themselves low paid – in Ireland as elsewhere – but very few employees are actually in such households.

7.5 The minimum wage

Most countries in the European Union have either statutory minimum wages set by government or minima set by collective agreements, and until very recently Ireland and the UK were the long-standing exceptions. For many years, both operated a limited system of minimum wage regulation that covered only specific jobs, sectors and in some cases geographical areas. This was implemented through Wages Councils in the UK and through Joint Labour Committees (JLCs) in Ireland, each consisting of trade union and employer nominees, together with independent members nominated by the state. Each committee covered a specific occupation/sector, and set legally-binding minimum wages and conditions of employment for the relevant workers, constituting only a small minority of all workers. Each JLC set a range of minima varying with experience and level of skill/responsibility, and the level of minimum payment also varied considerably across JLCs.

In the UK Wages Councils were abolished by the Thatcher government, but a national minimum wage had been a long-standing commitment of the Labour Party. On coming to power, the Labour government made clear its intention to establish a national minimum wage and established a Low Pay Commission to recommend how it should be structured. This marked a major change in the context in which a minimum wage could be considered in Ireland, and a commitment to introduce a national minimum wage was included in the programme of the in-coming government in 1997. A National Minimum Wage Commission was set up and reported in 1998, recommending that the minimum should be set at around two-thirds of median hourly earnings (with a lower rate for those aged under 18). On the basis of a study for the Commission using Living in Ireland survey data for 1994 (Nolan 1998), the Commission saw this rate as about £4.40 per hour at that date.

Compared with other industrialised countries, two-thirds of median earnings would be a very high level for the minimum wage. The government then announced that the national minimum would be introduced at £4.40 but in April 2000 – and this was subsequently implemented. A study on the likely impact of the minimum wage (Nolan et al, 1999) projected forward from the distribution of earnings in the 1997 ESRI survey, taking into account the exceptionally rapid growth in median earnings and the likelihood that the bottom of the distribution probably rose more rapidly. This suggested that the minimum wage on introduction would represent about 56 per cent of median earnings for those aged 18 or over. It was likely to affect about 13 per cent of all employees, and produce an immediate increase in gross earnings of about 1.6 per cent of the total wage bill. By comparison the minimum wage introduced in the UK in 1999 at stg £3.60 for those aged 22 or over was estimated to represent 47 per cent of their median hourly wage, to affect about 9 per cent of employees aged 18 or over, and to immediately increase the wage bill by about 0.6 per cent.

The study also concluded that the minimum wage would lead to a significant improvement in the incentive to be in paid work facing the unemployed or those working full-time in the home, while also improving the reward to employment for those who are currently employees. These improved incentives would be expected to increase participation in the labour force, the largest response being an expected increase in the participation rate of women. A decline in demand for low-wage labour in industry due to the direct impact of the minimum wage, and a decline in the demand for higher-wage labour due to the indirect impact on inflation, increasing wage demands and reducing competitiveness, were suggested by analysis using the ESRI's HERMES macromodel. However, the positive impact a minimum wage might have on effort, productivity levels and turnover of employees, and the monopsony power that employers in parts of the low-wage labour market may have, were also noted. Three effects have been at the centre of renewed debates among economists about the impact of minimum wages in recent years, and have sparked off a good deal of research, particularly in the USA and the UK. In a survey of firms carried out as part of the Irish study, substantial numbers of employers did indicate that they expected *inter alia* some cutting-back on profit margins, improved staff morale, productivity increases, reduced staff turnover, and more investment in retraining/upgrading the work of current staff. This survey also provides a basis for monitoring the actual impact of the minimum wage by re-interviewing the same sample some time after its introduction.

Under the terms of the Partnership for Prosperity and Fairness, the agreement reached between the social partners in early 2000 and discussed in detail in Chapter 16, it is likely that the minimum wage will be increased in two steps to reach £5 per hour in late 2002. Given the scale of the wage increases agreed under that programme, this should not exceed the rate of increase in average earnings over the period. The approach to further up-rating of the minimum wage remains to be seen, and will very much depend on whether collective agreements continue to operate: no formal indexation procedure has been adopted.

The minimum wage, like other policy instruments, does not always have a single clearly articulated objective. One obvious concern is with 'fairness' and the elimination of exploitation at the level of the individual earner, and in that context other earnings in the economy in question seem the most relevant point of comparison. Given the preponderance of women among the low paid, gender equality considerations may also loom large. The minimum wage is often advanced as an anti-poverty policy, but most families gaining from the minimum wage in terms of disposable income are in fact in the middle of the income distribution. As noted earlier, only a small minority of the low paid are in households which would generally be identified as 'poor'. The implication is not that minimum wages do not matter for poverty, but rather that they can form only one element in an anti-poverty strategy, in tandem with for example tax and welfare policies, treated in depth in Chapter 11.

7.6 Conclusions

Increasing earnings dispersion and rising returns to education and skill have received a great deal of attention internationally, and the aim of this chapter has been to document what has been happening in Ireland in this regard. We saw that over the period from 1987 to 1997 there was a substantial widening in earnings dispersion in terms of hourly wages among all employees. This was more pronounced in the 1987-94 period than from 1994 on, so rapid economic growth did not lead to an acceleration in the trend. It was primarily driven by relatively rapid increases for those towards the top of the distribution, with no indication that the bottom has been falling behind the median. Ireland already had a relatively high level of earnings inequality in 1987 compared with other OECD countries, and the increase in earnings dispersion was also relatively rapid.

From the early 1970s the supply of skilled labour in Ireland has risen rapidly as a consequence of educational expansion, with immigration becoming an important factor in the 1990s. The supply of unskilled labour, on the other hand, fell quite rapidly from the early 1980s as a result of increasing educational participation at second level. As regards labour demand, rising demand for skilled labour occurred throughout the industrialised economies over the 1980s and the 1990s but in Ireland this has been accentuated by the scale of foreign direct investment in the high-technology sector. To tease out the relative impacts of increasing labour supply and labour demand on the returns to education, we estimated earnings functions and examined the return to different levels of educational attainment in the ESRI surveys for 1987, 1994 and 1997. The results suggested an increase in returns to third-level education between 1987 and 1994, but this was confined to the middle or older age groups and did not continue from 1994 to 1997 – indeed declining returns for the middle-age ranges were then seen.

This could be because the skilled labour market differentiates between the newly skilled and the more experienced skilled employees. An increasing supply of skilled workers from the education system might then have sufficed to offset rising demand for younger skilled workers whereas the older and more experienced saw an increase in their returns up to 1994. From then on, though, immigration of skilled and experienced workers – particularly returning migrants – became substantial and this may explain the stability or even decline in the return to university education for this group over that period. Such an immigration effect on the differential between skilled and unskilled wages was seen to be consistent with the results from a simple model of the Irish labour market, with parameters estimated using data from 1971 to 1996, that allowed outcomes with and without an inflow of skilled immigrants to be compared.

Turning to low pay, we saw that about 11 per cent of employees were on hourly gross pay below half the median in 1987, 1994 and 1997. While 20 per cent of employees were below two-thirds of the median in 1987, this had risen to 23 per cent by 1994 and was 22 per cent in 1997. On this basis Ireland in the mid-1990s had one of the highest levels of low pay of the countries covered by OECD comparative figures, similar to the UK though lower than the USA and Canada. Part-time employees – many of them married women – employees aged under 25, and those in certain sectors such as retailing and personal services were at high risk of being low paid. Most low paid employees are not in poor households, though employees in poor households are often low paid. The introduction of a national hourly minimum wage in Ireland in 2000, following on the UK, is a major policy innovation. It is unlikely to have had a significant negative impact on employment so far, given the strength of the economy and the tightness of the market for unskilled labour. The key issue for the future is how the minimum wage changes over time: while increases over the life of the current social partnership agreement have been flagged, at this stage a formal indexation procedure or revision process has not been adopted.

NOTES

1 See for example Gosling, Machin and Meghir (1994) and Schmitt (1995) for the UK, Levy and Murnane (1992) and Juhn, Murphy and Pierce (1993) for the USA.

2 US studies assessing such explanations include Bound and Johnson (1992), Borjas and Ramey (1994), and Burtless (1995).

3 The role of institutional versus other factors in producing cross-country variation in the level and trends in earnings dispersion is discussed in for example Freeman and Katz (1995), Blau and Kahn (1996), and Gottschalk and Joyce (1997).

4 The recent study for the OECD by Baslelaer, Lemaitre and Marianna (1997) on how best to distinguish part-time from full-time employees for comparative purposes recommended that this 30 hours usual work per week be used.

5 Here total labour supply is defined as the labour force, as estimated by the CSO, for each year. The data used in the graph up to 1987 are obtained from successive censuses by interpolation. From 1988 onwards the numbers are taken from an analysis of the Labour Force Survey micro data.

6 The logarithm of hourly earnings is used so that the coefficients on the dependent variables can be interpreted as percentage effects.

7 All figures are derived from a CSO (1999) release on migration statistics.

8 The wages of the unskilled are assumed to be a fixed mark-up on social welfare payments.

9 However, recent evidence suggests that this may no longer be the case and that the tightening of the unskilled labour market is exerting upward pressure on wage rates.

8

Income Inequality

BRIAN NOLAN AND BERTRAND MAÎTRE

8.1 Introduction

As earlier chapters have described, the 1980s and 1990s saw Ireland on a macroeconomic roller-coaster ride, with stagnation through much of the 1980s, economic growth accelerating from 1987, stop-starting in the early 1990s, and then reaching and sustaining exceptionally high levels from 1994. Household income inequality increased very sharply during that time in a number of industrialised countries, notably the UK and the USA. One of the main factors underlying the increase in household income inequality in those countries has been increasing inequality in the distribution of earnings, with a widening gap between the more and less skilled and educated. We have seen in Chapter 7 that earnings dispersion also increased markedly in Ireland from the mid-1980s to the mid-1990s. Against the background of dramatic changes in the macroeconomy and with earnings inequality rising, has Ireland also seen such an increase in household income inequality?

We begin this chapter by discussing how the income distribution is conventionally measured and inequality assessed. We then examine how the distribution evolved in Ireland during the 1980s and 1990s, using household survey data up to 1997. As well as seeking to understand the factors underlying this evolution, we then place Ireland in comparative perspective both in terms of level and trends in inequality, drawing on recently-available comparative data from Eurostat and the OECD. Against this background some intriguing aspects of Ireland's recent experience are brought out. For example, this experience serves to demonstrate that the links between trends in the distribution of earnings and the overall household income distribution are more complex than is often casually assumed, and that – as developed in depth in Chapter 10 – the tax and welfare systems have an important role to play in influencing the shape of the income distribution and how it evolves.

147

8.2 Measuring income inequality

Since the previous chapter was concerned with the distribution of earnings, it is worth noting at the outset the differences between that and the distribution of overall household income. The earnings distribution relates only to one income source – albeit the most important one in industrialised economies – and to the way income from that source is spread across individual employees. Households on the other hand may receive market income from a variety of sources – earnings, self-employment income, pensions, rent, interest and dividends – and often contain more than one income recipient. This means that both the distribution of each of these income sources and the way their individual recipients are clustered together in households – including perhaps two or more employees – are key influences on the household income distribution. Further, in studying the distribution of earnings the focus is generally on the employee's gross wage, whereas from a welfare perspective it is the distribution of household income after state cash transfers are added and direct taxes (including social insurance contributions) are deducted that is of most interest. Finally, again from a welfare perspective one has to take into account the fact that a given household income may be supporting households of varying size and composition, an issue that does not arise when the focus is simply on the employee and his or her earnings.

Studies of the distribution of income in Ireland, like many other countries, rely on household surveys rather than administrative tax or social security records.[1] The Household Budget Survey (HBS) carried out by the Central Statistics Office is primarily an expenditure survey but also contains detailed income data, and has been carried out nationally in 1973, 1980, 1987 and 1994/95 (see Murphy, 1984).[2] Surveys carried out by the Economic and Social Research Institute represent the other main source of data, and these have already been employed in earlier chapters. Briefly, the Survey of Income Distribution, Poverty and Use of State Services was carried out in 1987 (and described in Callan, Nolan et al, 1989), while the Living in Ireland Survey (LII) is the Irish element of the European Community Household Panel (ECHP), an annual longitudinal survey that commenced in 1994 (see Callan et al, 1996). Here we will be using data from the LII from 1994 and 1997. The latter has been weighted along a number of dimensions to account for attrition among the original sample and the addition of new individuals and households (where households in the original sample split or join new households). Detailed validation suggested that attrition up to 1997, while substantial, was not associated with characteristics such as income or deprivation levels or social welfare recipiency, and appears not to have a significant impact on the structure of the sample. In particular, the pattern of attrition does not appear likely to have biased the picture provided by the surveys of the distribution of income or the extent of income poverty in 1997 versus 1994.

Disposable income is the core measure employed here, that is income from the market plus social welfare payments less income tax and employees' social security contributions; we also use gross income, before deduction of tax and contributions, and direct income, which is gross income less cash transfers. The time-period these cover is important. Both the ESRI surveys and the HBS obtained information for most sources of income (earnings, social security transfers, pensions) in respect of the amount received in the current pay period (usually previous week, fortnight or month). For income from self-employment, farming, rent and investment income, on the other hand, details were recorded on the basis of the most recently available annual figures. In constructing household income all these are converted to a weekly average, which we will call current income. In some other countries and some of the main sources of international comparisons on income inequality, however, an annual accounting period for income from all sources is adopted. Data on that basis were also obtained in the LII surveys, since an annual accounting period is the one Eurostat wished to focus on in the ECHP. Estimates of annual income were also constructed from the 1987 ESRI survey in order to provide data for Ireland for that year to the Luxembourg Income Study database, now widely employed in cross-country studies of income distribution.

A range of methodological issues arises in describing the shape of the income distribution and measuring income inequality (see for example Jenkins, 1991; Cowell, 1995; Atkinson, Rainwater and Smeeding, 1995). We cannot discuss these in any depth, but simply note the key ones and set out the approaches followed. While the ultimate source of concern is the welfare of the individual, income is generally shared among members of a given family or broader household, and we follow common practice and use the household as income recipient unit.[3] The extent to which income is actually shared within the household so as to equalise living standards is an empirical question which has recently been receiving some attention (see for example Lundberg, Pollak and Wales, 1997; Cantillon and Nolan, 1998) but is particularly difficult to address.

Since a given income will provide a different living standard to the individuals in a large versus a small household, equivalence scales are used to adjust income for differences in household size and composition. Actual household income is then divided by the number of equivalent adults in the household (rather than simply the number of persons) to produce equivalised income. There is no consensus as to which method for estimating these scales is most satisfactory, and studies such as Buhman et al (1988) and Coulter, Cowell and Jenkins (1992) have shown the extent to which the scale used can affect the measured income distribution. A variety of equivalence scales has been used in research on the Irish income distribution and in cross-country studies, and here we make reference to four. One is the square root of household size, without distinguishing between adults and children. The second is widely known as the OECD scale: where the first adult in the household is given a value of 1, each other adult is attributed a value of 0.7 and each child is attributed a value of 0.5. The third is the 'modified OECD' scale, where each additional adult is attributed a value of 0.5 and each child 0.3.[4] The final one was derived from the scales implicit in Irish social security rates some time ago, and has been one of those employed in research on poverty here: it gives each additional adult a value of 0.66 and each child 0.33.

The distribution of income among households and/or persons may then be portrayed and summarised in a number of different ways. Following conventional practice we present decile shares – the share of total income going to the bottom 10 per cent, the next 10 per cent, …. top 10 per cent. As summary measures of inequality we employ the Gini coefficient and Theil's entropy measure.[5] Comparison of Lorenz curves, showing the cumulative proportion of total income received by the bottom x per cent of persons, provides a way of ranking distributions in terms of the economist's concept of social welfare. A distribution with a higher proportion of total income going to the bottom x per cent than another for all x 'Lorenz-dominates' it, and is associated with a higher level of social welfare (where the ranking is being made independently of the levels of mean income, and given certain assumptions about the social welfare function). Where Lorenz curves cross, no such unambiguous welfare ranking is possible (Atkinson, 1971).

The final issue worth dealing with before turning to our empirical results is not so much about how inequality is measured but what it means and why we might want to know about it. The term inequality is used in two quite different ways in talking about the distribution of income (or wealth). It can be used in a purely descriptive and neutral fashion, to refer simply to the fact that income is distributed unevenly across the population – everyone does not have the same. It can however also be used to express a normative judgement about those distributions, that they are more or less inequitable or unfair. Merely finding an uneven distribution does not of course in itself provide a basis for such a judgement; one needs to bring additional information and values to bear. At that point there are many competing views, and debating these has long absorbed not only economists but also (and perhaps more importantly) philosophers, social scientists and those directly engaged with the political process. Some would argue that poverty rather than inequality should be of concern, and that ensuring that everyone meets a minimum standard would meet society's distributional objectives. Poverty is the focus of the next chapter, but such a position ignores the fact that the notion of equity or fairness – over and above the desirability of alleviating poverty – seems to be deep-rooted in human societies of very different types. While fairness may not be interpreted in the same way across societies, its applicability would not in general be restricted to the treatment of those at the bottom, applying instead to the overall distribution of society's rewards. That is fundamentally why the distribution of income is of concern, and capturing how it is changing over time is so important.

8.3 Trends in income inequality in Ireland

We begin by looking at the shape of the income distribution going back to 1973, in the years the Household Budget Survey was carried out. Table 8.1 shows the decile shares in disposable income among households, without adjustment for size or composition, from the 1973, 1980, 1987 and 1994/95 Household Budget Surveys, together with Gini and Theil summary measures.[6]

Table 8.1: Decile shares in disposable income among households, 1973-1994/95 Household Budget Surveys

	Share in total disposable income (%)			
Decile	1973	1980	1987	1994-95
Bottom	1.7	1.7	2.2	2.1
2	3.3	3.5	3.7	3.5
3	5.0	5.1	5.0	4.8
4	6.5	6.6	6.3	6.0
5	7.8	7.9	7.6	7.6
6	9.2	9.3	9.2	9.2
7	10.9	11.0	11.0	11.3
8	13.0	13.0	13.4	13.6
9	16.2	16.2	16.6	16.7
Top	26.4	25.7	25.0	25.1
All	100.0	100.0	100.0	100.0
Gini	0.367	0.360	0.352	0.362
Theil	0.221	0.211	0.200	0.210

Source: Decile shares for 1973 and 1980 from Rottman and Reidy (1988) Table 7.4, for 1987 and 1994/95 from microdata tapes (with correction for top-coding).

We see that from 1973 to 1980 the shares of deciles 2-7 all rose slightly, at the expense of the top decile. This is reflected in falling Gini and Theil inequality measures, and 1980 Lorenz-dominates 1973. Between 1980 and 1987 the share of the bottom two deciles rose substantially and that of the top decile again fell, but the Lorenz curves cross and there is no unambiguous dominance. From

1987 and 1994, there was now a shift away from the bottom 40 per cent and the summary measures rose, but the Lorenz curves again cross. Over the whole period 1973-1994/95 the shares at the bottom rose and at the top fell, and the inequality measures are lower at the end of the period, but the Lorenz curves actually cross in the middle.

It is important to place these trends in inequality in the context of the evolution of average real incomes, because the pattern of real income growth was very different in the sub-periods covered by these figures. Between 1980 and 1987, for example, average disposable household incomes actually fell in real terms. With the income share of the bottom deciles slightly higher, Generalised Lorenz curves for the distribution of disposable income in the 1980 and 1987 HBS cross: no unambiguous ranking is possible on this basis. Between 1987 and 1994, on the other hand, average household income rose substantially in real terms and Generalised Lorenz curves show an increase in social welfare.

Table 8.2: Decile shares in disposable income among households, 1987 and 1994 ESRI and HBS Surveys

| | Share in total disposable income (%) | | | |
| | 1987 | | 1994 | |
Decile	ESRI	HBS	ESRI	HBS
Bottom	2.0	2.2	2.3	2.1
2	3.4	3.7	3.3	3.5
3	4.8	5.0	4.6	4.8
4	5.9	6.3	6.0	6.0
5	7.3	7.6	7.5	7.6
6	8.8	9.2	9.1	9.2
7	10.7	11.0	11.1	11.3
8	13.2	13.4	13.5	13.6
9	16.5	16.5	16.5	16.7
Top	27.4	25.1	26.4	25.1
All	100.0	100.0	100.0	100.0

Since ESRI surveys are also available for 1987 and 1994, the next step is to compare the distribution in these surveys with the Household Budget Survey, and that is done in Table 8.2. We see that in each year the share going to the top decile is rather higher in the ESRI surveys, particularly in 1987. One important difference is in the timing of the fieldwork, and this may have had an impact on farm incomes in particular, but the reasons for this divergence merit further investigation.[7] As far as trends over the 1987-94 period are concerned, the HBS show a shift away from the bottom half of the distribution towards the top, though not the very top. The ESRI surveys also suggest some increase in the shares of deciles 7 and 8, but now at the expense of deciles 2 and 3 with the very bottom gaining. It would be unwise to read much in welfare terms into these distributional changes, because up to this point incomes have not been adjusted for differences in household size and composition.

Unfortunately, only limited results on an equivalised basis are available from the HBS,[8] and we concentrate from here on the ESRI surveys. We have derived the distribution of equivalised disposable income among households in the 1987 and 1994 ESRI surveys using the four sets of scales described earlier. In all cases the share of the bottom decile increases and the top falls over this period, but otherwise there is something of a shift from the rest of the bottom half to the rest of the top half. Both the Gini and Theil measures show a slight decline in overall inequality, which is greatest with the square root scale, but the Lorenz curves intersect for all the scales.

We now move on to the 1994-97 period, comparing the distributions shown by the Living in Ireland Surveys for these years. Table 8.3 gives the decile shares in disposable income among households, and we see that the distribution was generally rather stable over the period, though the middle did gain at the expense of the top. The two summary inequality measures both show about the same level of inequality in the 1997 survey as in 1994. When we turn to the distribution of equivalised income among households, the share of total equivalised income going to the bottom two deciles now falls between 1994 and 1997, with the top half of the distribution but not the top decile gaining.

While there are some differences across the scales in the exact pattern of change, all show a marginal increase in inequality as measured by the Gini and Theil summary indices. When equivalent income is used, focusing on persons may be more appropriate since we are primarily concerned with the distribution of welfare or living standards among persons rather than households. Counting persons rather than households and attributing the equivalised income of the household to each individual does not substantially alter the shape of the distribution in either year, though it does reduce the share of the top 30 per cent and increase the share of middle income groups. Comparing the distribution among persons in 1994 with 1997, there is now even less change with the bottom decile losing slightly but the share of the top decile unchanged.

Table 8.3: Decile shares in disposable income among households, 1994 and 1997 Living in Ireland Surveys

	Share in total disposable income (%)	
Decile	1994 LII	1997 LII
Bottom	2.3	2.1
2	3.3	3.3
3	4.6	4.5
4	6.0	6.0
5	7.4	7.7
6	9.1	9.5
7	11.1	11.2
8	13.5	13.4
9	16.5	16.5
Top	26.4	25.8
All	100.0	100.0
	Inequality measures	
Gini	0.377	0.374
Theil	0.238	0.237

8.4 Explaining the trends

A wide range of different factors affect how the income distribution evolves over time, and these operate through a variety of channels of influence. We now point towards some important factors and suggest how they may have been operating in the Irish case over the 1980s and 1990s.[9]

The single most dramatic element in the macroeconomic background over the two decades was the extent to which the level of unemployment fluctuated in Ireland. As we have seen in detail in Chapter 4, unemployment rose from about 8 per cent of the labour force in 1980 to 17 per cent in 1987, before falling back to 15 per cent in 1994 and declining much more sharply to about 10 per cent in 1997. While the level of unemployment compensation as a proportion of average earnings or take-home pay fluctuated a good deal over the period, unemployment would have entailed a significant loss of income for most of those affected. (The evolution of conventional measures of this income effect – a policy concern as often from the perspective of work incentives as income adequacy – are discussed in Chapter 10.) None the less, the impact of unemployment on the overall shape of the income distribution may be more muted than is often assumed, as studies of for example the UK (Nolan, 1987) and the Scandinavian countries (Aberge et al, 2000) have suggested. Finland and Sweden saw sharp increases in unemployment in the early 1990s but their income distributions remained quite equal. The Irish experience is consistent with that pattern, and reinforces Aberge et al's suggestion that the effect of unemployment compensation is only part of the story, with a complex set of interactions between different components of household income needing to be understood.

Up to this point we have been focusing on disposable income, that is after cash transfers have been received by households and income tax and PRSI contributions deducted. To understand what lies behind it, the obvious place to start is with the distribution of income from the market, and market income plus cash transfers, to see how these have been evolving. As is commonly the case in industrialised countries, both cash transfers and direct tax have an equalising impact on the shape of the income distribution, with the effect of transfers being substantially more pronounced. The bottom 30 per cent of the distribution has virtually no income from the market, while the top 10 per cent has about 35 per cent of the total. State cash transfers bring the share of the bottom 30 per cent of households up to about 10 per cent of total income. Income tax and employee's social insurance contributions move the distribution further in the direction of greater equality, but have a less pronounced impact than transfers.

Comparing 1994 and 1997, we find that the distribution of direct (market) income looks rather similar in the two years, but both the Gini and Theil coefficients suggest that inequality fell. Turning to gross income, the summary inequality measures suggest little change in inequality. This reflects the fact that the redistributive impact of social welfare transfers, as measured simply by the fall in the Gini coefficient they produce, declined marginally over the period (from a reduction of 25 per cent in the Gini in 1994 to one of 22 per cent in 1997). As far as income tax and employee PRSI contributions are concerned, they produce about the same further reduction in the Gini coefficient in each of the two years (i.e. 10 per cent), so the overall relationship between gross and disposable income distributions was broadly unchanged. Over the longer span of years from 1980, however, the redistributive impact of income tax and social insurance contributions had risen significantly, reflecting an increase in the proportion of household income going in tax and increasing progressivity in its structure during the 1980s. As discussed in detail in Chapter 10, while we cannot yet measure changes in the distribution of income after 1997 we can see that the distributional effects of tax and welfare changes since then have favoured higher income groups.

It is also illuminating to look at the distribution of the different types of income coming from the market. Income from earnings represents by far the most important source of income for households in Ireland, as in other industrialised countries, and marked changes in the distribution of earnings have been shown to be a major contributor to the increase in household income inequality in the United States and the UK. Chapter 6 has shown that there was a substantial widening in earnings dispersion in Ireland over the period from 1987 to 1997, with this trend being pronounced between 1987-94 but continuing at a slower pace from 1994 to 1997. Why then did increasing earnings dispersion among employees not feed through to greater inequality in the distribution of market income among households between 1994 and 1997? In contrast to the UK and the USA, between 1987 and 1994 the substantial increase in labour force participation by married women has been shown to have had if anything an equalising effect on the household income distribution (Callan et al, 1998). This was because the married women most likely to have entered the labour force during that period had spouses in the lower rather than upper half of the male earnings distribution.

Some further insights into the factors affecting the income distribution can be obtained by decomposition of inequality between and within particular population sub-groups, and by income source.[10] In decomposing by sub-group we have used the mean logarithmic deviation to look at a range of household characteristics for 1994 and 1997, categorising households by the age, sex, and labour force status of head, and by composition type. Distinguishing three age groups, for example, we find that with this measure inequality within each of the age groups and between them all rose slightly between 1994 and 1997, with the most pronounced change being increased inequality among the elderly. Perhaps the most interesting results are when households are categorised by the labour force status of the head. In each year, there is more inequality among households headed by a self-employed person (including farmers) than among those headed by an employee, and relatively little inequality among households headed by someone who is unemployed or ill, or engaged full-time in working in the home. There are also major differences across the groups in mean equivalised income: households headed by an employee or a self-employed person have much higher mean incomes than those with an unemployed or ill head or one working full-time in the home. In 1994, these differences in mean income across the groups accounted for about 27 per cent of the inequality in the overall sample. By 1997, the inequality produced by these differences in mean income had fallen slightly, so they accounted for 23 per cent of overall inequality. This was offset by increases in within-group inequality, which rose for the self-employed and unemployed. The size of some of the groups had also changed substantially, with the proportion of household heads in employment increasing and unemployed falling.

Decomposition by income source provides an alternative perspective, and here the summary measure commonly employed is the squared coefficient of variation. The share of income from employment in total disposable income rose by almost 3 percentage points from 1994 to 1997, with the share of social welfare transfers declining. This reflects both rising employment and declining unemployment, and the fact that, as we have seen, social welfare support rates lagged behind the very rapid pace of growth in earnings. When one looks at the distribution of each income type across all households (rather than just recipients), earnings, social welfare transfers and Child Benefit are the most equally distributed income types, with income from self-employment and property (interest, dividends and rent) very much more unevenly spread across households. Between 1994 and 1997, this inequality measure rose quite sharply for income from self-employment and property, though it declined for earnings. The other key element from this perspective is the correlation between income from each source and total household income. Social welfare transfers is the only type to be negatively correlated with total income, and this correlation was fairly stable between 1994 and 1997. Earnings, on the other hand, became less highly correlated with total income while income from self-employment and property became more highly correlated.

8.5 A comparative perspective on income inequality in Ireland

In order to be able to assess the implications of both the level of inequality in the distribution of income in Ireland and how it has been changing over time, one needs to employ a comparative perspective. How does the distribution of income in Ireland compare with other industrialised countries, and are trends in the Irish distribution merely a reflection of what has been happening elsewhere? In this section we address these issues, drawing on some recent data sources and studies.

It has become clear in recent years that great care is needed in making cross-country comparisons of income inequality levels and trends. Without careful attention to maximising the degree of comparability of the estimates in terms of income concept, income unit, time period, nature and coverage of data source, equivalence scale (where relevant) and so on, misleading conclusions can be reached. The income distribution database assembled by the Luxembourg Income Study (LIS) is designed to overcome these obstacles to the greatest extent possible. The preferred income concept in the LIS is annual rather than weekly, but the 1987 ESRI survey has been used to estimate the distribution of annual income in Ireland, and that data is included in the LIS database. The comprehensive comparative study of income inequality based (mostly) on LIS data by Atkinson, Rainwater and Smeeding (1995) for the OECD thus provides a reference point for the mid- to late-1980s.

Their results on inequality in the distribution of equivalised disposable income (using the square root equivalence scale and with person weighting), as summarised in the Gini coefficient, are shown in Table 8.4. Ireland is seen to have an exceptionally high level of inequality compared with the other OECD countries covered, with only the USA having a higher Gini coefficient.

Table 8.4: Gini coefficient for distribution of equivalised disposable income among persons, various countries, mid/late 1980s

Country	Year	Gini
Australia	1985	0.295
Belgium	1988	0.235
Canada	1987	0.289
Finland	1987	0.207
France	1984	0.296
Germany	1984	0.250
Ireland	1987	0.330
Italy	1986	0.310
Luxembourg	1985	0.238
Netherlands	1987	0.268
Norway	1986	0.234
Portugal	1989/90	0.310
Spain	1990/91	0.310
Sweden	1987	0.220
UK	1986	0.304
USA	1986	0.341

Source: Atkinson, Rainwater and Smeeding (1995) Table 4.4, except Spain from Table 5.21 and Portugal from Table 5.20.

This reflects the fact that the lower parts of the Irish income distribution have a relatively low share of total income, but even more important is the fact that the top decile has a larger share in Ireland than in any of the other countries covered. This is subject to the caveat that, as noted earlier, the top decile has a smaller share in the 1987 Household Budget Survey than in the ESRI survey, but even so the Irish distribution was clearly among the more unequal in the LIS dataset in the mid- to late-1980s.

A more up-to-date comparative picture can be obtained from data from the European Community Household Panel survey, which got under way in 1994. In the ECHP survey, like the LIS, the reference period is annual for all income sources, in the case of Wave 1 relating to the calendar year 1993 and Wave 2 1994. The ESRI Living in Ireland Survey constitutes the Irish element of the ECHP, and collected income information on both a (largely) current and an annual basis: the former was used earlier (consistent with the HBS), but the latter will be used here for comparability with other countries in the ECHP. Table 8.5 shows the Gini coefficient and the share of the bottom and top decile for the distribution of equivalised disposable income, now using the modified OECD scale, in Wave 1 of the ECHP.

Table 8.5: Distribution of equivalised disposable income among persons, 1993 from ECHP

Country	Gini	Share of bottom decile	Share of top decile
Belgium	0.28	3.0	21.9
Denmark	0.22	4.4	19.8
France	0.31	3.1	24.3
Germany	0.29	2.6	22.4
Greece	0.35	2.1	26.1
Ireland	0.34	3.3	26.4
Italy	0.32	2.3	23.5
Luxembourg	0.31	3.3	24.4
Netherlands	0.27	3.7	21.7
Portugal	0.39	1.9	29.3
Spain	0.34	2.6	25.5
UK	0.35	2.7	26.3
Average	0.31	2.9	23.5

Ireland is still shown as having a relatively high Gini coefficient, but it is now rather lower than Portugal, and similar to a group that includes the UK, Spain and Greece. The level of inequality rose quite sharply in the UK between the mid/late 1980s and the mid-1990s,[11] but it would be surprising if it had increased in for example Luxembourg and Portugal by as much as the comparison of the ECHP and Atkinson et al's results suggest. A good deal of work on reconciling data from different sources remains to be done, but the picture of Ireland's relative position in terms of inequality is consistent in the first two waves of the ECHP. It is worth noting that the share going to the bottom decile is in fact relatively high in Ireland: the share going to the top decile, though no longer the outlier portrayed in Atkinson et al, is still among the next-highest to Portugal.

A recent study on trends in income distribution and poverty by the OECD (Forster, 2000) provides another basis of comparison for the level of inequality in Ireland versus other countries, and is also particularly valuable in terms of a comparative picture on recent trends. It does not include some of the EU countries with relatively high levels of inequality – notably Spain and Portugal – but it does include Greece, Italy and the UK. It relies on figures supplied to the OECD by national experts, including for Ireland results from the 1994 Living in Ireland survey. On this basis Ireland is shown as having the same level of inequality as the UK in the mid-1990s, lower than Greece and Italy. However, the OECD study also shows that Ireland has a higher level of inequality than non-EU countries such as Australia and Canada, though lower than the USA.

While the OECD study tried to harmonise the measurement procedures adopted across countries, differences inevitably remain; one is that while annual disposable income was the main focus, for a number of countries – including Ireland – current income had to be used.

As far as trends in income inequality are concerned, for the ten countries for which data were available from the mid-1970s to the mid-1990s no general trends emerged, with inequality falling or stable for more countries than it was increasing. In the period from the mid-1980s to the mid-1990s, though, for which data on 20 countries were available, more of a common trend is apparent. Inequality increased in twelve countries – in half of these by considerable amounts – while it remained stable in 4 and decreased only slightly in another 4. Ireland is shown in the study as belonging to this last group, registering a slight decrease in inequality. Several other aspects of the trends shown are worth highlighting. The UK was the only country displaying marked increases in inequality both from the mid-1970s to the mid-1980s and from the mid-1980s to the mid-1990s. The USA saw a substantial increase in inequality during the earlier period, but the OECD's figures suggest only a marginal further increase there by the mid-1990s. The notion that the UK's experience in particular represents a pattern which other countries will necessarily experience in time seems a highly partial reading of the evidence. However, the fact that the majority of countries experienced increases in inequality in the later period does clearly suggest an underlying dynamic in terms of economic forces, policy or both.

The OECD study also explores the extent to which common factors were at work in influencing the income distribution across countries. It finds some very important common features, but also many intriguing differences over the mid-1980s to mid-1990s period. Perhaps the most notable common feature is that the share of earnings going to the lower income groups among the working population decreased in all the countries covered in the study, and the share going to middle income groups generally declined as well. The same was true of market incomes generally, including income from self-employment and capital, but earnings dominate that total. This was not, or not entirely, translated into higher inequality of disposable incomes because both transfers and taxes off-set its effects, and indeed in many countries the redistributive effects of taxes and transfers increased over the period. Ireland's experience during the 1980s and into the 1990s would be broadly consistent with that pattern, although from 1994 to 1997 we have seen that market incomes did not become less equally distributed whereas the redistributive effects of taxes and transfers declined – the scale of the decline in unemployment in particular being quite exceptional in comparative perspective.

The OECD study shows that there was a quite widespread tendency towards polarisation into work-rich and work-poor households. Among households with children, in the mid-1990s the proportion with no-one in paid work in Ireland was among the highest in the OECD, and even with substantial declines in unemployment this remains an important issue for further study. However, the OECD income distribution study showed that the more important contributor to increasing inequality in household incomes among the countries examined was increasing inequality within fully-employed versus workless versus 'mixed' households.

Another important pattern common to many of the countries covered in the study was an increase in the average incomes of the elderly towards the overall average. (The main gains here were for those aged between 66 and 74 rather than those aged 75 and over, so it was recent retirees who were doing better.) Once again, that would only be true of certain sub-periods during the 1980s and 1990s in the Irish case, and not the most recent one from 1994 to 1997 where the relative position of the elderly disimproved because earnings increased so rapidly that state pensions did not keep up. This was particularly important in the evolution of poverty assessed simply in terms of relative income position, as we shall see in the next chapter.

8.6 Conclusions

Increasing income inequality, driven by rising earnings inequality, has occurred in some major Western economies towards the end of the twentieth century. A fairly widespread though not universal trend towards increased inequality in the period from the mid-1980s to the mid-1990s is found in a forthcoming OECD study. Against this background, this chapter has used household survey data to provide a comparative picture of the distribution of household income in Ireland and how it evolved over the past two decades.

We have seen that Ireland's distribution is among the more unequal in the European Union, together with the UK, Greece and Spain, though less unequal than Portugal. As far as trends over time are concerned, we saw that the distribution of income among households was relatively stable during the 1980s and into the 1990s, certainly with no suggestion of the marked increase in inequality seen in the USA and the UK. From 1994 to 1997, as the pace of economic growth accelerated, the distribution once again was rather stable with little change in summary inequality measures such as the Gini. When income is adjusted to take the greater needs of larger households into account, there was some tendency for the share of the bottom one-fifth of the distribution to decline.

This broad stability in the overall shape of the distribution masks some significant fluctuation over time in the underlying distribution of income from different sources and among different groups in the population. Increasing dispersion of earnings among individual employees, although it occurred, has not been associated with increasing household income inequality in Ireland – at least so far – because of the particular manner in which labour force participation has risen. The redistributive impact of social security cash transfers may have fallen as support rates lagged behind rapidly-increasing incomes from the market, a point to which we return in the next chapter in focusing on poverty. The detailed discussion of tax and social welfare structures and policies presented in Chapter 10 will also throw further light on the trends discussed here.

NOTES

1 Nolan (1978) and Callan (1991) discuss the relationship between Irish data on incomes from household surveys and tax/social welfare records.

2 The frequency with which the HBS is carried out has been increased to every five rather than seven years, starting with 1999/2000.

3 Persons living at the same address with common housekeeping count as a household even if not related.

4 As in studies for Eurostat such as Hagenaars, de Vos and Zaidi (1994), we take adult here to be age 14 years or over.

5 These and other commonly-used summary inequality measures are fully described in e.g. Cowell (1995).

6 It was necessary to calculate these summary inequality measures from the decile shares rather than from microdata; while this will understate the extent of inequality at each point in time (because inequality within each decile is ignored) it should capture trends over time.

7 The 1987 ESRI survey measured farm income for 1986, a particularly bad year, whereas the HBS used accounts for 1987 when farm incomes were on average over 25 per cent higher. The 1994 ESRI survey was carried out in the second half of that year, whereas the HBS went from then well into 1995. A handful of households in each ESRI survey have very high incomes from self-employment, and estimates of the share of income going to the top are very sensitive to the sampling and subsequent treatment of such high-income 'outliers'. The very top of the HBS distribution is difficult to investigate because the microdata released to researchers has been top-coded.

8 The top-coding of the 1987 and 1994/95 HBS microdata released to researchers makes equivalisation problematic at the top. The only equivalised results available from 1980 were produced by the CSO for Roche (1984).

9 See Callan and Nolan (1997, 1999) for further discussion of the pattern up to 1994.

10 Decomposition of inequality by sub-groups is discussed in, for example, Shorrocks (1980), (1984) and Cowell (1995); decomposition by source is discussed in Shorrocks (1982).

11 See for example Goodman, Johnson and Webb (1997).

9

Trends in Poverty

RICHARD LAYTE, BRIAN NOLAN AND CHRISTOPHER T. WHELAN

9.1 Introduction

Earlier chapters have described how growth and unemployment rates have fluctuated dramatically in Ireland over the past quarter-century. While earnings dispersion increased markedly in Ireland from the mid-1980s, as in many other industrialised countries, the overall distribution of income among households has been rather more stable than in the UK or the USA, where income inequality also increased very sharply during that time. Against this background, a key concern is what has been happening to poverty. That is the question this chapter seeks to answer, and it is a particularly challenging one. While a broadly relative conception of poverty now appears to be widely accepted, seeking to apply that notion of poverty in a society moving from stagnation to very rapid growth highlights a variety of conceptual, methodological and data issues facing poverty research.

As we try to bring out in this chapter, the way these issues are treated is not simply of concern from an academic perspective; it can fundamentally affect how one interprets the experience of the past two decades and how anti-poverty policy is formulated. With the launch of its National Anti-Poverty Strategy Statement (NAPS) in 1997, Ireland became the first European Union member state to adopt a global poverty reduction target. This target is framed in terms of a poverty measure incorporating both relative income and direct measures of deprivation, which we will be describing in detail. As we will also see, this measure shows a very different pattern over the period to conventional poverty measures based on income alone, and teasing out the implications is a central theme of this chapter.

We begin by focusing on poverty measures based on income alone, and examine how income poverty evolved in Ireland during the 1980s and 1990s, using household survey data up to 1997. As well as seeking to understand the factors underlying these trends, we place Ireland in comparative perspective drawing on recently-available comparative data from the European Community household panel survey. We then broaden the focus by incorporating non-monetary indicators of deprivation and incorporating them into the measurement of poverty. Having examined the evolution of these measures in recent years, we conclude by focusing on the implications for understanding the underlying causal processes and for poverty targeting in the anti-poverty strategy.

9.2 Income poverty

Measuring income poverty

Various approaches to the measurement of poverty in developed countries have been proposed and applied in empirical research, most relying on income to capture a household's command over resources or living standards. These involve for example income poverty lines based on subjective views about adequacy, on social security rates, on budget standards, or on proportions of average or median income or expenditure (see Callan and Nolan, 1991, for a review). While the advantages of going beyond income in measuring poverty and exclusion are discussed in some detail later in this chapter, at this point we concentrate on conventional income poverty lines, both because the patterns we observe can be linked back to our earlier discussion of income distribution, and because it allows Ireland's experience to be placed firmly in a comparative context.

We therefore look first at relative income poverty lines, constructed as a given percentage of average equivalent income. In making comparisons over time or across countries, this approach has the advantage that the identical procedure can be readily applied in each case, and the sensitivity of the results to the particular line or equivalence scale chosen can also be examined. Having presented results on this basis we then look at how real incomes, and therefore the absolute rather than relative position of those on low incomes, evolved over the period. As in the analysis of income inequality in the previous chapter, the household is taken as the income recipient unit – so all members of a particular household are assumed to share the same standard of living – and household income is equivalised using a variety of equivalence scales to test for the sensitivity of the results.

Trends in income poverty in Ireland

We now look at the numbers falling below relative income poverty lines constructed as 40 per cent, 50 per cent and 60 per cent of mean equivalent household income. The equivalence scale employed is the OECD one, and these lines were applied to the Household Budget Survey for 1973 and 1980, and the ESRI samples for 1987, 1994 and 1997. (Results from the 1987 and 1994/95

Household Budget Survey show a similar general pattern to the ESRI surveys for those years.) Table 9.1 presents the percentage of households falling below each line, and the percentage of persons in these households.

Table 9.1: Percentages below relative income poverty lines, Ireland, 1973-97

	1973 HBS	1980 HBS	1987 ESRI	1994 ESRI	1997 ESRI
	per cent	*per cent*	*per cent*	*per cent*	*per cent*
40 per cent line:					
per cent of households	8.5	8.5	8.9	7.1	9.1
per cent of persons	9.0	10.4	11.8	10.9	12.5
50 per cent line:					
per cent of households	18.9	17.2	17.6	18.4	20.4
per cent of persons	18.6	19.2	21.8	22.7	23.3
60 per cent line:					
per cent of households	28.8	27.9	27.7	33.4	36.0
per cent of persons	29.4	29.7	32.2	35.2	36.6

From 1973 to 1987, the Household Budget Survey shows a decline in the percentage of households falling below each of the three lines, but the average size of these households rose so that there was an increase in the percentage of persons they contain. Between 1987 and 1994 the poverty rate for households and persons fell with the 40 per cent line, was broadly stable with the 50 per cent line, and rose quite sharply with the highest, 60 per cent line. From 1994 to 1997, relative income poverty rates rose consistently for households and persons across the three lines.

Simply counting the number of persons below an income threshold takes no account of how far below it they fall, and as highlighted by Sen (1976) this can give a misleading picture. We therefore also use the summary poverty measures developed by Foster, Greer and Thorbecke (1984), which also reflect how far the poor are falling below the poverty line. These are the per capita income gap and a depth and distribution-sensitive measure of poverty which gives additional weight to those with the largest income gaps. Between 1973 and 1980 these summary measures both rose consistently across the poverty lines. Between 1980 and 1987 they both fell with the 40 per cent line, were little changed with the 50 per cent line, and rose with the 60 per cent line. From 1987 to 1994, both measures fell with all three relative income lines, at a time when the numbers below the 60 per cent line were rising quite sharply: households below that line were a good deal nearer it by 1994. Between 1994 and 1997, on the other hand, both the per capita income gap and the weighted gap rose quite sharply. By 1997, indeed, these measures were in some cases back above the levels found for 1973.

Relative income poverty lines are sometimes constructed as proportions of the median of the distribution (the income level above and below which half the sample fall) rather than the mean. This can have some advantages in statistical terms in tracking changes over time, since the median tends to be less volatile than the mean (not being affected by fluctuations at the top or bottom of the distribution in survey data which may be due to sampling variation rather than genuine movements in the population). When this is done with the Irish data, the percentage below 60 per cent of the median still increases from 1987 to 1997.

As emphasised in earlier chapters, growth in average incomes fluctuated a great deal in Ireland over the period we are analysing. In the surveys we have been using here, mean household income in real terms (deflated by the increase in consumer prices) rose a good deal between 1973 and 1980. It actually fell slightly between 1980 and 1987, followed by rapid growth between 1987 and 1994 and an even faster pace of increase from then to 1997. This means that relative income poverty lines benchmarked on mean income will have followed that pattern in real terms. Poverty lines held constant in real terms, rather than changing *pari passu* with average income, would then show a very different picture. In the 1980-87 period, the number below lines held constant in real terms increased slightly more than with relative lines. Between 1987 and 1994, and again from 1994 to 1997, a substantial fall in the numbers below such lines was seen. To illustrate the scale of this fall, suppose we take the half average income poverty line in 1987 as a point of departure. We have seen that about 20 per cent were below that line in 1987. If one indexes that poverty line to the increase with prices only, by 1997 only about 7 per cent were below this 'constant real income' standard.

While it makes sense to see poverty primarily in relative terms, concentrating entirely on relative income poverty lines will miss the serious implications of periods when real incomes for the poor actually fall – which can happen even in the rich countries of the world. It is also particularly problematic though when real incomes are rising rapidly throughout the distribution, as they did in Ireland between 1987 and 1997, so that growth in incomes may for a time run ahead of the rising expectations about what is 'adequate'. Going beyond income to focus also on non-monetary indicators of deprivation may then be particularly illuminating, both in terms of the identification of those in poverty and understanding the processes at work. Before turning to that, though, we want to get behind the overall trends in income poverty to see what has been driving them, and also see how Ireland looks in comparative perspective.

Explaining trends in income poverty

Trends in the extent and nature of poverty are influenced by a complex mix of macroeconomic, microeconomic and institutional factors. Two key factors have driven trends relative to income poverty in Ireland over the past two decades: unemployment and social welfare policy. This can be seen by looking at discrete sub-periods that displayed quite different features in terms of these two central influences. The period from 1980 to 1987 was dominated by the dramatic increase in unemployment described earlier in this volume. It saw a sharp rise in the proportion of all poor households (below relative income lines) that were headed by an unemployed person, and a fall in the proportion headed by the elderly. Thus in 1980 15 per cent of the households below half average income were headed by an unemployed person, but by 1987 this had risen to 37 per cent. This reflected simply the scale of the increase in unemployment, rather than a rise in the risk of poverty for those who are unemployed.

This shift in the composition of the poor population carried with it an increased risk of poverty for families with dependent children. By 1987, one-quarter of all children were in households below average income. The elderly, on the other hand, did relatively well in terms of levels of welfare support and became less important among the poverty population. About one in four households headed by an elderly person fell below half average income in 1980, but by 1987 this was down to only 7 per cent.

The period from 1987 to 1994 was different. Although the unemployment rate did fall, in 1994 unemployment remained the single most important cause of poverty. The risk of income poverty for the retired rose but was still well below average. The evolution of social welfare rates for different categories of recipient *vis-à-vis* mean income for all households played a crucial role. As discussed in more detail in Chapter 10, priority during this period was given to raising the lowest social welfare rates, for means-tested Unemployment Assistance. These actually increased a good deal more rapidly than mean incomes between 1987 and 1994. At the same time support rates for other groups, notably the elderly and widows, rose by a good deal less than mean incomes (though still ahead of inflation). By 1994 many of those relying on old age or widow's pensions were at or about the 50 per cent line and below the 60 per cent one. This helps to explain the fact that poverty measures taking the extent to which people fall below the relative income lines were stable or fell, while the headcount of numbers below those lines rose during this period.

From 1994 to 1997, the percentage of persons or households below relative income poverty lines generally rose but the poverty measures also taking into account how far incomes fall below the poverty line now rose more sharply. How can this have been happening at a time when unemployment was coming down rapidly and economic growth soared? It reflects the fact that incomes for those relying on social welfare lagged behind the exceptionally rapid growth in earnings over the period. While consumer prices rose by only about 6 per cent and social welfare rates rose by about twice that figure, average household income rose by over 20 per cent. The risk of relative income poverty remained very high for households headed by an unemployed person, but the numbers in that situation declined as the unemployment rate fell sharply. Whereas in 1994 about one-third of all households under half average income were headed by an unemployed person, by 1997 this was down to one in five. In terms of the overall poverty rate, though, the fall in unemployment was not enough to fully offset the increasing proportion of the other groups depending on social welfare who fell below the relative income lines. In addition, those on social welfare who were already below the lines in 1994 fell further below by 1997, contributing to the increase in poverty measures incorporating poverty gaps.

The risk of being below half average income thus rose rapidly for households where the head is aged 65 or over, and fell for households with children. By 1997 about 30 per cent of households headed by an elderly person were below half average income, even higher than back in 1980 before unemployment soared. The percentage of children in such households, on the other hand, fell back though it was still over 20 per cent.

A more detailed treatment of tax and social welfare policy over the period, providing the background to these trends, is given in Chapter 10. Since cross-country comparisons of the extent of poverty most often rely on the relative income poverty lines, we now turn to Ireland's situation in comparative perspective.

Income poverty in Ireland in international perspective

To see the extent of relative poverty in Ireland compared with other EC member states in the mid-late 1980s, one can draw on a number of cross-country studies carried out for the EC Commission or Eurostat, by O'Higgins and Jenkins (1990), ISSAS (1990), and Hagenaars, de Vos and Zaidi (1994). Key results from the comprehensive analysis presented in Hagenaars et al are summarised in Table 9.2. The relative position of the different countries varies somewhat with the line chosen. The European Commission tends to place most emphasis on the half average income standard, and on that basis Ireland is shown as having about the same percentage of households in poverty as Greece, Portugal and the UK, with Denmark, the Netherlands and Luxembourg having much lower rates. As far as non-EC countries are concerned, the study by Atkinson, Rainwater and Smeeding (1995) using the LIS data set also includes the percentage falling below various proportions of the median in the mid-late 1980s. Their results suggested that around 1987 the proportion of persons below half or 60 per cent of median income was higher in Ireland than most of the European countries covered, about the same as Australia and Canada, and lower than the USA.[1]

Table 9.2: Relative income poverty rates in the mid-late 1980s (modified OECD scale)

	per cent below relative line		
	40 per cent	50 per cent	60 per cent
Denmark (1987)	3.3	8.8	17.6
Netherlands (1988)	2.2	7.1	18.1
Luxembourg (1987)	1.9	5.7	14.9
France (1989)	7.1	14.4	23.4
United Kingdom (1988)	8.8	19.0	28.1
Ireland (1987)	6.7	16.9	27.6
Italy (1988)	5.6	13.0	23.7
Greece (1988)	10.2	17.3	26.7
Spain (1988)	7.0	13.7	22.3
Portugal (1989)	8.8	17.2	26.8

Source: Hagenaars, de Vos and Zaidi (1994)

More recent results are now available from the first wave of the ECHP, for income in calendar year 1993. Table 9.3 shows Ireland with a particularly low percentage, below 40 per cent of mean income. With half mean income as the standard, Ireland has a rate similar to the UK, Greece and Spain, lower than Portugal but higher than the other EU members covered. With 60 per cent of the mean, Ireland has the same poverty rate as Portugal, slightly higher than the UK, Greece and Spain.

Table 9.3: Relative income poverty rates in wave 1 ECHP, 1993 (modified OECD scale)

	per cent of persons below proportion of mean		
	40 per cent	50 per cent	60 per cent
Germany	9.9	15.2	21.4
Denmark	2.9	6.0	12.2
Netherlands	4.7	8.8	19.1
Belgium	7.3	13.3	21.5
Luxembourg	6.5	15.4	25.9
France	7.7	14.9	24.5
UK	12.3	21.3	30.8
Ireland	7.7	21.6	32.9
Italy	11.2	17.7	26.2
Greece	14.8	21.8	29.3
Spain	11.0	19.8	29.1
Portugal	17.1	25.2	32.9

An interesting perspective on the implications of taking differences in real incomes into account in such cross-country poverty comparisons is provided by results for the percentages in each member country below a poverty line set at a particular fraction of mean or median income across all the member states. The divergence in poverty rates across countries is then very much wider than with country-specific relative lines, since the countries with low poverty rates also tend to be those with relatively high income per capita (adjusted for purchasing power), and *vice versa*.

9.3 Measuring poverty using income and deprivation indicators

Low income on its own may not be an entirely satisfactory measure of exclusion arising from lack of resources. This is not primarily because of the (real) difficulties in measuring income accurately in household surveys, but also because a household's command over resources is affected by much more than its current income. Long-term factors, relating most importantly to the way resources have been accumulated or eroded over time, play a crucial role in influencing the likelihood of current deprivation and exclusion (Layte et al, 2000 and Whelan et al 2000).

This provides the rationale for making use of non-monetary indicators of deprivation, as well as income, in measuring poverty. Townsend (1979) and Mack and Lansley (1985) pioneered the use of non-monetary indicators of deprivation in this context, and other studies in that vein include Townsend and Gordon (1989), Frayman et al (1991) and Gordon et al (1995) with British data, Mayer and Jencks (1988) with US data, Muffels and Vrien (1991) using Dutch data, and Hallerod (1995) with data for Sweden. Since Irish data was first available from the 1987 survey, this has also been pursued in ESRI research. Callan, Nolan and Whelan (1993) used that data to implement Ringen's (1987) proposal that both income and deprivation criteria be used to identify households excluded from society due to lack of resources. Nolan and Whelan (1996) used the same data to provide an in-depth analysis of the relationship between deprivation indicators, household income, and wider resources. This research has sought to construct a more reliable measure of poverty by combining low income with suitable direct indicators of deprivation.

Factor analysis of data from the 1987 survey revealed three underlying dimensions of deprivation, to which the terms basic, secondary and housing dimensions were applied. The 'basic deprivation' cluster included not being able to afford heating, a substantial meal once a day, new rather than second-hand clothes, a meal with meat, chicken or fish every second day, a warm overcoat, two pairs of strong shoes, a 'roast' or equivalent once a week, and falling into arrears or debt paying everyday household expenses. These items were perceived to be social necessities by respondents in the sample – that is, 'things that every household should be able to have and that nobody should have to do without'. They were possessed by most people, reflected rather basic aspects of current material deprivation, and clustered together. On this basis they were taken to be most suitable as indicators of the underlying generalised deprivation one is trying to measure.[2]

Those both below relative income poverty lines and experiencing basic deprivation were then identified as experiencing generalised deprivation or exclusion due to lack of resources. Comparing the households who were counted as poor on this measure with the corresponding numbers at the bottom of the income distribution, the combined income and deprivation measure captured a higher proportion of the long-term unemployed and a lower proportion of the self-employed and farmers. When other features that one might expect to be associated with exclusion – such as low levels of savings and high levels of economic strain and psychological distress – were examined, this combined measure performed much better than income on its own in identifying high-risk groups.

So what happened to deprivation levels, and to numbers below this combined relative income and basic deprivation measure, between 1987 and 1997? (Few of these indicators were included in the Household Budget Survey, so it is not possible to look back before 1987.) Deprivation levels, as measured by the full range of non-monetary indicators available in our surveys, fell substantially between 1987 and 1994 and even more so between 1994 and 1997. The percentage reporting basic deprivation in particular fell from 33 per cent in 1987 to 25 per cent in 1994 and 15 per cent in 1997. Poverty as measured by the combined income and deprivation measure also depends on the numbers falling below the relative income lines, and thus does not show such a consistent fall. In 1987, about 16 per cent of households were below the 60 per cent relative income poverty line and experiencing basic deprivation, while 10 per cent were below half average income and experiencing such deprivation. By 1994, the corresponding figures were only slightly lower at 15 per cent and 9 per cent. By 1997, by contrast, they had fallen to 10 per cent and 7 per cent respectively. Over the decade as a whole, then, this measure suggests a substantial fall in poverty, concentrated mostly in the 1994-97 period when economic growth accelerated.

When deprivation is falling markedly in this way, many people may not regard rising numbers falling below a relative poverty line as an unambiguous increase in poverty. This may be true even if they accept that, over a lengthy period as new patterns of living standards emerge, societal expectations may indeed catch up and adjust fully to higher average incomes. In terms of the conceptual underpinnings of the measure – starting from a relative definition of poverty – it is clear that the non-monetary deprivation indicators used to capture generalised deprivation need to be adapted and augmented in the light of improved living standards, changing perceptions about what constitute necessities, and potential transformations of the underlying structure of deprivation. Significant change within one of these areas could lead to the need for a revision and adaptation of the deprivation component of the poverty measure. However, so far the set of indicators included in our basic deprivation measure has remained unchanged since 1987. One needs to be sure that this measure is not missing fundamental changes in living patterns and expectations captured by the relative income line approach.

We have explored this by looking over the whole period from 1987 to 1997, and found that expectations have indeed followed the general upward trend in the extent of possession of items. As a result, items such as central heating, a telephone, a car, a colour TV, and presents for friends and family at least once a year came to be perceived as necessities by a substantial majority of households. However, not all socially perceived necessities are suitable for incorporation into the combined income/deprivation measure, but only those tapping the underlying generalised deprivation one is attempting to capture. Factor analysis shows that these five items continue to load on what we have called the secondary deprivation dimension, rather than cluster with the basic items (Layte et al, 2000). This supports the argument that the basic deprivation index should not at this point be expanded to include these additional five items.

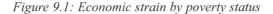

Figure 9.1: Economic strain by poverty status

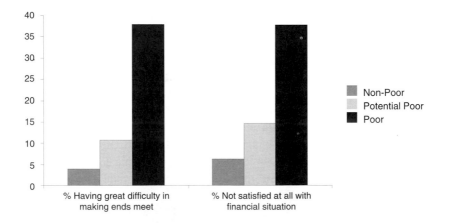

We have also examined the households who would be counted as poor if one did indeed broaden the deprivation element of the measure by incorporating these five additional items – the 'potentially poor'. In terms of self-assessed economic strain, psychological distress and fatalism the consistent picture was that the profile of these households was similar to that of the 'non-poor' and strikingly different from the 'poor' (see Layte et al, 2000). For example, Figure 9.1 shows that almost 40 per cent of those counted as poor with our current combined income and deprivation measure report 'extreme difficulty' making ends meet. This compares to only about 11 per cent of the additional group who would be counted as poor if the deprivation criteria were expanded and under 5 per cent of those who are non-poor even with the expanded criteria.

Figure 9.2 shows that very much the same pattern is found when we look at levels of psychological distress for these groups with information obtained in the ESRI surveys.[3] Using what is known as the General Health Questionnaire, there is a clear distinction between the poor and the potentially-poor in terms of numbers over the threshold value on this measure of distress. The combined income and deprivation measure as originally constituted thus continues to identify a set of households experiencing generalised deprivation resulting from a lack of resources, suffering a degree of economic strain and general psychological difficulties that mark them out from the rest of the population. The decline in numbers poor by this measure between 1987 and 1997 captures the effects of improvements in living standards that are not reflected in relative income poverty rates. This is particularly important because this measure has been adopted in the official National Anti-Poverty Strategy, to which we now turn.

Figure 9.2: Psychological distress and poverty status

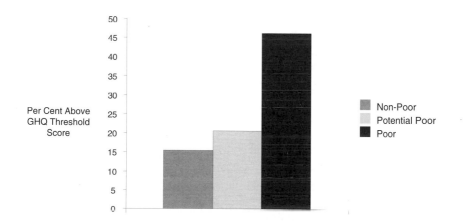

9.4 The National Anti-Poverty Strategy

Following the United Nations Social Summit in Copenhagen in 1995, the Irish government decided to drawn up a strategy to combat poverty in the medium to long term, which would provide a framework for the efforts of various government departments and agencies and non-governmental actors. The National Anti-Poverty Strategy was launched in 1997 following a process of widespread consultation including those affected by poverty. Presenting an overview of evidence on the extent, nature and causes of poverty and social exclusion in Ireland, the strategy sets out the definition of poverty on which it has agreed:

> People are living in poverty if their income and resources (material, cultural and social) are so inadequate as to preclude them from having a standard of living which is regarded as acceptable by Irish society generally. As a result of inadequate income and resources people may be excluded and marginalised from participating in activities which are considered the norm for other people in society.

The Strategy then set out its strategic aims and targets. The centrepiece was a global target for the reduction in poverty to be achieved over the period from 1997 to 2007. Ireland thus became the first European Union member state to adopt such a poverty reduction target. This overall or global target was:

> Over the period, 1997-2007, the National Anti-Poverty Strategy will aim at considerably reducing the numbers of those who are 'consistently poor' from 9 to 15 per cent to less than 5 to 10 per cent, as measured by the Economic and Social Research Institute.

This target related to the numbers both below relative income poverty lines and experiencing basic deprivation, as outlined above.

In addition to the global poverty reduction target, the strategy also contained a number of supplementary targets for what it identifies as key areas. These covered educational disadvantage, unemployment, income adequacy, disadvantaged urban areas and rural poverty. These specific targets were rather a mixed bag, with the crucial issue of what happens to social welfare support rates relative to average incomes left open and the urban and rural disadvantage targets being extremely vague.

When the strategy was initiated in 1997, the extent of poverty used as the baseline for the target was taken from the 1994 Living in Ireland Survey, the most recent then available. When the results from the 1997 round of that survey were published in 1999 (Callan et al, 1999), they showed as we have seen a significant reduction in the numbers 'consistently poor' – so that the target for 2007 had effectively been reached by 1997! In addition, unemployment was falling so rapidly that the unemployment target was also reached. Reflecting this progress the government decided to revise the global poverty and the unemployment targets. The current global poverty target is to reduce 'consistent poverty' to below 5 per cent by 2004. Unemployment is to be reduced to below 5 per cent by 2002, and long-term unemployment is to be reduced to below 2.5 per cent by the same date. Both the global target and the sub-targets are also to be re-examined in the context of the newly-agreed Programme for Prosperity and Fairness.

The fact that the government acknowledges its responsibility for reducing the overall extent of poverty is the single most important element of the anti-poverty strategy. It is by setting out explicitly an overall standard against which success or failure of the national effort to combat poverty can be assessed – both by those framing policy and the general public – that this is given content and meaning. The adoption of a national poverty target alters the nature of the national discourse on poverty and the way anti-poverty policies are assessed. The poverty definition and target become the touchstone for discussion – even for those who reject them, because they have to say why. Indeed, some suggest that official poverty targets are unworkable because it is impossible to obtain sufficient consensus about what poverty means and how it should be measured. In the Irish case, obtaining widespread agreement on the broad definition to be attributed to the term poverty did not prove to be the major obstacle one might have expected. There are certainly those who would quarrel with the resolutely relative conceptualisation spelt out in the definition quoted earlier. However, that definition emerged from a consultative process and was accepted with little apparent difficulty by the government of the day. Even more interestingly, the strategy – and by implication the definition – were endorsed by the new government which subsequently took office in 1997. Both the out-going and in-coming governments were coalitions, and between them included all the main political parties.

It remains to be seen how deep-rooted this acceptance proves to be under the pressure of events. This is where the formulation of targets and their interpretation are crucial. What is required is a set of poverty targets to which people can relate, but which still capture key elements of the complexity of the underlying reality. The rationale for adopting the combined low income plus deprivation measure is not set out in the Strategy, and a cynic might point to the scope for different interpretations and the fact that the poverty rates it produces are lower than the half average income standard. It does however have the great merit of focusing attention firmly on those most in need of sustained intervention.

The key difficulty with the combined income and deprivation measure as the sole poverty target – rather than as a poverty measure – is specific to Ireland's unusual situation. Average incomes are growing exceptionally rapidly; those on low incomes share in that growth and see their real living standards rise significantly, but are lagging somewhat behind the mean. As a result, deprivation levels are falling while relative income poverty is rising. Even augmenting the set of deprivation measures to take into account changing expectations may not then be enough to alter this picture, since expectations themselves probably lag behind such rapid income growth.

This could be seen as simply a problem with the measure, which using a purely relative income poverty standard such as half average income would avoid. However, if it is to achieve its core objective a national poverty target has to be seen as broadly acceptable by the general public. When deprivation is falling markedly, many people may simply not regard an increase in numbers falling below a relative income line as an unambiguous increase in poverty. Over a lengthy period when living standards stabilise, societal expectations may indeed catch up and adjust fully to higher average incomes. Higher real incomes and lower deprivation levels, however welcome, would not then mean that everyone was able to participate fully in society: they would not represent a sustained reduction in poverty. In the shorter term, however – over which a poverty target may be operating – the fact that real and relative income levels are diverging so markedly cannot be simply ignored. The key challenge in setting and monitoring poverty targets is to capture these realities, but also take into account the long-term consequences of lower incomes, and social security rates in particular, lagging behind the average.

Capturing this complexity may be too much to ask of any one measure, and an alternative is to broaden the scope of poverty targets to encompass distinct elements. One could have a set of tiered and inter-related poverty reduction targets ensuring first that those on low incomes see their real incomes rise and their deprivation levels fall, next that the combined income/deprivation measure declines, and finally that over the medium to long term the proportion of the population falling below relative income poverty lines should decline. The final element reflects the assumption that in the long term, people will not be able to participate in what comes to be regarded as ordinary living standards if their incomes fall too far below the average. Seeing this as a key medium- to long-term poverty target in no way contradicts the arguments we advanced earlier about the limitations of relative income poverty rates in capturing poverty trends from year to year, particularly in a rapidly-growing economy.

One important role a global poverty target can play is highlighting the limitations of specific policies which, however valuable in themselves, cannot realistically be expected to have a substantial impact on the overall numbers in poverty. It makes clear that policies targeting very specific groups or areas do not in themselves constitute a credible national anti-poverty strategy. The fact that most poor people do not in fact live in 'black spots' of concentrated poverty

– as discussed in detail in the following chapters – means that policies focusing on those areas, however valuable in themselves, will not on their own have a major impact on the global poverty target. It becomes impossible to ignore the big, expensive issues – most importantly, redistribution through the tax and welfare systems.

The poverty target, and the anti-poverty strategy more generally, should also act as a lever for institutional change. The Irish strategy gives a prominent place to the need for strong institutional structures to underpin its development and delivery. A cabinet sub-committee has been set up to deal with poverty and social exclusion, chaired by the Taoiseach. The day-to-day responsibility for oversight of the strategy has been allocated to the Department of Social, Community and Family Affairs, and the Minister has to report to a parliamentary committee on the development of the strategy. An inter-departmental committee of officials from the various government departments has been set up, in which the advisory Combat Poverty Agency is also involved. Each government department, state agency and local and regional authority is obliged to address the question of poverty in the overall strategy statements they are now required to produce, and departments will also have to produce annual statements to the inter-departmental committee setting out progress achieved over the previous year in relation to the strategy. Further mechanisms for 'poverty proofing' policy decisions, including in the annual Budget, are currently being developed.

It is too early to say how much impact the Irish anti-poverty strategy, and the adoption of a global poverty reduction target, will have on poverty (see Johnston and O'Brien (2000) for an initial assessment). In a sense one could say that the easy part has been done, and that delivery as the strategy faces the test of time – and in particular bad times – is what counts. On the other hand, obtaining such widespread acceptance across the political divide for a concrete definition of poverty, and recognition of the need for a co-ordinated strategy to combat it, represents an achievement that should not be undervalued. A considerable degree of political and broader societal commitment to tackling poverty is a prerequisite rather than a product of a national poverty target. There is however reason to hope that adopting such a target will help to crystallise such a general commitment into concrete action.

9.5 Conclusions

This chapter has examined trends in poverty in Ireland as the macroeconomy fluctuated throughout the 1980s and 1990s. The overall percentage falling below relative income poverty lines was seen to be fairly stable, if anything trending upwards through 'good times and bad'. There were however major changes in the composition of the households found below a threshold such as half average income, as unemployment and the relative position of the elderly fluctuated. The importance of the relationship between the level of social transfers and mean income in driving these trends was brought out. Ireland was seen to have a high rate of relative income poverty compared with other European Union members, now similar to the UK though lower than Portugal.

The importance of going beyond relative income – particularly when average income is growing very fast – in measuring poverty was brought out by a poverty measure incorporating non-monetary indicators of deprivation. This showed a significant decline from 1994 as rapid growth in real incomes brought deprivation levels down. In 1997 Ireland adopted a National Anti-Poverty Strategy, which frames its global poverty reduction target in terms of this combined income and deprivation measure. As growth slows, expectations about minimum standards may catch up with average incomes. High relative income poverty rates are thus a concern for the longer term even when deprivation levels are falling, and this needs to be taken into account in the way the anti-poverty strategy – and its targets – is formulated.

NOTES

1 Atkinson, Rainwater and Smeeding (1995), Table 4.2.
2 Most of the items in the secondary dimension, such as a car or a telephone, were not overwhelmingly regarded as necessities in 1987. The housing and related durables indicators, while generally regarded as necessities, appeared to be related to very specific factors, and so while providing valuable information about one important aspect of living standards were not satisfactory as indicators of current generalised exclusion.
3 For a more detailed discussion of the relationship between poverty and psychological distress see Whelan (1992, 1994).

10

Taxation and Social Welfare

TIM CALLAN AND BRIAN NOLAN

10.1 Introduction

In terms of the extent and nature of its welfare state, Ireland is generally categorised as among the liberal/minimal states, together with the UK and other Anglo-Saxon countries. Unlike many of those countries, an explicit policy of cutting back the welfare state has not been adopted in Ireland in recent years, though the challenge of stagnation and high unemployment in the 1980s caused a good deal of soul-searching. While significant changes in tax/welfare structures have been implemented, these have been presented in terms of a rather different rhetoric, as aiming to promote both growth and social inclusion. This chapter aims to place Ireland's tax and welfare structures in comparative perspective, examine the way these structures have evolved over the 1980s and 1990s, and explore the implications for poverty and income inequality.

Over that period Ireland has seen very considerable fluctuations in tax and welfare levels and rates. There were major increases in taxation during the 1980s versus cuts in the 1990s, fluctuating levels of welfare provision relative to earnings or average incomes, a changing balance between insurance versus means-tested support, and swings in support for the elderly versus others depending on social welfare. As well as describing these changes and bringing out the way the underlying strategies have shifted over time, we use a tax/benefit simulation model to explore their impact on the distribution of income and on economic incentives. The chapter also seeks to bring out the implications of the Irish experience for current welfare state regime theory, exploring the extent to which that theory has explanatory power when comparing the responses of states with similar regimes to the emergence of sustained high unemployment in the 1980s.

10.2 Social welfare

The Irish Social Welfare System

We begin with a thumbnail sketch of the Irish social welfare system. Ireland on Independence inherited a social welfare system essentially identical to that of the United Kingdom at the time, and many later structural developments also mirrored those in the UK. The broad structure comprises a system of social insurance, with contributions from employers, employees and the state financing contributory benefits, and a system of social assistance, with means-tested payments for many of the same contingencies (old age, unemployment). A universal child benefit payment was introduced as early as 1944, but operates alongside payments made as 'child dependant additions' to recipients of most social welfare schemes. Social welfare recipients with a dependent spouse also receive an additional 'adult dependant' payment. Payments are almost always flat-rate rather than earnings-related.

The safety-net Supplementary Welfare Allowance scheme was established in 1975, replacing the old 'home assistance' service with a payment rate equal to that for short-term unemployment assistance. A number of smaller schemes were put in place during the 1960s and 1970s, including provision for deserted wives and an 'Unmarried Mother's' Allowance subsequently subsumed under the broader Lone Parent's Allowance. In the early 1980s, concerns about financial incentives to take up employment led to the introduction of the Family Income Supplement, paid to those with child dependents whose income from employment was low relative to their family size. A Carer's Allowance payable on a means-tested basis to those who live with and look after people who need full-time care was introduced in the early 1990s. Social insurance contributions became pay-related in 1979, and a number of changes in the contribution structure have been made since then which we will discuss later together with income tax.

Recent research on the welfare state – of which social security forms a central element – has expended a good deal of energy on typologies aiming to distinguish and group countries with similar regimes. In these terms, the Irish welfare state is generally categorised with the UK, though there appears to be some confusion and uncertainty about where it best fits. This is the case in Esping-Andersen's (1990) influential study distinguishing three different regimes, 'liberal', 'conservative' and 'socialist'. Ireland appears in the liberal group of 'Anglo-Saxon' countries, with the UK, USA, Australia, Canada and New Zealand, at one point in his discussion but elsewhere is said to be among the strongly élitist and corporatist with Austria, Belgium, Finland, Italy and Japan. The influence of Catholicism and the role of the family certainly distinguish Ireland from the UK, and some have extended this to class Ireland as having a 'Southern European' model of welfare. Whatever about the broader welfare state, as far as income maintenance is concerned that seems unhelpful. Unlike Italy or Spain, for example, Ireland's income maintenance system is highly centralised, with little or no regional differentiation (Cousins, 1999). Focusing simply on the social welfare system, Ireland does seem to fit comfortably with the UK as aiming to provide universal minimum protection with an emphasis on means-testing and flat-rate rather than earnings-related provision. As we shall see later, though, sharing a similar structure does not mean that the effectiveness of the system will necessarily also be similar across countries: how the parameters of the system are operated also matters a great deal.

In terms of the overall scale of social welfare expenditure as a proportion of Gross National Product or Gross Domestic Product, Ireland ranked as a relatively low-spending country even before the full effects of the economic boom were felt. In the mid-1990s, Ireland spent about 10 per cent of GDP on social insurance plus social assistance, and among our EU partners only Portugal and Greece were spending that little: the Netherlands was spending more than twice that share of GDP, but a more typical share was about 16-18 per cent. This was despite the fact that Ireland was then spending a relatively high proportion of national income on income support for the unemployed – about 3 per cent of GDP. Spending on old age and widow(er's) pensions was a substantially lower share of GDP in Ireland than in any other member state, and spending on disability-related income support was also among the lowest. While demographic factors clearly play a major role in determining pension expenditure, the fact that Ireland's social insurance system pays a flat-rate rather than an earnings-related pension is also very important. By 2000, with unemployment very much lower and social welfare rates lagging behind other incomes as we shall see, Ireland's total social welfare expenditure was down to about 7 per cent of GDP.

Trends in social welfare support 1980-2000

Moving on from structures, we now describe the rates of support provided by the main schemes in the social welfare system and how they evolved over the past two decades. In doing so we distinguish four distinct sub-periods: 1980 to 1987, 1987 to 1994, 1994 to 1997, and 1997 to 2000. These are usefully distinguished because we have household survey data for 1980, 1987, 1994 and 1997, and because they also do display some different features. We look first at how the rates payable for single adults by some of the most important social welfare schemes evolved from 1980 to 2000 in real terms. Table 10.1 shows the actual rates, while Table 10.2 shows the percentage change in the rate, deflated by the increase in consumer prices, in each sub-period and over the period as a whole.

We see that at the outset, in 1980, there was in effect a hierarchy of payment levels with three groupings. The elderly and widows in receipt of contributory pensions – with entitlement through social insurance contributions – were the most generously supported. Next came the unemployed or ill in receipt of insurance-based support, together with the elderly or widows on means-tested social assistance pensions. Those on means-tested unemployment assistance received rather lower levels of support and the safety-net Supplementary Welfare Allowance (SWA) scheme received least. The weekly payment for a single adult on SWA was only two-thirds the level of the contributory old-age pension. This brings out the scope for significant differences across these groups in poverty, measured in terms of the comparison between current weekly income and an income poverty line.

What is most striking then is the extent of variation in the rate of increase across the different schemes, within the sub-periods. Table 10.2 shows that from 1980 to 1987, the real increase in the basic personal rate was about 21 per cent for both the contributory and non-contributory Old Age Pensions. Insurance-based income support for unemployment or illness, and means-tested support for the short-term unemployed, rose by only half that amount. The long-term unemployed, on the other hand, also received relatively substantial increases. This reflected a combination of relatively generous treatment of pensions for the elderly in the early 1980s, and growing concern about the living standards of the long-term unemployed from the mid-1980s as unemployment stabilised at a very high level.

Table 10.1: Social welfare rates 1980 -2000

Scheme	Personal rate				
	1980	1987	1994	1997	2000
Social Insurance:					
Contributory Old Age Pension	24.5	55.1	71	78	96
Contributory Widow's Pension	22.5	49.5	64.5	71	81.1
Unemployment/Disability Benefit	20.45	42.3	61	67.5	77.5
Invalidity Pension	22.05	48.5	62.6	69.2	79.2
Social Assistance:					
Non-contributory Old Age Pension	21	47.1	61	67.5	85.5
Non-contributory Widow's Pension	21	46.2	61	67.5	77.5
UA short-term*	17	35.1	58.9	65.4	76
UA long-term*	17	37.8	61	67.5	77.5
Supplementary Welfare Allowance	16.45	34	58.9	65.4	76
Lone Parent's Allowance, 1 child	27.9	57.8	76.2	82.7	92.7

* In 1980 and 1987 separate UA rates operated for urban and rural areas; the urban rate was slightly higher and is shown here.

Table 10.2: Percentage real increase in social welfare rates 1980 -2000

Scheme	per cent increase in Personal rate, deflated by CPI				
	1980-87	1987-94	1994-97	1997-2000	1980-2000
Social Insurance:					
Contributory Old Age Pension	21.44	5.40	3.94	14.87	52.82
Contributory Widow's Pension	18.80	6.58	4.14	6.61	40.57
Unemployment/Disability Benefit	11.69	17.95	4.69	7.16	47.80
Invalidity Pension	18.77	5.57	4.58	6.82	40.08
Social Assistance:					
Non-contributory Old Age Pension	21.11	5.93	4.69	18.22	58.79
Non-contributory Widow's Pension	18.80	8.00	4.69	7.16	43.93
UA short-term*	11.49	37.26	5.05	8.46	74.35
UA long-term*	20.07	32.00	4.69	7.16	77.79
Supplementary Welfare Allowance	11.61	41.70	5.05	8.46	80.18
Lone Parent's Allowance, 1 child	11.87	7.83	2.68	4.62	29.58

Between 1987 and 1994, on the other hand, all schemes saw an increase in the real value of their payment rates but the elderly fared worst. The elderly saw real increases of only 5-6 per cent while the unemployed saw their support rates rise by 18-37 per cent depending on the scheme and duration. Those on Supplementary Welfare Allowance Assistance now saw the largest increase, of over 40 per cent in real terms. The increases for schemes for widows/widowers, lone parents and those on Invalidity Pension were towards the bottom of the range. This pattern reflects the deliberate strategy adopted over the period from the late 1980s, to give priority to bringing up what had been the lowest rates of social welfare. That was influenced by the recommendations of the government-appointed Commission on Social Welfare (1986), which highlighted what it saw as the inadequacy of these lowest payment rates. Rather than increasing these rates to the levels recommended as adequate by the Commission on Social Welfare as part of a general up-rating in support levels, however, the policy adopted was to bring the lowest rates up towards the rest. By 1994 there had therefore been a good deal of convergence in the rates paid across the different schemes. By that date, the lowest basic personal rate – still for Supplementary Welfare Allowance – was 83 per cent of the highest one, which was still the contributory Old Age Pension

By 1994, means-tested support for the long-term unemployed had reached the same level as the insurance-based payments to the unemployed or ill, so the limit had been reached in terms of convergence there (though means-tested pensions for the elderly and widows remained below contributory pensions).

There was a fairly consistent pattern of increases across the schemes between then and 1987, representing a 4-5 per cent rise in real terms. From 1997 on, with unemployment continuing to fall rapidly and the elderly seen to have done relatively badly over the previous decade, the 1987-94 policy went into reverse. Between 1997 and 2000, pensions for the elderly rose by 15-18 per cent in real terms, whereas the unemployed and sick – whether on insurance or social assistance – saw increases of about 7 per cent.

By 2000, the pattern of support rates had some similarities with the one right back in 1980, at the start of the period we are considering, but there were also some important differences. There was once again a hierarchy of three groups. Those on contributory old-age pensions were once again doing rather better than others, receiving about 12 per cent more than those on the means-tested pension who were in the second group. However, widows had lost ground compared with the elderly, whether on contributory or means-tested payments. Furthermore, the unemployed and ill on insurance-based payments were now in the group with the lowest level of support, doing no better than their means-tested equivalents. The lowest rate of weekly payment had reached 83 per cent of the highest rate in 1994. By 2000 this had fallen to 79 per cent, though the gap from top to bottom was still rather less than it had been in 1980.

The extent of divergence across the different schemes within sub-periods was sufficiently pronounced to produce marked changes in the position of one group of social welfare recipient versus another over time. The position of the elderly versus the unemployed, for example, will have fluctuated very considerably, and this will have been a major influence on the profile of the low income population. As well as variations across schemes in the increase in social support levels and prices over the period, though, the relationship between these increases and other incomes in the economy is clearly of central importance. Support levels increased in real terms in each of the sub-periods examined for all schemes, though at different rates across the different schemes within sub-periods and over the entire two decades. A real increase of up to 78 per cent was registered over the twenty years, which is an impressive rate of growth by any standard. In considering the relative position of those depending on social welfare, however, it is how that compared with other incomes that matters, and there was also a great deal of variation across the sub-periods in the evolution of those incomes.

The first available point of comparison here is with average earnings. A series compiled by the Central Statistics Office shows average weekly earnings in industry, and once again this can be deflated by the increase in consumer prices. This shows some increase between 1980 and 1987 but a particularly rapid increase between 1987 and 1994, with much slower growth from then up to 1997 and then some acceleration. That is in fact rather deceptive in terms of the evolution of disposable income, because the average tax rate also fluctuated very considerably over the period, as discussed in detail later in this chapter. As a result, average earnings after tax showed little or no growth from 1980 to 1987, then a still significant increase to 1994 but from 1994 and particularly 1997 tax reductions made a major contribution to the rate of increase in after-tax earnings.

The second point of comparison, available up to 1997, is average household disposable income from the Household Budget Surveys of 1980, 1987 and 1994/95, and the ESRI household surveys for 1987, 1994 and 1997 described in detail in previous chapters. Disposable income averaged over households in the Household Budget Survey showed virtually no increase in real terms between 1980 and 1987. From 1987 to 1994, by contrast, the ESRI surveys show average household disposable income increasing by over 20 per cent in real terms – rather faster than old age pensions but more slowly than means-tested income support for the unemployed. Over the shorter period between 1994 and 1997, average household income rose by about 10 per cent in real terms, when we saw most social welfare rates increased by about half that figure.

So far we have concentrated on the rate paid for a single adult by the various schemes, but there were also significant changes over time in the rate paid for a couple versus a single adult. Especially from 1987 on, as payment levels for the lowest-paying schemes were brought up, the percentage increase awarded for a couple was often lower than that for a single adult in some of the main schemes. In effect, the equivalence scale implicit in these schemes changed over the period. In 1980, and still by 1987, a couple on Unemployment Benefit received 1.65 times the basic adult payment, and the figure was as high as 1.72 for couples on means-tested Unemployment Assistance. By 1994 this ratio had fallen to 1.6 for both these schemes, and that was where it remained by 2000. This was consistent with the Commission on Social Welfare's suggestion that the appropriate ratio was 1.6, but that was not based on an in-depth empirical examination of the issue by the Commission or on Irish evidence. A commitment to increase this ratio back up towards 1.7 was included in the Partnership for Prosperity and Fairness. (This was not an issue for contributory old age pensions, where couples actually received larger percentage increases than single adults over the period, or for non-contributory pensions where both spouses usually receive the full personal rate.)

As far as child income support is concerned, there was an important structural change early in the period we are considering. At the outset, child income support was provided through universal payments called children's allowances, through additional payments to those relying on social welfare called Child Dependant Additions, and through tax allowances for those with children and liable for income tax. In 1984, mirroring an earlier shift in the UK, these child tax allowances were abolished and the revenue saved was used to finance an increase in the universal cash payment, which was re-labelled Child Benefit. As a result, the universal payment had risen from £4.50 per month in 1980 to £15.05 in 1987. The increase to 1994 was then quite limited, bringing the figure to £20; by 1997 it was £30 and by 2000 had reached £42.50. Over the whole period, then, this universal payment increased ten-fold at a time when prices went up by a factor of approximately two and a half. For those in the tax net, however, the loss of child tax allowances for children partially offset this increase.

Finally, there was also an expansion over the period in the additional cash payments or non-cash benefits available to social welfare recipients or low income households generally. As well as new schemes and an expansion in the coverage of some pre-existing ones, payments under the Supplementary Welfare Allowance scheme for rent and mortgage supplements and exceptional needs rose particularly rapidly. Local authority differential rents also provide a subsidy to low-income tenants which can be substantial. Analysis of the ESRI surveys suggests that these can make a significant difference to the position of certain groups, notably the elderly, and that this needs to be taken into account to get a full picture of trends over time (Nolan and Russell forthcoming).

The anti-poverty effectiveness of the social welfare system

The social welfare system has a range of objectives, including the alleviation of poverty, protection of living standards and redistribution across the life-cycle. A comprehensive analysis of the effectiveness and efficiency of the system would require a specification of its multiple objectives, their relative importance, and the nature of any trade-offs between them. Without down-playing the other objectives – and their importance in sustaining support for social welfare spending – alleviating poverty may be seen as central. It is particularly important to assess how effective (and efficient) the Irish system has been in terms of that aim, and how this has changed over time and compares with other countries. For this purpose we can employ the approach developed by Beckerman (1979). It begins by defining the pre-transfer income of each household or tax unit as disposable income less social security transfers received. An income poverty line is applied for households of differing size and composition. The pre-transfer poverty gap is then calculated as the difference between the household's pre-transfer income and the poverty line, and the aggregate pre-transfer poverty gap is the sum of all these gaps across households. This provides a measure of aggregate pre-transfer poverty in money terms, which can be related to social welfare spending also in money terms. The Beckerman measure of effectiveness is then the percentage of the aggregate pre-transfer poverty gap which is eliminated after social welfare transfers are added to household income. The Beckerman measure of efficiency is the percentage of total social security spending which goes towards the elimination of poverty, i.e. serves to reduce the pre-transfer poverty gap.

It is helpful in interpreting these measures to think of households as falling into three categories, illustrated in Figure 10.1. Type 1 have income below the poverty line even after transfers, so all the transfers they receive (A_1) contribute to reducing their poverty gaps, but they still have a poverty gap post-transfers (D). Type 2 have pre-transfer income below the poverty line but post-transfer income above it, so some of the transfers received (A_2) contribute to reducing their poverty gaps, but the remainder (B) do not. Type 3 have pre-transfer income above the poverty line, so all the transfers they receive (C) do not contribute to reducing poverty gaps. The Beckerman measure of effectiveness is then the ratio of (A_1+A_2) to the total pre-transfer poverty gap (A_1+A_2+D). The Beckerman measure of efficiency, on the other hand, is the ratio of (A_1+A_2) to total social welfare expenditure (A_1+A_2+B+C).

Figure 10.1: Classification of households for effectiveness and efficiency analysis

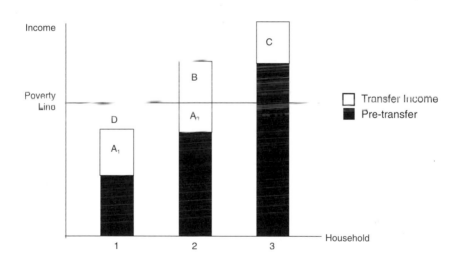

The implicit assumption that the income of recipient households would have been unchanged in the absence of income support from the state is clearly unrealistic. However, the difficulties involved in estimating what the world would actually look like in the complete absence of transfers are obvious, and this is not in any case the comparison in which one is interested. The measures are thus to be taken as providing a picture of the overall performance of the social welfare system allowing for comparisons over time and across countries, rather than absolute measures of effectiveness and efficiency. Since spending bringing people over the line, or going to those already above it before transfers, is to be considered 'inefficient', the precise location of the income poverty line may be crucial. Calculating the effectiveness and efficiency measures with a range of income poverty lines allows us to assess the sensitivity of the results to precisely where the cut-off is located, and as in other chapters lines set at 40 per cent, 50 per cent and 60 per cent of average equivalent household income are employed.

The equivalence scales to be used have also been described in Chapter 8. Where the first adult in the household is given a value 1, we present results for the scale which allow 0.66 for each extra adult and 0.33 for each child, but comment on the sensitivity of the results to the alternative scales. These results cannot be derived for 1980, but Table 10.3 shows the effectiveness and efficiency measures calculated from the 1987 ESRI survey and 1994 Living in Ireland survey samples. We see that in each year, as one would expect, poverty reduction effectiveness is greatest with the lowest income poverty line. Comparing 1994 with 1987, the consistent pattern is that poverty reduction effectiveness increased with each of the relative income poverty lines. Turning to poverty reduction efficiency, we see that – again unsurprisingly – spending is more efficient the higher the poverty line, in that more of it goes to reducing poverty gaps. Comparing 1994 with 1987, efficiency is also up consistently across each of the poverty lines.

Table 10.3: Poverty reduction effectiveness and efficiency at different income poverty lines, 1987 and 1994

	1987	1994
	per cent	*per cent*
Poverty reduction effectiveness		
per cent of pre-transfer poverty gap eliminated by social welfare		
40 per cent line	91.5	96.6
50 per cent line	84.7	89.7
60 per cent line	75.8	78.6
Poverty reduction efficiency		
per cent of spending going on eliminating pre-transfer gap		
40 per cent line	44.6	52.0
50 per cent line	56.0	65.3
60 per cent line	65.6	74.2

Note: Equivalence Scale 1/0.66/0.33.

The fact that the increase in efficiency was greater than the increase in effectiveness reflects the growth in the size of the aggregate pre-transfer poverty gap. The pattern shown by these results reflects the strategy employed *vis-à-vis* social welfare rates over the period, which as we have just seen was to concentrate resources on more rapid increases for what were in 1987 the schemes paying the lowest rates of support. Particularly given the means-tested nature of the schemes involved, this had the effect that support became more concentrated on the households with relatively low incomes.

It is also interesting to disaggregate social welfare spending in the two years into the components A_1, A_2, B and C distinguished earlier, and this is done in Table 10.4 for the highest relative income line. We see that the proportion of spending going to those who remain below the poverty line (A_1) increased markedly from 1987 to 1994. The proportions going to bring households up to the line (A_2), going to bring them above the line (B) and going to those already above the line before transfers (C) all fall.

Table 10.4: Classification of social welfare spending in terms of poverty reduction with 60 per cent relative income poverty line, 1987 and 1994

	1987	1994
	per cent	per cent
A_1	38.9	54.0
A_2	26.7	20.3
B	11.4	8.2
C	23.0	17.5

Note: Equivalence Scale 1/0.66/0.33.

These results help to explain the pattern of results on aggregate measures of income poverty presented in Chapter 9. There we saw that poverty measures based on relative income poverty lines and poverty gaps had remained static or fallen between 1987 and 1994, whereas headcounts of the percentage of households below the 50 per cent and 60 per cent lines had risen. Social welfare spending clearly became more tightly focused on reducing poverty gaps between 1987 and 1994, and this was the major reason for the decline in gap-based measures, but with growing numbers below the higher lines, effectiveness in terms of reducing gaps did not increase as much as efficiency. While the exact level of measured effectiveness and efficiency varies somewhat depending on the choice of equivalence scale, the pronounced change from 1987 to 1994 is seen when alternative scales are employed.

International comparisons of analyses of this type are dogged by problems of comparability. However, the Irish data and analysis for 1987 formed part of a harmonised international project on measurement of poverty and the effectiveness of social security in a number of European countries (Deleeck et al, 1992). This suggested that the Irish social welfare system at the time was markedly more efficient, in the Beckerman sense, than those of the Benelux countries over a wide range of poverty lines, but was also somewhat less effective. The implication is that a given proportion of national income devoted to social welfare, at any given level of efficiency, was less effective in Ireland than in countries such as Belgium and the Netherlands, with a lower pre-transfer poverty gap.

A more up-to-date comparative perspective on anti-poverty effectiveness is available only for a specific aspect of the income maintenance system, namely income support for the unemployed. Nolan, Hauser and Zoyem (forthcoming) look at the impact of cash transfers on poverty rates for the unemployed in the mid-1980s and mid-1990s in six European countries: Ireland, the UK, Denmark, Sweden, France and Germany. To measure the impact of transfers on poverty, it focuses not on poverty gaps but on the numbers in poverty, and in particular on the percentage of the pre-transfer poor unemployed who are lifted above the poverty line by cash transfers received by their household. Using a poverty threshold of half average income, Table 10.5 shows that in the mid-1980s transfers were most effective in alleviating poverty for the unemployed in Denmark, where more than 80 per cent of those who were poor before transfers had been lifted out of poverty by transfers. In France, Germany, Ireland and the UK, about 40-45 per cent of the pre-transfer poor were lifted above the poverty line by transfers, while in Sweden the figure was only about one-quarter.

By the mid-1990s, the impact of transfers on this measure had increased in France, Ireland and particularly Sweden, where a much larger proportion of the pre-transfer poor unemployed were being lifted above the poverty line. In Denmark the very high 'escape rate' seen in the mid-1980s was maintained. In Germany and even more so in the UK, however, the percentage of the pre-transfer poor lifted above the poverty line by transfers fell sharply. In Denmark, France, Ireland and Sweden, the pre-transfer poverty rate rose but cash transfers either became more effective or (in the Danish case) remained very effective in lifting the pre-transfer poor above the poverty line, so the post-transfer poverty rate for the unemployed fell or at worst increased only marginally. In Germany and the UK, the pre-transfer poverty rate rose while cash transfers became much less effective, so the post-transfer poverty rate rose a good deal more.

Table 10.5: The impact of transfers on poverty rates for the unemployed, 50 per cent line, selected European countries

	per cent of pre-transfer poor unemployed lifted above line		per cent of all unemployed lifted above line	
	1980s	1990s	1980s	1990s
Denmark	87.0	88.6	50.9	59.0
France	44.5	52.4	18.5	25.7
Germany	47.0	32.0	22.6	17.8
Ireland	47.1	58.0	34.4	46.2
Sweden	26.4	51.2	9.8	31.9
UK	38.2	19.0	20.3	11.6

Both the scale of unemployment and the extent of pre-transfer poverty among the unemployed obviously differ across countries, and thus so does the size of the problem being tackled by the cash transfer system. The table also shows the absolute reduction in the poverty rate for the unemployed which transfers succeed in bringing about in each country. We see that in the mid-1990s cash transfers lifted half or more of the unemployed out of poverty in Denmark and in Ireland, considerably more than in the other countries. This reflects the very high level of effectiveness of transfers in the Danish case, but in Ireland reflects a lower (though still relatively high) level of effectiveness together with a very high pre-transfer poverty rate for the unemployed. In Germany and even more so in the UK the percentage of the unemployed lifted out of poverty by transfers in the mid-1990s is relatively low. In each case this is not because the pre-transfer poverty rate was low, but rather reflects the ineffectiveness of transfers in lifting the substantial numbers in pre-transfer poverty above the poverty line.

The relationship between these results and the nature of the welfare regimes in the different countries is worth bringing out. The relationship between welfare regime and the extent of poverty and unemployment is itself of course highly controversial. Much of this debate, particularly among economists, has concentrated on the links between the level of unemployment and the generosity of welfare provision for the unemployed. Taking the level of unemployment in different countries or at different points in time as given, however, the pattern across the countries in the effectiveness of cash transfers in lifting the unemployed out of poverty does not fit neatly into a welfare regime framework. In terms of conventional typologies, Sweden and Denmark are both countries that aim to provide a high level of protection of living standards to all unemployed people. Germany and France both have systems based on the protection of living standards of those with longer-term experience of employment and minimum protection for those who have not. The UK and Ireland, as we have seen, both have systems of universal minimum protection with an emphasis on means-testing.

The results suggest that effectiveness is not predictable simply on the basis of welfare regime: it varies a good deal both within each of these groupings, and over time. Denmark is consistently highly effective, but Sweden, where unemployment rose very sharply from a very low level over the period, was less so. In France the effectiveness of cash transfers increased, so post-transfer poverty rates for the unemployed remained stable between the mid-1980s and the mid-1990s despite an increase in pre-transfer poverty, but for Germany effectiveness fell over the period so that post-transfer poverty rose quite sharply.

The divergence in experience between Ireland and the UK was even more pronounced. Between the mid-1980s and mid-1990s pre-transfer poverty rose in both countries – as it did in the other four – but the transfer systems responded very differently. The Irish cash transfer system became more effective in lifting the pre-transfer poor unemployed out of poverty, while the UK saw a marked decline in the effectiveness of its transfer system. As a result, poverty rose sharply for the unemployed in the UK, whereas it fell in Ireland. The two transfer systems were very similar in structure at the outset, and evolved over the period in a similar manner, with greater reliance on means-testing and a reduced role for social insurance-based unemployment compensation. The crucial difference between the two countries was quite simply trends in the level of cash transfer paid relative to other incomes: not structures.[2] We have seen that in the Irish case transfers to the unemployed, particularly means-tested support, rose a good deal more rapidly than average household income over the period, but in the UK the level of safety-net support lagged significantly behind mean incomes. Callan and Sutherland (1997) show that in 1987 the level of safety-net support provided to a couple with three children was about 50 per cent of average weekly earnings in manufacturing in both countries; by 1994, the UK figure had fallen to 43 per cent, whereas for Ireland it had risen to 60 per cent. This, rather than the increased role of means-testing or changes in structures, had the most direct impact on poverty rates for the unemployed producing such divergent trends in the two countries.

Similar institutional structures and welfare regimes have thus responded in very different ways to the changing labour market of the 1980s and 1990s. The implication is that governments have considerable scope in the way they operate within the structure of their welfare regimes to affect crucial outcomes, notably through the level at which social welfare rates are set relative to other incomes.

10.3 Taxation

The Irish tax system

The Irish tax system incorporates the main elements familiar across industrialised countries – namely taxes on income, goods and services, capital transfers, profits, and property together with a system of social insurance contributions. Particular features of the Irish system, and the balance between these types of taxation, merit brief discussion before we turn to a detailed examination of income taxation. The most important of these is the particularly prominent role that income tax itself plays, accounting for a larger share of total tax revenue than in most other European countries. This does not reflect any disinclination to tax goods and services – value added tax and excise taxes are a more significant source of revenue in Ireland than in many other industrialised countries. Rather, Ireland is unusual in having a relatively very low share of revenue coming from social insurance contributions.

Social insurance contributions are indeed made by both employers and employees in Ireland (unlike for example Denmark), but they account for about half as much of total revenue as in the EU as a whole. Whereas the standard contribution rate for an employee in Ireland is under 7 per cent and for an employer about 12 per cent, in many other EU countries the corresponding figure for employees is twice as high, and for employers a rate of one-third is not uncommon. This reflects the fact that much of social welfare spending in Ireland is funded directly by the Exchequer, but it also reflects the more modest level of social insurance benefits paid relative to average earnings compared with countries such as Belgium, the Netherlands, France or Germany. It also reflects the influence of the British model and the long-standing desire to maintain competitiveness of labour-intensive firms against British competition.

The other most striking feature of the Irish tax environment over the past two decades has been the extent of the fluctuation in the overall tax burden. Measured as a proportion of GDP, the tax burden has been falling rapidly in Ireland during the 1990s, having risen very sharply in the 1980s. Towards the end of the 1990s, when 29 OECD countries were ranked from the largest to the smallest share going on taxation, Ireland ranked twenty-second, with all the other EU member states having a higher share. Taxes represented about one-third of GDP in Ireland, with the EU average over 40 per cent. During the previous decade, the Irish figure had fallen by about 4 percentage points, whereas in the OECD area as a whole the tax burden was still trending upwards.

Trends in income tax and PRSI 1980-2000

We now turn to the specifics of developments in the Irish tax system from 1980 to 2000, focusing on income tax and employee social insurance contributions. Table 10.6 shows the income tax rates and basic allowances in place in 1980, .1987, 1994, 1997 and 2000. We see first that there were significant changes in the tax structure over the period. In 1980 there were five income tax rates, ranging from 25 per cent up to 60 per cent. By 1987 this had been reduced to three rates, though this reflected the disappearance of the bottom rate, leaving the standard rate at 35 per cent and a significant proportion of taxpayers liable to 48 per cent or 58 per cent. By 1994 the number of rates was down to two, with the standard rate down to 27 per cent and the top rate at 48 per cent. These two rates were reduced throughout the remainder of the 1990s until by 2000 they stand at 22 per cent and 44 per cent respectively, with the government committed to further reductions.

Table 10.6: Income tax rates and allowances 1980, 1987, 1994, 1997 and 2000

Rates and allowances	1980	1987	1994	1997	2000
Tax rates	25 per cent	35 per cent	27 per cent	26 per cent	22 per cent
	35 per cent	48 per cent	48 per cent		44 per cent
	45 per cent	58 per cent			
	50 per cent				
	60 per cent				
Single allowance	£1,115	£2,000	£2,350	£2,900	£4,700
Married allowance	£2,230	£4,000	£4,700	£5,800	£9,400

Turning to the allowances which are deducted before tax liability is computed, we see that personal allowances almost doubled between 1980 and 1987 but were then increased only marginally between 1987 and 1994, below the rate of increase in prices much less that of incomes. They increased more significantly between 1994 and 1997 and then much more rapidly to 2000. In 1999 there was a major change in the way allowances operated, as we discuss below, as part of a move towards a tax credit system. In addition, the evolution of the bands between which the different rates are payable has been important. Because these bands were not increased in line with incomes through the 1980s and into the 1990s, the numbers paying tax at the higher rates rose very substantially, and it is only in the second half of the 1990s that a major effort to reverse this trend has been made. Further, scope to transfer bands between spouses began to be restricted in 2000, as part of a move towards greater individualisation of the income tax code which once again is discussed in greater detail later.

Finally, the pay-related social insurance contributions and associated levies paid by employees are also relevant, and the period saw some significant changes in their structure. In particular, a lower exemption limit – below which PRSI was not payable – was introduced and an allowance structure subsequently put in place. PRSI is not payable over an earnings ceiling, and this has been increased over time broadly in line with earnings, but the corresponding ceiling over which the Health levy was payable was abolished in the early 1990s.

10.4 The distributional impact of tax and welfare changes

Having examined the way the social welfare and income tax systems evolved over the past two decades, we now examine the distributional impact of these changes. This is done using a tax-benefit simulation model developed at the ESRI, called SWITCH, which we describe shortly. This model is based on micro-data from the ESRI household surveys, initially from 1987, and has only been used to analyse changes from that point on. We therefore look first at the 1987-94 period, then at the impact of the rather different policies implemented since then.

Distributional impact can mean different things to different people, and the first requirement for analysis is a benchmark against which to assess the budgetary measures actually implemented. A useful benchmark is a budget that ensured that growth in disposable income was the same for all major population groups, and shares of income for those groups remained the same after the budget as before. This 'distributionally neutral' benchmark provides one yardstick against which changes can reasonably be measured. To implement such a benchmark, we index tax and social welfare to the growth in wage income, the predominant element in national income. For wage earners, this is achieved by increasing tax-free allowances and the standard rate band in line with the growth in gross wages. For those depending on social welfare payments, welfare rates are increased in line with pre-tax wages.

The impact of budget tax and welfare changes is often assessed by looking at their effects on a small number of supposedly 'typical' families, for example a one-earner couple on average earnings with 2 children. This may miss important effects for significant groups, and cannot provide an overall picture of the distribution of gains and losses. Microsimulation models have been developed and used in many countries to overcome these shortcomings. Being based on large-scale representative samples of the population, they automatically take account of the wide diversity of circumstances in the population. The overall pattern of gains and losses from tax and welfare changes can then be identified, as well as their impact on financial incentives to work. SWITCH, the ESRI tax-benefit model (the acronym stands for *S*imulating *W*elfare and *I*ncome *T*ax *CH*anges) is based on the nationally representative surveys of households undertaken by the ESRI, first in 1987 and then in 1994. For analysis after 1994 the underlying database has been uprated in line with external trends in employment and unemployment, demographics, income from different sources, etc.

We now use this model to look first at the net distributive effect of the changes in the parameters of the tax and welfare systems between 1987 and 1994, described earlier, as measured against the benchmark of indexing tax and welfare policies in line with earnings growth. Figure 10.2 shows considerable gains on average for the poorest 20 per cent of families, reflecting the exceptionally large increases in the lowest rates of welfare payment. There were however losses relative to the indexation benchmark for many low and middle income earners, and for those welfare recipients (including many pensioners) whose payments did not increase as fast as earnings. The tax cuts implemented over the period also gave rise to substantial gains for higher earners, these gains being greatest for those at the top of the income distribution.

Figure 10.2: Distributive effects of 1987-1994 changes against policy indexed to earnings

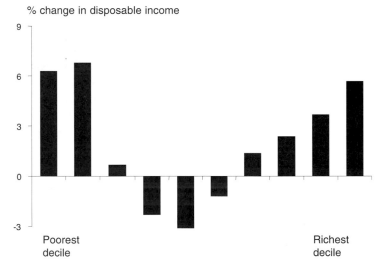

From 1994 to 1998, the pattern of policy change was somewhat different, as we saw in detail earlier. In general, welfare rates now rose by more than prices but not as fast as other incomes, though some special increases for pensioners were implemented. On the tax side, tax rates were coming down but there was also now significant widening of the standard rate band and increases in personal allowances, as well as further restructuring of the PRSI system. Figure 10.3

looks at the distributional impact of the changes introduced from 1994 to 1998, against the benchmark of indexation to earnings growth. This brings out the fact that budgetary policy has, in general, allowed the incomes of welfare recipients to fall further behind average incomes, and has, through tax cuts, particularly favoured top income earners. The richest 10 per cent of families gained about 4 per cent from Budget day changes, over and above what they would have gained from the simple indexation rule. But the poorest 30 per cent of the population gained 2 per cent less from the more complex and costly Budget day changes actually introduced than from indexation. They would have fared better if successive Ministers for Finance had simply indexed social welfare and taxes to average income growth.

Figure 10.3: Distributive effects of 1994-1998 changes against policy indexed to earnings

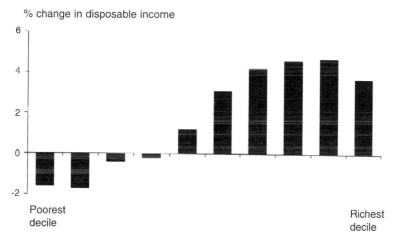

Partly in reaction to this, the 1999 budget aimed at concentrating tax relief on low and middle income earners, and restricting gains to those at the top of the income distribution. This was to be achieved by restricting the value of personal allowances to the standard rate of tax – as the start of a move to a system of tax credits – and focusing tax relief on increasing this standardised personal allowance. Figure 10.4 shows that the overall package did indeed give the greatest gains in proportionate terms to those in the middle reaches of the income distribution, with substantial gains for low earners and lesser gains for high earners. It also shows that the bottom 20 per cent of the income distribution did not share to the same extent in the gains, relative to the wage indexation benchmark.

Figure 10.4: Distributive impact of 1999 Budget against policy indexed to earnings

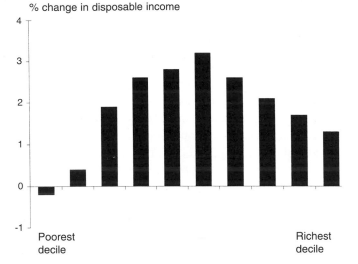

The Budget coming into operation in 2000 marked another reversal in direction, with the emphasis on cutting tax rates once again. Both the standard and top tax rate were cut by 2 percentage points, to 22 per cent and 44 per cent respectively. Figure 10.5 shows the first-round impact of the budget across the income distribution, measured once again against the neutral budget benchmark. The average percentage gain for the poorest 20 per cent of families was below 1 per cent. Middle income groups saw their income rise by between 2 and 3 per cent. The greatest gains were for the highest income groups, with the top 30 per cent of the distribution gaining about 4 per cent in disposable income.

Figure 10.5: Distributive impact of 2000 Budget against 1999 policy indexed to earnings

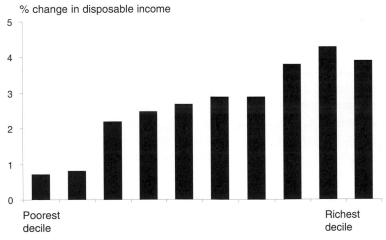

The relatively low gains for the poorest income groups reflect the balance that was struck between increased welfare expenditure and tax cuts. The fact that high income earners gained more than the low paid and middle income earners is due to the structure of the tax cuts, with the focus on rate cuts and band widening rather than increasing the standardised personal allowance introduced by Budget 1999. Indeed, Budget 2000 can be seen as reverting to the trend of policy from 1994-98, with Budget 1999 being the one to stand out as unusual.

The major structural innovation in the 2000 Budget, and the element receiving most attention in the immediate aftermath, was the start of a move towards individualisation of the standard rate tax band by restricting transferability of allowances across spouses. Despite cuts in tax rates and the application of significant resources to tax-cutting packages in recent years, a persistent feature of the Irish income tax system has been the relatively low income at which single persons pay the top rate of tax. A comparison with the situation in the UK, in Figure 10.6, shows stark differences in the marginal tax rates facing single persons at incomes between about IR£15,000 and IR£35,000 – before the 2000 Budget took effect. The difference is much less marked for one-earner couples.

Figure 10.6: Marginal income tax rates for single persons, Ireland and UK, 1999

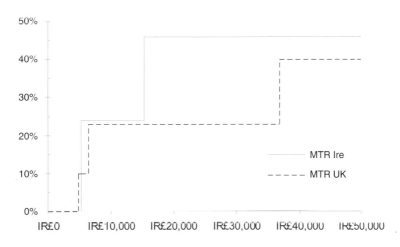

Note: UK figures converted to Irish pounds using purchasing power parity exchange rate derived from European Economy, December 1998: this exchange rate was IR£1=UK£0.92.

Until the late 1970s, there was a similar approach to taxing couples in the two countries, built around the 'male breadwinner' idea. In the Irish case, this system was then deemed unconstitutional in the way it treated married two-earner couples, and the policy response was to move to what is known as an 'income-splitting' system. This involves aggregating family income and splitting it equally between the partners for income tax purposes, and can be characterised as involving full transferability not only of income tax allowances, but of rate bands as well. In the UK, reform of the tax treatment of couples came later, and involved a move towards independent treatment of each partner's income.

The shift in policy introduced in the 2000 Budget involves restricting the extent to which tax bands are transferable between spouses, to be phased in over three years. The stated objective is to arrive at a position after three years where each individual, whether single or married, has his/her own standard rate tax band which can be set off against his/her own income but cannot be transferred between spouses. The uproar in response to this proposal when the Budget was announced was such that the government felt obliged to introduce a 'balancing' £3,000 tax allowance for one-income families where a spouse is working in the home to care for children, or an aged or handicapped person.

10.5 Tax, welfare and work incentives

As elsewhere, a central theme in debates about tax and welfare policy in Ireland has been the promotion of work incentives and avoidance of 'dependency'. In assessing the impact of changes in the tax and social welfare systems on work incentives, a variety of complex methodological issues must be faced. Empirical studies of the incentive to take up or stay in work generally measure the financial incentive facing individuals in the form of replacement rates, the ratio of income when unemployed to income when in work. The incentive to work more hours when in work is often summarised through marginal tax and benefit withdrawal rates. Simply looking at averages or at hypothetical 'typical' cases can be misleading, since they fail to capture the complexity of the situations of different individuals and families in the population. Tax-benefit micro-simulation models can thus be particularly valuable in this context, and the SWITCH model has been used to study the evolution of financial incentives to take up work in the Irish case (Callan and Nolan, 1999).

Over the 1987-94 period, concern about the potential disincentive effects of the welfare and tax systems was at its peak in Ireland as unemployment remained stubbornly high. Analysis of various hypothetical example families suggested that replacement rates went up significantly, as Unemployment Assistance in particular rose more rapidly than take-home pay of the average industrial worker. The impact of improvements in in-work benefits or alterations to income tax bands, allowances and exemption limits may not be reflected in calculations focusing on the average, and many unemployed may face wage offers well below the average industrial wage. Estimates produced by microsimulation using information on the representative sample, and predicted wages from estimated earnings equations, suggest that the average cash replacement rate facing the unemployed in Ireland was roughly constant between 1987 and 1994. An increase on average for those in receipt of Unemployment Assistance was seen, but this was offset by a decline for those relying on Unemployment Benefit, particularly since the pay-related additions to those social insurance-based payments were phased out.

The microsimulation approach also has the advantage that the distribution of replacement rates as well as the mean can be studied. Analysis for the representative sample incorporated into the tax/benefit model shows that tax/welfare policy between 1987 and 1994 served to reduce the incidence of replacement rates above 80 per cent. However, an increase in the numbers with replacement rates between 70-80 per cent, still rather high, was also seen.

These calculations are based on cash income in or out of work, whereas incentives to work will also be affected by any non-cash benefits available to the unemployed but lost when taking up a job – because they are either directly linked to labour force status or subject to a means test. In the Irish case, the most important of these non-cash benefits in this context is entitlement to free medical care. The valuation of such non-cash benefits, assigning them a cash value to include in the calculation of replacement rates, poses particularly complex problems. These valuation issues have been explored in some depth in the USA where such benefits play a significant role, but less often in the European context. Unemployed respondents in the ESRI's 1994 household survey were asked what wage they would require to make it worth taking a job, and how much less that would be if they were able to retain their health care entitlements. The responses, also analysed in Callan and Nolan (1999), suggested that retention of medical card cover is likely to directly influence the reservation wage of only a relatively small minority of the unemployed, but that for that minority the amounts involved are quite substantial.

Since 1994, average after-tax earnings have risen a good deal more rapidly than weekly welfare rates for the unemployed, and earnings towards the bottom also appear to have increased more rapidly than those in middle of the distribution (Nolan and McCormick, 1999). A number of different reforms to the way the tax and welfare systems operate have also worked to widen the gap between low-paid employment and unemployment. In addition, individuals going from long-term unemployment into work have been allowed retain entitlement to free health care for themselves and their families for several years, and also to retain additional cash support for children. While concerns about incentives and dependency have not disappeared, with unemployment down to about 5 per cent they are now expressed in a very different context, and relate for the most part to the rapidly-diminishing stock of long-term unemployed and to those parenting alone and depending on welfare. They also arise in respect of an element of the Irish income support structure which has assumed increasing importance in recent years, namely direct and indirect support for housing costs. With the dramatic escalation in rent and house prices in the late 1990s, potential loss of this support may be a serious disincentive but one which has not as yet been studied in depth.

Microsimulation models have also been used to provide a comparative perspective on incentives in Ireland. A recent study by the OECD draws on models for 12 countries, including SWITCH for Ireland. Where the point of comparison is the median full-time wage, the microsimulation results show that the replacement rate is under 40 per cent for most unemployed Australians and Americans, much higher for Danes and Swedes, and somewhere in between for other countries studied including Ireland. High replacement rates tend to be concentrated in particular family types, but in a manner which varies across countries. Another comparison of microsimulation-based replacement rates for Ireland and the UK, using consistent definitions, suggested that in the mid-1990s a considerably higher proportion of the unemployed in Ireland faced rates above 60 per cent. The replacement rate was strongly influenced by family composition in each country, primarily because of the impact of extra income support payments for dependants. The fact that income support for the long-term unemployed is a good deal more generous relative to average earnings in Ireland was the single most important difference identified between the two tax/benefit systems. (The corollary was that the Irish system was more effective in reducing poverty among the unemployed, as detailed earlier.)

The OECD, in the course of its Jobs Study, also produced time-series on average hypothetical replacement rates for most member countries. The overall index for Ireland in the mid-1990s was at about the same level as in the mid-1980s. This left Ireland below the average for OECD countries though above the UK. The index does not take into account the impact of taxation, housing benefit, or benefits to children (as brought out in other work by the OECD), and Callan and Nolan (1999) discuss how apparently minor issues of definition and measurement can make a major difference to the comparative picture provided by these hypothetical calculations.

10.6 Conclusions

Over the past two decades Ireland has seen very considerable fluctuations in tax and welfare levels and rates. There were major increases in taxation during the

1980s versus cuts in the 1990s, fluctuating levels of welfare provision relative to earnings, and a changing balance between insurance versus means-tested support and in support for the elderly versus others depending on social welfare. During the period since the start of the boom, their overall impact has been to produce or permit a redistribution of income from the bottom of the distribution towards the top, though maintaining a social protection floor. The tax-cutting strategy in particular has favoured higher incomes through its concentration on cutting tax rates. With unemployment increasing dramatically and then falling even more so, the focus on work incentives and welfare dependency has waxed and waned, but as yet a coherent overall strategy for the social welfare system in particular has not emerged.

NOTES

1 An earnings-related supplement to Unemployment Benefit operated in the 1970s and 1980s, but was phased out due to concerns about work disincentive effects.

2 In the Irish case this largely reflected sustained long-term unemployment bringing about exhaustion of benefit entitlement rather than a deliberate and explicit policy choice as in the UK, but the net result was a substantial increase in the proportion of the unemployed relying on means-tested assistance. A similar benchmark is among those used by Redmond, Sutherland and Wilson (1998).

11

Cumulative Disadvantage and Polarisation

BRIAN NOLAN, RICHARD LAYTE AND CHRISTOPHER T. WHELAN

11.1 Introduction

Though the immediate cause of poverty may be a lack of resources relative to needs, it may well be that other, less visible factors lay behind and structure poverty statistics. Concern about these factors is implicit in the concept of 'social exclusion' which has gained increased currency in recent years, particularly since Ireland's unprecedented economic growth. The term social exclusion has generally been employed to denote multiply deprived groups, trapped in cycles of fatalism, concentrated in the worst housing estates and at risk of transmitting their fate across generations. One consequence of this manner of defining social exclusion is that it defines the key social cleavage as between a comfortable majority and an excluded minority.[1] In the midst of increased prosperity, many argue, we are seeing a new kind of poverty, qualitatively different from traditional forms in that it is based upon two different, but related forms of *cumulative disadvantage*. The first relates to the accumulation of disadvantage over time, whilst the second relates to the concentration of disadvantage geographically. The former suggests that the impact of earlier disadvantages persist and as a consequence produce a form of isolation from the mainstream more extreme and perhaps qualitatively different from that associated with any particular disadvantage. The latter suggests that individual disadvantages may be exacerbated for those living in communities where poverty is concentrated. Both express the notion that particular groups in Irish society are being socially excluded, and increasingly so, by structures beyond their control.

If true, such processes have important implications for social policy since they prioritise the processes through which 'problem' groups develop, such as the emergence of alternative value systems and other vicious circle processes, rather than the general disadvantage experienced by other, broader groups, such as the manual working class, in areas such as access to education and exposure to unemployment (Paugam, 1996). Here we examine the reality behind these concerns using data from two nationally representative social surveys, the first conducted after a period of economic crisis (1987) and the second after roughly four years of consistent growth (1997).

11.2 Poverty and social class

In Chapter 9 we argued that the NAPS poverty measure had continued to be successful in capturing a set of households who experience a combination of low income, levels of deprivation and related phenomena that set them apart from other households. The number of households below this line had declined significantly but the life-style gap between such households and all others had widened significantly. How was this decline in poverty distributed across the class hierarchy? Is it possible that although poverty levels were lower, the more extreme life-style disparities that it implied were concentrated to a greater extent among those at the bottom of the class structure? In Figure 11.1 we show the distribution of poverty by social class in 1987 and 1997. Our analysis for the most part will involve use of the following four-category scheme.[2]

1. Professional and Managerial or Service Class
2. Higher White Collar and Petty Bourgeoisie
3. Skilled and Semi-Skilled Manual and Lower White Collar which combines falling below the 60 per cent income line and experiencing basic deprivation.
4. Unskilled Manual

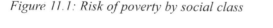

Figure 11.1: Risk of poverty by social class

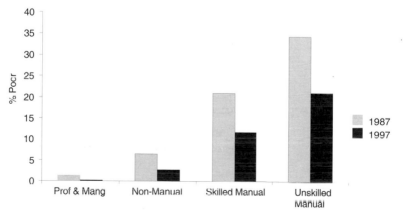

For convenience we will refer to Class 3 as the *skilled manual class*, and Classes 3 and 4 taken together as the *manual or working class*. It is clear that the reduction in poverty levels has operated across the class system. The rate for the professional and managerial class, which was already extremely low, approaches zero and that for the non-manual group falls from over 6 per cent to less than 3 per cent. The skilled manual group experienced a decline in the rate from 21 to 12 per cent with the unskilled group having a corresponding drop from 34 to 21 per cent. In absolute terms, the extent of improvement clearly increases as one descends the class hierarchy.

However, taking a relative perspective we find the *proportionate* reduction in poverty was least in the unskilled manual classes and the disparity in the rate of poverty experienced in comparison with other classes increased. Thus, in 1987 they displayed a poverty rate approximately five times that of the higher white collar class and one and a half times that of the skilled manual class, whereas by 1997 the comparable figures were over seven to one and just less than two to one. Similarly the gap between the skilled manual class and the higher white collar widens from just above three to one, to just less than four to one. Thus substantial absolute gains for working class groups are accompanied by polarisation in relative terms. The changes in risk levels are reflected in the changing composition of poor households. While in 1987 the non-manual classes constituted 16 per cent of poor households, by 1997 this had fallen to 9 per cent. For manual households there was consequently an increase in the proportion they constituted from 84 per cent to 90 per cent.[4] As the unskilled manual class decreased in size between 1987 and 1997, the increased proportion of poor manuals was mostly made up from the skilled manual class.

Figure 11.2: Class composition of the poor

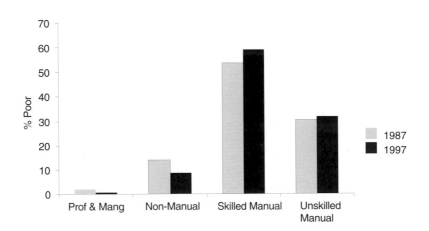

11.3 Cumulative disadvantage

To what extent does the polarisation we have just seen reflect the emergence of cumulatively disadvantaged groups of the kind discussed earlier? Do, as most people would expect, working class origins, low education and the absence of educational qualifications and unskilled manual work combine to create a distinctively disadvantaged group? While a *priori* this hypothesis appears eminently plausible, in practice we do not observe an increasing accumulation in the risk of poverty associated with each additional disadvantage. There are two reasons for this. Firstly, most of these characteristics are correlated and do not exert an additional effect of their own in any simple manner. For example, almost all heads of households currently in the working class have working class origins. Thus specifying the presence of both attributes simply succeeds in identifying the unskilled manual class as a whole. Secondly, the consequences of earlier variables are sometimes implicit in later statuses.

Figure 11.3: Risk of poverty: cumulative impact of class and education

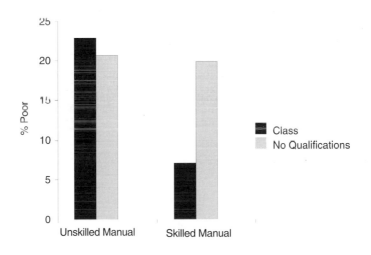

We illustrate this latter point in Figure 11.3 where we show the cumulative impact of current class position and the absence of educational qualifications for both the skilled and unskilled working classes. For the unskilled working class there is no significant difference in poverty rate between those with and without qualifications. If qualifications have not led to an exit from the unskilled manual class, no return is observed in terms of a lower poverty rate. In itself this says volumes about the nature of the occupations within this class, but the extent of overlap precludes the operation of cumulative processes. Among the skilled manual class, on the other hand, a quite different outcome is observed. Within this class variations in poverty rates are closely connected to the presence or absence of qualifications. The former is associated with a poverty rate of 7 per cent while in the latter case it soars to 20 per cent. It is clear then that if we are to pursue issues of cumulative disadvantage, it can be more fruitfully done among the working class as a whole where overlap between characteristics is more modest and greater variability in impact is observed.[5]

In Figure 11.4 we show the cumulative impact of manual class position, the absence of educational qualifications, long-term unemployment, being a local authority tenant and living in an urban centre.[6] As we have already seen being in the manual class is associated with a poverty risk of 14 per cent. This rises to 21 per cent for the sub-group with no educational qualifications and then climbs sharply for the sub-set who are long-term unemployed to 57 per cent.[7] A further increase is observed to 68 per cent of these who are also local authorities' tenants and are located in urban centres. An accumulation of disadvantages does therefore lead to a situation where certain groups are almost doomed to poverty. However, as is clear from Figure 11.4, as the magnitude of the poverty risk escalates the size of the group, and consequently the proportion of poor households that it constitutes, declines sharply. Thus the manual class constitutes nine out of ten poor households but this falls to one in two for the sub-group with no qualifications and to one in five for those also experiencing long-term unemployment.

Figure 11.4: Cumulative disadvantage among the manual working class

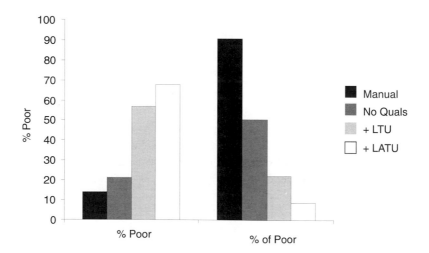

If we further specify urban local authority tenancy it falls to less than one in ten. Thus while we can identify sub-sets of cumulatively disadvantaged households, who experience strikingly high rates of poverty, they constitute a small, though important, minority of households. Poverty is spread fairly widely across the manual class. Households within this class that lack qualifications and are exposed to labour market marginalisation experience distinctively high rates of poverty. The unskilled manual group are most likely to experience such disadvantages but where they are encountered by the skilled manual class their consequences are no less severe, ensuring that poverty is by no means confined to the unskilled manual class.

It could be argued that processes which are not class based may have a significant impact on the risk of poverty and that by focusing on such factors we provide a distorted view of the causes of poverty. In particular we may miss the impact of life events that have particularly negative consequences for women such as lone parenthood and separation/divorce. Our analyses do show that the risk of poverty is particularly high for such groups. However, although the risk of poverty is high among lone parents, this follows the patterns already outlined in being much higher among lone parents without qualifications. Similarly, among the separated or divorced, the risk of poverty rises sharply for those from non-manual backgrounds. Thus even though we have difficulty assigning class positions to such households their destinies are clearly strongly shaped by class processes.

11.4 Concentration of poverty and the role of vicious circle processes[8]

As we can see from Figure 11.5, being a local authority tenant and, in particular holding such a tenancy in an urban centre, is associated with particularly high levels of poverty. In 1987, 48 per cent of local authority tenant households fell below the consistent poverty threshold compared to 14 per cent of other rural households. This constituted a ratio of 3.5:1. For urban households the corresponding figures were over 48 per cent and less than 8 per cent, giving a ratio of over of 6.4:1. In 1997 the comparable rural figures were just less than 34 per cent and over 6 per cent, resulting in a disparity ratio of 5.3:1. For urban respondents the 1997 figures were 47 per cent and almost 6 per cent leading to a disparity of 8.1:1. Thus for both types of tenants their relative level of disadvantage increased over time.

Figure 11.5: Risk of poverty by location and tenure

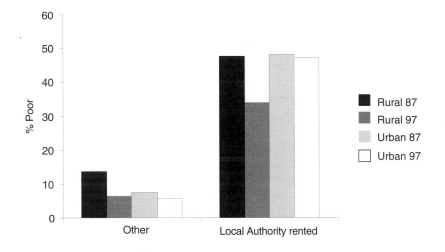

For the rural tenants this reflected the fact that the rate of decline in their level of poverty was proportionately less rapid than it was for other households. In the urban situation increased inequality was a consequence of the fact that the poverty rate remained stable for such tenants while it declined for other households.[9]

In order to develop our understanding of these effects, and the manner in which they have changed over time, in Figure 11.6 we set out for urban and rural households some of the key socio-economic disadvantages suffered by local authority tenants in 1987 and 1997. In 1987 both areas had in the region of six out of ten household heads lacking qualifications (NQ) and four out of ten of those active in the labour market were unemployed (U). Between 1987 and 1997 the number with no qualifications increased in rural areas to almost two out of three while in urban areas it declined to one in two. In both areas the number unemployed increased to one in two. Thus in terms of these characteristics urban local authority households were not disadvantaged in comparison with their rural counterparts. Where urban households differed from rural was that they had significantly higher numbers in full-time unpaid household duties (HD) and larger numbers of lone parents (LP). In rural areas in 1987 the respective figures were 12 per cent for the former and 5 per cent for the latter. In urban centres the corresponding figures were 13 per cent and 22 per cent.

Figure 11.6: Changing disadvantage profile of local authority tenants

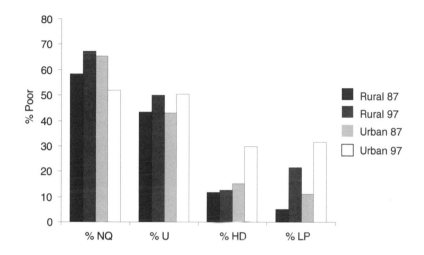

By 1997 these figures had increased to 15 per cent and 11 per cent in rural areas and to 30 per cent and 32 per cent in urban areas. These changes are not surprising given trends in housing policy over the period. As Fahey and Watson (1995:10) have stated, the pre-eminence of home ownership as an objective of social policy relegated social housing to a marginal position in the system: 'Schemes such as shared ownership, local authority house purchase loans and the provision of low-cost sites have the effect of increasing residualisation in the local authority rented sector since these schemes *cream off* the tier of housing applicants.'

The overall improvement in the economic situation between 1987 and 1997 ensured that the poverty rate for rural tenants declined and that for urban tenants remained stable during a period when their socio-economic profile deteriorated.

As we shall see, the fact that there is a greater disparity in poverty ratios between local authority tenants and other households in urban rather than rural areas is accounted for in large part by socio-demographic characteristics. However, an additional impact of urban tenure is observed even when we control for level of disadvantage. This finding might encourage interpretations in terms of additional contextual effects associated with location *per se*. Concern with the consequences of the spatial concentration of disadvantage has been reflected in the growth of an extensive literature on topics such as the 'urban ghetto', 'dependency culture' and most controversially the 'emerging underclass'. This concern is not confined to the USA, though the debate has a particular emphasis and flavour there. Kleinman (1998) notes the extent to which imagery of an 'urban underclass' that is 'shut out' or 'cut off' from society has also become common in Britain. However, two factors are crucial to understanding the manner in which this process operates. First, as Nolan, Whelan and Williams (1998) and Fahey and Williams in this volume have shown, poverty is not spatially concentrated to any great extent in Ireland.[10] Most poor people do not live in areas with very high poverty rates. In addition local authority tenant housing is fairly equally distributed between urban centres and more rural locations. Finally the processes of marginalisation that we have observed, in terms of detachment from the labour market, are equally evident among rural and urban tenants.

However, the residual or additional effect of urban local authority tenure does leave open the question of the extent to which such locations are associated with contextual and sub-cultural effects that make it more difficult to escape from poverty. The most fruitful development of such an approach is by Wilson (1987,1991) who notes that the term 'underclass' was actually coined by Mrydal to describe those who had been driven to extreme economic marginality because of changes in 'post-industrial society'. Such an interpretation focuses on the unintended consequences of economic change. Wilson's central propositions are as follows.[11]

- Economic change leads to a demand for different forms of labour and is associated with significant institutional change in labour market arrangements. These changes have a disproportionate effect on particular groups.
- The major changes involve a weakening of attachment to the labour market among such groups, with a dramatic decline in the proportion of stable, reasonably paid jobs.
- These effects are aggravated by outward migration.

The effects of economic change are compounded by social isolation. Joblessness, particularly of a prolonged nature, leads to increased levels of fatalism. People come to seriously doubt that they can accomplish what is expected of them, whether because of their damaged self-image or their perception of environmental constraints. It is also anticipated that this orientation is reinforced by the feelings and values of others operating in the same social context leading to 'lower collective efficacy'.[12]

What is crucial in this framework is the combination of labour force detachment and social isolation. Unlike 'culture of poverty' type explanations this form of interpretation sees behaviour and orientations as being in the first place a consequence of factors such as poverty and unemployment. Only subsequently do the latter play an independent causal role as vicious circle processes emerge. For urban local authority housing to play a crucial role in the process of cumulative disadvantage it must be established that the observed effects of urban local authority tenancy are mediated by the consequences of social isolation such as a reduction in perceived self-efficacy or detachment from mainstream values.

- It must have either an independent influence on labour market marginalisation, or interact significantly with it, so that marginalisation produces more severe poverty risks; or
- It must have an effect independent of labour market marginalisation which produces high poverty rates; and
- The evidence must be consistent with interpreting these as genuine contextual effects rather than as an outcome of selective movement of households with different characteristics into and out of such housing.

In attempting to provide an empirical assessment of the possible impact of 'vicious circle' processes associated with social milieu in our earlier work, we proceeded to develop a set of measures intended to reflect the processes through which such effects operate. The theoretical perspective that we have outlined would lead us to expect that residing in a rented urban local authority household could have an impact on labour market disadvantage and poverty through:

- *Perceptions of environmental constraints:* particularly of lack of employment opportunities in the area; may affect behaviour and coping capacity
- *High levels of fatalism:* may be exacerbated by perceptions of prevailing norms and values in the immediate environment
- *Increased detachment from dominant societal values:* may arise from the erosion of neighbourhood resources and the scarcity of appropriate role models.

In an attempt to tap these attributes we drew on a range of measures in the LIPS survey. Since our interest is in the determinants of labour market marginalisation, we concentrated our attention on households where the head of household is less than sixty-five. The first measure we employed was a set of items that measure the respondents' degree of fatalism that has been fairly widely used in the research literature. This included items such as 'I often feel helpless in dealing with the problems of my life', 'I have little control over the things that happen to me' and 'what happens in the future depends on me'. In addition we drew on a range of questions dealing with perceived problems in the neighbourhood. The first assessed the extent to which absence of paid work was perceived to be a very general problem in the area in which they lived. They were asked to assess the proportion of people wanting paid employment who were actually in work. It was not necessary to assume that such perceptions conform perfectly to reality, since it is precisely the degree of perceived constraint that is of interest to us. A further set of questions was intended to provide indicators of detachment from dominant values in the area. Here we made use of a set of questions relating to perceptions of problems loosely associated with disorder such as crime, vandalism, drunkenness, graffiti and rubbish. Respondents were asked how common each of these was in the neighbourhood.

In Figures 11.7 and 11.8 we provide a summary of the outcomes on these indicators, providing in each case a comparison of local authority urban tenants (LATU) and other urban respondents (OU). Figure 11.7 shows that in each case local authority tenants display levels of fatalism that are close to twice that of their urban counterparts. Somewhere between 50-60 per cent of such household heads are likely to feel that they have little control over their lives, to feel helpless in dealing with problems, to feel there is not a lot that they can do to change their lives and that there is no way they can solve their problems. Figure 11.8 demonstrates how a whole range of community problems are between two to four times more common in such neighbourhoods than in other urban areas. Thus almost seven out of ten local authority tenants think that less than half of those wanting employment in their area have access to it compared to one in six in other urban areas. Similarly, approximately one in two consider graffiti, rubbish and litter and vandalism to be problems in these areas compared to between one in four and one in six of other urban households. Four out of ten think public drunkenness is a problem; a rate that is over three times higher than for other urban residents. Finally four out of ten also consider crime to be a problem compared to one out of six of those in other types of tenure.

Figure 11.7: Fatalism levels for urban respondents

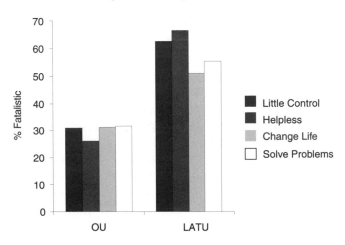

Figure 11.8: Neighbourhood problems in urban areas

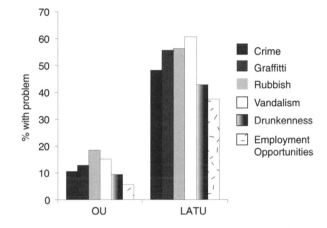

The distinctively high levels of poverty observed for local authority urban tenants, compared to other urban households, cannot be entirely accounted for by controlling for differences in socio-demographic profile. It is this independent or residual effect that must be interpreted if we are to assess the possible role of vicious circle processes. The distinctive levels of fatalism and perceived neighbourhood problems in such areas are entirely consistent with such a possibility. In order to examine whether that possibility is translated into reality we make use of a statistic known as an odds ratio, which has already been employed in our earlier analysis of social mobility. The notion of an odds is very familiar to all gamblers. Suppose 20 per cent of the population are poor. Instead of saying that the probability of being poor is 0.2 and of not being poor is 0.8, we can say that the odds on being poor is 0:25 (that is, 0.2/0.8) and the odds on being non-poor is 4:1 (0.8/0.2). In our present example, we can then take into account the disparities between local authority urban tenants and other urban residents not only in their likelihood of being poor, but also in their likelihood of being non-poor. If we transform poverty rates into an odds ratio summarising the extent to which local authority urban dwellers are poor rather than non-poor compared to other urban dwellers we obtain an odds ratio of 19:1.[13] The question is, does this large risk of poverty remain once we have controlled for other individual and household socio-demographic characteristics that may explain the effect? Figure 11.9 gives the results of just such an analysis and shows that the 'odds' of local authority tenants being poor is much reduced, down to 5.5:1. This constitutes a reduction of over 70 per cent in the effect and demonstrates that the major part of the poverty differential is explained by these other characteristics.

Nonetheless, we still have a residual effect that equals about 30 per cent of the original effect that, in principle, might be interpreted as being due to contextual, or 'vicious circle' processes. If so, then we would expect to observe a substantial reduction in this residual effect when we control for perception of 'problems' in the neighbourhood (vandalism, drunkenness, etc), levels of unemployment and their own level of fatalism contributing substantially to the explanation of levels of poverty.

The results of just such an analysis are presented in Figure 11.9. This shows that the net effect of urban local authority tenancy on the risk of poverty is again reduced by the inclusion of these variables to an odds of around 3.5:1. The reduction is equal to around 10 per cent of the original effect. A further 18 per cent of the original effect remains unexplained. In other words two-thirds of the effect unaccounted for by the socio-demographic variables remains unexplained. This final residual is most plausibly interpreted in terms of the impact of unmeasured variables that are associated both with poverty and selection into urban rented local authority housing. One third is accounted for by the additional variables we have included in our attempt to capture the possible operation of underclass processes.

If we compare these results with those we have reported earlier using the 1994 wave of the LIPS we find the following pattern. The overall impact of being a local authority tenant in an urban centre increases, with the odds ratio going from 15:1 to 19:1. This occurs in the context of a decline in the size of the urban rented public sector. Our surveys covering this period show a decrease from 15 per cent in 1987 to 11.6 per cent in 1994 and finally to 9.9 per cent. We might expect such a decline to be associated with a process of residualisation resulting in a sharper contrast on a range of poverty-related characteristics between such tenants and others. However, in rural areas a similar decline occurred without any corresponding increase in the degree of inequality. In both 1994 and 1997 the socio-demographic variables accounted for just over 70 per cent of the gross urban local authority tenant effect. The set of variables intended to capture potential underclass 'effects' accounted for 6 per cent of the original effect in 1994 and 10 per cent in 1997. There was a corresponding fall in the scale of the final residual effect from 23 per cent to 19 per cent.

Thus in the context of an overall increasing disparity between public sector tenants and all urban residents and a continued contraction of this sector we do see evidence that is consistent with the emergence of 'vicious circle processes'. However, the scale of the change is modest and care must be exercised in interpreting the results. One additional piece of evidence that is relevant to such interpretation is that perception of neighbourhood problems has no role in mediating the effect. This is the variable that we might expect to most strongly tap the role of alternative value systems. Its failure to achieve significance makes such interpretations less plausible. The variables that are highly significant are fatalism and perception of neighbourhood. The possibility remains that, rather than such variables having a causal impact, respondents are selected into urban rented public sector housing on the basis of characteristics that lead them to have more pessimistic views about their environment both local and general and to have a higher risk of poverty.

However, the evidence is consistent with the argument that increased affluence and reduced rates of poverty have gone alongside the emergence of additional advantages. These go beyond those arising from their socio-demographic characteristics. Such effects would impact on only a small minority of poor households. They are also modest when compared to the impact of factors such as social class, education, unemployment, separation/ divorce and parenthood. They are indeed only about half the size of those associated with other unmeasured characteristics that lead households to be selected into local authority tenure. However, it should clearly be an objective of social policy that groups that are already suffering multiple disadvantages should not be exposed to a further exacerbation of their situation. To the extent that community or neighbourhood interventions can address such issues they are clearly to be encouraged. We must acknowledge that the evidence is not conclusive and the issue will probably be only finally settled by the availability of panel data, which allows us to entangle the causal sequence.

Figure 11.9: Gross and net effects of local authority tenancy on poverty

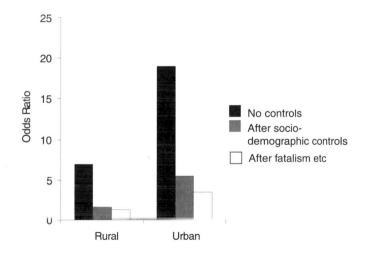

11.5 Conclusions

The central concern of this chapter was the extent to which vicious circle processes, or contextual effects of a particular kind, apply in the Irish situation. Could it be that despite unprecedented levels of growth we are seeing the emergence of new forms of poverty, which involve even greater detachment from the mainstream? We distinguished between two different but related conceptions of cumulative disadvantage. The first relates to the accumulation of disadvantage over time, and the second relates to the notion that geographical concentration of disadvantage generates vicious circle processes whereby existing individual or household disadvantages are reinforced by neighbourhood effects. Establishing the role played by these processes is of major importance from a policy perspective. If they are seen to be central, attention may be directed to the manner in which 'problem' groups emerge, the transmission of disadvantage across generations, the emergence of alternative value systems, the spatial concentration of deprivation and the need for interventions which break the vicious circle of poverty. In that context, policies relating to the disadvantage experienced by broad class groups in relation to access to education and unemployment and the operation of the taxation and transfer system may come to receive less attention.

In exploring whether cumulative disadvantage increased in significance over time, we examined whether persisting effects of working class origins and educational disadvantage combined with current membership of the unskilled working class to produce such a group. We found that these disadvantages are so common among unskilled working class households that very little extra information about their poverty risk was afforded by knowing whether or not the household head possessed a qualification or was from a working class background. It was in the middle range of the class structure that a good education, in particular, was seen to significantly reduce the risk of poverty. We then proceeded to look at the consequences of accumulated disadvantage in the labour market including being in a manual class, having no qualifications, being long-term unemployed, and being a local authority tenant in an urban centre. Rates of poverty are seen to escalate as disadvantages accumulate but there is a corresponding decline in the proportion of poor households being accounted for. The risk of being exposed to poverty is spread across the manual class rather than being concentrated in a subset of multiply deprived households. The disadvantages associated with having a head of household in full-time unpaid home-duties and, in particular, being a lone parent are not reducible to class related factors. However, such households are disproportionately drawn from disadvantaged backgrounds in terms of both class origin and level of education and the risk of poverty associated with either status is influenced to a significant degree by such prior disadvantage.

The form of coincidence of economic marginality and social isolation receiving most attention is that arising from concentrated pockets of urban deprivation. Rising levels of urban deprivation and a perception that poverty has both become more concentrated in such areas and taken on a qualitatively different form have provoked a variety of popular and academic responses. Drawing on Wilson's (1987, 1991) work, the potentially most fruitful hypotheses focus on the unintended consequences of social change: a combination of weak labour force attachment and social isolation are perceived to lead to behaviour and orientations which contribute to a vicious circle of deprivation. We know from previous work that poverty in Ireland is not heavily concentrated in urban 'black-spots', so any explanation focusing on households in those areas can apply to only a minority of the poor. However, evidence of the emergence of 'underclass processes' could still have considerable significance in terms of policy. The most plausible location of an Irish 'underclass' is in public sector rented households in major urban centres.

Our approach to establishing the relevance of the 'vicious circle' framework to such households does not involve a direct attempt to measure the impact of living in specific spatial units. Instead, on the basis of our understanding of the relevant theoretical framework, we attempt to measure directly the factors which are hypothesised to underlie the process. These include levels of fatalism, neighbourhood problems that are seen to reflect deviation from mainstream norms, and neighbourhood employment opportunities. Our analysis showed that urban local authority tenant households did have high levels of fatalism and neighbourhood problems and fewer employment opportunities than others. Strikingly, the objective patterns of disadvantage associated with public sector tenure – in terms of social class, education, labour market disadvantage and single parenthood – are remarkably similar in urban and rural locations. In particular there is no evidence, when we control for other factors, that the risk of unemployment is higher for local authority household heads in urban centres. Where there is some difference is in frequency of heads of households being in full-time home duties and being lone parents.

Urban local authority households are distinctive in terms of their high level of poverty. If 'underclass' type processes were contributing significantly to such disadvantage, one would expect the introduction of variables measuring levels of fatalism and perceptions of neighbourhood employment opportunities and other problems to substantially contribute to predicting this group's poverty risk. Their introduction does produce a modest further reduction in the unexplained residual disadvantage over and above that accounted for by socio-demographic factors. Their role seems to be somewhat greater than that observed in the past. The results are consistent with an increased tendency towards the emergence of vicious-circle processes in the context of the contraction of the urban local authority sector and widening inequalities between such tenants and other urban residents. Any such tendency is obviously a matter of serious policy concern. However, in interpreting this finding we must keep in mind that the effect remains modest in relation to the role of other factors. It should certainly be a priority, however, to provide a more definitive answer to this question as appropriate panel data become available.

The relatively modest role of neighbourhood effects may come as a surprise to many, but it is entirely consistent with a recent review of the evidence by Friedrichs (1998). In the first place he notes the dangers of generalising from US experience, pointing to Wacquant's (1993) conclusion, based on a comparative study of a Chicago and a peripheral Paris neighbourhood, that there is no European counterpart to the Afro-American experience of long-term negative discrimination and restriction of opportunity. Glennerster et al (1999:5-6) also note that the high concentration of poverty in the United States is restricted to blacks and Hispanics and that consequently reading across from US experience can be misleading. Even in the United States conclusions regarding neighbourhood effects have been hedged by a variety of caveats relating to, among other things, difficulty in identifying the appropriate spatial unit, in specifying intervening mechanisms, and guarding against the role of selection into neighbourhoods on factors associated with the outcome of interest (Jargowsky, 1996, Brooks-Gunn et al, 1997)

As Portes (2000:5) notes there is a long tradition in the US of characterising poor inner-city areas as places of social disorganisation and attributing the problems of such areas to the personal and social shortcomings of their inhabitants. This he notes has led to the search for the 'missing element' in impoverished areas with the latest candidate being the alleged absence of 'social capital' that is a collective spirit and solidarity. Recent studies he notes have found that the problem in poor areas 'is not that people do not know each other or help each other, but that the resources to do so are meagre and the social ties so insulated as to yield meagre returns'.

In evaluating the European evidence that is available, Friedrichs (1998) cautions that it is also necessary to take into account that many of the most frequently cited sources are descriptive and small-scale studies which are highly selective since only neighbourhoods with high poverty rates are sampled. Taking into account such caveats, he concludes that the available evidence suggests there is substantial differentiation within poor neighbourhoods. A number of studies identifying contrasting groups, the first of which manage their lives according to mainstream norms and the other which is more marginalised, suggest that the former group actively avoid contact with the latter (Paugam, 1991). Such an outcome, Friedrichs notes, would inhibit any automatic diffusion of values within a neighbourhood. Dominance of deviant norms he suggests occurs only via selective population exchange. His most general conclusion is as follows: 'The general evidence presented on neighbourhood effects indicates low or negligible effects; most context effects can be explained by either individual or institutional effects.' (Friedrichs, 1998:93)[14] Poor neighbourhoods, he concludes, substantially aggravate the risk of poverty only where residents have their action spaces and their social networks restricted to the neighbourhood. The recent study of social housing in Ireland by Fahey, ed., (1999) reaches similar conclusions regarding the heterogeneity of neighbourhood.

The implication of these findings for strategies of spatial or community intervention is that a case can be made that the distinctive profile of urban local authority tenants provides a rationale for correspondingly tailored forms of intervention with an emphasis on empowerment.[15] However, in assessing the nature of the interventions required, it is necessary to remember that there is only weak evidence to suggest that the distinctive nature of the environment in which public sector tenants live has any independent influence on their risk of poverty or their psychological state.

Our findings point to the limitations of specific policies which, however valuable in themselves, cannot realistically be expected to have a substantial impact on the overall numbers in poverty. It becomes clear that policies targeting very specific groups or areas do not in themselves constitute a credible national anti-poverty strategy. This is particularly important given the recent emphasis in both Ireland and the UK on area-based policies to tackle 'social exclusion' by targeting the 'worst estates' Whatever about the merits of the proposed policies and the way target areas are selected, the fact that most poor people do not live in such estates means that this will not on its own have a major impact on the global poverty target. It becomes impossible to ignore the big, expensive issues – above all what happens to unemployment and the up-rating of social security benefits.

NOTES

1 See Kleinman (1998:67).

2 This scheme is an aggregated version of the seven class schema employed by Erikson and Goldthorpe (1992). The skilled working class constitutes a rather large group of households but we could find no significant differentiation in terms of poverty rates between classes in the group.

3 Throughout this analysis we use the social class of the head of household. Alternative approaches using the household reference person or what has been described as the

dominance approach would lead to broadly similar approaches. All of these approaches recognise that members of a household share a joint fate.

4 These figures are based on all households where we could establish a class position.

5 For more detailed discussion of these issues see Nolan and Whelan (1999).

6 Urban centre is defined as being resident in Dublin, Cork, Galway, Limerick or Waterford.

7 Long-term unemployment is defined as being unemployed for over a year. Most of the unemployed who are also unskilled and lack qualifications are long-term unemployed.

8 For a more detailed discussion of the issues covered in this section and an elaboration of the technical issues see Nolan and Whelan (1996 and 2000) and Whelan (1996).

9 This picture of stability for urban tenants is somewhat deceptive. In fact their poverty rate rose rapidly between 1987 and 1994 and then declined sharply between 1994 and 1997.

10 Fahey and Williams provide a detailed treatment of the issue of geographical concentration of disadvantage and deprivation in chapter 12 of this volume.

11 See Petersen (1991).

12 See Bandura (1982).

13 This figure differs from that deriving from the results reported in Figure 11.5 because it is based on the coefficients in the multivariate logistic regression rather than the cross-tabulation.

14 A range of other arguments can also be made regarding the value of area based interventions. See the concluding chapter of Nolan and Whelan (1999).

12

The Spatial Distribution of Disadvantage in Ireland

TONY FAHEY AND JAMES WILLIAMS

12.1 Introduction

Much of the debate about the impact of economic restructuring, industrial modernisation and infrastructural development in Ireland has a strong spatial dimension. The concern is that the effects of socio-economic change vary not only by social group but also by place. In popular discourse in Ireland, certain places (often quite vaguely defined) are often said to have fared badly, such as 'the west', 'remote rural areas', or 'poverty black-spots' in the cities, while others, such as 'the east', 'the Dublin area', or cities generally, are sometimes said to have done better. Concerns of this kind are nothing new. The 'congested districts' in the western half of the country were already a subject of public debate and state intervention in the late nineteenth century, while the slums of Dublin and other Irish towns and cities had become infamous by the early decades of the twentieth century.

It is not our intention here to review the long history of these spatial patterns. Rather, our concern is to examine spatial inequalities in the distribution of social disadvantage over the very recent period – the ten years from the mid-1980s to the mid-1990s. The latter part of this period witnessed the onset of the present economic boom. It thus gives an opportunity to consider how rapid economic growth has affected patterns of spatial inequality. Research on poverty in Ireland in the depression years of the late 1980s and early 1990s had shown that poverty was spatially pervasive. This body of work showed that the poor were not concentrated in urban areas nor in 'backward' rural areas but were found virtually everywhere in the country. Some regions were poorer than others but many of the households which were poor lived *outside* the worst-off regions (Nolan, Whelan and Williams,1998; Jackson and Haase, 1996; SAHRU, 1997).

The pattern in urban areas is of particular interest in this regard, since much recent international research has suggested that social polarisation in western cities has increased during the recession of the 1980s and the weakening of welfare states (OECD, 1996). There is some evidence in Ireland that socio-spatial segregation is more pronounced in urban areas than it is elsewhere in the country (Nolan, Whelan and Williams, 1998; McKeown, 1991). The urban poor may not be wholly segregated into deprived areas, and those who are may form only a minority of the poor in the country as a whole, yet the spatial dimension of disadvantage in urban areas appears quite strong.

The issue does not end there, however, since the chapter by Nolan, Whelan and Layte in this volume raises uncertainties about the precise significance of urban social segregation. They question whether the poor who live in deprived urban neighbourhoods are any worse off on key dimensions of life than similar house-holds that live in the countryside or in better-off urban areas. They argue, in short, that the characteristics of households and their members are the main predictors of risk in this regard and neighbourhood seems at most to have only a small additional impact (see also Nolan and Whelan, 1999). This argument is in keeping with a substantial body of international quantitative research on neighbourhood effects on poverty and life-chances. As one review of American research on the impact of neighbourhood deprivation put it, 'a sceptical reader might easily conclude on the basis of available research that neighbourhoods matter rather little, if they matter at all' (Furstenberg and Hughes 1997: 346; see also Friedrichs, 1998 for a similar conclusion). This 'non-effect' of neighbourhood disadvantage raises the somewhat puzzling possibility that urban social segregation may not be nearly as great a social evil as is often thought, since it does not seem to have significant negative consequences for the lives of those who live in deprived areas.

The purpose of this chapter is to explore these issues. It first examines national spatial inequalities at a number of different spatial levels – the regions, counties, rural/urban districts and district electoral divisions (DEDs). This analysis examines both the extent of spatial inequality and the degree of change which is evident in the period from the mid-1980s to the mid-1990s. The chapter then looks in more detail at spatial inequalities in Dublin city and county based on quantitative analysis and mapping of census data for the area (both for 1986 and 1996). That is followed by a brief review of some qualitative evidence about the nature and significance of neighbourhood processes in disadvantaged urban areas. It attempts to explores how the apparent non-effect of neighbourhood quality on residents' lives as revealed by Irish and international research might be understood. The final section summarises the main points of the chapter.

12.2 Poverty – regional patterns

Risk of poverty by planning region

Table 12.1 presents details on the risk of poverty by planning region in both 1987 and 1997 based on the Living in Ireland Survey data. Two lines are presented, namely the 60 per cent relative income line and the 60 per cent line combined with basic deprivation indicators.[1]

Table 12.1: Risk of poverty by planning region, 1987 and 1997

	60% Income Line		60% Income Line & Basic Deprivation	
	1987	1997	1987	1997
	Per cent in poverty			
East	19.3	31.6	13.6	8.9
South-West	31.0	34.4	16.3	11.1
South-East	33.3	47.9	16.9	13.4
North-East	35.7	51.1	20.6	14.0
Mid-West	32.9	36.3	19.7	7.3
Midlands	41.1	38.6	19.7	9.1
West	31.0	36.3	13.8	4.8
North West and Donegal	42.6	44.0	22.9	11.5
Total	29.0	36.7	16.4	9.8

The picture of regional inequality emerging from these data varies somewhat by year and indicator and shows no strong consistent trend in any direction. According to the 60 per cent relative income line, there was a slight narrowing in the risk of poverty across regions, mainly because the gap between the East and the rest of the country narrowed over the period. The East region had by far the lowest risk of poverty in 1987 but its risk level had risen much closer to the national average by 1997. In 1987, the North-West and Donegal was the most impoverished region according to both indicators in Table 12.1, but by 1997 it had been overtaken by the North-East. Between 1987 and 1997, all regions showed an increase in the risk of poverty as measured by income alone. This indicates that economic growth had the effect of widening income inequalities within regions over that period, even though, as already noted, there was a certain measure of convergence in poverty risk between regions.

The 60 per cent income line plus basic deprivation measure combines elements of relative and absolute poverty into a single indicator. The inclusion of an absolute poverty element has the consequence that the indicator shows quite different trends than the relative income measure alone. First, all regions experienced a fall rather than a rise in risk levels, indicating a general decline in absolute poverty (or, in other words, a general rise in absolute living standards). Some of these falls were quite large (more than half in the case of the North West & Donegal, the West, the Midlands, and Mid-West regions), while others were much lower (as low as one-fifth in the case of the South-East). Furthermore, the combined line showed no indication of convergence in risk levels between regions – if anything, there was a higher degree of regional differentiation in 1997 as compared with the situation 10 years earlier, though the shifts in this direction were not large.

Incidence of poverty by planning region

Where risk of poverty by region refers to the proportion of the population in each region who are poor, the *incidence* of poverty by region refers to the proportion of the poor who are found in each region. Figures 1 and 2 present comparative distributions of the poverty population and all households by region for 1987 and 1997, using the combined 60 per cent income line plus basic deprivation.

These graphs show the heavy, and rising, incidence of poverty in the East region and a fall in incidence in the Mid-West, West and North-West & Donegal. The East region accounted for almost 30 per cent of the poor in 1987 and 36 per cent in 1997. However, the East accounted for 36 per cent of households in 1987 and 40 per cent in 1997 so that the proportions of poor in the region, though large, amount to an 'under-representation': they are below what one would expect from the distribution of households alone. Poverty is under-represented in the same sense in the Mid-West, Midlands, and West regions, while it is somewhat over-represented in the North-East, Mid-West, Midlands, North-West & Donegal and (marginally) the South-East.

In summary, therefore, there would appear to have been some shifts in both the risk and incidence of poverty over the period 1987 to 1997. In line with national trends, all regions have shown an increase in the risk of poverty measured on the basis of income alone (with the exception of the Midlands area), indicating a general rise in income inequality over the period. However, a convergence of the East region towards the average income-poverty risk level for the country as a whole had the effect of slightly narrowing income inequalities *between regions*. The combined income and deprivation indicator showed the opposite trends – a sharp overall decline in risk levels (indicating a fall in absolute poverty) coupled with a barely detectable widening in risk levels between regions. One-third of the poor are found in the East region, but since that region accounts for a slightly higher proportion of all households it actually has a slight under-representation of the poverty population (though that under-representation decreased in the period 1987-97).

Many other regions had an over-representation of the poverty population. In some of these – the South-West, South-East and North-East – over-representation increased over the years 1987-97, while in others – the Mid-

West, Midlands, West and North West & Donegal – it was substantially reduced or reversed over the period. Notwithstanding the minutiae of these distributions and trends over time, the overall picture to emerge from these data is one which suggests that poverty is experienced in all parts of the country in both years with some trends to suggest a moderate equalisation of its risk and incidence across the regions over the period 1987-97.

Figure 12.1: Distribution of households in poverty (60 per cent line plus basic deprivation) and all households, 1987

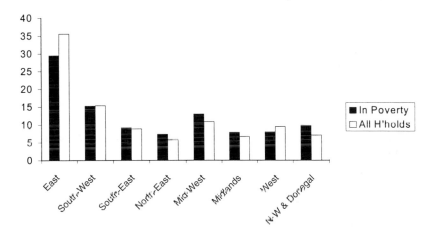

Figure 12.2: Distribution of households in poverty (60 per cent line plus basic deprivation) and all households, 1997

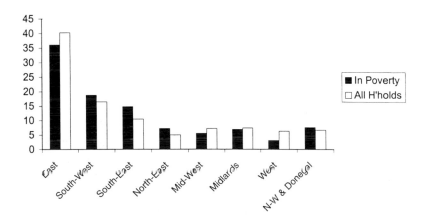

12.3 The national distribution of unemployment

To consider spatial variations in poverty or disadvantage below the level of the region, one must look to another data source, the Small Area Populations Statistics (SAPS) based on the Census of Population. The most recent Census data relate to 1996. Census data constitute the most geographically disaggregated and comprehensive information on national socio-demographic patterns, though they contain no information on income. Given constraints of space, we will focus here on only one indicator of disadvantage – unemployment. A great deal of research in Ireland has shown that unemployment is perhaps the single most important cause of poverty and disadvantage.[2] There is thus some justification in treating spatial variation in unemployment as a proxy indicator for spatial patterns of disadvantage more generally.

The smallest area unit for which SAPS data are available is the District Electoral Division (DED) of which there is a total of just over 3,400 in the country. Here we make some use of data at the DED level, but for mapping purposes the DEDs are aggregated into 159 rural/urban districts (which we will refer to here as rural districts).[3]

The geographical distribution of unemployment rates at the rural district level in 1986 and 1996 is presented in Maps 12.1 and 12.2 respectively. Two caveats are needed in reading these maps. The first is that they do not capture the full picture of spatial inequalities in unemployment risk since they fail to reflect the strong spatial differentiation in unemployment rates which is found in Dublin and other cities. As we will see below in connection with Dublin, spatial inequalities within Irish cities are quite sharp, but these are washed out in the aggregations up to district level used in the present maps. This is an important qualification since large numbers of unemployed and many instances of locally high unemployment rates are found in urban areas – and it for this reason that the situation in Dublin is examined separately below.

The second caveat concerns the low unemployment rates found in some rural areas, as reflected for example in the light shadings for many midland districts (particularly along the Shannon basin) in Maps 12.1 and 12.2. It is notable also that county Roscommon, which is largely rural and quite underdeveloped, had the lowest county-level unemployment rates in the country in 1996 (at 9.6 per cent, compared to a national average of 17.9 per cent). In these instances, unemployment rates are likely to be less effective as indicators of spatial disadvantage than elsewhere, largely because of the high incidence of small farming (and probably high levels of outward migration) in the areas in question. In other words, relatively low unemployment in these areas may mask high levels of underemployment in small farming coupled with weak demand for labour as reflected in high outward migration.

Despite these limitations, the maps provide a useful general indication of the geographical spread of unemployment risk. They show a wide variation in unemployment rates across the 159 districts, running (in 1996) from a low of 6 per cent to a high of 35 per cent. In general, in both 1996 and 1986, high levels of unemployment are found scattered along the west coast – in parts of Donegal, north and west Mayo, west Galway, north and south-west Kerry – and also, more surprisingly, in a long tract through the South-East and into the midlands – in parts of Wicklow, Wexford, Waterford, Kilkenny, Kildare and Offaly. Although many western rural districts have high unemployment rates, they generally have small populations and account for only small proportions of the unemployed (all of Mayo, for example, accounted for only 3.1 per cent of the unemployed in 1996). Dublin City and county, by contrast, accounted for 33.1 per cent of the unemployed in 1996 (compared to just under 30 per cent of the population aged 15 and over).

Map 12.1: National unemployment rates in 1986

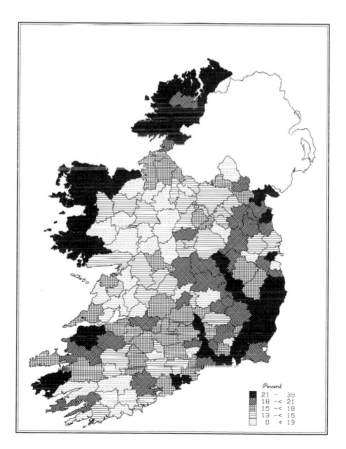

Map 12.2: National unemployment rates in 1996

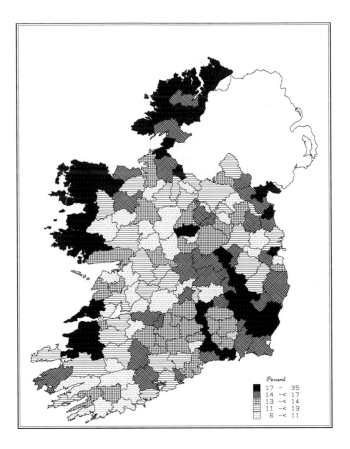

The most significant aspects of these maps is, first, that high rates of unemployment are widely dispersed throughout the country rather than being restricted to any particular region. Thus, for example, there is no east-west gradient in the distribution of high unemployment rates. Secondly, it is clear from the maps that the spatial structure of unemployment has remained largely unchanged over the decade 1986-96 despite the very substantial changes which took place in the macroeconomy over the latter part of the period.

Concentration of unemployment by DED

In addition to visual representation through mapping, we can also explore the degree of concentration of unemployment within quite small areas by examining unemployment rates at the level of District Electoral Divisions

(DEDs). Here we do so by grouping the DEDs into deciles on the basis of their unemployment rates, that is, by grouping together the one-tenth of DEDs with the highest unemployment rates, the next tenth and so on. We then consider the percentage of the unemployed who are contained within each of the deciles and compare that with the percentage of persons aged 15 years and over who are in the same areas. The DEDs contained in any decile of unemployment rates are not necessarily contiguous, so this analysis cannot be used to identify larger spatial clusters of high unemployment. It does, however, indicate the degree to which high unemployment is concentrated within smaller areas.

The results are outlined in Figure 12.3. This figure presents a comparison for 1986 and 1996 of the unemployed with the population aged 15 years and over who are located in the 30 per cent of District Electoral Divisions which have the highest unemployment rates. In 1986 a total of 56.5 per cent of the unemployed fell into the relevant group of high unemployment deciles while a total of 38.4 per cent of all persons aged 15 years and over were located in the same group of DEDs. By 1996 the comparable figures were, respectively, 59.5 per cent of the unemployed and 38.6 per cent of the population aged 15 years and over.

Figure 12.3: Comparison of national distribution of the unemployed and the total population aged 15 years and over in the top three unemployment deciles at the DED level

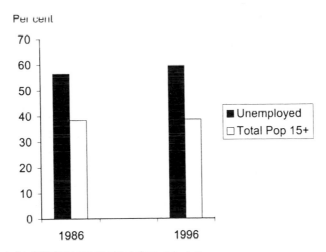

This analysis highlights two main points. First, there is some over-concentration of the unemployed in the 30 per cent of DEDs with the worst unemployment rates. In 1996, there are 1.5 times more unemployed in the three deciles with the highest unemployment rates than there ought to be on the basis of population share. As one moves to the fourth highest and subsequent deciles in both 1986 and 1996, however, the level of over-concentration falls off substantially. For example, the fourth highest decile in 1996 (not shown here) contains 8.2 per cent of the unemployed and 8.6 per cent of persons aged 15 years and over. Secondly, there was relatively little change in the decile distribution of the unemployed over the decade 1986 to 1996. For example, in 1986 the worst-off decile accounted for 28.5 per cent of the unemployed, compared to 27.9 per cent in 1996.

The spatial stability in the distribution of unemployment over the period in question is also shown by the correlation coefficient of 0.96 between the absolute numbers of unemployed at the DED level between 1986 and 1996. The corresponding figure for unemployment rates is 0.78.[4] These are extremely high correlations and indicate a very strong relationship in the spatial structure of unemployment over the decade in question.

12.4 Spatial inequalities in Dublin

The suggestion in international research that the trend towards socio-spatial segregation in western cities is intensifying is hard to sustain in Dublin. Dublin has been a spatially divided city at least since the nineteenth century and its level of polarisation in the past has often been extreme (Daly, 1984; Bannon et al, 1981). Its slums were extensive by the early decades of the twentieth century and were widely viewed as one of the greatest social evils afflicting the city. Slum clearance programmes which began in the 1930s dramatically improved the housing conditions of the poor but did little to reduce spatial segregation. Former slum dwellers were re-housed *in situ* or, in later decades, were moved to large new local authority housing areas on the landward side of the city to the south-west and north-west.

Quantitative analysis and mapping of spatial differentiation in Dublin in the 1970s confirmed a picture of marked segregation.[5] This work identified a central corridor of disadvantage running westwards from the docks along both banks of the Liffey. That corridor divided in two at the Phoenix Park, with one peninsula of disadvantage running northwest above the Park with the other belt running southwest below the Park. The coastal belts to the northeast and southeast of the port along with a fairly large hinterland inland from those coastal belts contain the main concentrations of higher class households.

Unemployment data for Dublin in 1996 shows that the range of employment rates over the 322 wards in the Dublin City & County was extremely wide, running from a low of 3.4 per cent to a high of 59.0 per cent. These are massive differentials and indicate that spatial inequalities within Dublin on its own were as great as any within Ireland as a whole. Wards with very high unemployment rates in 1996 included Mountjoy A (59.0 per cent unemployment rate), Cherry Orchard C (52.9

per cent), Priorswood C (51.2 per cent) and Tallaght-Fettercairn (47.9 per cent). At the other end of the spectrum, wards with unemployment rates in the region of 3–4 per cent included Firhouse-Ballycullen; Blackrock-Glenomena; Churchtown-Landscape; Foxrock-Beechpark; and Clonskeagh-Roebuck.

The diversity and geographical spread of unemployment rates in Dublin is shown in Maps 12.3 and 12.4.[6] Map 12.4 shows that in 1996 there was a central corridor of wards with high unemployment running north and south of the quays and extending outwards to the south and west through parts of Kilmainham, Crumlin and Drimnagh, stretching into Inchicore, Ballyfermot and Cherry Orchard. In addition, there is an outer ring of high unemployment wards encompassing Finglas, Ballymun and Darndale to the north of the city, Blachardstown – in particular Coolmine, Corduff, Mulhuddart and Blakestown – to the north-west, and Clondalkin and Tallaght (especially the Fettercairn and Jobstown wards) to the south-west.

Map 12.3: Unemployment rates in Dublin city and county, 1986

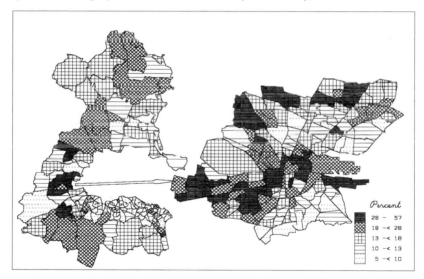

As well as being quite extreme, it also appears from the maps that the structure of spatial inequalities in Dublin was quite stable over the period 1986-96. This is confirmed by correlation analysis. The correlation coefficient in ward-level unemployment rates in Dublin between the two years is 0.93 while the correlation coefficient between the total numbers of unemployed persons was 0.91.

Map 12.4: unemployment rates in Dublin city and county, 1996

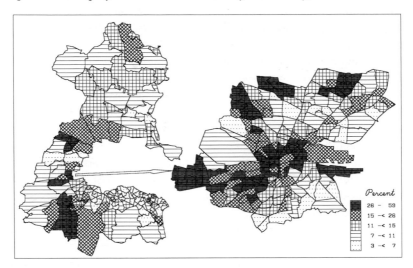

We earlier discussed the spatial concentration of unemployment at the national level by examining the proportions of the unemployed and of the population aged 15 years and over who were located in the decile of DEDs with the worst unemployment rates, the second worst and so on. Here we do the same for the 322 wards of Dublin for 1986 and 1996. Figure 12.4 presents details on the concentration of both the unemployed and the population aged 15 years and over on the basis of the unemployment rate deciles at the electoral Ward level. The chart shows the percentage of both who fall into the 30 per cent of Wards with the highest unemployment rates.

Figure 12.4: Comparison of distribution of the unemployed and the total population aged 15 years and over in the top three unemployment deciles at the electoral Ward level in Dublin

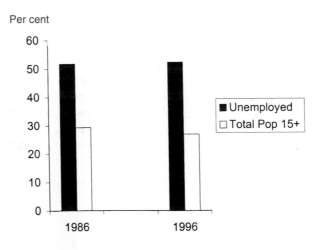

In 1986 a total of 51.8 per cent of the unemployed fell into the relevant group of high unemployment deciles compared with a total of 29.4 per cent of all persons aged 15 years and over. By 1996 the comparable figures were, respectively, 52.2 per cent and 27.0 per cent. This implies an over-concentration in 1996 of 1.93 times as many unemployed in the 30 per cent of Wards with the highest unemployment rates as would be expected if they were distributed across the Wards on a population basis. These figures and the relevant chart indicate a higher level of concentration of the unemployed in Dublin than was the case at the national level. Having noted this relatively greater level of over-concentration in Dublin, however, one should note that it falls off substantially in the fourth and subsequent unemployment deciles. For example, in 1996 the fourth decile contained 9.9 per cent of the unemployed compared with 8.6 per cent of the population aged 15 years and over while the corresponding figures for the fifth decile were 8.7 per cent and 9.7 per cent respectively.

As was the case with the national picture, a particularly important point to emerge from our discussion of the maps, the correlation analysis and decile distributions of the unemployed is the highly consistent nature of the spatial structure of unemployment in Dublin between 1986 and 1999.

Clearly, unemployment is only one measure of disadvantage. Other equally valid measures which one might use and which are available from the Census material include social class, educational disadvantage, etc. Space does not permit a detailed consideration of these in this chapter. An analysis of these variables highlight the same basic patterns of concentration/dispersal of disadvantage throughout the Dublin region (see, for example, Nolan, Whelan and Williams, 1998). In addition, such an analysis clearly indicates a strong relationship in the geographical pattern of disadvantage when measured using the various indicators in question. Finally, and most importantly, a broader analysis of disadvantage based on a wider set of social indicators shows a remarkable geographical consistency over the period 1986-96 in terms of the full range of indicators chosen.

International comparisons

How segregated is Dublin by the standard of other cities in the developed world? This question is difficult to answer, since standardised statistical measures of the extent of segregation in cities have not yet been devised. From the information so far available, it appears that European cities in general are less segregated than their American counterparts, though studies of this issue have so far focused on only a small numbers of cities (Duerloo and Musterd, 1998; Kaufman, 1998; Musterd et al, 1999). Mills and Lubuele's (1997) comparison of social indicators for American and European inner cities also suggests that deprivation in European inner city areas is less extreme than in American. An on-going comparative study of seven European cities, of which Dublin is one, suggests that there is considerable variation across Europe in urban social segregation (Flatley and McIntosh, 2000). According to this study, some cities (Helsinki being a particular example) experience very little spatial segregation, while others (such as Dublin and London) are quite polarised. In the case of Helsinki, segregation is minimal because a strong welfare state has kept social inequalities within relatively narrow ranges, while urban planning (at least up to the late 1980s) promoted social mixing as an important plank of urban housing policy. In Dublin and London, by contrast, weaker welfare states allowed a wider degree of social inequality, while urban housing policy allowed a greater role to market forces in determining the spatial pattern of housing (Flatley and McIntosh, 2000).

Even if Dublin is relatively segregated on certain measures, there is one respect in which Dublin can be thought of as a highly *integrated* city by European, and even more, by American standards. This is in its cultural, racial and ethnic homogeneity. The vast majority of Dubliners are native born, English speaking, white and of Christian religious background. Until recently, they would rarely have seen a non-white person on the streets of the city. This feature has begun to change with the influx of refugees and asylum seekers from eastern Europe and Africa in the past few years. But even this change is of too recent origin to have yet resulted in the build-up of substantial pockets of ethnic populations in Dublin. Social inequality and spatial segregation in the city thus so far lack any overlay of racial or ethnic differentiation. Dublin provides a rare instance of a capital city in the developed world where social differences between categories of the population are wide and where spatial segregation of those categories is marked, even though the cultural and ethnic differentiation which is so typical of socio-spatial differentiation in other cities is largely absent.

12.5 The significance of urban spatial segregation

We now turn to the puzzling issue mentioned earlier – the inability of statistical analysis to show any consistent relationship between neighbourhood quality and various indicators of the well-being of households in urban areas. Taken at face value, the lack of such relationship might suggest that urban spatial segregation is less of a concern than has often been thought. If the poor who live in socially mixed neighbourhoods do no better than those who are concentrated together in disadvantaged neighbourhoods, why be worried about the spatial concentration of poverty in cities?

Despite the statistical results, researchers have been slow to draw conclusions along these lines. One reason is the rather crude nature of the data so far available and the hesitancy researchers would feel in asserting that those data adequately capture the full complexity of neighbourhood characteristics and their effects on well-being (Friedrichs, 1997; Furstenburg and Hughes, 1998). Another is that there are too many neighbourhoods in real life where the environment is so unpleasant that it would seem impossible for it not to have a negative impact on residents' lives. Popular views about the unpleasantness of life in such places may contain a large element of prejudice and unjustified fear, but academic research clearly shows that instances of serious neighbourhood deprivation are real and clearly are felt by residents to have a damaging effect on their lives.[7]

Local authority housing estates as deprived neighbourhoods

In the case of Irish cities, some recent qualitative research on social conditions in local authority housing estates gives some clues to resolving the conflict between statistical evidence on the 'non-effect' of neighbourhood and everyday experience (Fahey, 1999b; Bartley, 1998). A focus on local authority housing is relevant in this regard since the spatial pattern of local authority housing development has played a major role in sustaining spatial segregation in Dublin (Bannon et al, 1981, McLaran, 1996). About a quarter of the dwellings in use in Ireland today (that is, some 330,000 dwellings) originated as local authority housing. In many respects, that housing amounted to a major contribution to social progress. It cured the problem of slum housing which bedevilled Irish cities and towns in the first half of the twentieth century. It subsequently went on to provide generations of low-income families with secure tenure in good quality affordable accommodation (while problems of poor build quality did sometimes arise in local authority dwellings, they were confined mainly to housing built in the late 1960s and early 1970s).

However, despite the long and successful record of local authority housing, its role in the housing system has become increasingly residualised in recent years – it has evolved into a small housing sector targeted heavily on the poor and unemployed (see Harloe, 1995 on this trend in social housing in Europe generally). This is so in part because of privatisation of local authority dwellings. Generous tenant purchase schemes have been available in urban areas since the early 1970s and in rural areas since 1936 (Walsh, 1999). These have led to the purchase by residents of more than two-thirds of the local authority housing stock, leaving only about 100,000 units – some 8 per cent of the national housing stock – in local authority ownership. In addition, the share of social housing in new build has been cut back to less than 10 per cent of the total since 1987, a sharp reduction from the levels of 20-30 per cent which it accounted for in earlier decades (Fahey, ed., 1999). Recent policy developments, particularly the National

Development Plan (1999) and the Planning Bill (1999), indicate an intention on the government's part to reverse the contraction of social housing and give it a major role in dealing with the current housing shortage. But these plans have not as yet had an impact on the residualised character of social housing.

The consequence is that at present local authority tenure has strong links with poverty and disadvantage, and this link is especially marked in urban areas (Layte, Nolan and Whelan, this volume; Nolan, Whelan and Williams, 1998). In 1996, according to Labour Force Survey data, only one in four local authority households had anyone in the household at work (O'Connell and Fahey, 1999: 41). Local authority housing has traditionally tended to be located where building land was cheapest, either in deprived inner city neighbourhoods or in low-amenity peripheral areas. This has produced a spatial clustering effect which is an important contributor to the overall pattern of spatial segregation in urban areas and which means that many urban local authority housing estates can justifiably be regarded as deprived areas.

Diversity in deprived areas

The key to understanding the character of such areas as neighbourhoods is that, while they may show a great deal of uniformity of disadvantage and segregation according to standard indicators, they are quite diverse as social and physical environments. This was evident from a detailed examination of seven urban local authority estates in Ireland reported in Fahey (1999) (three of the seven estates were in Dublin, and there was one each in Cork, Limerick, Sligo and Dundalk). Across these seven estates, one extreme of social conditions was represented by a high-demand estate in Cork (Deanrock in Togher, a mixed estate of flats and houses on the edge of Cork city) which had a low turnover of residents, reasonably settled social conditions and a long waiting list to get in. This estate had become popular in spite of the poor initial build quality of the dwellings – the social stability of the estate had outweighed its building defects in determining its attractiveness to residents. At the opposite extreme was an estate in Dublin (Fatima Mansions, an estate of flats in Dublin's southwest inner city) which was troubled and difficult to let. Almost half the tenants in this estate had applied for transfer elsewhere, about 15 per cent of dwellings were vacant, some blocks of dwellings were falling into dereliction and heroin usage was widespread. The other estates ranged more or less between these two extremes, though complex patterns of popularity and unpopularity attaching to them meant that they could not easily be ranked in a uni-dimensional way.

Along with diversity between estates, there was also a great deal of diversity *within* most of the estates. This diversity is significant from the point of view of statistical analysis of neighbourhood effects, since the estates in question were generally either of about the same size or smaller than the wards used in the statistical analysis and mapping referred to earlier in this chapter.[8] Even the smallest estates were comprised of spatial and social sub-units. Social and physical conditions could vary sharply across these sub-units. Status hierarchies often emerged between areas within estates, with some areas being more settled and successful than others. Residents in the higher status areas often went to considerable lengths to minimise their contact and identification with lower status areas.

These divergences appeared to have little or no linkage with variations in the conventional indicators of social disadvantage such as poverty rates, unemployment levels, incidence of lone parenthood, and so on – all of which tended to be quite uniform in the estates studied. In some cases, the status gradations were subtle and difficult to relate to externally observable distinctions, and might have reflected vague prejudices on the part of residents who have little contact with or knowledge of parts of the estate which may be quite close to them but which they rarely have occasion to visit. In other cases, however, there are striking visible differences between higher and lower status areas within the same estate, mainly in regard to the neatness and external appearance of houses, the presence/absence of litter or graffiti, the degree of planting in front gardens or public green spaces, and so on. Even in Fatima Mansions (the worst of the estates), which was comprised of 320 flats laid out in 14 blocks, some of the blocks had a well-kept appearance and were more settled and stable than the worst-off blocks in the same estate (the former were referred to by some residents in the estate as the 'yuppie blocks'). Similar sharp diversity within a confined area could also arise in estates outside the larger cities. In Crannmore estate in Sligo town, for example, which was an estate of 499 houses well-located close to the centre of the town, one small section of the estate had experienced serious decline and unpopularity, even though other parts of the same estate were quite settled and successful.

What is neighbourhood?

These strong internal variations within estates suggest another important point which is relevant to the analysis of neighbourhood effects. This is that the core neighbourhood unit within estates was usually quite small – a particular drive or road (or segment of a road), or a block of flats. These amounted to micro-neighbourhoods where the dwellings would be counted at most in dozens rather than in hundreds. It was at the level of these micro-neighbourhoods that the great diversity of disadvantaged areas was evident, as reflected in the sharp differences often found between one road or block of flats and the next within the same estate. Residents tend to identify most closely with these small units, to have most of their neighbourly contacts within them and to have greatest immediate concern for their social and physical quality. Estates which from the outside might appear as homogeneous spatial entities thus in the minds and day-to-day experience of residents were broken up into a mosaic of much smaller and in some cases quite diverse units. This is not to say that the wider estate had no significance or effects for residents. But that wider impact, whatever it might be, was heavily mediated by the character of the immediate environs (the micro-neighbourhood) of the individual household. That character in turn could vary quite widely even within what from the outside might appear as a confined and uniform larger neighbourhood.

12.6 Conclusion

This chapter has considered the spatial distribution of poverty and disadvantage in Ireland from the mid-1980s to the mid-1990s. It first examined the national picture at a number of different spatial levels – the regions, rural/urban districts and district electoral divisions (DEDs). It then looked in more detail at spatial patterns in Dublin city and county. The main concerns of the chapter were to examine the extent of spatial inequality in Ireland (both at a national level and in Dublin), to assess the degree of change in spatial inequalities which occurred between the mid-1980s and mid-1990s, and to consider some qualitative evidence on the nature and impact of spatial differentiation in Dublin, as a complement to quantitative analysis.

The analysis showed that the picture of spatial inequalities depended in some ways on the level of spatial unit which is the focus of study. At the regional level, for example, spatial inequalities in the risk of disadvantage seemed to be modest and to have decreased somewhat over the period 1987-97. Thus, the East region has a lower poverty rate than the other regions, but its advantage in this regard had reduced sharply between 1987 and 1997.

However, when we look at smaller spatial units, and especially the smallest spatial unit of all – the DED – spatial differentiation becomes more marked in some respects but in addition regional patterns break up and yield a more scattered overall picture of spatial inequality. This is exemplified by the situation in Dublin. Though Dublin is located within the East region – the region with the lowest poverty risk overall – it contains as much internal spatial differentiation as is evident across the country as a whole. Thus, for example, some wards in Dublin have among the highest unemployment rates in the country, while others have among the lowest. The national picture is slightly akin to a partially patterned mosaic: the DEDs with the highest unemployment rates are far worse off than those with the lowest unemployment rates and there is some tendency towards a clustering of the worst with the worst and the best with the best. However, the clustering effect is relatively modest in the overall, so that effect is not of large sharply delineated blackspots in which the bulk of the poor or unemployed are concentrated. Rather, it is of a complex, graduated picture in which some blackspots occur but also in which there are many shades of grey and where many of the disadvantaged live in the grey – or even white – areas rather than the blackspots. The general conclusion is, therefore, that while some concentration of disadvantage does exist, poverty and deprivation are still spatially pervasive and affect almost all parts of the country at all levels of geographical disaggregation.

One feature of spatial inequalities in the years 1987-97 which is quite consistent across spatial levels is the stability in the geographical pattern of the distribution of disadvantage. The same areas which were badly off in 1987 were badly off in 1997, whether one looks at counties, rural/urban districts or DEDs/wards as area units (some shifts were evident at the regional level but these were too indeterminate to amount to a clear trend). It would thus appear that the emergence of the economic boom in the 1990s did not produce either an immediate widening or narrowing of inequalities between areas but rather left the structure of spatial inequality more or less intact.

The chapter also looked at some qualitative evidence on the significance of neighbourhood disadvantage in urban areas. This evidence was viewed in the context of quantitative evidence that the poor who live in deprived urban neighbourhoods do not seem to be significantly worse off in major dimensions of life than similar households who live in better-off neighbourhoods (see Layte, Nolan and Whelan, this volume). The conclusion reached here was that neighbourhood may matter but perhaps in a more complex and fine-grained way than has been captured in the statistical analysis of neighbourhood effects. The key point is that deprived areas should not be thought of as large uniform social environments but as complex composites of micro-areas – individual streets or blocks of flats rather than whole estates, each micro-area having its own character and neighbourhood quality. Since such micro-spatial variations are hard to capture in statistical measures, it is to be expected that statistical analysis will find it hard to identify neighbourhood effects.

The existence of such micro-areas also implies the possibility of micro-segregation. Physical contiguity between different social groups gives no guarantee of positive social interaction or a sense of commonality between them. Even where the social inequalities between groups are narrow (as is often the case with the sub-groups within local authority housing estates), social barriers can easily arise, and these social divisions can lead to forms of micro-segregation within what otherwise might seem like compact, socially uniform neighbourhoods. This is not to say that larger-scale spatial segregation is of no importance, but rather that social differentiation and social segregation in urban areas take more complex forms and are due to a more complex range of factors than the size and location of housing areas alone.

NOTES

1 For a full discussion of the definitions of these lines see Callan et al (1996).

2 See, for example, Rottman et al (1982); Roche (1984); Callan et al (1989); Whelan et al (1991), Nolan and Callan (1994), Callan et al (1996), Callan et al (1999).

3 There is, in fact, a total of 217 rural and urban District (RDs and UDs) in the country. For mapping purposes, since urban districts are generally quite small, we have incorporated them into their neighbouring rural districts. The four local authority areas in Dublin are included as separate districts (see Nolan, Whelan and Williams, 1998: 107-109 for details).

4 The correlation between *rates* is lower than that between *levels* because in many DEDs the rates are based on a relatively small labour force. Consequently, even small changes in the absolute number of unemployed persons may result in a disproportionately large change in the *rate* for any given DED. This introduces 'noise' with the 1986-96 comparisons of rates which is not apparent in the analysis based on *levels*.

5 Brady and Parker (1975) and Breathnach (1976) used composite indices of social disadvantage based on Ward level data from the 1971 Census to map social segregation in Dublin. Mac Gréil (1973) used survey data from 1972 to map educational disadvantage by postal district in the city (postal districts are much larger in area and fewer in number than Wards). Breathnach (1976), in addition to her own Ward-level analysis, replicated Mac Gréil's postal district analysis on the basis of 1971 Census data and arrived at broadly similar conclusions. Bannon et al (1981) used both survey and census data from the 1970s to provide detailed social profiles of different areas of the city.

6 As was the case with Maps 12.1 and 12.2 the maps showing unemployment rates in Dublin are based on quintile distributions. In other words, the areas with darkest shading show the 20 per cent of Wards with the highest unemployment rates; the next darkest areas show the next 20 per cent of Wards according to unemployment rates and so on.

7 Much of the relevant academic research in European countries has focused on 'problem estates' in the social housing sector, though neighbourhood regeneration which extends beyond social housing estates has become an important element of British policy in recent years. For an overview of the relevant literature, see Fahey (1999).

8 The average population size of the Dublin Wards was 3,300, which was the equivalent of about 1,000 households. Of the seven estates referred to here, two had populations at or above this average, while the remaining five were below it (Corcoran and Fahey, 1999: 96).

13

Gender Equality, Fertility Decline and Labour Market Patterns Among Women in Ireland

TONY FAHEY, HELEN RUSSELL AND EMER SMYTH

13.1 Introduction

From the 1960s onwards, debates about social equality in Ireland have often extended to include the question of gender equality. By the time Charles J. Haughey, as Minister for Finance, set up the Commission on the Status of Women in March 1970, a wide range of prohibitions and disabilities which shaped women's lives had become a focus of protest and had pushed the 'woman question' onto the political agenda. In that year, to cite some examples, the importation and sale of 'artificial' contraceptives were still illegal, women in the civil service and in a wide array of white collar jobs in the private sector were obliged to leave those jobs if they married, pay scales in many jobs routinely discriminated between men and women (or, in many cases, between married men on the one hand and single men and women on the other),[1] and children's allowances were normally paid to fathers rather than mothers.

The following decade witnessed considerable institutional change in these areas. In the *McGee* case in 1973, the Supreme Court declared that the legal ban on the importation and sale of contraceptives was unconstitutional (though it was to take another twenty years before health legislation was to bring about full liberalisation of the law on contraception – Hug, 1999: 84-108). The marriage bar in the public service was lifted in 1973, pay discrimination was proscribed in 1974, other major forms of discrimination against the employment of women were outlawed in 1977, and the right to maternity leave for women was introduced in 1981. Children's allowances were made payable to mothers rather than fathers and an allowance for unmarried mothers was introduced in the early 1970s.

244

However, broad social change moves at a different pace to institutional change and questions remain about how much gender equality has emerged in Irish society. Despite transformation of various areas of law and social provision affecting women and despite the impact of economic development and cultural change, some have strongly doubted that female disadvantage has been fundamentally reduced. There are many areas where women's position of weakness seems stubbornly resistant to change and where, to use O'Connor's phrase, a 'patriarchal dividend' persists (O'Connor, 2000; see also Pyle, 1990; O'Connor, 1998). Alongside the question of *how much* gender equality has emerged, there are also questions as to *why* gender relations have changed – what are the driving forces that cause shifts in the balance of advantage between men and women? In the case of Ireland, this translates into questions about the relative importance of a whole range of influences: the economic shift from agriculture to industry and services, growth in productivity and the consequent rise in wage rates, the particularly sharp expansion of demand for women's labour, the rising educational levels of the population, the emergence of the women's movement, the influence of EU equality directives, the impact of the media, and so on.

As the space available here precludes a full overview of these questions, the present chapter focuses on two issues which have long been at the heart of debates about women's position and which are closely intertwined with each other – fertility and women's place in the labour market. Women's role as bearers and rearers of children has long been pointed to by feminists as a key element of their social subordination. As a corollary, the demand that women should have full control over their own fertility has been seen as a necessary, though not sufficient, condition for their emancipation. Likewise, full access to the labour market has been regarded as a means of escape from male domination within the household and a foundation for women's economic equality (for an Irish feminist statement on these questions, see the six-point manifesto of the Irish Women's Liberation Movement 1970). Furthermore, these two aspects of emancipation are normally thought to be mutually reinforcing: declining fertility frees up women to participate more fully in paid work, while increasing demand for female labour (as reflected both in higher wage rates and higher participation rates) gives women the incentive to have fewer children. Thus the interconnections between fertility and female labour force patterns, over and above each of these matters separately, form a major focus of interest in tracking change in women's social position.

The purpose of the present chapter is to trace developments on these two central issues over recent decades in Ireland and assess their significance for gender equality. The next (second) section of the chapter begins the analysis by taking up the question of fertility, the third deals with trends in female labour force participation, the fourth with issues of gender equality in the labour market, and the final section provides a summary and conclusion.

13.2 Fertility

General trends

The universal decline in fertility and mortality in developed countries since the nineteenth century – the 'demographic transition' – is one of the great social transformations of modernity. The decline in fertility began first in France and the United States in the early decades of the nineteenth century, and was in train more or less everywhere in Europe by the end of the nineteenth century. By the 1930s, fertility had fallen to 50 per cent or less of its pre-transition level in almost every European country, a decline which in most cases had taken no more than three or four decades to achieve (the standard account is Coale and Watkins, 1986; see also Gillis et al, 1992). Pre-transition fertility in Europe had itself been subject to various limits and controls, the most important of which took the form of social restrictions on access to marriage – women married late by comparison with non-Europeans and many (usually between 10 and 20 per cent) never married at all. The net effect was that, at any given time in pre-transition Europe, up to one third of the female population of child-bearing years was unmarried and this had the effect of suppressing fertility by something close to a corresponding amount.

As the modern fertility transition took root in the late nineteenth century, the pre-transition restrictions on access to marriage gradually lost their pre-eminence in fertility control. They became secondary to a broad array of 'modern' fertility control practices, which have the common feature of seeking to limit conceptions (or, in the case of abortion, births) within marriage or, more generally, within a sexually active life. In the long initial phase of this new regime, fertility control was couple-based, or even, to a great extent, male-based. That is to say, they relied on methods such as *coitus interruptus*, periodic abstinence within marriage and, to a much lesser extent, condoms, which required the man's active participation in avoidance of conception. It was only in the second half of the twentieth century, when the fertility transition was far advanced, that a wholly woman-based fertility control technology became available. The contraceptive pill, various new barrier methods of contraception, and widely available and relatively safe abortion gave women the freedom to determine their own fertility outcomes – without the knowledge, much less active participation, of their male partners if that was what women wished. It was in this new era of female-centred fertility control that fertility fell to the very low levels that had become characteristic of western countries by the late 1980s.

The Irish exception

Ireland's position in this history is peculiar, at least in matters of timing and degree. By the late nineteenth century, Irish fertility had fallen to quite low levels by contemporary European standards (and by the standards of its own history). However, this 'modern' outcome of relatively low fertility was achieved by distinctly non-modern means. It relied not on the emergence of widespread fertility control behaviour within marriage, as was beginning to occur elsewhere in Europe, but on an intensification of the traditional European pattern of marriage avoidance. Marriage rates had been falling in Ireland since the Famine and by the 1930s they had reduced to levels that were among the lowest in recorded human history. The average age of marriage for Irish women at that time was 29 years, and for Irish men it was nearly 35 years. In the 1936 Census of Population, 34 per cent of men and 25 per cent of women in the age-group 45-54 were single and so would be counted as 'permanent celibates' in demographic terms. At the same time, fertility within marriage was exceptionally high and remained so throughout the first half of the twentieth century. But high marital fertility provided only partial compensation for the high proportions who were not married, so that overall fertility remained at modest levels (Coleman, 1992).

By the 1960s, Irish women had among the least 'modernised' fertility patterns in the western world. Though marriage rates had risen somewhat since the trough of the 1930s, they were still low by international standards. Those who did marry still had exceptionally high fertility rates. For Irish women, therefore, the dominant choice was still between either having no children (through non-marriage) or having a lot (if they did marry), between sexual denial or a fertility regime where they had only limited personal control. The overall fertility rate in the 1960s had changed little since the early twentieth century, but by then had been made to appear relatively high by the receding tide of fertility elsewhere in Europe (Coleman, 1992).

Convergence

Since the 1960s, Ireland has gradually converged on European fertility norms and lost its former outlier status. As had happened in other European countries decades earlier, this movement at first entailed two counterbalancing shifts in the fertility regime: average family size declined sharply but there was a compensating surge in the proportion of women who married. Growth in the number of women of childbearing age also helped push up the total number of births. The annual number of marriages reached a twentieth-century peak in 1974 and, despite falling family size, the annual number of births did so six years later (1980).

It was only in the 1980s, as the marriage surge petered out and the decline in family size persisted, that marriage trends and fertility trends joined together in a common downward movement. The impact on the total fertility rate (TFR) is shown in Figure 13.1. The Irish TFR remained high until the early 1970s but by 1990 had fallen to half the level of 1970 and had come within the range common among western countries. It thus conformed with the general trend among developed countries of homogenisation of fertility rates around very low levels.

Today, Irish fertility rates, though low by historical standards, are just about the highest in Europe (if we discount Iceland, which at present is marginally higher than Ireland). However, fertility is lower in Europe than in America, and fertility rates in the US have been slightly higher than in Ireland since 1993. Furthermore, as Figure 13.1 indicates, there has been a trend towards some divergence in fertility rates among developed countries in the 1990s, following tight convergence in the 1980s. This is largely due to the stability in fertility rates in some countries (particularly the US) and continuing decline in others (particularly in southern Europe – Italy, Greece and Spain).

Figure 13.1: Total fertility rate

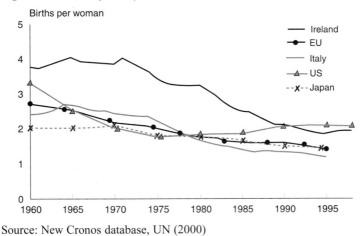

Source: New Cronos database, UN (2000)

Though the divergence of recent years is small in absolute terms, it is surprisingly wide in relative terms. The TFR in the US today is 70 per cent higher than that of Italy and 43 per cent higher than that of the EU. California, the most populous state in the United States (32 million people) has a TFR of 2.2 (80 per cent higher than Italy), and Texas, with a population of 19 million people, has a TFR of 2.4 (double that of Italy) (National Centre for Health Statistics, 2000). Taking major regional differences in the US into account, therefore, the upper limit of period fertility across the industrialised world is double the lower limit, a degree of *relative* divergence in fertility rates across countries that is not radically different from that of earlier eras. Ireland's position in this picture could perhaps be characterised as mid-Atlantic rather than wholly European. The Irish TFR in 1960 was 40 per cent higher than that of the later EU countries combined; by 1995 that differential had reduced, but only to 31 per cent (following a considerable but temporary widening during the 1960s). The continuing extent of the differential, rather than its modest reduction since the mid-twentieth century, might be considered the more remarkable.

Births outside marriage

The decline in fertility to low levels could be interpreted as an expression of women's control over their own fertility and as a fulfilment of their demand for this particular aspect of liberation from traditional constraints on female behaviour. However, a number of aspects of fertility behaviour have emerged over recent decades which clouds this interpretation and raises questions about the nature and significance of what has occurred.

Here we will mention only one of these, the rapid rise in the proportion of births occurring outside of marriage, which is part of the general increase in lone parenthood and the loosening association between marriage and child-rearing. More and more children are being born outside of marriage, and of those born within marriage or a stable marriage-like relationship, more and more are likely to have their parents separate. Apart from the implications for children, these developments are significant for the relative position of men and women. The commonest pattern in western countries is that the primary burden of parenting in lone parent situations falls on women. From a gender equality perspective, this has led to a concern that while women may have widely escaped the pressures of large families they experienced in the past, these have been replaced in many cases by new pressures arising from carrying an excessive share of the responsibility for much smaller families.

Looking at broad international trends in the proportion of births occurring outside marriage (Figure 13.2), we can see that some countries have long had and continue to have low scores on this indicator (see especially Greece and Italy in Figure 13.2). Others have soared from relatively low to high percentages. Norway, for example, showed a large absolute increase between 1980 and 1996 (from 14 to 48 per cent of births), while Ireland showed a five-fold *relative* increase (from 5 to 25 per cent of births) over the same period. However, there is one strong common feature to the trend across countries shown in Figure 13.2 – it is universally upwards. Apart from that, the pace of increase varies so widely that cross-country differentials have increased rather than declined over time.

Figure 13.2: Births outside marriage as per cent of all births in the EU and the US, 1980 and 1996

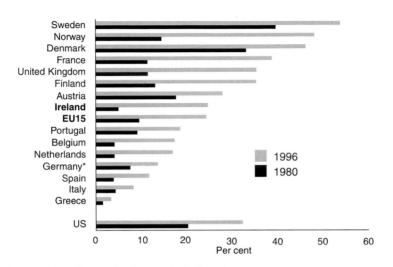

Source: New Cronos database: *Excluding former GDR.

Ireland's position on this indicator was low in 1980 and was similar to the levels in Belgium, the Netherlands, Spain and Italy (Figure 13.2). By the mid-1990s, those countries no longer clustered together. The value for Ireland was three times that of Italy, while the other countries in the group were spread between the Italian and the Irish values. At the same time, despite the sharp increase in the value for Ireland by 1996, it was still only at the average for the EU.

The social significance of high proportions of births occurring outside marriage is difficult to interpret and is likely to vary from country to country. Non-marital births often occur to cohabiting couples rather than to solo mothers (though perhaps less so in Ireland, where census data suggest that cohabitation is relatively uncommon – CSO 1997). In a study of nine European countries in the early 1990s, births to solo mothers generally accounted for between 5 and 12 per cent of all births, a level that is much lower and less variable across countries than the proportion of births outside marriage (Kiernan, 1999b). However, this fact itself does not have clear implications, since it is uncertain how far non-marital cohabitation can be considered the functional equivalent of marriage. Cohabitation is less stable than marriage (Kiernan, 1999a), and there is some evidence also that unions which commenced in non-martial cohabitation and subsequently entered marriage are less stable than those which commenced as marriages. A US study in the 1980s showed that the proportion of unions surviving ten years was 59 per cent in the case of married couples who had never cohabited compared to only 30 per cent of couples who started out in cohabitation, whether or not they subsequently married (Bumpass and Sweet, 1989). In Britain in the early 1990s, 92 per cent of married families survived for at least five years after the birth of their first child compared to only 48 per cent in the case of cohabitees (Kiernan, 1999b: 19). Apart from the greater instability of cohabiting relationships, questions have also been raised as to whether they practise the same level of income-pooling as married couples do (Blau, 1998).

Thus, however one might qualify the social significance of non-marital fertility, it does seem to be part of a general pulling back from a life-time commitment to joint parenthood on the part of men and women. Since this generally throws a greater share of the parenting task on women, the degree to which women can be said to have increased their control of all the circumstances surrounding their child-bearing and child-rearing becomes open to question. The advent and widespread adoption of fertility limitation practices undoubtedly represented a massive extension of women's freedom to shape their own lives. But new imbalances in the way women and men share responsibility for their children create new forms of constraint and complicates the question of how far recent fertility trends have furthered the cause of equality between the genders.

Fertility and female labour force participation

A further puzzle about the significance for women's social position of declining fertility arises when we look at what it means for their position in the labour market. As already mentioned, the conventional view is that declining fertility and rising female labour force participation are mutually reinforcing: each facilitates and gives the incentive for the other. As is illustrated further below in connection with Ireland, there is abundant evidence from cross-sectional analysis within countries to support this view.

However, the picture becomes less clear-cut when comparisons are made across rather than within countries. In empirical cross-national research, it has proved extremely difficult to find robust links between fertility decline and *any* socio-economic variable, either across time in developed countries or across countries in the world today (Hirschman, 1994; Alter, 1992). In Europe, fertility decline emerged and developed at a similar time and pace in countries at quite different levels of socio-economic development, and the same seems to be true in many parts of the developing world today (Hirschman, 1994: 213). It is hardly surprising, therefore, that in the broader cross-national picture, the relationship between fertility levels and socio-economic variables such as the rate of women's participation in the labour force is weak and is difficult to interpret.

The plot of the association between fertility levels and female participation rates across developed countries today shown in Figure 13.3 bears this out. The

Irish position in this plot, along with that of Luxembourg, is most in keeping with expectations: female participation is low and fertility rates are high, as conventional views would lead us to expect. However, Ireland and Luxembourg are outlier cases. Italy, Spain Greece have low levels of female participation but also low fertility levels. At the other extreme, the US, with the highest fertility, also has quite high female participation, while in the Scandinavian countries, both female participation and fertility are relatively high. If Ireland and Luxembourg were removed from the plot in Figure 13.3, the relationship between fertility and female participation would appear to be in a positive direction – the more women participate in paid work, the *higher* their fertility.

Figure 13.3: National fertility rates and female activity rates, 1997

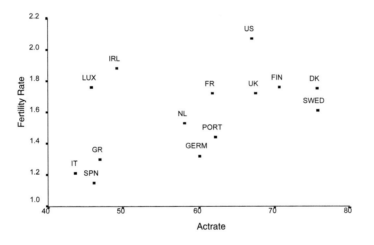

Source: Council of Europe, 1998; European Commission, 1999

Another way of stating this is that the sharpest collapse in fertility across developed countries today occurs in those cases where women's options, as reflected by the level of market demand for women's labour, are narrowest (as exemplified at present by the Mediterranean countries of Europe). This is contrary to expectations, since the standard view is that the decline of fertility is associated with the widening of women's options and the consequent increase in the opportunity cost of having children. Attempts to date to account for this paradox generally do not abandon cost-benefit explanations, but point to the complex range of factors which shape the cost-benefit balance regarding fertility and which vary widely across developed countries (Esping-Andersen, 1999; Bettio and Villa, 1998; Calhoun, 1994). The interest of these analyses from the present point of view is the implication they carry that falls in fertility to Mediterranean levels may not reflect an emancipatory expansion of women's options but rather a new set of constraints which closes off child-bearing options that women might otherwise wish to pursue. They remind us, in other words, that women today who fully control their own fertility may choose on average to have far fewer children than their grandmothers did, but that does not always mean that they would be fully happy to choose the very low fertility levels that have emerged in some countries in recent years.

13.3 Female labour force participation

We now turn more directly to labour market patterns as a dimension of equality between men and women. This section looks at the evolution of female labour force participation rates, while the next examines related changes in the type of jobs held by women and men and the levels of pay they command.

Marxist-feminist theorists have argued that industrialisation tends to result in an initial decline in female labour force participation as production moves from the home to the factory but that subsequent industrial expansion tends to lead to a long-term increase in female employment rates (see, for example, Humphries and Rubery, 1984). Similar predictions of a gradual integration of women into the paid labour force have been evident among modernisation theorists who also tend to emphasise the role of associated attitudinal changes in transforming gender roles. Such assumptions of cross-national convergence have been criticised by Maurice, Sellier and Silvestre (1986) who analyse how systems of education, occupational training and workforce stratification interact to produce 'certain specific national patterns' (p. 54; see also Wilkinson, 1983). The gender dimension of this cross-national diversity has been elucidated in more recent research, which has examined how gender relations have been constructed historically and shaped in specific institutions, such as the family and the labour market (O'Reilly, 1996; Connell, 1987). Contrary to Marxist and modernisation predictions, comparative research has indicated no simple relationship between the process of industrialisation and women's labour force participation (Tilly and Scott, 1978). Instead, research has shown how gender differences are constructed within specific societal contexts (see, for example, Bradley, 1989; Rubery and Fagan, 1995) and how female labour force participation trends vary according to national labour market structures, education/training systems, the policy environment and family systems (Lane, 1993; Daune Richard, 1998).

Long-term trends in Irish female labour force participation

The long-term evolution of women's participation in the labour force in Ireland is difficult to trace because, until recently, the available data provided only partial coverage of women's economic role. Official statistics appear to indicate that trends in women's labour force participation since the nineteenth century have followed a U-shaped pattern rather than showing a simple increase over time. This may be seen in the context of a marked decline in some of the traditional 'female' employment areas (domestic service, agriculture and textiles) during the nineteenth century (Daly, 1981). Census data also indicate a relatively static, if not declining, level of female labour force participation over the early twentieth century, with particularly low rates apparent among married women. However, there are good reasons for regarding official statistics as underestimating the actual level of female labour force participation. The biggest gaps in coverage related to women's (and especially married women's) participation in the farm labour force, as well as to female unemployment and part-time work in industry and services (Daly, 1997; Fahey, 1990; Walsh, 1993). Taking all forms of labour force activity into account, it is likely that married women's labour force particpation rates in the 1960s were above 25 per cent, and perhaps even 30 per cent, so that rates around 5 per cent derived from Censuses of Population data for that period should be regarded as serious underestimates (Fahey, 1993). Furthermore, such statistics tend to underestimate the numbers of women actively seeking work. From 1880 onwards, emigration was female-dominated and the number of female emigrants was very high in relation to the numbers of women in the Irish labour force (Fitzpatrick, 1984; Rhodes, 1986).

Recent trends in female labour force participation

Figure 13.4: Female labour force participation (FLFP) rates 1983-1998

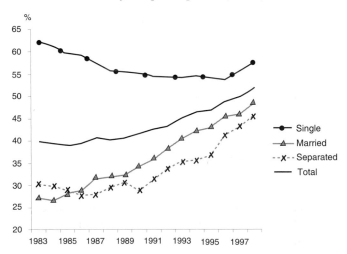

Source: New Cronos database: European LFS

Nevertheless, it is clear that since the 1970s, and more especially since the late 1980s, women's presence in the labour force has increased sharply (Figure 13.4). All of the increase has been due to rapidly rising participation among ever-married women, since participation rates among single women dropped in the 1980s and have only turned upwards again since 1996. Marital status now has much less bearing on participation rates among women than it had in the past, since the differentials between single and ever-married women have narrowed sharply. Labour force participation among married women has risen for all women in the child-bearing years, with particularly strong increases among women aged 25-34 between 1983 and 1998.

Placing Ireland in comparative perspective, participation rates remain relatively low by European standards although there would appear to be some convergence towards the European 'average' over the recent period. Activity rates among married women have increased in all European countries (with the exception of Denmark) and cross-national differences in levels of participation among married women are less pronounced in 1998 than in 1983 (see Figure 13.5). Absolute increases have been greatest in the Netherlands and Ireland. In addition, the relative position of Ireland has changed somewhat. In 1983 Ireland had the lowest rate of married women's participation.[7] However, by 1998 rates were higher in Ireland than in a number of Mediterranean countries (such as Italy and Spain).

Figure 13.5: Married FLFP rates across Europe

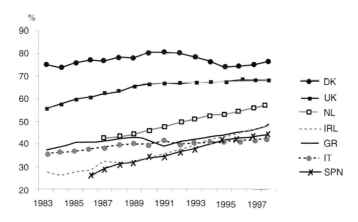

Ireland's position within Europe looks somewhat different when we consider women's parental status rather than marital status. While activity rates among Irish women aged 25 to 45 years with no children are very close to the European average, among women with children under 5 years of age, Ireland still has the lowest activity rate in Europe (see Figure 13.6). In Ireland, along with Italy and Greece, less than half of this group are active in the labour market. At the other extreme, almost 80 per cent of Danish mothers with 'pre-school' age children are in the labour market. A similar pattern is found when mothers of children up to 10 years of age are considered, with rates remaining lowest among Irish mothers. In the majority of EU countries there is a gradual decrease in women's labour market participation with each additional child. Further analyses indicate that the decline in activity rates for each additional child is more dramatic among Irish women than in most European countries (ECHP data, special tabulation by authors). EU-wide information on trends in maternal participation rates could only be located for the period 1991 to 1996. These figures show that, although the participation rate among Irish mothers is low, it has been drawing closer to the European average in recent years. In 1991 the Irish activity rate was 19 percentage points below the European average;[3] however, in the space of just five years the gap had closed to 14 percentage points. National figures for 1997 show that maternal participation rates in Ireland continued to increase to 49 per cent, but comparable EU figures are not yet available.

Figure 13.6: Female activity rates by age of youngest child (Women aged 25-45)

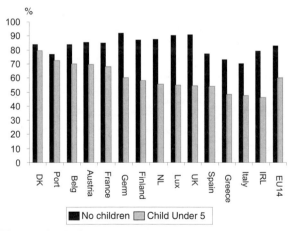

Source: ECHP Wave 3, 1996.

Analyses of trends in Irish women's labour force participation highlight two questions which require exploration. Firstly, what factors were associated with the sharp rise in married women's participation rates from the early 1970s onwards? Secondly, in spite of these significant changes, why are women's participation rates much lower in Ireland than in Europe?

Factors shaping participation patterns

As has already been mentioned, rising female participation rates can be linked to changes in fertility patterns and also to related factors such as increasing educational attainment, changes in legislation and social provision, and changes in the nature of labour demand. Human capital theory maintains that educational attainment has significant effects on participation decisions; women's labour force participation will increase with education (because more educated women can expect higher wages) and decrease as family size grows (due to the increased time that must be allocated to childcare) (Becker, 1981). Furthermore, increasing levels of education among women will tend to result in smaller families due to the increased opportunity cost of taking time out of the labour market. From an institutional perspective, it is argued that educational participation among women acts as a 'qualifications lever', with access to occupations following from women securing access to qualifications (Crompton and Sanderson, 1990).

To some extent, the Irish situation is consistent with these predictions; cross-sectional evidence indicates that women with higher levels of education tend to have lower fertility rates and higher labour force participation rates than other groups. However, the pattern of change over time is more difficult to explain in these terms. Historically, female education expanded a long time before their employment rates rose. From 1881 onwards, female school attendance rates were higher than male rates, a pattern which was strongly related to the lack of employment opportunities for women (especially in Connaught and Munster) (Rhodes, 1986). The participation of girls in secondary education increased throughout the first half of the twentieth century with girls making up 47 per cent of those passing the Leaving Certificate by 1949 (Finnegan, 1985). The increasing participation of women in second-level education, paralleled by a growth in the numbers entering higher education, took place at a time when female labour force participation rates were virtually static. It appears, therefore, that it is not supply factors *per se* that influence female participation rates but their impact in the context of labour market, legislative and other socio-cultural constraints on female employment (see Beechey, 1987; Tilly and Scott, 1978). In more recent years, a much higher proportion of young women than young men have completed second-level education with entry to higher education among females now outstripping male entry levels (see Smyth, 1999a). This pattern is likely to have on-going consequences for the level and nature of female employment in Ireland.

The growth in married female employment was further facilitated by the overall impact of changes in marriage and fertility patterns. Declining marital fertility rates and earlier completion of families from the 1960s onwards occurred at a time when the potential supply of single female labour was reduced (through increased educational participation and a reduction in the proportion of the single population). Thus, to a certain extent, the increased proportion of married women in the labour force can be related to the decline in the supply of single female labour (among other factors). For the later period, however, the pattern was much more complex. Fertility decline in Ireland was rapid when growth in female labour force participation was relatively modest in the 1980s. But fertility has stabilised (at moderately high levels by European standards) as female activity rates have increased markedly in the 1990s. Increases in female participation rates over time, therefore, cannot easily be linked in a consistent fashion to declining fertility rates.

The growth in the number of women in work since the 1970s must also be seen in relation to overall trends in the Irish labour market. If demand for labour is seen as segmented (see Dex, 1998), then rates of female labour force participation will be influenced by the nature of industrial and occupational change. The growth in female employment during the 1970s was primarily driven by the expansion of traditionally female jobs in the clerical and service sectors. The pattern changed in the 1980s and 1990s, however, as female employment grew in a wide range of occupations (see Smyth, 1993; Hughes et al, 2000). There is also some indication that a growth in third-level participation has been associated with the increasing feminisation of some professional occupations, such as medicine, law and accountancy.

The growth of educational participation and the nature of labour market restructuring go some way towards explaining the increase in female labour force participation in the absence of declining fertility levels. This increase was also facilitated by the progressive removal of legislative constraints on female employment and the introduction of employment equality legislation, most of which occurred in the 1970s (as mentioned earlier). However, it should also be recalled that married women's participation rates remain low by European standards. This suggests that the overhang effects of long-established disincentives to married women's employment should not be forgotten. High marginal rates of income taxation for married women have long discouraged women from labour market (re)entry while similar barriers affect women whose spouses are dependent on social welfare payments. Furthermore, the provision of early childhood education and publicly-funded childcare services is extremely low in comparison with the rest of Europe. Reliance on privately funded childcare increases the costs attached to maternal employment and forms a particular barrier to mothers who cannot command high levels of pay.

In summary, economic growth in the Irish context has been accompanied by a trend towards somewhat greater equality in participation rates between women and men, and among groups of women. However, participation continues to be strongly influenced by women's parental status, a pattern that is related to the nature of the welfare régime in Ireland.

13.4 Female labour market patterns and gender equality

In this section we consider the consequences of the rapid growth in female participation for gender equality, taking particular account of pay differentials, occupational segregation and working hours. Has women's increasing presence in the labour market been accompanied by a decrease in the gap between men's and women's pay? Has increasing female participation diluted the gender segregation in the Irish labour market? Are women's hours of work approaching those of men or has increased participation (especially among mothers) widened the gap between men's and women's hours?

Gender differentials in pay

Assessing the long-term trends in gender pay differentials in Ireland is difficult due to the lack of appropriate data. Consistent information on earnings back to the 1950s is available only for those in the manufacturing sector (CSO series on Industrial Earnings, Employment & Hours Worked, published annually in the *Irish Statistical Bulletin*). These figures show that the ratio of women's wages to men's wages amongst this group has increased since 1955. However, the rise has not been a continuous one (see figure 13.7). The size of the wage ratio remained relatively stable at 56-57 per cent between 1955 and 1972. The most dramatic rise occurred between 1972 and 1980 when the ratio increased from 57 to 69 per cent. In the early 1980s there was very little change or even small declines in the ratio. However, in 1988 the ratio started to improve again and gradually increased to 75 per cent in 1998.

Figure 13.7: Trends in the Irish female to male hourly wage ratio among industrial workers and trends in female labour force participation

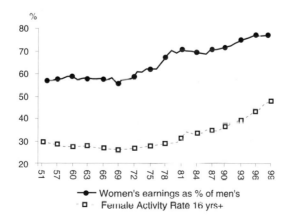

So how do trends in the gender wage gap relate to the trends in female participation outlined earlier? The most dramatic change in the wage ratio occurred in the 1970s which was also a period of rapid growth in female participation. During this period trends in both participation and in the gender wage gap are likely to have been affected by equality legislation, which outlawed pay discrimination and increased women's access to the labour market. We can compare trends in the gender wage gap and in female labour market participation more accurately for the period 1983 to 1998. Figure 13.7 suggests that there is a relatively strong relationship between these two factors. In the early- to mid-1980s there was little change in either the female participation rate or the gender wage gap (in the manufacturing sector), while in the late 1980s and 1990s both indicators increased steadily. However, there is some sign that the wage ratio is flattening off while female participation rates continue to rise.

The figures on the gender wage gap among industrial workers are of limited value because employment in this sector encompasses less than one-third of total employment in Ireland, and an even smaller minority of female employment (18 per cent) (Ruane and Sutherland, 1999). The female-to-male wage ratio in the industrial sector bears no necessary relationship to the economy-wide ratio. Callan and Wren (1994) and Barrett et al (2000) have produced estimates of the gender wage gap for a more representative sample of employees in Ireland, though the figures cover a much shorter time period (see Table 13.1). The gender wage gap for all employees is substantially smaller than for industrial workers in the same year, but is consistent in the trends identified: both sets of figures suggest that the gap has been narrowing since 1987. The research by Barrett et al (2000) further shows that the portion of the wage gap that is not attributable to the differences in individual characteristics has fallen since 1987. In other words there has been a decrease in the portion of the wage gap that could be most directly attributed to discrimination.[5]

The analysis of changes over time conducted by Barrett et al (2000) suggests that the wage gap narrowed in part because women were spending more years in the labour market (increased participation) and because of increased female educational qualifications. However, the report is cautious on whether continuing increases in participation will lead to further improvements in the gender wage gap. At present there is a very strong relationship between educational level and participation among Irish women. If continuing labour market expansion means that women with fewer qualifications are attracted back into the labour market or do not leave work when they have children, then the gender wage gap may widen or remain static.

Table 13.1: Female to male wage ratios* – all employees

	Wage Ratio (%)
1987	80.1
1994	82.4
1997	84.5

* Calculated from gross hourly wages.

Source: Barrett et al (2000).

Occupational segregation

The persistent gap in men and women's hourly wages in part reflects the segregation of men and women into different types of jobs, and perhaps more importantly, into different levels within occupations. Here we assess whether the degree of gender segregation has declined with women's increased presence in the labour market. Women's share of total employment increased from 26 per cent in 1971 to 38.3 per cent in 1997. Over that period, women's share of employment within occupational categories has varied very widely, and occupations have fared quite differently over the 26-year period.

Table 13.2: Female share of employment within occupational categories 1971-97

	1971	1981	1986	1990	1997
All Employment	26.4	28.9	32.1	33.0	38.3
Personal service (catering, cleaning, etc.)	77.4	71.9	73.1	71.6	75.9
Associated professionals*	64.0	68.0	69.3	73.0	66.6
Clerical workers	59.4	65.9	68.5	69.8	73.5
Professionals	42.4	39.6	42.8	42.2	43.8
Sales workers	38.7	40.3	42.7	41.9	53.0
Skilled production workers	32.9	20.3	22.6	17.3	15.4
Production operatives	30.7	24.9	28.0	27.8	30.5
Managers/prop	18.7	17.7	18.5	22.5	29/33
Agric. workers	9.1	6.6	7.1	7.9	8.7
Foremen/supervisors man**	8.4	8.0	10.3	16.4	
Security workers (inc. gardaí)	2.5	3.1	4.0	4.9	10.0
Labourers	0.9	0.9	1.7	2.6	4.4
Transport/communications	0.6	1.1	1.8	2.1	5.6
Skilled maintenance	0.0	0.4	0.6	2.4	2.7

Source: Corcoran et al (1992); Hughes et al (2000).

* Includes occupations such as nursing, physiotherapy and computer programming
** In 1997 foremen/supervisors are grouped with skilled production workers.

We focus first on the period from 1971 to 1990 for which consistently defined data are available. These data show that in 1971 women were under-represented (compared to their share of the workforce in that year) in seven of the 14 categories: agricultural workers, managers/proprietors, skilled maintenance, 'foremen'/supervisors, transport/communications, security workers, and labourers. Women were over-represented in another 6 occupations: professionals, associated professionals, clerical workers, skilled production workers, sales and personal service occupations. Only in the semi-skilled 'production operatives' category was women's share roughly proportional to their presence in the labour market.[6]

By 1990 women had increased their share of employment in most of these occupational categories. However, the broad picture of gender segregation remained intact. The main change was that women came to be under-represented among skilled and semi-skilled production workers, due largely to the decline in the textile/clothing industry. Otherwise, women continued to be over-represented or under-represented in the same occupations as in 1971.

The occupational coding has changed slightly for the 1997 data.[7] However, except in the case of transport these changes are unlikely to have been responsible for any shifts in the female share of occupations. The figures for 1997 show that women have continued to make significant inroads into a number of male-dominated occupations. For example, in 1997 women made up 29 per cent of managers, which represents an increase of seven percentage points since 1991. There was also a significant increase in the women's share of the male-dominated security occupations. Between 1990 and 1997 women also increased their share of a number of female-dominated occupations: sales-work, clerical and personal service occupations. Therefore while increased female participation has reduced segregation in some occupations, it has enhanced segregation in others.

From a gender equality perspective an increasing female share in labouring jobs is not the same as an increase in professional and managerial positions. Women's growing representation in managerial occupations and their stable but high representation within professional and associate professional jobs, is very positive. Nevertheless there is evidence of considerable vertical segregation within these occupations, and women are severely under-represented in the very top layers of those occupations (Ruane and Sutherland, 1999; O'Connor, 1999). Furthermore the relatively low status and pay of female-dominated 'associated professional' groups such as nurses, compared to similar level occupations, have been highlighted in recent industrial disputes. The strong growth in the share of clerical jobs and sales jobs held by women may have less positive implications for gender equality since the status, pay and level of control exercised are much lower; again the impact of this change will depend on sex divisions within these occupational groups.

If we consider the distribution of female workers we can see that while there have been some substantial changes in the occupational structure of female employment such as the decline in agricultural and manufacturing employment (skilled production workers and operatives) women remain concentrated in a relatively small number of occupations (see Table 13.3). In 1971, 50 per cent of working women were employed in clerical, sales or personal service activities. In 1997, 53 per cent of employed women were located in these occupations. Furthermore little change in this proportion is forecast for 2005 (Hughes et al, 2000).

Table 13.3: Distribution of female and male workers by occupational group 1971-97

	Women					Men				
	1971	1981	1986	1990	1997	1971	1981	1986	1990	1997
Personal service	15.9	13.5	14	13.6	16.7	1.7	2.1	2.4	2.7	3.3
Associated professionals	6.6	9.7	9.9	10.9	10.8	1.3	1.9	2.1	2.0	3.4
Clerical workers	25.1	31.6	30.2	28.4	25.5	6.2	6.7	6.6	6.0	5.7
Professionals	11.3	12.7	14.1	15.1	13.9	5.5	8.0	8.8	10.2	11.1
Sales workers	9.1	9.1	9.8	9.0	10.8	5.2	5.5	6.2	6.1	5.9
Skilled production workers	8.3	5.7	5.1	4.5	3.4	10.4	11.3	9.8	10.8	11.7
Production operatives	9.4	7.5	6.9	6.7	6.9	7.6	9.2	8.3	8.6	9.7
Managers/prop	4.5	5.1	5.1	6.5	7.8	7.0	9.6	10.5	11.0	11.2
Agric. workers	9.1	3.8	3.4	3.6	2.2	32.4	22.1	21.2	20.6	14.5
Security workers (inc. Gardaí)	0.2	0.3	0.4	0.4	0.7	2.5	3.7	4.5	3.9	3.8
Labourers	0.2	0.1	0.2	0.3	0.0	9.1	6.3	5.4	4.8	5.4
Transport/communications	0.1	0.2	0.2	0.3	0.7	6.2	6.1	5.9	6.0	6.8
Skilled maintenance	0.0	0.1	0.1	0.3	0.3	4.9	6.9	7.4	6.9	7.4
	100	100	100	100	100	100	100	100	100	100

Source: Corcoran et al (1992); Hughes et al (2000)

Part-time employment

The final labour market 'outcome' we address is working hours. We consider whether increased labour market participation among women has been associated with increased divergence in the working hours of men and women. Ireland has a lower incidence of part-time work than many other European countries. For example, in 1985 only 6.5 per cent of Irish workers were employed part-time compared to an average of 12.7 in the EU.[8] By 1997, 12 per cent of Irish workers were working part time compared to 17 per cent in the EU. As in other countries, part-time employment in Ireland is primarily a female activity: in 1997 nearly one in four women were working part-time compared to only 1 in 20 men. However, the proportional increase in part-time working between 1983 and 1997 has been greater amongst Irish men than Irish women (Table 13.4).

Table 13.4: Percentage of male and female workers working part-time, 1983-97

	1983	1990	1993	1997	Diff. 83-97 % points	Ratio 1997/83
Men	2.7	3.3	4.8	5.4	2.7	2.0
Women	15.3	16.8	21.1	23.1	7.8	1.5
All	6.7	8.0	10.8	12.3	5.7	1.8

Source: Sexton et al (1998)

The increase in part-time employment has undoubtedly facilitated mothers of young children to participate in the labour market, especially given the low level of publicly provided childcare and the expense of private provision.[9] Analysis of the 1996 Living in Ireland Survey suggests that women with children aged under 10 make up 41 per cent of those women working part-time although they represent only 31 per cent of the female workforce. However, the growing proportion of women working part-time is significant for gender equality for a number of reasons. Firstly, this trend may reinforce gender segregation in the labour market. Part-time work is most prevalent in personal service occupations and sales (Sexton et al, 1998), which we have seen have a high female share of employment. Rubery et al (1999) found that in all EU countries except Italy, the proportion of women part-timers working in female dominated occupations (i.e. occupations in which over 60 per cent of the workforce was female) was much higher than for full-timers. Secondly, although the hourly earnings of part-timers are no lower than full-timers when individual characteristics have been controlled (Barrett et al, 2000) there is evidence that part-time workers lose out in terms of promotion opportunities, training and non-wage compensation (Dex, 1992; O'Connor, 1995). Thirdly, it has been found that part-time employment does little to undermine gender inequalities in the domestic division of labour (Layte, 1999).

To summarise, increased female labour force participation in Ireland has been associated with a number of important qualitative changes in employment, which have significant implications for gender equality. Firstly, the gap between men's and women's hourly wages has been declining since the late 1980s, which is undeniably good news for working women and gender equality in the workplace (although there is still a gap of 15 per cent to close). This improvement may encourage more women to join the labour market. However, it is debatable how far further increases in female participation will go to reducing the remaining pay gap. There is already some evidence from the manufacturing sector that increases in the ratio of women's to men's wages are tailing off. Secondly, the impact of increased female participation on gender equality in occupational positions has been mixed. Growing female activity rates have been associated with an increased female presence in a wide range of occupations, but in many cases this increase has not been enough to over-turn long-standing patterns of under-representation of women. There is also evidence of increased feminisation of some traditionally female occupations and a continuing concentration of women in a limited number of occupations. Finally, the growth in female participation has been associated with a rise in part-time employment; while this facilitates the combination of paid work and caring responsibilities, its long-term consequences for gender equality are ambiguous.

13.5 Conclusion

Greater control over fertility and more equal access to the labour market have surfaced as classic concerns of the women's movement from the nineteenth century to the so called 'Second Wave feminism' in the 1960s and 1970s. The transformations which have occurred on these fronts in Ireland since the 1960s have been dramatic. In 1960, women were still faced with the choice of staying single and childless (which usually meant staying sexually inactive) or marrying and having little personal control over the number of children they had (although some degree of fertility control within marriage had emerged by then). Today, the starkness of these options has dissolved: marriage is no longer the critical gateway to either sex or child-bearing, nor does it entail such a surrender of control over the precise number of children to have. Women bear far fewer children as a result, and the child-bearing function has ceased to have such a dominating position in their lives, both in day-to-day practice and in the imagery of what women's role ought to be. This is a transformation of major proportions, and represents a fulfilment of key elements of the historic feminist project.

Women's economic role and position in the labour market has also changed dramatically and has greatly advanced the cause of women's economic equality with men. Women's secondary qualifications and participation in higher education has overtaken men's, female labour force participation rates have risen, wage differentials have narrowed, and women have increased their share of a number of high status occupations.

Do these changes mean that gender equality has arrived and that the 'woman question' which was pushed onto the political agenda in the 1960s has been resolved and disposed of? Few would answer 'yes' to that question and a number of issues identified in the present chapter give reasons why. On the fertility front, though old questions of contraceptive rights have been dealt with and are no longer controversial, new ones have emerged. These keep issues associated with child-bearing and child-rearing at the centre of debates about gender equality (this is over and above the question of abortion, which continues to divide opinion in Ireland to the present). The rapid rise in lone parenthood, caused in part by a movement of child-bearing outside of marriage, is one instance which has been pointed to here. Lone parenthood has implications for gender sharing of responsibility for children which remain fundamental to the question of gender equality and which are far from satisfactory resolution.

Within the labour market there remains a substantial gap in men's and women's wages, and while less of this gap can be attributed to direct discrimination, its continuing existence undermines women's bargaining power and reinforces the unequal distribution of domestic and caring work and leisure time. Despite women's gains in a wide number of occupations, including managerial positions, the Irish labour market remains highly segregated by sex and there is little prospect of significant change in the near future. The continuing sex-stereotyping of occupations limits the choices of both men and women in the labour market, while the persisting male dominance in the highest level jobs also highlights that equal numbers within occupations does not imply equal access to power or rewards. The continued separation of men and women into sex-typed occupations may be partially fuelled by the growth in part-time work noted above. This rise in part-time employment has uncertain consequences for gender equality both within the labour market and in the domestic sphere. These trends in the Irish labour market, encompassing growing numbers of highly qualified, professional and managerial level women and a growing band of female sales workers, personal service workers and part-time workers, suggests there is also a potential for increased divisions between different groups of women within the labour market.

NOTES

1 The pay differential at the top of various pay scales in the public service was generally about 20 per cent in favour of either men or married men – Commission on the Status of Women (1972: 28, 55-57).

2 Comparable data on female labour force participation in Spain is only available from 1985 onwards but it is likely that it would have been lower than for Ireland in 1983.

3 In the analysis of trends, the EU average excludes the three new member states, Sweden, Austria and Finland.

4 Callan and Farrell (1991) argue that increasing female wages in the 1970s were responsible for a large part of the rise in female participation. However, the discussion in section 13.3 above suggests that this is just one of a wide range of factors.

5 Of course differences in the characteristics of men and women (e.g. qualifications, work experience, etc.) may in part arise from discriminatory processes.

6 Within this broad occupational group, however, there is a high degree of gender segregation (see Corcoran et al, 1992: 118).

7 The most significant of these were, separating proprietors from managers, grouping foremen/supervisors with other skilled manual workers, moving farm managers and farm labourers from 'agricultural' category to the management and labourers groups (see Sexton, Canny and Hughes, 1996, Appendix II, for further details).

8 Relates to the current 15 EU members (European Commission, 1998).

9 The Expert Working Group on Childcare 1999 report that the cost of childcare as a proportion of average earnings in Ireland is among the highest in the EU.

14

Political Culture, Growth and the Conditions for Success in the Irish Economy

RONA FITZGERALD AND BRIAN GIRVIN

14.1 Introduction

The Irish economy has experienced unprecedented economic growth during the 1990s. Various factors have contributed to this outcome, including substantial FDI, European Union funding, social partnership and good luck. However, an important question is how and, indeed why, these factors came together during the 1990s to facilitate the job-rich growth that now characterises the Irish economic success story. This chapter suggests that an important element of the Irish success story is the interaction between political culture, expressed through the core values of the society, and the policy and decision-making process. This interaction means that not all policy options are available to policy-makers at all times. Nor does this imply that rejection of some economic maximising strategies is an irrational choice for a society; on the contrary, it is to acknowledge that economic modernisation imperatives may clash with other policy priorities.

The chapter provides an historically nuanced explanation of how Irish political culture mediates change, how it can constrain policy choices and how it affects the pace as well as the scale of change. To assert that certain core values persist in the Irish political culture is not to imply inability to change, or lack of change. What is important is to understand that this persistence can determine what policy options are available to policy and decision-makers at various times. Rather than assert political culture as a causal variable in the explanation of Irish growth, we suggest that it is another explanatory variable complementing those identified in the other contributions to this book. The causal variable is the imperative for change posed by modernisation and industrialisation and accelerated through Ireland's involvement with the European Union. What we suggest is that Ireland has mediated change, in general, and economic growth in particular, in a distinctive manner. Further, we wish to propose that while culture provides the environment in which society operates, political action can change the nature of the decisions made within the culture and can in time also change aspects of the culture itself. Political culture provides a means of understanding the interplay between the two and an explanation of the constraints and possibilities experienced in a specific context.

Three interrelated elements can be identified in the Irish context. First, the forging of consensus on economic management that begins with the agenda-setting changes of the 1960s is contested up until the late 1980s and is positively adopted in the 1990s. The second element is social and constitutional change which until the mid-1980s was resisted and in some cases curtailed by the assertion of the dominant political culture. The third element is membership of the European Union. The EU is crucial as both an external force for policy and agenda setting through Structural and Cohesion fund interventions and as a promoter of social and constitutional change and review. The provision of financial resources and the imposition of programming following the 1988 reform of the Structural Funds, provided the context for national policy-making for a range of spheres from innovation through social inclusion, equality and employment This agenda setting coincided with and contributed to Ireland's distinct resolution of internal crisis and pressure for change. In addition, the adherence to the Maastricht criteria after 1992 provided a framework for macroeconomic policy.

The late 1990s demonstrate how these elements came together, in Ireland, to provide the basis for substantial economic growth and social change. However, the concluding section of the chapter will highlight the tensions, some evidenced in the recent response to the budget proposal on individualisation of tax allowances, that still persist between economic modernisation and growth and the retention of core values in the Irish context.

14.2 Culture and economic success

It is sometimes assumed that economic success is a relatively straight-forword process. If a society seeks comparative advantage, accepts the discipline of free trade and keeps state interference to the minimum, then considerable benefits will be gained. However, while not wrong, such a view has to be modified by the experience of successful economies in northern Europe and in Asia (Sørensen, 1993, Weiss 1997: 3-27) as well as by historical studies of the developmental process (Harrison, 1992; Landes, 1998). One of the key assumptions of this chapter is that successful economic development is not easy. Growth in isolation may produce what Mjøset (1992: 5) has described as 'auto-centric development (growth with development)'. Auto-centric development is a qualitatively distinct process incorporating such outcomes as sustained growth, high levels of employment creation, widespread welfare and the elimination of forced emigration. Most states have not achieved this qualitative level of development, nor is there any guarantee that those who do can maintain it with ease (International Monetary Fund, 2000). Landes (1998: 512-14) claims that 'If we learn anything from the history of economic development, it is that culture makes all the difference.' He rejects the view, as we do, that culture is destiny but suggests that there is a complex relationship between economic opportunity and the cultural values of a society, that underwrite success or failure (see also Harrison, 1992). Culture may empower or it may constrain economic development and its impact on the decision-making process will give to a society its particular dynamic. Furthermore, comparative advantage is not fixed, but can move in favour or against a state or region. Scotland and Northern Ireland achieved comparative advantage between the eighteenth and twentieth centuries, but lost it in the second half of the twentieth century (Devine, 1999). While market signals may appear the same, they are interpreted and internalised through a specific framework. Consequently, economic success or failure cannot be attributable to any one set of factors, but to the interaction with and response to internal and external forces.

Each political culture has also to be placed in an historical context, reinforcing the claim that while a culture may endure it is not impermeable to change. Modern political culture is a product of the response to the break-up of the agrarian world in the eighteenth century and the growth of the industrial urban world of the following two centuries (Gellner, 1988). Adaptation to this challenge was mediated in a fashion which drew on pre-existing cultural norms and values. A comparison of the way in which the United Kingdom, the United States, Germany and Japan negotiated this period highlights both the contrasts and the similarities (Moore, 1966). The contrast may also be measured by the way ethnic identity and nationalism were used to meet the challenge of this changing world, though in different ways. In most cases, nationalism emphasised difference between peoples, even when these differences might have appeared insignificant to the outsider (Smith,1991; Gellner, 1983).

Political culture is generally associated with norms, values and beliefs, implicitly of a long standing and deeply rooted nature (Almond and Verba, 1963; Verba, 1965: 512-60; Woshinsky, 1995). These features are not the only focus for political culture; institutional arrangements will also be included as will mass political action. Thus, a political culture will have a normative, institutional and mass level, which has been described as the macro, meso and micro (Girvin, 1989b; 1997b). This is a multidimensional process, one that provides for interaction between the different levels. The macro level preserves the deeply rooted values of a specific society, such as religion or national identity, while also transmitting a normative context to each generation. These norms and values are what Collingwood (1940: 31-2) described as Absolute Presuppositions, providing the foundations of a belief system. The meso level includes institutional arrangements for the continuity of the society and could include the constitution, the form of the political system or more generally the rules of the game for political behaviour. The micro level is where individualistic and mass political behaviour occurs, though short-term considerations are probably primary at this level.

While each level can be autonomous, there is also a degree of interaction between them. However, change is more likely to occur at the meso or micro level than at the macro level. Change can be driven by mass or élite concerns, but change that is too rapid, unrepresentative or in conflict with the core values of the macro level will be countered by political mobilisation at either or both the meso and micro levels. Gradual change can be more easily accommodated but not without strain if the consequence of change is to transform the core values. Different strategies will be pursued at the mass or élite level to achieve particular political objectives, but not all (or even most) of these will have an impact on the macro political culture. Clearly the relationship between the three levels is a complex one and we do not intend to explore it in more detail here. However, it is sufficient to claim that all societies have Absolute Presuppositions that, though not unchanging, do have a powerful normative impact on society. In turn the nature of the Absolute Presupposition will influence the institutional arrangements of the society and inform the possible options available to both élite and mass at times of change.[1]

14.3 Irish political culture

Ireland provides a test case for the claim that there is a relationship between the political culture and the performance of the economy. Historically, Irish nationalists have claimed that the Union with the United Kingdom retarded Irish growth and that independence would unleash the economic potential of the society (O'Brien, 1921; O'Malley, 1981; Girvin, 1997b). However, Lee (1989: 528) provided a very pessimistic assessment of Ireland's economic performance after independence, concluding that 'it is at the human level that the solution to the mystery of the mediocrity of Irish socio-economic performance seems to lie'. This suggests that there were constraints other than the Union that blocked Irish economic progress. Irish political culture is normally associated with a number of characteristics including nationalism, religion, the land, authoritarianism and patriarchy (Chubb, 1982; Coakley 1993: 25-48; Girvin, 1997a: 122-38, Galligan 1993). For the most part, these features had been well established by the time the Irish Free State was founded in 1922. Subsequently the new state reinforced most of these values institutionally, culminating in the introduction and ratification of a new constitution in 1937 (Keogh, 1988: 4-84).

The constitution gave express recognition to Irish nationalism in a number of articles and also to the family, the farm and religion. It provided a template for an agrarian, conservative, catholic, communalist and patriarchal society with the role of women firmly proscribed within the family and the home. Article 41.2 of the 1937 Constitution set the context for policy-making that has resulted in discriminatory treatment of Irish women in law and public policy (Galligan, 1993; Scannell, 1988), while other articles reflected the dominant traditional and pre-industrial culture. In the Irish case, the different levels of the political culture remained in harmony with one another and with the values expressed in the constitution until the 1960s. A number of studies have emphasised the popular acceptance of these values (Biever, 1976; Whyte, 1971; Inglis, 1998). The Irish political culture that was in place in 1960 was shaped by the adaptive strategies pursued by Irish nationalism in a predominantly agrarian society following the famine, the industrialisation of Britain and the loss of the gaelic language by the majority of Irish people.[2]

While the main challenge to Ireland came after World War Two, the nationalist strategy promoted by Fianna Fáil after 1932 weakened the economy, making it less capable of responding to change. The commitment to economic nationalism and protection was based on ideological considerations – the Fianna Fáil leadership continued to believe that the links with the United Kingdom were the cause of Ireland's economic problems. Consequently, the so-called 'economic war' was a wound inflicted by a government driven by nationalist presuppositions. It is probable that the long decline of Irish agriculture and of Ireland's relative decline in respect of Europe can be dated from this conflict. State-supported industrialisation hid some of the accompanying difficulties, but could not postpone the crisis indefinitely (Girvin, 1989a). The role of the state was also enhanced between 1932 and 1961, as most economic sectors became dependent on the state for their income and market. Between 1945 and 1961, Ireland's development path diverged significantly from other small export-dependent democratic states in Europe. In most cases (Norway, the Netherlands, Denmark and Finland) these states integrated into the world economy, industrialised and developed new export markets. The Irish economy remained dependent on agriculture, on farm exports to a single market, and on a heavily protected, but small, industrial sector. By the beginning of Ireland's New Economic Policy in the 1960s, the income gap between Ireland and the European average had widened appreciably. Nor did the economic changes introduced between 1959 and 1973 or membership of the EEC thereafter change this situation (NESC, 1989: 117). By 1989 Ireland still lagged behind average European Union income by over a third. Ireland did narrow the gap with the

United Kingdom, but this can be attributed to Britain's relative decline rather than to any significant improvement in Ireland's overall positions.

14.4 Modernisation Irish style, 1959-73

Despite renewed optimism in the early 1960s there does not appear to have been any easy answer to Ireland's continuing difficulties. Irish policy making was successful during this decade only when compared to the failures of the 1950s and not if compared with other developing European states or those already participating in the long boom prompted by European industrialisation. Moreover, the Irish state was now operating in an environment that was increasingly outside its control and one which from an Irish viewpoint was more unstable. This was brought home to Irish policy makers in 1961 when the United Kingdom decided to apply for membership of the European Economic Community. Prior to this the only body of opinion in favour of membership was the National Farmers Association (NFA later the Irish Farmers Association, IFA), on the grounds that they would benefit from the Common Agricultural Policy (Murphy, 1997: 57-68). While the government quickly recognised the attendant benefits of membership, the primary reason for the application remained the need to defend Irish access to United Kingdom markets, rather than any positive assessment (Girvin, 1996b: 247-62). This priority was maintained into the 1970s, remaining a prominent feature of the campaign in favour of joining in 1972. Such a defensive response characterised much of Irish policy making during the 1960s, though changing circumstances did provide the stimulus to introduce new policies in respect of industry, trade and education. The decade should also be seen as a point of departure in some policy areas – during the 1960s and early 1970s the Irish élite began to experiment with more innovative policies and to recognise the importance of the European dimension for growth.

In political terms continuity is the main feature of the time, with Fianna Fáil re-establishing its traditional dominance at the 1969 election (Gallagher, 1981). Social change is incremental and cannot be compared with the considerable disruption experienced by most European states at this time (Post, 1989; Bax, 1990; Eatwell ed., 1997). In economic terms, change is more in evidence. The most important change was the successful negotiation of the Anglo Irish Free Trade Agreement which came into operation in 1966. In policy terms this confirmed the formal abandonment of economic nationalism and protection, as well as the belief that an independent Ireland could follow a successful economic policy in isolation from the rest of Europe (Girvin, 1989a; Horgan, 1997; Murphy, 1996). The return to free trade coincided with a growing commitment to the European departure, but it also overlapped with the failure to realise a domestically generated economic expansion. While the Irish economy recovered between 1959 and 1966, self-sustained growth had by no means been achieved. Participation in the European economy benefited Ireland, but its late entry deprived it of the benefits generated earlier by other similarly placed small, open economies. Even more seriously for the future, there is little evidence that Ireland was developing a national system of innovation identified by Mjøset (1992: 5-22) as the key to successful growth with development.

This weakness can be explained by a number of contributory factors. The original objective of Lemass's economic policy failed to be realised, as this presumed that domestic industry could make the transition to export-led growth. Domestic Irish industry remained 'resistant' to this transition, in large part because of its protected nature and continuing reliance on the state. Consequently, in general Irish industry did not develop a propensity to export at a time when most economic benefits were being derived from export strategies (Committee on Industrial Organisation, 1965; Committee on Industrial Progress, 1973). The continuing commitment to agriculture compounded this problem as its exports and output were stable, while the sector continued to shed labour. In addition, agriculture was now a well organised interest group committed to enhancing its income by using its political influence. Throughout the decade the NFA insisted that farm income should be subsidised by the state, a demand that became more difficult to resist on the part of the government (National Archives, 1962 S11563 B-E; Manning, 1979; Murphy, 1996:156-98). The situation was further aggravated at the end of the decade by increased militancy on the part of the trade unions, which led to a number of serious disputes (McCarthy, 1999; Hardiman, 1988). These three factors contributed to a serious policy dilemma for the government. Fianna Fáil continued to insist that the party was a national as well as a nationalist one and this entailed convincing the electorate that the changes would benefit all sections of society. As Whyte (1973: 619-51) has shown, Fianna Fáil drew support from most social classes, but so too did Fine Gael. If Ireland indeed had a 'politics without social bases' (Whyte, 1973) then it was politically important for Fianna Fáil, as the largest party, not to alienate any specific sector of the electorate.

This dilemma was resolved between 1966 and 1973, but by external intervention rather than domestic initiative. Most of the manufacturing growth by 1967 was accounted for by foreign direct investment and this recognition led to the reorientation of industrial policy, in particular the restructuring of the Industrial Development Authority while giving it control over industrial policy. The Irish state used its resources to compete internationally for mobile capital, to assure Ireland's further industrial growth (Survey of Grant Aided Industry, 1967; Industrial Development Act 1969; Telesis, 1982). The decision to join the EEC resolved the potential distributional conflict between urban and rural interests. Consequently, the Europeanisation of agricultural policy transferred the cost of agricultural subsidies to the richer regions of Europe at little cost in the short term to Ireland. This imperative to sustain Irish agriculture, rather than a commitment to European integration, was acknowledged by Garret FitzGerald (1991b:1-15), as a key factor in the decision to join the EEC. The limited nature of Irish integration becomes more obvious when it is recognised that Ireland was unlikely to have been invited to join as a full member without its existing close ties to the United Kingdom economy.

14.5 The impetus for change 1973-87

Irish belief systems, behaviour and attitudes were undergoing some modification during the 1970s, but in general terms, more traditional norms and values maintained their strength among the population. Mac Gréil (1977: 362-427) identified continuing authoritarian attitudes among his Dublin sample, but his research also highlighted the emergence of a liberal-conservative division on core issues such as Northern Ireland, the Catholic church and moral issues. The evidence we have for the 1970s suggests that some institutional change was taking place, prompted for the most part by modernising élites but also in response to membership of the EEC. In particular, a range of European directives on pay and conditions, judicial decisions in the Irish Supreme Court and the European Court of Justice, allied with demands from the Irish women's movement, provided a strong impetus for change in the area of women's rights (Scannell, 1988). Nevertheless, the evidence suggests that the impact of this was quite limited with regard to the majority of the electorate. Probably more representative was the decision of the Taoiseach Liam Cosgrave and six of his fellow Fine Gael TDs to vote against a motion in favour of legalising contraception supported by the government parties (Girvin, 1986: 61-89). This episode provides an important example of how deeply rooted values can obstruct change introduced by élites at the meso level. On Northern Ireland a similar pattern of reinforcement of traditional norms was the main feature of this period, though Fine Gael was developing a more moderate view on the problem (Girvin, 1994b). On most issues this was a period of conflict avoidance on the part of the political parties if not actual consensus. While Irish political culture was experiencing more disharmony, at the end of the decade the core values remained largely impervious to criticism or amendment.

This tenacity had consequences for economic policy. If in 1973, FDI and membership of the EEC promised to provide Ireland with a positive sum outcome, avoid distributional conflict and secure internal political stability, the onset of recession after 1973 undermined this prospect. By 1973 the Fianna Fáil government was running a deficit on current expenditure (as distinct from capital for investment) and this change in budgetary policy initiated a borrowing and expansionary process that continued for over a decade (Whitaker, 1986: 12-15). This shift in policy can be attributed to the desire to offset the electoral threat from Fine Gael and Labour, but there was also considerable public expectation that the state should extend public services, increase income and expand consumption. While Fianna Fáil lost the 1973 election, the new Coalition government followed a broadly expansionary path in 1974 and 1975. Nor did membership of the EEC constrain national macro-economic policy, as European regional policy at this time mainly co-funded national projects (Fitzgerald and Michie, 1997: 14-28). The oil crisis and the recession forced the Coalition, under Fine Gael pressure, to adopt a more restrictive policy (Economic and Social Development, 1976: 5-12), a recognition of the threat to economic stability. However, the inevitable competition resumed once a new electoral cycle began in 1977. In February the Coalition budget was well received (Irish Marketing Surveys, 1977a), but Fianna Fáil responded with an election manifesto which promised, in effect, to eliminate unemployment, promote further growth and protect society from the threat of recession (Fianna Fáil, 1977; Sinnott, 1978). This proved extremely successful and Fianna Fáil quickly built up a commanding lead in the polls on the main issues (IMS, 1977b).

Fianna Fáil may also have benefited from its emphasis on state action to achieve development, an emphasis that received considerable support in a survey carried out by the ESRI not long before the election (Davis, Grube and Morgan, 1984). There was widespread agreement that the state could achieve particular objectives; 74.6 per cent agreed that inflation could be cured, 'If the state would take the right steps', while 71 per cent considered this to be the case for unemployment. Furthermore, approximately 60 per cent agreed that given the state of the economy Ireland would be better served by a 'good strong leader rather than the existing political system'. This view is given added force by the 58.5 per cent who agreed that 'The majority of people are not capable of determining what is, or is not, good for them'. While there is considerable support for wage control, only 51 per cent would accept a reduction in their standard of living if this helped to reduce unemployment. There is little evidence in this sample that the Irish believed in merit as a criteria for advancement; 78 per cent agreed that 'It's who you know not what you know that is important for getting on in life'.

That these beliefs were widespread does not mean that all sections of the population would gain equally from state intervention. In fact for most of this time the evidence suggests that property owners generally and farmers in particular were extremely successful at mobilising to achieve their objectives, certainly more so than other groups. As Ireland moved from growth (up to 1973) to recession there was a return to traditional zero-sum assumptions on the part of the electorate. In a context where employment and resources are in short supply, there will be a tendency for those with organisational strength to mobilise to achieve redistribution in their favour (Olson, 1982). Corporate, property and consumption taxes all declined as a proportion of tax revenue while income tax and social security contributions increased significantly (Maguire, 1986: 269; Breen, et al, 1990: 196-212). The IFA demonstrated its effectiveness in the run up to the 1977 election by organising opposition to Coalition plans to tax the farming sector, a strategy which led to a substantial decrease in support for Fine Gael among large farmers (Gibbons, 1989: 15-17; Sinnott, 1978: 53). This influence was maintained into the 1980s and can be contrasted with the ineffectiveness of trade union mobilisation on tax and other issues, despite the huge demonstrations in favour of tax reform in 1979 and 1980 (Jacobson, 1994: 130-43; Girvin, 1984).

Although Fianna Fáil's developmental strategy failed, both because of its internal contradictions and the second oil crisis, it draws attention to the continuing attractiveness of state-based solutions to Irish problems among the electorate. If, as Breen et al (1990: 211) suggest, Irish governments have tried to avoid distributional conflict by promoting growth, this strategy failed after 1973. However, one of the consequences of this was that the cost of the recession up to 1983 was transferred to the state. In turn this led to further borrowing which increased debt and contributed to a deteriorating economic environment by 1980. Nor did FDI or EEC membership provide a positive answer to these difficulties. Indeed, when measured by employment creation, linkages to the Irish economy or research investment, FDI's impact remained limited (Telesis, 1982; O'Malley, 1992c). By the early 1980s Ireland was in crisis, increasingly the problem economy of the EEC. If membership of the EEC is measured in terms of convergence, employment or living standards, then Ireland did not benefit significantly between 1973 and 1989. The Irish experience demonstrates that membership alone is not enough to secure the benefits of integration and free trade – this process needs to be accompanied by an active domestic policy.

In contrast to the electoral competition between 1969 and 1977, the period 1981 to 1989 can be characterised as one where the political foundations for an anti-inflationary coalition were established. There is the significant surge in support for Fine Gael between 1977 and November 1982, placing it in direct competition with Fianna Fáil's. Moreover, Fine Gael attracted support from all social groups, but was especially successful with the middle class, the skilled working class and large farmers (Sinnott, 1987: 70). Fine Gael now provided a serious alternative to Fianna Fáil and its traditional politics. On economic issues, it built an anti-inflationary majority, on Northern Ireland it successfully negotiated the Anglo-Irish Agreement in 1985 and in the 'Constitutional Crusade' FitzGerald focused on divisions between liberals and conservatives in

Irish life. Yet, FitzGerald was unable to maintain an electoral majority for the Coalition, even if its economic and Northern Ireland policies acquired widespread political support, nor was his constitutional crusade successful in changing Ireland in a liberal direction (Girvin, 1987; FitzGerald, 1991b). While this draws attention to elements of continuity in Irish political culture (Fogarty, Ryan and Lee, 1984), serious strains had appeared and these were driving the emergence of a political division between liberals and conservatives.

Haughey opposed the Anglo-Irish Agreement on traditional nationalist grounds, yet failed to generate support even among Fianna Fáil supporters (Irish Political Studies, 1986:144; Irish Political Studies 1987:155). In fact, disagreement within Fianna Fáil on this issue was one of the contributory factors to the establishment of the Progressive Democrats. A more complex division emerged on issues associated with the Catholic church, the Constitution and the moral agenda. In this context, Haughey and Fianna Fáil were very successful in neutralising the 'Constitutional Crusade', adopting the referendum on abortion and defeating the referendum to introduce divorce (Girvin, 1986: 61-86; Hesketh, 1990; Hug, 1999). Carroll (1991: 53-72) has emphasised the considerable rhetorical and emotive appeal that traditional values retain in the Irish context. The abortion and divorce referenda support this view, especially when the issue divides the main political parties on core normative values.

The Coalition was more successful on the economic front though it did not gain electoral advantage from this. In the European context, the agenda in the 1980s was about lack of competitiveness and the cost of *Non-Europe*. Member states agreed reforms that were necessary to bring about the Single Market – originally called the Common Market in the Treaty of Rome 1957 – and were gearing up for the Single European Act (1986) and the proposed reform of the Structural Funds in 1988. These developments provided an impetus for the internal debate on better management of the economy. As noted above, Fine Gael received strong support from the middle class, large farmers as well as the skilled working class. This provided the core support for its anti-inflationary, anti-borrowing strategy, but it was not enough to secure a consensus on what was essentially a deflationary policy. To do so the Coalition, and especially the Minister for Finance, Alan Dukes, stressed the threat to Irish sovereignty that borrowing and debt presented. While pursuing a neo-liberal policy, the Coalition emphasised that its approach would maintain Irish policy-making autonomy that had been eroded by Fianna Fáil (O'Malley, 1989: 31-56; Farrell, 1987: 1-30). Though successful in exploiting these concerns in the electorate, a consensus did not at first emerge. ICTU was explicitly excluded from influence (FitzGerald, 1991b: 454) and the neo-corporatist institutions downgraded. The 1983 budget was particularly severe, with the middle class and large farmers satisfied with it, and the working class and small farmers least satisfied.

Although Fianna Fáil had adopted a deflationary stance during the 1982 election campaigns, in opposition it reverted to a cautious reflationary policy. The key Fianna Fáil criticism was not that control of the public finances was not necessary, but that there was no developmental aspect accompanying it (*Irish Times*, 7 February 1985; Girvin, 1987: 9-29; Mair, 1987: 30-47). Opinion poll evidence on budgetary strategy remained seriously divided for the remainder of the decade, but a more positive assessment is in evidence after 1987.

Nor had views changed significantly on the role of the state in job creation. The MRBI (1983) twenty-first anniversary poll reported that 87 per cent agreed that 'Every person leaving full time education has a right to a job'. When this sub-group was asked who was responsible for providing the employment, 64 per cent replied the government and 5 per cent business or industry.

The 1987 general election draws attention to a number of distinctive features in the Irish political process. Though the Coalition government was unpopular, it was the Progressive Democrats rather than Fianna Fáil that benefited from this. Yet the Progressive Democrats' individualistic and neo-liberal policies were not universally endorsed, even by its own supporters. This may be because sections of the middle class were reluctant to accept radical tax reform if this entailed significant cuts in public services (Laver, 1987:113-26; Lyne, 1987: 107-14). Furthermore, during the election campaign Haughey was placed on the defensive on the Anglo-Irish Agreement and on Fianna Fáil's proposals in the economic sphere. The main consequence of this was the extension of the anti-inflationary coalition to include Fianna Fáil by election day, as well as Haughey's acceptance that a Fianna Fáil government would maintain the Anglo-Irish Agreement in place (Girvin, 1987: 9-29). While Haughey was in a position to form a minority government in 1987, he was dependent on the support of Fine Gael and the Progressive Democrats to remain in office. Alan Dukes, the new leader of Fine Gael, deepened the macro-economic consensus by agreeing to support the government on spending cuts in the 'Tallaght Strategy'. Dukes' policy was approved by a majority as well as by 52 per cent of Fine Gael supporters (*Irish Political Studies*, 1988:142). This arrangement reinforced the consensus that had emerged at the 1987 election, though it did not extend to moral issues.

This agreement on macro-economic policy and Northern Ireland did not limit the possibilities for the Haughey government to act in an innovative fashion. In sharp contrast to the Coalition government, he initiated a return to corporatist arrangements with the Programme for National Recovery (1987). In contrast to earlier attempts to achieve national agreements, the PNR proved to be more successful in achieving its goals. A plurality (45 per cent) agreed that the PNR would 'contribute to the economic recovery of the country', while 24 per cent believed that it would not. The 31 per cent with no opinion probably reflected a genuine level of uncertainty after previous experience of similar arrangements. Surprisingly the middle classes and large farmers were more likely to agree than were the working class, while agreement was low among Labour Party supporters (*Irish Political Studies*, 1988:142).

The policy mix adopted by Fianna Fáil in 1987 had more in common with some social democratic governments (such as the Australian Labour Party) than with neo-liberal regimes. The former included a deflationary element (particularly savage in 1987-88), but it also promoted corporatist arrangements with the trade unions and other interest groups. Furthermore, commitments to welfare provision were maintained to avoid social disruption and to maintain national inclusiveness in the face of unemployment. It was easier for Fianna Fáil to pursue this strategy as it fitted in with that party's belief in national cohesion and consensus rather than confrontation between competing interests. It also provided opportunities for state involvement, important for a party not wedded ideologically to neo-liberalism. By acting in this fashion, Fianna Fáil changed the nature of the consensus and Ireland's economic recovery. In effect, Haughey's minority government generated the political and social foundations to accompany the economy's success and gave it an institutional form. Consequently there was no Thatcherism Irish style; indeed ICTU enhanced its institutional weight, achieved at considerable cost, which allowed it to counter the long-term influence of farmers and property owners. ICTU had a valuable asset to trade: wage restraint, industrial relations stability and social consensus. The agreements became more sophisticated and detailed over time, allowing the trade unions to promote their agenda; this included tax reform, improved welfare provision and job creation (see Hardiman, this volume).

If the main gain for ICTU was access and influence, Fianna Fáil benefited by dividing ICTU from the Labour Party, which remained sceptical of corporatism. Another important factor is that while the electorate was deeply concerned about inflation and rising taxation, a significant section continued to value state intervention in various policy areas, mainly but not exclusively in the social policy sphere. The government seemed to have got the balance right by 1989 (Girvin, 1990:7-9). Considering the harsh nature of the deflationary policies, their popularity was not affected. Gallagher (1990:101-02) has shown that the gap between those satisfied or dissatisfied with the government narrowed appreciably between February 1987 and January 1989, although those registering dissatisfaction increased once Haughey decided to call a snap election for June of that year. In contrast to the experience of the Coalition, this government, despite its severe deflationary policies, maintained its popularity for a considerable period.

14.6 Reinforcing consensus and the modification of political culture in the 1990s

From the 1960s to the 1980s Irish economic development was generally obstructed by the way in which the political culture was configured, by the distribution of power and resources and by the priorities associated with the national interest. However, the crisis during the 1980s, the response of the élite to this and the role of the European Union as an agenda-setting agency combined to provide the basis for the political and social consensus that reinforced economic success during the 1990s. After the 1988 reforms of the Structural Funds and the Treaty on European Union in 1992, European Union membership provided Ireland with both a limited range of policy choices and a clear set of policy objectives (Fitzgerald, 2000).

Furthermore, the specific political and social patterns established by the end of the 1980s were quickly institutionalised and extended during the early 1990s. One consequence of this has been the erosion of difference between the political parties and the main interest groups. In 1992 ICTU and the Labour Party supported a referendum on the European Union for the first time, a position maintained and deepened during the referendum on the Amsterdam Treaty in 1998. The Labour Party also accepted social partnership, despite previous misgivings with it. When the Rainbow Coalition was formed in 1994, Fine Gael readily accepted the need to continue the social partnership – a distinct shift in policy on its part. In addition, the participation of Democratic Left extended this consensus further to the left (Girvin, 1999a). In terms of government formation, it seemed that by 1997 any variety of coalition, except between Fianna Fáil and Fine Gael, was possible. In part this was a consequence of Fianna Fáil's assessment of the electoral arithmetic, but it was also a recognition that the difference between the parties was now so narrow. The 1997 election campaign confirmed the narrowness of the difference between all but the smallest parties (Girvin, 1999a: 3-28; Garry and Mansergh, 1999: 82-106).

The 1992 election and the surge in support for the Labour Party did not break the patterns established in the party system over the past 40 years. Despite Fianna Fáil's loss of votes in that election, by 1997 Fianna Fáil and Fine Gael still attracted 67 per cent of the vote and this increases to 78 per cent if the Labour Party is included in the calculation. The surge in support for the Labour Party in 1992 can be compared to that for the Progressive Democrats in 1987, involving a temporary swing which was not maintained. This is not to claim that there has been no change or that what change there has been is patternless.

Marsh and Sinnott (1999: 160-61) report considerable volatility in 1997, a finding which may point to greater complexity within the party system rather than significant change. The political system has been modified somewhat as a consequence of voter volatility and a greater number of parties in competition, but the widespread consensus and the continuing dominance of the traditional parties reinforce continuity rather than change in this area. Indeed, Whyte's (1973) characterisation of a politics without social bases retains its importance. Table 14.1 provides data on the support received by the parties in terms of class.

Fianna Fáil continues to attract a plurality of support in each category except farming, where it lags behind Fine Gael. Together Fianna Fáil and Fine Gael continue to gain the support of over two-thirds of each social class.

Table 14.1. Party and class in 1997* (per cent by column)

	Upper and Middle classes	Skilled Working Class	Unskilled Working Class	Farming
Fianna Fáil	38	51	49	41
Fine Gael	31	18	23	46
Labour Party	9	14	9	4
Progressive Democrats	7	3	4	3
All Others	15	14	15	6

Source: Irish Marketing Surveys, 'Election Poll No. 5, June 3 1997. *Excludes undecided.

Fianna Fáil remains the party of the skilled and unskilled working class, if not a working class party. The distribution of support for the Labour Party is also of interest as it receives approximately the same level of support from the upper and middle classes as from the unskilled working class. Although both Fianna Fáil and Fine Gael have lost some support since the 1970s, both can still claim to be national parties drawing support, if somewhat unevenly, from most sections of the Irish electorate.

While the consensus has been largely élite-driven, there have also been changes in mass opinion. In respect of the economy, opinion has shifted from one of cautious pessimism at the beginning of the 1990s to a more optimistic, if still cautious, view at the end. After the 1993 budget, 39 per cent still believed that the standard of living would fall while 54 per cent considered that it would remain the same. In 1997 the figures were 12 per cent and 67 per cent respectively (*Irish Political Studies*, 1994:207; *Irish Political Studies*, 1998: 238). In 1994 two thirds of respondents concluded that the budget would not help employment, but a year later this had dropped to 51 per cent with some 34 per cent now agreeing that the budget would improve employment opportunities (*Irish Political Studies*, 1995:280; *Irish Political Studies*, 1996:231). A majority continued to believe that the government or the IDA had the responsibility to provide more jobs, while just 12 per cent considered that it was the employer's responsibility (*Irish Political Studies*, 1992:161). However, two thirds agreed with the view that 'The political parties could find an answer [to unemployment] if only they agreed to work together' (*Irish Political Studies*, 1995:280).

One by-product of this is the continuing endorsement of social partnership; 53 per cent of those interviewed in 1994 favoured it, but among the middle classes support rose to 66 per cent and among Progressive Democrat supporters to 69 per cent (*Irish Political Studies*, 1995:300). By 1999, 78 per cent agreed that social partnership was important for Ireland's economic development, with the middle classes providing the most consistent support. In contrast to previous polls Labour Party support for social partnership increased significantly, placing it ahead of Fianna Fáil and just behind the Progressive Democrats. Respondents in this poll made an important distinction between the importance of social partnership in general and who would benefit from the arrangements; 33 per cent considered that the gap between rich and poor would be widened as a consequence of the agreements, while 44 per cent believed it would make no difference. Labour Party supporters were more likely than any other party supporters to adopt the view that the gap would widen (MRBI Poll, 1999). This confirms an earlier finding that three quarters concluded that the 1997 budget would most benefit those on high income (MRBI Poll, 1997). In 1997 also a relatively small proportion of the Irish electorate considered that they had benefited positively from economic expansion. Two-thirds of those questioned believed that neither they nor their families' living standards had improved as a consequence of any 'economic boom'. Opinion poll evidence demonstrated the differential impact of changing economic circumstances, with the middle classes reporting an improvement to a greater extent than other social groups. About three-quarters of the unskilled working class and over 70 per cent of farmers reported no improvement (Irish Marketing Surveys, 1997).

This may also have had an impact on the election, as those who did not feel better off were more inclined to vote for the Fianna Fáil/Progressive Democrats Coalition than the Rainbow Coalition. Consequently, for most Irish people, it is probable that the full impact of economic success and prosperity has only been felt since 1997 and it is likely that this will play a considerable part in the evaluation of parties at the next election. By early 2000, the government was maintaining a high satisfaction rating as was the Taoiseach, Mr Ahern (MRBI Poll, 2000b).

The evidence suggests that at the economic level, success and prosperity gradually penetrated the consciousness of the mass of the population. The recognition that Ireland is now an affluent society and the consequences of this is likely to alter the actions and behaviour of individuals in the future. This, however, does not entail that the political culture has been altered radically; rather it has been modified in a number of respects. If the 1990s was a decade of economic achievement, it was also a time when the social conservatism of the previous decade was in large part reversed in respect of divorce, contraception and homosexuality (Girvin, 1996c; Hug, 1999). Yet abortion remains an active and controversial issue, one which is only likely to be resolved by another referendum (Green Paper on Abortion, 1999; MRBI, 1999). This draws attention to the continuing salience of moral issues in the political culture.

14.7 Conclusions

The chapter set out to chart the interaction between political culture and the policy-making process in Ireland and to suggest that this interaction affects the range and the timing of policy options available to policy makers. We have also set out to show that while change and development are possible, given time and attentive management, the dilemma is exacerbated when economic modernisation imperatives clash with core values. This is evident in Ireland from economic nationalism as pursued in the 1930s, 1940s, and 1950s, through the primacy of farming interests in policy making until the 1980s, the constitutional provision on property that even now could affect the timing of policies to address infrastructural deficits, and the response to the recent budget proposal to individualise tax allowances.

We would suggest that the élite political culture (meso) has changed most, prompted by both internal and external forces. The mass political culture (micro) has also changed, but this level has divided between liberals and conservatives as well as between those who do or don't benefit from prosperity. National identity remains the most cohesive core value and is likely to continue to be the case. Most of the changes that have taken place since the 1960s occur at the lowest level of the political culture, the micro level. Here attitudes have become more fluid, more heterogeneous and most controversial.

There has also been change at the institutional level, though even here, the vote on divorce and important amendments to the Constitution highlight the constraints on change. We would argue, however, that there has been relatively little change in the core values of the society at the macro level, and it is here that the most serious questions arise. If this realm of political culture is fairly immune from change, what impact can it have on behaviour at the lower levels? While there is no clear answer to this, what does seem to be the case is that the macro level will maintain its hegemonic/ordering role even while considerable changes are occurring at the lower levels as long as these changes are gradual and do not openly challenge traditional values (Dowding and Kimber, 1983: 229-43). The attempts to change the Constitution in respect of divorce and the recent controversy concerning the budget illustrate this enduring tension. In the case of divorce, after the rejection of divorce in 1986, considerable care had to be taken before and during the second referendum campaign in 1995. This included introducing legislation to meet the concerns of existing families and assurances to the electorate that removing the prohibition would not undermine the family.

In the case of the recent budget proposals it seems that the need for negotiation and time to filter through the policy process were ignored. The proposal in the January 2000 Budget, to provide an individual allowance to married women who enter the labour market, had to be modified in response to public and political reaction. The scale of the negative response was considerable despite active consideration within the Irish policy process of issues around equality, childcare and barriers to labour market participation. However, those who rejected the proposal articulated concern about the fundamental tax and constitutional issues involved in a move to individualise tax allowances and reiterated the policy of successive governments to refocus tax and social welfare in favour of the family unit. This piece of cultural defence underlines the enduring capacity of the Constitution to inform responses to policy making and to constrain policy choices.

NOTES

1 Other distinctions can be applied when discussing political culture. One would be that between the political culture of liberal democracy, authoritarianism or totalitarianism. Within liberal democracy, distinctions might be drawn between a political culture which is primarily individualistic, hierarchical, parochial or collectivist. At the most general level all societies have Absolute Presuppositions within the macro level.

2 Ireland and Irish is used exclusively in this chapter to refer to the catholic nationalist majority on the island. It does not refer to the protestant unionist nation, largely concentrated in the north east and whose political culture has more in common with Scotland than with the rest of Ireland (Girvin, 1999b).

ACKNOWLEDGEMENTS

Brian Girvin wishes to acknowledge support from the Robertson Bequest, University of Glasgow, in funding research for this chapter.

15

Social Partnership, Wage Bargaining, and Growth

NIAMH HARDIMAN

15.1 Introduction

Many commentators have accorded the practice of social partnership an important place in explaining the Irish *Wirtschaftswunder* of recent years. This chapter seeks to explore the nature of the social partnership process and how it has contributed to the economic success story. It also seeks to locate social partnership in the wider context of political representation and decision-making, and to ask how firmly institutionalised it has become in the framework of national policy development.

Section 15.2 outlines the model of national-level co-ordinated pay bargaining which underlies the Irish process of social partnership. The next section surveys the pay agreements negotiated in Ireland since 1987. This is followed by an exploration of the difficulties inherent in the process, and an examination of how well the problems have been dealt with to date.

15.2 'Co-ordinated' pay policy

The resumption of a centralised approach to pay-bargaining in 1987 and the integration of pay policy with issues such as tax reform and welfare spending commitments may in some respects appear anomalous in the period since the late 1980s. All the western economies have been subject to new pressures arising from moves toward free trade and free capital mobility, or 'globalisation'. The need to improve competitiveness within national boundaries has led to a disruption of national-level processes of wage determination (Traxler, 1995). The need for increased flexibility has given rise to pressures to make wage-setting more responsive to company-level variations in profitability and competitiveness. Where centralised bargaining was unable to respond to these needs, as in Sweden, the centralised agreements collapsed altogether, giving way to a more decentralised locus of pay bargaining (Thelen, 1993; Locke and Thelen, 1995; Pontusson, 1996; Lange, 1996; Iversen, 1998).

Pay bargaining practices in Britain and the USA come close to the model of market-led outcomes, where the weakness of trade unions has enabled employers to achieve significant flexibility in pay and work practices. However, there is little reason to expect that all pay bargaining systems must or should converge on this neo-liberal model, or that the only alternative to market regulation is direct state intervention. State and market should not be thought of as antithetical; and there are other modes of regulation of economic performance (see, for example, Regini, 1995: 4-5).

An alternative model is the more co-ordinated approach to wage bargaining, common to much of continental Europe and to Japan, which can produce outcomes that are compatible with promoting economic competitiveness, but which avoid the socially and politically divisive consequences associated with the neo-liberal model. This co-ordination need not necessarily be provided by a centralised trade union movement; it may arise from employer-led co-ordination, and may result in industrial or sectoral-level bargaining (Soskice, 1990, 1999).[1] As Soskice, among others, has pointed out, business interests in the co-ordinated market economies of continental Europe and Japan have increasingly sought, not deregulation on the British or American models, but reregulation of industrial relations and product markets, 'to preserve for their companies long-term financial frameworks, co-operative skilled workforces, and research networks in order to remain competitive in world markets where such resources give them a competitive advantage' (Soskice, 1999: 134).

Among the co-ordinated responses to changes in the international economy, national-level politically-mediated agreements have not been rendered obsolete. A new form of national-level social pact has emerged which combines adaptation to competitive needs with an explicit political commitment to social protection and social equity. This model of 'competitive corporatism' (Rhodes, 1998), or what Regini (1999) has termed 'organised decentralisation', accommodates employer concerns about competitiveness and flexibility. It also involves government commitment to maintaining social spending and minimum welfare standards that are not present in decentralised market-liberal models of wage determination, and which typically do not feature explicitly in sectoral or industrial-level bargaining systems. The emergent model of 'competitive corporatism' may be identified in the agreements governing pay bargaining and social policy issues in the Netherlands, in Finland, and to some degree (with much weaker union involvement) in Spain and in Italy. It is the contention of this paper that the Irish experience of social partnership can be understood as an experiment in 'competitive corporatism', and that the dual commitments to competitiveness and social equity have contributed to the successful period of growth and unprecedented job creation (see also Aust, 1999).

'Competitive corporatism' was worked out in response to domestic economic problems. But the wide European context also provides new challenges to which national economies have to adapt, and which affect the kind of 'domestic coalitions' that are put together. Katzenstein (1985) argued that the vulnerability of small, open economies to external constraints tends to induce the principal economic interests to forge consensus-oriented domestic coalitions, co-ordinated at national level, to mediate the impact of international pressures on the domestic economy.

There may be a pressing logic to the argument, but this is no guarantee that the functional imperative will be met (Crouch, 1994:178). The role of political leadership in enabling employer-labour pay co-ordination may prove crucial. In Ireland, for example, union and employer organisations are strong but not highly centralised and may find it difficult to achieve co-ordination autonomously.[2] The adoption of shared macroeconomic priorities in pay bargaining makes it easier for employers and unions towards a centrally negotiated framework pay agreement. But the intervention of government may be necessary to make it a reality.

Pérez (1999) has argued that attempts in both Spain and Italy to adjust to developments in the wider European economy, especially the need to adapt to the requirements of monetary union, had far-reaching consequences for remodelling the conduct of pay bargaining. She argues that in neither country did employers or unions have much capacity to co-ordinate wage bargaining themselves. Government initiative played an important role in bringing it about. She argues that 'the imposition of a tight monetary policy ... is likely to allow sheltered sectors to set the pace of inflation, and hence, eventually, that of nominal wage growth throughout the economy ... It is only through framework bargaining or a re-centralisation of bargaining that the exposed sectors of an economy have a chance to regain some say over this pace' (p.30). The interest of the trade union leadership in sustaining employment led them to seek to balance the competing points of view of exposed and sheltered sectors, through national-level framework pay agreements. There is indeed some more general evidence that where the exchange rate is fixed or non-accommodating to inflationary pressures, a co-ordinated approach to pay bargaining works better than a market liberal or non-coordinated approach – and better than a highly centralised approach too (see, for example, Iversen, 1998:3).[3]

This perspective may throw some light on the renewal of a centralised approach to pay bargaining in Ireland from 1987 onwards. The principal macroeconomic constraint was that of extreme fiscal difficulty – very much a domestic political issue. But throughout the late 1980s and the 1990s, pay bargaining was also conducted in the context of the need to adjust to broader European economic constraints, in which exchange rate policy featured increasingly strongly.

The domestic adoption of externally-induced constraints was an important influence on centralised bargaining from 1987 on. All the actors recognised the depth of the domestic economic crisis of the 1980s. They came to share a common view of Ireland as a small, open economy whose fortunes were ever more deeply implicated in those of the wider European economy. This recognition of the extent to which domestic economic performance depended on externally given circumstances marks a distinctively new phase in the development of social partnership. Its origins in the deep fiscal and economic difficulties of the mid-1980s profoundly marked the character of the social partnership process.

15.3 The Irish experience: from managing crisis to managing growth

Internal crisis, external constraints: the origins of social partnership

A series of four three-year pay agreements has been negotiated in Ireland since 1987, with a fifth ratified in March 2000. Over this time, the economic climate has been transformed, from the dark days of fiscal crisis, perennially high unemployment, and little hope of improvement, to the heady experience of economic boom, steady growth in population and employment levels, and a new confidence in the country's performance and prospects. Social partnership agreements, worked out originally to meet the first set of problems, have adapted in form and content to deal with the new challenges.

Centrally negotiated pay agreements had a precedent in Ireland's 'policy repertoire'. Collective bargaining over the postwar decades had taken the form of a loose sequence of pay 'rounds'. During the 1970s, in an attempt to dampen wage inflation and contain industrial conflict, governments had sponsored the negotiation of a series of national wage agreements, through which pay and tax had come to be explicitly linked. But it has been argued that these never really approximated to the continental European model of 'societal corporatism' or 'social concertation' (Hardiman, 1988). In view of the upward trend in nominal pay increases, rising inflation, and mounting strike rates, private sector employers withdrew their support in 1981. They were determined to make pay settlements more responsive to firm-level conditions and to ensure that real concessions were secured in exchange for productivity-based pay increases. A period of decentralised bargaining ensued between 1981 and 1987. High and rising unemployment dampened wage pressures. But a sense of escalating economic crisis, and the apparent inability of government to devise a convincing strategy in response to extreme fiscal difficulties, changed the context of pay bargaining quite profoundly (see Hardiman, 1988:231-4; Hardiman, 1992).

By the mid-1980s a real sense of crisis pervaded the country. Unemployment stood at over 227,000, or 17.4 per cent of the labour force, in 1986 (Sexton et al, 1996:42, 43), and almost two-thirds of these were classified as long-term unemployed (ibid: 48). Emigration increased steadily, taking many of the 'best and brightest'. By 1987 a sense of hopelessness reminiscent of the worst days of the 1950s was widespread, summed up in the phrase 'the country is banjaxed'.[4]

The tripartite consultative body, the National Economic and Social Council (NESC), originally established in 1973, now took on a new role. It developed an analysis of the nature of the country's economic problems and the priorities that needed to be addressed. Its document, *A Strategy for Recovery* (1986), set out the analysis agreed on by all participants. It recognised that reform of the public finances was imperative. It accepted that moderation in pay increases would be essential to improve competitiveness and thus generate the necessary economic improvement, though it did not explicitly advocate an incomes policy. This NESC report committed the participant organisations to the attainment of specific performance targets on the public finances, expressed in figures: 'NESC developed the debt/GNP ratio as a performance measure long before Maastricht.'[5]

The minority Fianna Fáil government that took office in 1987 accepted the terms of the NESC report, and convened the tripartite talks that led to the negotiation of the Programme for National Recovery (PNR). The intervention of government was crucial to achieving co-ordination, the need for which had already been recognised in principle.

Yet the contingency of the first agreement is easy to forget in hindsight. Considerable misgivings were expressed within the Irish Congress of Trade Unions (ICTU). The Irish Business and Employers' Confederation (IBEC) was initially reluctant to be involved and sceptical that the agreement would hold. The deal combined a moderate pay deal with tax concessions to boost take-home pay. What secured the success of the package was an upturn in the international economy and a drop in the inflation rate which turned a very modest pay settlement into an increase in real disposable income (see Honohan, 1999). This contrasted with the period 1981-87, when the nominal earnings of manual workers rose by 101 per cent but real take-home pay dropped by 7 per cent (NESC, 1999: 237). Fortuitous external circumstances helped the PNR to initiate a 'virtuous circle' of improved domestic economic performance, which paved the way for successor agreements (see also Prondzynski, 1997; Durkan, 1999: 47).

Undoubtedly the shared sense of economic crisis helped to bring trade union and employer leaders together; in this sense, patriotism and a sense of responsibility to the wider community played an important part in shaping participants' views (see also Dore, 1994: 29). But the institutional and political bases for maintaining the 'virtuous circle' were now in place. While the negotiation of a new agreement could never be taken for granted, there was certainly a bias in favour of renewal of the process with the expiry of each old agreement. Furthermore, all parties participated in government over the period since 1987, which tended to further stabilise the social partnership approach to pay determination. Despite criticism from individual commentators, there was no organised bloc of political opposition either to the process of social partnership or to its outcomes.

The negotiation of the next two three-year programmes, the Programme for Economic and Social Progress (PESP, 1990-93) and the Programme for Competitiveness and Work (PCW, 1993-96) broadened the range of bargaining issues surrounding the central framework pay agreement. The process of social partnership, it may be argued, gained in problem-solving capacity.

Those negotiating the pay terms of the PESP had to deal with the uneven performance of the economy during the course of the PNR. While some enterprises were clearly profitable and able to pay more than a moderate pay settlement would permit, recovery in economic growth was producing very little in the way of additional employment – fears of 'jobless growth' were widely shared. The PESP permitted a 3 per cent element of local bargaining to accommodate the need for company-level flexibility. Evidence on the extent to which it secured worthwhile productivity increases in exchange for this is mixed, but on balance favourable (Taylor, 1996: 269; Roche, 1997: 212). But, overall, IBEC was concerned that instead of functioning as an exceptional outlet, it had come to be expected by all bargaining groups. Anxious about the possibility of a return to the two-tier bargaining of the 1970s, the employers opposed any new local bargaining clauses under the PCW. Despite intense pressure on the leadership of ICTU during the currency crisis of the early 1990s, when members suffered from short-term but painful increases in interest rates, the agreement held firm. Evidence suggests that the wage drift was in general relatively low under the first three agreements (Sheehan, 1996; Roche, 1997).

Turning the corner: managing prosperity

By 1996, when the PCW was nearing expiry and NESC was preparing its background strategy document for a new agreement (NESC, 1996), the sense of economic crisis, of an economy near collapse, of a polity running out of ideas, had receded into the past.

Against this backdrop, commitment to the 'virtuous circle' was maintained: a new pay agreement was negotiated, termed Partnership 2000 (1996-99). Despite the fairly modest nominal pay terms, the total increase in take-home pay was estimated to average 14 per cent for single people and 16.2 per cent for married people. In fact, cumulative increases in real take-home pay over the whole period 1987-99 for an employee on average manufacturing earnings was estimated to amount to over 35 per cent (NESC, 1999: 237).

Pay determination in a new era

Ireland became a member of the European Monetary Union (EMU) in January 1999. With no further domestic control over monetary or exchange rate policy, adjustment to external shocks could only be mediated through fiscal policy or pay adjustments. This gave pay agreements an even more important role in economic management than hitherto. A new pay agreement was negotiated, under the title of Programme for Prosperity and Fairness (2000-2003). The pay terms, at about 15 per cent over 33 months, were a good deal higher than in any previous agreement. Tax cuts were due to give a further substantial boost of about 10 per cent to disposable income. The rather high nominal pay terms reflect the tightness of the labour market – pay trends have always, of course, been subject to market forces as well as to pay agreements (see Fitz Gerald, 1999). The economic projections continued to forecast high and steady growth into the future.

Successes and stresses

In summary, the pay agreements negotiated through the evolution of social partnership since 1987 undoubtedly contributed to the remarkable turnaround in the economy. Real increases in disposable income were delivered while keeping industrial conflict at low levels; inflation was curbed effectively, at least until early 2000; the national finances were transformed. The national framework of pay bargaining made it possible for the far-reaching trade-offs between wage moderation and tax reform to take effect. Once growth began in earnest, the pay agreements helped to ensure that the gains were not dissipated by wage inflation and industrial conflict.

Critics of social partnership such as Teague (1995) argue that it amounts to little more than an 'institutional adjunct to a harsh and uncompromising competitive disinflation strategy'; that it was driven by enthusiasm, misplaced on the unions' part, for European integration, involving adherence to a hard monetary regime which bore heavily on workers' living standards; that employment growth was negligible; and that considerations of equity were completely overlooked.

However, the evidence does not support such an interpretation. The exchange rate regime was a good deal less rigid than Teague assumes and disinflation was not secured at the expense of living standards. Although the expansion in employment did not become apparent until the mid-1990s, the foundations for the remarkable performance in job creation had been laid during the period in which Teague argues that nothing happened (see Barry, 1999).

The trade union movement recognised that the economy had entered a 'virtuous circle'. The unions particularly welcomed the opportunity to influence the wider terms of political debate on issues of unemployment, education, income maintenance policy, and a host of other issues relating to economic and social policy. The process of consultation itself broadened from 1997 onwards to include the community and voluntary sector, reflecting 'the concern to ensure the fairness necessary for social cohesion, an essential underpinning to successful policy implementation' (McCarthy, 1999: 9).

But the overall experience of social partnership should not be construed as a frictionless exercise in consensus. Even though NESC had provided a forum within which a consensual analysis of economic and social issues could be worked out, there were some systematic sources of difficulty that made it difficult to keep the agreements working according to plan. By and large, the institutions of social partnership have proven able to respond flexibly to new challenges. Some of the issues thrown up proved easier to resolve than others. Six sources of difficulty may be identified, which will be considered over the following sections. These are:

- Industrial sectoral conflicts – traditional manufacturing versus modern high-tech
- Differences between the bargaining systems in public and private sectors
- In the private sector, conflicts between business interests and employees over workplace social partnership
- Difficulties arising from growing income dispersion
- Problems accommodating the priorities of the community and voluntary sector
- Conflict between governments' electoral priorities and the partnership process.

15.4 Sectoral conflicts

Any pay agreement purporting to span the whole economy is likely to encounter problems accommodating the diverse needs of different sectors. The Irish economy has been experiencing profound structural change since 1987. Some sectors have been very successful indeed, generating large productivity gains and profits. The foreign-owned sector overall has been far more successful than the indigenous sector (NESC, 1999: 241, 325). This is partly a function of enterprise scale, but is also a feature of the industrial sectors in which they are concentrated, among them pharmaceuticals and chemicals, and microelectronics. On the other hand, some parts of the traditional manufacturing sector were hard-pressed to accommodate the terms of the pay agreements.

The high-tech sector, labour scarcity and upward pay pressures

In much of the software industry, the supply of skilled labour was at a premium from the mid-1990s on. Most of this sector is not unionised, and wage increases in excess of the pay agreement norms were common. It was estimated that wage cost increases were running at between 10 per cent and 15 per cent per annum in the latter part of the 1990s (Ó Riain, 1999: 37-42). Labour shortages in a range of skill areas began to emerge as a serious problem in the late 1990s, earlier in some sectors. It would appear that the 'expectations consensus' (Dore, 1994: 29) essential to maintaining the cohesion of pay pacts had begun to unravel. At a time when wage flexibility has become more necessary, not less, in view of Ireland's membership of European Monetary Union, market pressures increased the diversity in the terms on which firms can settle.

A further feature of the pay agreements in general is that employee expectations are more keenly shaped by the experiences of the recent economic situation than by anticipation of the conditions that a new pay agreement must meet. The surge of growth in GDP, in exports, and in employment, between 1997 and 2000 made many bargaining groups feel dissatisfied with the terms of Partnership 2000. Their keenness to 'catch up' makes it more difficult to build up a new consensus around the requirements of life within the Euro-zone. The pay agreements are future-oriented but backward-looking. This may give rise to more pay conflict in the course of the Programme for Prosperity and Fairness.

The traditional manufacturing sector

Cost competition in the more labour-intensive, lower-productivity and low-paid traditional manufacturing sector was keenly felt. Even the modest basic pay increases of the framework agreements constituted a threat to the viability of some enterprises. These employees also found themselves at the critical edge of the conflicting exchange-rate priorities which Irish governments were trying to balance during the 1990s. The Irish pound approached parity with sterling for a time during the mid-1990s. The value of non-sterling exports was growing in significance compared with the value of exports to Britain. But a disproportionate number of jobs in marginally profitable and labour-intensive firms in traditional industries such as clothing, textiles, and food production depended on sales in Britain. Nevertheless, job losses continued in the traditional sector during the 1990s, in which low cost was crucial to competitiveness.[6]

The main participants in the partnership process accepted that low-cost-based competition was not sustainable in the long run, and that these sectors were in irreversible decline. On balance, the risk of job losses was outweighed by the benefits of securing sustainable agreements throughout the rest of the economy. The emphasis was placed instead on pressing for skills upgrading and improved productivity in the small-enterprise and low-skill sector, complemented by politically-initiated task forces to seek to find replacement industry for regional job losses.

15.5 Public sector versus private sector

The framework pay agreements since 1987 were supposed to facilitate improvement in the competitiveness of the national economy. This implies giving priority to the needs of the market-oriented sector. The size of the public sector pay bill makes its management a priority issue for government: it amounts to some 60 per cent of current supply services expenditure (NESC, 1999:6.4.3), and about 40 per cent of total current government spending (Gunnigle and Roche, 1995:11).

But control over public sector pay proved a recurrent problem. Public sector pay determination had neither market disciplines to respond to, nor any tradition of productivity-based assessment. Pay bargaining was mainly driven by well-established relativities, which had an in-built tendency to foster leap-frogging pay claims. It was further complicated by 'special' pay increases which tended to spread through the relativities networks.

Compared with pay trends in the economy as a whole, the public sector displayed 'steady and consistent' pay increases throughout the period from early 1988 to the start of 1999: it experienced 'real increases noticeably greater than the general body of employees in manufacturing industry and in financial and insurance industries' (Sexton, Nolan and McCormick, 1999). This does not necessarily only reflect preferential pay increases going to the public sector; issues of public sector workforce composition are involved as well. Nevertheless, pay movements in the public sector proved – and continue to prove – a recurring problem for the social partnership process.

The dynamic set in train by traditional relativities proved to be very difficult to contain.[7] Government came under strong pressure to concede the 3 per cent productivity-based local bargaining provision under the terms of the PESP (1990-93), even though productivity increases were difficult to measure.[8] The issue was postponed until the negotiation of the PCW. The figure eventually conceded was closer to 5.5 per cent. But this then provided the basis for further catch-up relativity-based claims, prompting one commentator to conclude that 'the last attempt at public sector restructuring (under the PCW) was a disaster'.[9] High-profile industrial conflict by Gardaí and nurses in 1998 and 1999 secured them increases well beyond the guidelines. Teachers were among those next in line to submit a catch-up claim. One of the three teachers' unions, the Association of Teachers' Union of Ireland (ASTI), with over 15,000 members, disaffiliated from ICTU in late 1999, prior to the negotiation of the Programme for Prosperity and Fairness, in support of its claim for a 30 per cent[10] pay increase.

By the end of the 1990s, the principal cleavage in the trade union movement could be identified as running between the public sector and the rest (Roche, 1997: 218). Organisationally, public sector employees accounted for some 50 per cent of total trade union membership (Roche, 1997: 200). They continued to be highly unionised, whereas some of the newer sectors, especially in high-tech manufacturing and in private-sector services industries, proved difficult or impossible to unionise. Private sector unionisation is estimated to be about 30 per cent. Public-sector-only unions constituted a powerful bloc within ICTU. SIPTU, the single largest union, is estimated to have 80,000 members in the public sector and 120,000 in the private sector. On the trade union side, therefore, the leadership of ICTU has been hard-pressed to balance the interests of its public sector membership against the rest.

Usually kept muted in public, the conflict broke out in public during ICTU's Special Delegate Conference in November 1999 to vote on entering talks for a successor agreement to Partnership 2000. Des Geraghty of SIPTU issued a blistering criticism of public sector fixation on relativities, in response to the warning by a teachers' union leader that they intended to pursue a large claim to catch up with the nurses' settlement. To loud applause from a majority of the delegates he said:

> You don't live on the moon. Don't expect that private sector workers are going to sit back and see you going in for your special, and your other special and your other special, plus the other national pay agreements and say, 'That's grand. We don't notice.'... Survival into the next millennium is entirely dependent on our ability to manage economic success effectively ... We mustn't take the eye off the ball of the social wage ... If we descend into mere sectionalism, if we descend into differentials as we did in the past, if we descend into the worst form of dog-eat-dog capitalism, because that is what it is about, the strong will succeed and the poor will go to the wall.[11]

But the government had relatively little appetite to confront public sector pay claims during the 1990s. Strikes by Gardaí or nurses or teachers or transport workers are inevitably unpopular and politically difficult to withstand. The public sector Strategic Management Initiative (SMI) was intended to improve services and increase productivity. But while it was welcomed and supported by government, it had originated among senior civil servants and had no political 'sponsor' to drive through difficult institutional changes (Roche, 1998). It did not engage with the extremely difficult issues of relating pay to measurable productivity (see, for example the emphasis on service delivery in Teahon, 1998; *Administration*, 1995). No method had been found to ensure that public sector pay developments were responsive to trends in the wider economy.

The Programme for Prosperity and Fairness (2000-2003) finally committed the social partners to work on methods of reforming the system of public sector pay determination, to move it away from relativities-based bargaining and to tie it more closely to private sector pay trends. A report is due in 2002. The issue is being addressed, but it cannot be claimed that it has so far been satisfactorily resolved.

15.6 Business, employees, and workplace social partnership

The national context

Despite the consensual framework of the pay agreements, conflicting interests are inherent to some degree in employer-labour relations. Since 1987, Irish business has been improving its profitability; the OECD comments that this has undoubtedly been helped by the wage restraint entailed by the social partnership pay agreements. The share of capital income as a proportion of GDP rose from 25 per cent in 1987 to about 38 per cent in 1998, close to the European average (OECD, 1998; NESC, 1999: 240). The wage share has been correspondingly declining, especially in manufacturing. Over the same time-period, cost competitiveness has also been improving across the economy taken as a whole. Even though earnings in national currency rose faster than competitor countries in 1998 and 1999, exchange rate movements offset the negative consequences.

While the trade union movement must accept this as a condition of the ongoing growth in the economy, they are also keen to ensure that they protect their own interests adequately. The stream of scandals and revelations during the 1990s about the financial misdeeds of prominent business and political figures created a mood of disgust and disillusionment. Des Geraghty of SIPTU wrote about the latest revelations regarding prominent people holding enormous sums of undeclared income in off-shore bank accounts as follows:

The whole of Ireland is angry. We waited through a long and costly Beef Tribunal, we read media revelations about financial institutions and politicians; about planning corruption, rezoning and political donations; we waited for justice to be done, for some public acknowledgement of wrongdoing, some admission of guilt, and for recompense. And what did we get? – Ansbacher. ... Clearly, the 'little people' were the only ones who paid their taxes, accepted pay moderation and worked for the common good. They were also the ones to pay the price for economic failure. ... Their pay demands were always characterised as inflationary. ... Here was a classic case of one section of society writing the rules and ethics for the others, but not for themselves.

The trade union movement was committed to using its influence to bring about better outcomes through a process based on consensus. Peter Cassells, commending trade union delegates for their vote to enter new talks in late 1999, said that 'the decision was about more than pay. It was about trying to develop a fairer society purged of institutional corruption, the gold-collar fraud, the money politics, the abuse of power, the political croneyism and the massive tax fraud.'[12]

Thus the trade union movement was committed to the social partnership process as the best way of bringing these issues onto the political agenda. In order to keep the social partnership agreements on track, the unions needed to retain a lot of control over trends in basic pay. Increasingly, they took the view that this would only be possible if the commitment to partnership could be strengthened at firm level.

However, the trade union movement has made relatively little progress on the two issues it signalled as particularly important: developing institutions of workplace participation and consultation; and extending the opportunity for employees to benefit from financial participation in the firm's productivity gains.

Workplace participation

One commentator noted, 'when the Partnership 2000 deal was sold to members in January 1997, it was on the basis that it would allow for a qualitative shift in the nature of relationships between employers and workers.'[13] Chapter 9 of Partnership 2000 was devoted to the need to deepen partnership at workplace level. ICTU encouraged its affiliates to move away from adversarial industrial relations toward a new role as 'business partners' committed to quality improvement.[14] A number of workplace participation schemes were developed on a pilot basis (NESC, 1999: 308). A National Centre for Partnership was set up under Chapter 9 of Partnership 2000 to promote further initiatives on a voluntary basis.

For all that, specific measures to promote initiatives in workplace social partnership are still quite weakly developed, relative to European systems (NESC, 1999: 268). One authoritative investigation concluded that '"exclusionary" forms of decision-making are shown to dominate the postures of establishments towards the handling of change'. Furthermore, where change in workplace practices has taken place it tends to be in line with that of other Anglo-American industrial systems, 'which are not readily permeable to collaborative production', nor very favourable towards consultative or inclusive forms of decision-making (Roche and Geary, 1998).

The trade union movement is committed to expanding all forms of employee workplace involvement. But the key consideration from the employer point of view is that any developments must be wholly voluntary. They oppose the establishment of works councils, other than in the limited form required by EU legislation, or disclosure of company information to employees, on anything other than a voluntary basis.

Financial participation

Profit and gain-sharing schemes would appear to be an imaginative way of resolving the conflicts between the need to maintain high levels of compliance with a pay norm, and the inevitable employer-labour tensions in profitable sectors. Research evidence based on different samples produces very different estimates of the extent of all kinds of financial participation – estimates range from 22 per cent to 58 per cent of enterprises (NESC, 1999: 251-2). They are more common in larger than in smaller enterprises, but are more likely to apply to management than to all employees.

Profit-sharing schemes approved by the Revenue Commissioners numbered 28, covering 16,500 employees, in 1987; 134 covering 21,600 in 1994; and 292 covering up to 30,000 in 1999 (NESC, 1999: 255). This is still a fairly small proportion of all employees.

Among other forms of gain-sharing, employee share-option schemes have been growing in coverage. By the end of 1999, it was estimated that firms employing a total of about 200,000 workers were covered, a high proportion of the private sector. If about 22 per cent of the workforce is employed in PLCs, these figures would seem to be close to saturation point.[15] There is as yet no comparable provision for gain-sharing in privately-owned private sector companies.

SIPTU criticised the fact that more was not achieved during Partnership 2000. Des Geraghty argued that 'for such arrangements to succeed and become widespread, there must be far greater trust. … However, the stark reality is that only a small minority of agreements provided for profit sharing and other forms of financial participation.'

Trade union recognition

Of course the extent of trade union influence at workplace level depends on their having a presence there in the first place. Trade union recognition became a particularly difficult issue in the run-up to Partnership 2000 in the wake of a bitter dispute at Ryanair. The issue was referred to a high-level working group under the terms of Partnership 2000. Its report was accepted by both unions and employers: it set out a protocol for dealing with issues of recognition on a voluntary basis.

But some of the most highly profitable sectors of industry and services are ones in which trade unions have no presence at all, as a matter of company policy. A number of American microelectronic firms and software producing companies do not recognise trade unions and are opposed to union organisation in their enterprises (see, for example, Geary, 1999). The trade union movement has had to concede that the non-union status of such firms cannot be challenged.

15.7 Dealing with wage dispersion

ICTU's organisational capacity to hold diverse interests together has been greater during the current period of social partnership than it had been during the 1970s (see Hardiman, 1988, ch.5), partly due to rationalisation within the trade union movement, and partly due to the enhanced prestige of ICTU arising from the process of social partnership itself. Unions affiliated to ICTU numbered 77 in 1970 and 65 in 1983. In 1999 there were 63, 46 of which, with some 523,700 members, organised in the Republic. But these figures conceal a great many organisational changes. There were 30 amalgamations between 1989 and 2000; 10 new organisations affiliated to Congress. The most significant merger was the creation of SIPTU in 1990, whose 200,000 members in the Republic now constitute almost 40 per cent of total trade union membership. The organisational basis on which 'encompassing' analyses of the economy can be undertaken has grown.

However, the trade union movement sought to represent the interests of a membership the conditions of whose employment were growing more not less diverse. The tensions between higher- and lower-paid employees were not always easy to resolve.

Wage dispersion and low pay

The pay agreements provided a floor or flat-rate minimum increase to protect the low-paid. The agreements were not primarily designed to manage income distribution, but to prevent wage inflation through negotiation of moderate pay increases. But the combination of special provision for the low-paid and moderate settlements for everyone else might have been expected to result in some degree of wage compression in the economy. The main factors accounting for wage dispersion appear to be the compositional changes in the Irish economy, including the large increases in employment in high-tech employment, the continuing decline of the traditional sector, and the availability of a relatively highly-educated workforce (Barrett, Callan and Nolan, 1999).

The lowest-paid also experienced real wage gains under the terms of the agreements. It is generally agreed that the pay agreements prevented real income decline at the bottom of the wage distribution such as has been seen in Britain or the USA over the same time-period (Sexton, Nolan and McCormick, 1999: 64). However, real income growth at the bottom may still be experienced as inadequate when others are visibly doing so much better. Representatives of employees in some sheltered sectors expressed some of the most vociferous complaints about the gains made by their members relative to other groups.

Nor was dissatisfaction confined to the private sector. One of the largest public sector unions, the Civil and Public Sector Union (CPSU), organising some 14,000 employees, held a ballot at the end of 1998 to consider withdrawal from Partnership 2000.

The trade union movement pressed through partnership channels for adoption of a national minimum wage to assist the lowest-paid. On the advice of a working group, government introduced a statutory minimum wage in April 2000, and the terms of the Programme for Prosperity and Fairness (PPF) provide for further increases over the terms of the agreement. But in a climate of ongoing rapid economic growth, raised expectations may be difficult to meet. When pay expectations are heightened for all, the demands of the relatively low-paid, especially in sectors where productivity gains are difficult to measure, are likely to fall behind.

Tax reform priorities

The real disposable income of the low-paid depends heavily on the treatment of tax and social insurance. Despite repeated recommendations by NESC and other bodies, this issue received fitful political attention (Hardiman, forthcoming).

SIPTU withdrew from the Programme for Prosperity and Fairness (PPF) talks in December 1999 in protest at the lack of budgetary consideration for the low-paid in Budget 2000. But the trade union movement also has to pursue other tax reform priorities, including the issue of the threshold at which the higher rate of tax applies.[16] The PPF committed government to ensuring that at least 80 per cent of taxpayers are not subject to the higher rate of income tax (PPF, 1.1.4: 11). In comparison, the commitment that 'over time, all those earning the minimum wage will be removed from the tax net' appears a weaker and more modest aspiration (PPF, 1.1.3: 11).

15.8 'Social Modernisation': widening the partnership process

The first three social partnership agreements were negotiated by the 'traditional' social partners of government, employers, and unions (with farmers participating too). Representation at Partnership 2000 was extended to a range of groups representing a 'third strand', or the 'community and voluntary sector'. This reflected a shift in the emphasis of government policy, associated with the development of the National Anti-Poverty Strategy (NAPS), from 'social equity' to 'social inclusion', 'a strategic objective in its own right' (see NESC, 1999: 12).

The traditional social partners initially resisted the inclusion of the voluntary and community sector in social partnership institutions (O'Donnell, 1999: 21); the impetus came from government through the logic of widening the consultative process. But both unions and employers came to accept them for a combination of pragmatic and principled reasons. The trade union movement had long supported the role of social partnership in advancing discussion of the 'social wage'; including the voices of those outside the wage nexus was a logical corollary. Employer representatives supported them in part at least because of an acceptance that economic policy cannot work effectively unless social policy issues are also addressed. They endorsed the notion that having achieved greater-than-expected successes in economic development, it is appropriate to turn to issues of 'social modernisation'.[17]

Government supported the inclusion of the voluntary and community sector because although their criticism of government policy, expressed through the media, can discomfit government, their support can increase the perceived legitimacy of the social partnership agreements. These groups can command no direct electoral sanction. But the catch-all nature of Fianna Fáil, the weak ideological differentiation of the party system, and the fact that every political party has been in government during the period of the partnership process, leaves governments averse to conflict, keen to seek compromise positions, and anxious to defuse criticism. There has been no party-political disagreement on the desirability of including the community and voluntary sector either in the partnership agreements or in NESC. The reason for embracing this style of political inclusion may be traced back to the small scale of Irish society and the density of social interactions.

There is also a pragmatic justification for inclusion of the community representatives because valuable policy learning is involved. The voluntary sector's experience of the effects of various social policies can help in the design and adjustment of new programmes.[18] In the absence of other feedback mechanisms, this is one means whereby the bureaucracy can be held to account, however imperfectly.[19] Partnership 2000 gave rise to many new partnership-based working groups on diverse policy issues, including, for example, the Inter-Departmental Committee on Childcare, various initiatives on women's health, domestic violence, the needs of the travelling community, the needs of people with disabilities, and racism (see NESC, 1999). The Programme for Prosperity and Fairness makes commitments to about 35 partnership-based working groups at national level, some of them bodies set up under Partnership 2000, some new.

The inclusion of the community sector as 'new' social partners, alongside the 'traditional' social partners of unions, employers, and government, is for some an indication of the growing importance of the consultative process as a means of determining the most important policy choices facing governments. However, if we look at it a little more closely, a number of tensions arising from their participation are visible.

Included but still at the margin: traditional versus new social partners

In the wake of Partnership 2000, the organisations in the umbrella group Community Platform argued that their concerns had been treated as a 'residual category' in the course of the talks. Pay and tax issues were sorted out first, leaving issues of social inclusion to be dealt with afterwards; they wanted to be involved in setting the terms of the negotiations from the outset (Community Platform, 1997: 12-15). They have little 'clout' in the negotiations. As became clear during the talks leading to the PPF, they can threaten to withdraw to secure better terms, but are reluctant to carry out the threat.

Their concerns for better representative status were met by their inclusion in NESC in 1998. But their presence in NESC makes that body more diffuse in composition, and potentially less cohesive in its consensus-building on economic priorities. A more inclusive process is also a more unwieldy process.

Poverty and inequality: new social partners versus government

The participation of the community and voluntary sector has been linked with making progress on issues of poverty and inequality. However, there is little indication that the social partnership process is the principal forum within which social policy initiatives are actually developed. Insofar as the partnership agreements include concessions or promises in specific policy areas, such as changes to teacher-pupil ratios in schools, or additional spending on sport or recreational facilities, these have already been through the conventional governmental policy-planning process. PPF includes two global spending commitments on issues of 'Social Inclusion' (Framework III, section 3.1: 78). Pledges on other issues are uncosted declarations of principle. Details of administration and implementation are still very much decided on a ministerial and departmental basis.

Thus, even though the involvement of the community sector would purport to bring issues of poverty and social inclusion to the heart of the political process, the additional spending committed through this process is marginal, compared with departments' budgets on social policy. The agreements have not fundamentally altered the kind of spending priorities governments adopt. The involvement of the community and voluntary sector representatives gives a voice to the interests of marginalised groups. But this cannot be seen as any sort of 'functional substitute' for redistributive government policy commitments.

15.9 Politics versus social partnership

A plausible case may be argued that social partnership in Ireland has become thoroughly embedded in the political process. It may be seen to have evolved from a mechanism to deal with emergency to a more embedded set of institutionalised relationships (see, for example, Rhodes, 1998:198; for a critical evaluation of the same trend, see Ó Cinnéide, 1998).

One test of the institutional embeddedness of social partnership is a consideration of how difficult it might be for any of the participants in the process to exit unilaterally. Withdrawal by ICTU or IBEC in the course of an agreement would be interpreted as an extreme and disruptive move. Social partnership, principally through NESC, may be said to have developed a 'strategic capacity', that is, 'the actions of economic players have predictable and discernible effects on the welfare and decisions of other players' (Iversen, 1999: 94). To that extent, Ireland may be thought of as having moved some way towards developing a form of 'co-ordinated market economy' (Soskice, 1999).

Some commentators would contend that the process has gone even further. O'Donnell and Thomas (forthcoming), for example, argue that it represents 'innovative attempts to reconfigure the relationship between representative and participatory democracy which are fostering new forms of deliberative democracy'. This amounts, they argue, to a new 'hybrid' form of 'post-corporatist governance'. Problem-solving is only one element of the significance of social partnership; the commitment to engage in a continuous process of 'reworking identities' is equally important (O'Donnell, 1998: 19-20).

An alternative perspective suggests that social partnership is less securely anchored in the political process than might have been assumed, and much more heavily dependent on maintaining performance in the core areas of wage moderation, competitiveness, and productivity. With the expiry of each agreement, each party remains free to enter new talks, or not. Moreover, the influence of the consensus-building networks on government decision-making remains both limited and contingent. Government decisions can run counter to the priorities set within the context of social partnership.

The co-ordinating role of government

In one respect, it may be argued, government has played too weak a role in the social partnership process. Its contribution to consolidating the co-ordinating capacity of employers and unions has been crucial. On each occasion when a pay agreement is due to expire, governments of all political hues have indicated their strong preference for negotiation of a new one.[20] But government has not sought to exercise a strong discipline on the social actors to alter their own behaviour or preferences. As Visser and Hemerijk (1997: 182-3) note, all developed societies have many 'veto points' where social actors have the power to obstruct initiatives or pursue their own interests. 'The "problem solving style" of decision making which corporatism, or social partnership, can help produce is better than its alternatives, but it is inherently unstable and fragile. Corporatism easily produces policy stalemates.' Strong corporatism needs 'a strong state'. Governments must be prepared to use the 'shadow of hierarchy', that is, the threat of unilateral intervention, to achieve objectives it wishes to see attained.

As we have seen, public sector pay determination remains an important unresolved issue in the overall management of pay policy. Government's overt political preference for securing a consensus-style agreement may actually have postponed the need to take on an essential reform.

The policy autonomy of government: tax policy

If government may be said to have been too accommodating in one respect, it may equally be argued to be too removed from the process of social partnership in another: government has kept core functions of policy-making apart from the consultative and negotiating process. The serious process of policy development on issues as central to social partnership as tax policy and social spending are largely decided outside the parameters of social partnership.

The most striking example of this is tax policy. The overall direction of tax reform has developed in parallel with the centralised pay agreements. While tax concessions have been vitally important in securing union support for the moderate pay deals, budgetary tax cuts have been far more extensive and have significantly exceeded the levels promised in the agreements. But the priorities established through the partnership process were not consistently reflected in government actions. NESC reports repeatedly drew attention to the need to concentrate on two areas: reform of the tax situation of the lowest-paid, and reform of the low-to-middle-income threshold at which the higher rate of tax began to apply. Yet tax-cutting priorities paid relatively little attention to these arguments. Greatest emphasis was placed on cutting rates rather than increasing allowances or widening bands, which resulted in most benefits being channelled to those on higher incomes (Hardiman, forthcoming; Ruane and O'Toole, 1995; Cahill and O'Toole, 1998).

The budgetary decisions of the second Fianna Fáil-Progressive Democrat coalition, from 1997 on, display the limits of consultation. Three budgets in a row showed erratic priorities, alternately favouring higher and lower paid. Budget 2000 in particular caused a furore by embracing priorities quite at odds with those worked out through the consultative partnership process in NESC and endorsed by various independent policy commentators such as the ESRI.[21] In response, government did modify some of its tax plans; December 1999 was a critical moment for the negotiation of a new pay deal, and some concession was widely believed to be necessary. But the whole episode left many disillusioned with the seriousness of government's commitment to social partnership.

Other far-reaching decisions such as the tax amnesty of 1993, or individualisation of the tax system, were introduced without any prior consultation. What is striking is the ease with which governments can take decisions on these matters outside the parameters agreed by the process of consensus-oriented consultation – evidently responding more to specific electoral priorities than to the consensus-oriented partnership process. This is quite unlike the process of achieving tax reform in Sweden, for example, through negotiation with the social partners (see for example Steinmo, 1993), or in the Netherlands (Visser and Hemerijk, 1997).

Episodes such as these reveal the limits of the embeddedness of social partnership in the political arena.

Government and macroeconomic priorities

Government's role in co-ordinating pay bargaining with broader macro-economic priorities has become, if anything, even more important in the context of EMU. But there is some evidence that other domestic political priorities might under-cut its ability to do this effectively.

The government's capacity to provide large tax cuts underpinned the wage-moderating elements of social partnership. This has caused some commentators to wonder if there might be a limit to its ability to offset tax against pay, and whether policy must stabilise at a low-tax, low-social spending equilibrium (NESC, 1999). But while tax revenues as a proportion of a rapidly expanding GDP have fallen, gross tax receipts have continued to be very buoyant. Government spending commitments have not prevented it from running a fiscal surplus of over 2 per cent for several years running.

A more serious problem for the continuing viability of pay agreements is the co-ordination between pay agreements, tax cuts, and overall management of the economy. By 1999 and 2000, various commentators, including the European Central Bank, expressed concerns that the economy was at risk of over-heating, with growing inflation and capacity constraints particularly in the areas of labour supply, housing, and transportation. The NESC strategy documents argued, in 1996 and in 1999, that centrally negotiated framework pay agreements were not only possible in the context of a fixed exchange rate, but a necessary complement to it. They argued that such pay agreements could and must provide the means of negotiating flexible pay adjustments to respond to asymmetric 'shocks', such as a recession or a sudden drop in the value of sterling. The social partnership process has not yet been faced with the need to respond to an economic downturn with a renegotiation of the terms of the pay agreement. Neither has government yet been faced with the need to manage an economic downturn. But there are obvious dangers in the pro-cyclical policy stance of the early phase of the Programme for Prosperity and Fairness.

15.10 Conclusion

The process of social partnership has proved durable over quite a long time, and has undoubtedly contributed to the achievements of rapid growth and unprecedented job creation. It has adapted successfully not only to the exigencies of economic crisis, but also to the pressures of qualifying for Euro membership.

However, the process has not been without periodic difficulties, some more persistent in nature. The new era of managing membership of the Euro and dealing with the constraints of labour shortages presents new and formidable challenges.

It is hard to see what could replace social partnership, given the organised nature of the workforce and the aversion built into the party political system to overt manifestations of conflict. Nevertheless, the strains of accommodating very diverse pay pressures may well prove difficult to contain. The tensions between government's wish to support social partnership and its desire for policy autonomy may prove difficult to bridge. The capacity of social partnership to respond flexibly to an economic downturn has yet to be tested. Only time will tell.

NOTES

1 Calmfors and Driffill (1988) argued that a co-ordinated approach to pay policy depended mainly on the degree of centralisation of the trade union movement. But the case for according explanatory primacy to trade unions had been weakened by

the recognition that moderately centralised systems have proved capable of achieving much greater levels of pay co-ordination than Calmfors and Driffill predicted (Soskice, 1990, 1999; Swenson, 1989).

2 In contrast, the German industrial relations system does not depend on government intervention to manage employer-labour co-ordination, which has largely been achieved through 'autonomous' ·labour-market co-ordination within a highly distinctive legal and institutional context. See, for example, Streeck (1994).

3 Iversen argues that 'non-accommodating monetary regimes produce inferior employment performance in highly centralised systems, but superior performance in intermediately centralised systems' (Iversen, 1998: 3).

4 Gay Byrne, in an interview in 1986 with *Hot Press* magazine, as Ireland's most popular broadcaster, said '(Ireland) is banjaxed and washed out ... a man ... stood up in the audience at the Late Late Show three or four years ago and said that if we had any manners we'd hand the entire island back to the Queen of England at 9 o'clock the following morning and apologise for its condition. ... As every week passes, I think that guy had something' (O'Clery, 1986: 215-6).

5 Interview with Dermot McCarthy (Secretary-General to Government, vice-chair of NESC).

6 Regini (1999) thought that Ireland, like Britain, would need a lot of flexibility in wage structures, because of the importance of mass-production industry for employment (even if not as a contributor to GDP or total export value).

7 IBEC's commitment to social partnership agreements had always been conditional. Other things being equal, they prefer the predictability and orderliness of a central pay agreement, 'but not at any cost' – the cost being an inappropriately accommodating government approach to public sector pay (Interview with Turlough O'Sullivan, IBEC).

8 One senior civil servant described how the issue was continually postponed in the course of three-year-long agreements. Initially a lot of time is focused on the negotiations, and no time is available to think about reform; then once an agreement is in place, everyone becomes complacent and there is no impetus to get on with thinking about reform; then the pressure builds up again to negotiate a new agreement, and change is too sensitive an issue to broach (Interview with Paddy Teahon, former Secretary-General, Dept. of the Taoiseach and chair of NESC).

9 Pádraig Yeates, *Irish Times*, 8 February 2000.

10 ICTU estimate, cited in *Irish Times*, 22 October 1999.

11 *Irish Times*, 5 November 1999.

12 *Irish Times*, 5 November 1999.

13 Pádraig Yeates, *Irish Times*, 4 October 1999.

14 See, for example, ICTU policy documents *New Forms of Work Organization* (1999), *Profit Sharing Guidelines for Employee Share Ownership* (April 1999), *Challenges Facing Unions and Irish Society in the New Millennium* (June 1999). Productivity-

related bargaining at workplace level secured improvements for many employees in conditions of employment other than basic pay, such as pensions and sick pay schemes, holiday entitlements, and other issues.

15 Interview with Tom Wall (ICTU).

16 Des Geraghty (SIPTU) argued that the proportion of PAYE workers paying no more than the standard rate of tax was 56 per cent and that this represented a drop in the recent past. *Irish Times*, 5 October 1999. See also Tansey (1998).

17 Among the leadership of IBEC the view has been taken that 'we live in a society as well as an economy'; that it is incongruous to see people sleeping rough in the midst of a Celtic Tiger economy; that it is important to maintain social cohesion to be able to continue to make economic progress; and that consensus-building is the best way to pursue this. Interview with Turlough O'Sullivan (IBEC).

18 For example, government has been criticised for its lack of focus in implementing active labour market policies (O'Connell, 1998). But the case has been made that Irish governments have spent proportionately more on labour market measures than other countries, have initiated a range of different kinds of measures, and have sought to learn from this which work best to meet the principal local problems. The claim, in other words, is that 'government took on the problem', and that 'it worked', leaving Ireland with less severe problems of social inclusion and labour market integration that other OECD countries. Interview with Dermot McCarthy (Secretary-General to Government, vice-chair of NESC).

19 Interview with Dermot McCarthy (Secretary-General to Government, vice-chair of NESC).

20 A minority Fianna Fáil government negotiated the PNR; a Fianna Fáil-Progressive Democrat coalition negotiated the PESP; a Fianna Fáil-Labour coalition negotiated the PCW; a Fine Gael-Labour-Democratic Left government negotiated Partnership 2000; a minority Fianna Fáil-Progressive Democrat coalition negotiated the PPF.

21 There are of course other priorities that government must attend to. In late 1999, government had just completed its mid-term review of its coalition agreement, and had committed itself anew to the electoral promise of rate-cutting. The government had committed itself to convergence with British tax rates, in view of the shared labour market with Britain and the perceived need, in the context of labour shortages, to attract returning emigrants.

16

The Role of the State in
Growth and Welfare

SEÁN Ó RIAIN AND
PHILIP J. O'CONNELL

16.1 Introduction

The Irish economy has undergone a profound transformation in the past forty years. Ireland in the 1960s was comparatively underdeveloped industrially and economically and its welfare state lagged behind developments elsewhere in Europe. By the end of the 1990s, however, after decades of advances and reversals, Ireland was being hailed a success story within the global economy. Economic growth rates in the 1990s have been among the most rapid in the world and GDP has converged with the core European economies. This economic progress has not, however, been matched by a complementary development in social rights. The expansion of the welfare state in Ireland lagged behind developments elsewhere in Europe and its main period of growth took place against a background of very difficult economic circumstances, culminating in a fiscal crisis of the state in the 1980s. The Irish welfare state might therefore be characterised as a case of interrupted development which today falls far short of the European model, as overall state and welfare spending as a percentage of GDP falls closer to US than EU levels.

Over the past four decades Ireland has pursued an uninterrupted strategy of increasing integration into the global economy. However, this imbalance between growth and distribution is not a simple story that globalisation has forced the withdrawal of the state and other social actors and promoted the rise of neo-liberalism. In fact, the most dramatic changes have occurred under the guidance of neo-corporatist social partnership institutions and the state has been deeply implicated in the entire process of managing both economic development and the welfare state.

Ireland stands then as a particularly clear and interesting example of how a highly interventionist state can promote adaptation to the internationalisation of the economy (Katzenstein, 1984, 1985). Where core states play a critical role in generating processes of internationalisation, small states are pushed to adapt to these changing conditions. Successful adaptation may indeed depend on an active and effective state, rather than on the neo-liberal strategies prescribed by the dominant institutions of the global economy. To the extent that small states are successful in adapting to internationalisation of economic processes they create the basis for further extension of those processes – by providing new locations, labour forces and institutions that can support transnational economic processes. The Irish state has played a critical role in inserting Ireland into international economic processes, reshaping both the economy and the welfare state in the process.

16.2 State, society and the global economy

Globalisation has resulted in the weakening and even destruction of institutional buffers between national economies and global markets (Ruggie, 1982). States find themselves trying to respond to pressures from local societies and global markets simultaneously without the breathing room previously offered by controls on transnational trade, finance and production. The intensification of global processes has actually made the role of the state more important as an effective state becomes critical to promoting competitiveness within a global economy (Sassen, 1996). Some argue that this increased state role is limited to promoting economic competition and accumulation – even as the state becomes an increasingly critical enterprise association its role as a civil association diminishes (Cerny, 1995). Cerny argues that all states are now faced with the imperatives of global competition, causing a convergence around the model of the 'competition state' (Cerny, 1995). Certainly this resonates with aspects of the experience of recent years as states, both within and across national boundaries, compete to offer the greatest incentives and concessions to attract mobile investment.

Jessop's (1993) concept of the 'Schumpeterian workfare state' describes a state which combines the promotion of flexibility and innovation, oriented towards global markets, with punitive measures, such as workfare, directed towards those groups in society who fail to stake out a place in these markets. Although Jessop suggests that this kind of state may prove to be the universal mode of regulation for a Post-Fordist economy (with variations across different systems) it seems to be most advanced in the liberal states of the US and Britain, in particular the Thatcherite regime for which the analysis has been most comprehensively developed (Jessop, 1994; Peck, 1994). Liberal regimes have clearly moved in this direction, combining an intensified state promotion of markets with a more punitive relation between state and society. However, the

Schumpeterian workfare state may run into its own problems as the 'workfare' component proves insufficient to reproduce the labour force necessary for Schumpeterian innovation (Peck, 1994: 206-229).

However, these analyses go too far. Both the structure of the global economy and the space for local and national diversity are more varied and offer more opportunities than the concept of the 'competition state' allows. There remain a variety of ways of connecting to the global economy, with significantly different implications for local and national populations (Gereffi, 1994). Significant portions of economic activity are still shaped by local and national factors which are heavily influenced by national states (Weiss, 1998). Weiss argues that the role of the state remains significant both in shaping *development* outcomes and in negotiating the *distribution* of the rewards and costs of economic development.

Even in an era of globalisation, the state can still act to promote economic development by mediating connections between the local and the global and influencing how local-specific assets are mobilised within the range of opportunities available in the global economy. Despite the financial crisis of 1997/1998 in Asia, the demise of the 'developmental states' has been greatly exaggerated. Certainly, it has become much more difficult for states to take the tasks of development upon themselves through the use of public organisations. The state can continue to play a role in promoting economic development, however, by shaping the capabilities of society and the market to compete internationally. In particular the state pokes and prods domestic firms to compete in the global economy and to constantly upgrade their organisational and technical capabilities to that end.

The impact of progressive globalisation on the welfare state is believed to derive from two sources. First, the new international division of labour has led to the transfer of manufacturing employment, particularly low-skilled employment, from the advanced industrial societies to the newly industrialising economies that offer a low-wage, low-tax environment. The resulting shift in investment results in increased unemployment and falling tax revenues in the advanced societies, both of which undermine the welfare state. Second, increased international financial mobility increases the importance of policies to maintain national competitiveness and thus constrains the policy autonomy of national states, leading to a convergence towards a neo-liberal withdrawal of welfare provision (Cerny, 1995; Cox, 1993). Critics of this position, however, argue that globalisation is hardly a new phenomenon, and that while states have always been confronted by international constraints, they have retained sufficient autonomy and capacity to pursue national agendas (Hirst and Thompson, 1996; Pierson, 1998). Indeed, as Esping-Andersen (1999) notes, it was extreme vulnerability to international forces which led the small European societies to construct strong welfare regimes and protected labour markets after World War Two. In this respect Ireland shares a high degree of exposure to international trade competition with other open societies such as Denmark or the Netherlands with highly developed welfare systems. Rhodes (1998) argues that far from convergence to a neo-liberal roll-back of the welfare state, the future direction for many European countries may be one of 'competitive corporatism'. Such a proscription appears particularly applicable to the Irish strategy adopted since 1987, prioritising competitiveness and macro-economic stability and employment creation and redistribution, but downplaying the 'equity' function of more traditional 'golden age' forms of corporatism.

Weiss is correct then to argue that the state continues to play a central role in shaping development and distribution outcomes. However, she treats each of these state roles as points on either end of a continuum of state roles, with states being classified as developmental, distributional or 'mixed' cases (Weiss, 1998: 117). We prefer to treat these two state roles as largely referring to the relatively distinct and identifiable institutional realms of industrial and economic development policy and welfare state policy. Each may have a relatively autonomous logic from the other but developments in one institutional sphere may be critical to the ability to pursue certain strategies in the other. For example, the losses of the industrial working class in development policy may be compensated for by a generous early retirement scheme on the distributional side – much as in the German case (Esping-Andersen, 1990:151). In this chapter therefore, we first outline the Irish state's roles in the spheres of development and distribution separately and then go on to relate them explicitly to one another.

If the state continues to play a significant role in shaping socio economic outcomes within the global economy, the question remains as to how certain states are more effective in carrying out certain roles than others. Recent research has emphasised that the state cannot achieve these developmental and distributional ends in isolation but in fact depends on its relation to society for its success. In particular, effective states are characterised by 'embedded autonomy' (Evans, 1995). Such states are embedded in local social groups (usually, although not necessarily, capital) through close social or associational ties between state bureaucrats and domestic social classes, among other social groups. However, these states avoid being captured by social class interests by retaining their autonomy. For Evans, this autonomy is safeguarded by the presence of a classic 'Weberian bureaucracy' – based on meritocratic recruitment and promotion and norms of objective, procedural rationality (Evans, 1995; Evans and Rauch, 1999; Maxfield and Schneider, 1997). Of course, coherent Weberian bureaucracies are relatively rare. However, some research suggests that, under certain conditions, encompassing business associations and other associations which can monitor and sanction their members can promote a long-term developmentalist orientation to the market, even in the absence of a state which is able to enforce such an orientation

(Maxfield and Schneider, 1997: 25). In any case, the effective state is one which can pull off the delicate balancing act between the close ties to society necessary to generate 'state-society synergy' (Evans, 1996) and the 'autonomy' necessary to safeguard broader state development and distributional goals from simply becoming a function of the interests of the dominant class.

Accounts of 'successful' states often emphasise the coherence and cohesive character of the state bureaucracy as a critical element in securing state autonomy (Evans, 1995). For some, this coherence not only insulates state bureaucrats from 'capture' by dominant social interests but enables the state to impose its 'plan rationality' over the 'rationality' of the market (Johnson, 1982). However, this emphasis on the internal organisational coherence of the state is challenged by recent arguments that the state is increasingly moving towards a position as a network state, embedded in a variety of levels and types of governance institution (Castells, 1997; Ansell, 1999).

We argue that the various roles of states, particularly the developmental and distributive roles, may in fact be relatively autonomous from one another. 'Successful' states are, however, able to maintain complementarity or compatibility between these two roles. Indeed, states may be better able to manage any tensions or contradictions between the semi-autonomus roles of development and distribution if they are organisationally *less* cohesive. Therefore, 'successful' states need not be tightly coupled, cohesive organisational entities. Indeed, while a certain degree of bureaucratic coherence is essential, a more decentralised, 'loosely coupled' organisational structure may better facilitate the workings of a 'network state'. We can contrast the organisational structure of bureaucratic with flexible states, the former characterised by bureaucratic coherence compared to the more loosely co-ordinated, networked organisational structure of the latter (Ó Riain, 2000a).

Flexible state structures are characterised by significant decentralisation, close ties to social constituencies, and a high degree of flexibility in the relations between the units of the state apparatus. The internal accountability of cohesive Weberian bureaucracy is supplemented or even replaced by the external accountability of particular units of flexible states to external evaluations based on clear performance criteria. Such a state may also be better able to handle tensions between partly conflicting agendas within the state itself.

Rather than a cohesive and relatively insulated national state apparatus, the flexible state consists of a state apparatus which is deeply embedded in a 'network polity', forging socio-political alliances out of constantly shifting local, national and global components (Ansell, 1999). In transforming itself to operate within a locally and globally networked economy and polity, state governance itself is 're-scaled' as the prior privileged role of the national level gives way to a 'glocal' form of state (Brenner, 1998, 1999).

With a decentralised, flexible structure, change in any one part of the state apparatus is much easier to carry out than in a more highly integrated, bureaucratic structure. Where the bureaucratic state emphasises strategic planning and state leadership (at least in theory), the flexible state is better thought of as adaptive and responsive, evolving through learning and path-dependent evolution of institutions. Clearly these are not exclusive categories and any one state will incorporate elements of both. However, states can also be classified as more firmly within one or other of these models. We argue that the Irish state has been a relatively flexible state, especially in recent years. Its weakness has been the inability to take decisive steps out of crises or to pursue developmental or distributional goals against the resistance of powerful social groups. However, it has adapted successfully to a number of opportunities that have presented themselves at different stages of Irish development over the past forty years. In the 1990s, the adaptations undertaken in both the developmental and distributional realms complemented one another in such a way as to create a new dynamic of growth and improved living standards, within an ongoing process of integration into the global economy and increasing social polarisation.

16.3 The developmental state

Ireland experienced an economic and social crisis of enormous proportions in the 1950s, stimulating a range of changes in economic and industrial policy. At least partly in response to this crisis, industrial policy shifted dramatically between the mid-1950s and the early 1960s. After 1958 protectionist measures were eased for foreign investors and removed entirely in 1964. Full integration into the international economy has been a mantra of Irish economic policy since this period and protectionist measures were almost completely dismantled by the 1970s. The state became the key actor in attracting foreign direct investment (FDI) and creating a 'world class' location for mobile investment became a motivating policy goal for the following forty years. Among the critical elements of this locational advantage were generous tax incentives and grants, a transnational-friendly environment, a young and cooperative labour force and (later) a world class telecommunications system. The state was placed at centre stage in industrial policy by its efforts to continually upgrade these 'factors of production' and its assumption of the role of 'hunter and gatherer' of FDI.

However, this was not an inevitable, nor even particularly planned, outcome. By the time the crisis of the 1950s had prompted some action on economic and industrial policy, alternatives to concentration on attracting foreign investment had been effectively sidelined (O'Hearn, 1990). Attempting to revitalise the moribund domestic industrial sector was one option. While the state had largely viewed itself as complementing the market in the 1930s and the 1940s the then

Minister for Industry and Commerce (and later Taoiseach), Seán Lemass, became increasingly concerned with the inefficiency of protected indigenous industry. Lemass's vision was of a self-sufficient but efficient economy. To this end he made various attempts to introduce measures to support state intervention in Irish firms with a view to improving their efficiency. His efforts to form an Industrial Efficiency Bureau in 1947 failed in the face of resistance from a united domestic capitalist class and a deflationary coalition within the state headed by the Department of Finance (O'Hearn, 1990). Even so, when the Industrial Development Authority (IDA) was set up in 1956 it was initially envisaged to have two broad sets of objectives – firstly, the provision of incentives to industry (mainly Irish) to start new businesses and, secondly, a set of powers to call witnesses and investigate firms in relation to inefficiencies within the firm. Once again in the face of capitalist and Department of Finance resistance, the investigatory powers were removed from the IDA before it even began its duties. However, it should be noted that when the IDA was founded it was envisaged as an agency largely supporting indigenous industry. Political pressures to transform national institutions in order to build development upon a national system of innovation were constantly deflated by the 'safety valve' of emigration which facilitated the 'catch-all' politics of Fianna Fáil (Mjøset, 1992).

Why then did the FDI regime become so dominant within the Irish political economy? The key document said to have started the shift to export-led industrialisation – a paper called *Economic Development*, written by a senior civil servant – was in fact focused almost completely on agricultural exports. However, it did mark a shift in Department of Finance thinking towards a more expansionist agenda and a legitimation of economic planning. Furthermore, Ireland became eligible for Marshall Aid in the late 1940s and the expansionist coalition within the Irish state was anxious to use the funds to develop their agenda. However, there were a large number of conditions attached to Marshall Aid, the primary condition being a steady and significant move towards free trade. International agencies such as the IMF, dominated by the US government, pushed free trade measures through the 1950s until the restrictions on foreign investment and the tariffs and quotas around Irish industry began to weaken through the 1950s (O'Hearn, 1990; Girvin, 1989a).

It still remained unclear, however, where the firms would come from to fulfil this export-led expansion. The IDA had been left with the task of promoting new industry and soon filled this vacuum through its pursuit of foreign investment. Lemass still hoped to prod Irish-owned business into life and wanted to retain promotional capabilities within the Department of Industry and Commerce. However, he compromised with the IDA in the late 1950s, agreeing that it could focus on new industry. This effectively meant foreign investment and proved the basis of the IDA's narrow institutional focus on attracting FDI. Throughout the

1960s foreign investment grew rapidly, with foreign firms accounting for 2.3 per cent of gross output in 1960 but 15.9 per cent in 1973 (O'Malley, 1989: 102). This fuelled a period of rapid economic growth and with it the legitimacy and power within the state of the IDA.

In 1969 the IDA took on direct grant-giving powers and that same year it was restructured as a semi-state body outside the civil service but reporting to the Department of Industry and Commerce. This administrative independence and its exclusive focus on 'new' industry (mainly foreign) gave the IDA a specific corporate culture organised around a clear set of goals. It also became the centre of policy-making as the Department of Industry and Commerce became more marginalised: 'Our impression is that the Department's practice has tended more towards intervention in operational matters while devoting little attention to the strategic plans formulated by the agencies. We are not in a position to substantiate this impression, but to the extent that it may be true, it represents an inappropriate means of control' (O'Malley, Kennedy and O'Donnell, 1992: 132). Out of the adaptation to circumstances and learning through its early successes in attracting foreign investment, the IDA had taken on a strategic role in shaping industrial policy by the early 1970s. However, this outcome itself was not created by strategic planning but by adaptability and learning within these newly created arms of the state.

Through the 1970s the focus on attracting FDI was consolidated with the institutionalisation of the IDA's role as the leading strategic force in industrial policy. While the Department of Industry and Commerce had published a series of Economic Plans in the 1960s, it remained largely silent on policy issues through the 1970s and 1980s. It is noticeable that in public debates on industrial policy among the policy élites during the 1970s and early 1980s there is a clear expectation that the IDA is the body which must address these issues, with little mention of the Department of Industry and Commerce (SSISI, 1976, 1982).

Irish political and economic institutions were radically reshaped through the 1970s, in large part in pursuit of foreign investment. The structure of state finances has been transformed to greatly reduce taxes on capital and profits in an effort to attract foreign investment, leaving the state heavily reliant on revenues from personal income taxes. The education system has been transformed, largely through the creation of a large sector of the third-level education system which is oriented heavily towards business and technology. Heavy investments were made in upgrading the telecommunications system in the early 1980s.

The outcome of the institutional compromise surrounding the emergence of the FDI policy regime was to de-politicise and institutionalise the FDI regime while hyper-politicising indigenous development in the form of clientelism. The FDI regime dominated the traded sector of the economy while non-traded sectors contained primarily domestic firms and were dominated by clientelism.

Clientelism was the byword of state-business relations in sectors such as beef and property, much as it was in the polity at large (Higgins, 1982; Chubb, 1982). Agencies such as the IDA found it next to impossible to insulate themselves from political interference in these sectors. As a series of special tribunals established in the 1990s – the Beef, McCracken, Moriarty and Flood tribunals – have revealed, relationships between agriculture, construction and property development and certain politicians and public officials were of a highly dubious character (MacDonald, 1985; O'Toole, 1995). In the protected sectors extensive battles ensued in an attempt to prolong protection although these sectors ultimately had to face international competition, usually to their disadvantage (Jacobson, 1989). These sectors began to suffer in the mid-1960s, were faced with serious problems upon entry to the EEC in 1973 and collapsed during the recession of the early 1980s (O'Malley, 1981, 1989, 1992b). Before the industrial revival of recent years Irish industry had a very weak presence in the traded sectors of the economy and in some respects it could be said that no coherent policy regime existed to support potential firms which might emerge in these traded sectors.

As a result employment growth was largely stagnant through the 1970s and collapsed in the 1980s, with almost one quarter of domestic manufacturing jobs lost between 1980 and 1988. Even foreign investment suffered a downturn, with employment dropping 6.8 per cent in that period (O'Malley, 1998). The full implications of the industrial policy compromises of the 1950s were only now becoming clear. The existing industrial development regime was simply not up to the task of generating employment for a burgeoning population with significant financial problems – in fact employment was falling most disastrously as the largest demographic bulge pushed into the labour market in the 1980s.

It is important to note that this was not in itself a crisis of the FDI model. Although employment in foreign-owned firms declined in the 1980s this was still the most dynamic sector of the economy and provided the best chances of employment growth at any particular time. O'Malley (1989) argues that the TNCs did not have a damaging effect on indigenous industry even if they did not do much to stimulate indigenous development. However, this structural crisis in the Irish economy and society did point up the weaknesses of the FDI model as a model of national economic development, taken on its own as it had been for most of the 1970s.

These concerns came to a head with the publication of a report by the Telesis Consultancy Group in 1982 which was heavily critical of the prevailing model of development. Telesis were contracted by the National Economic and Social Council, a body representing the 'social partners', to carry out a study of the existing policies regarding industrial development. Telesis severely criticised the sole reliance on foreign-owned firms, arguing that 'foreign-owned industrial operations in Ireland with few exceptions do not embody the key competitive activities of the businesses in which they participate; do not employ significant numbers of skilled workers and are not significantly integrated into traded and skilled sub-supply industries in Ireland' (Telesis Consultancy Group, 1982; quoted in O'Malley, 1989: 167). Ultimately, the foreign investment-led model of development could not even begin to stem the tide of mass emigration, with an increasingly professional look to it, through the 1980s. By the late 1980s almost half of each cohort of new engineers and one quarter of computer science graduates were leaving the country within one year of graduation (HEA, various years).

The report was widely quoted in the media at the time and although a national debate could hardly be said to have ensued it did cause quite a stir within the policy community (see SSISI, 1982 for example). The IDA defended itself robustly at the time (White, 1982; *IDA News*, 1982, No.2). However, the hegemony of the FDI model and the IDA within the national policy regime was therefore somewhat shaken by the events of the early and mid-1980s. The FDI model now became one part, if still the dominant part, of industrial policy. The general tenor of policy did shift through the 1980s to take account of some of the recommendations of the Telesis Report – in the direction of greater selectivity in grant giving and a greater focus on marketing and technology and on indigenous firms (O'Malley, 1992b). A space had opened up therefore in which new models of economic development could be advanced as candidates for institutionalisation – a space which would prove vital to the institutional change underpinning the industrial change and economic boom of the 1990s.

Out of this disastrous situation came the boom of the 1990s. Looking at manufacturing industry, investment has increased by 91 per cent between 1991 and 1997.[1] This investment seems to have shifted towards 'intangible' investments as R&D spending has increased by over twice as much, 202 per cent (Breathnach, 2000). Unfortunately we have no information on other intangible investments in marketing and related business activities, which also seem likely to have expanded and which are increasingly critical sources of industrial competitiveness in technology-based sectors (Ernst and O'Connor, 1992). Manufacturing employment has expanded by 22 per cent over the period and has seen a significant degree of 'upskilling', at least as measured by occupational category. 'Administrative and technical' workers (these do not include clerical workers) have grown by 42 per cent across manufacturing, almost double the rate of general employment growth. Although output figures are relatively meaningless for certain 'entrepôt' sectors such as cola drinks and software reproduction, it is striking that output has expanded steadily across all nationalities of firms and almost all sectors. There has however been a marked sectoral shift with rapid decline in 'older' sectors such as textiles, clothing and leather, even as the 'high tech' sectors expanded rapidly. Furthermore, output per employee has been growing steadily, indicating an increased level of productivity in the Irish economy.

These figures also hold for those service sectors for which we have data for the period. Indeed, consistent with international trends, employment growth has been more rapid in most categories of service employment than in manufacturing. Over 5 years the number of persons engaged in 'all business services' expanded by 71 per cent and full-time employees by 69 per cent (CSO, 1992, 1997). This growth is even stronger in the most dynamic sub-sectors within these, such as computer services and management consulting. Employment in the less glamorous 'personal services' has also expanded rapidly, by 71 per cent, from 1993 to 1997 (CSO, 1993, 1997b). Here the expansion consists almost entirely of a boom in the employment of part-time workers. In addition therefore to the 'upgrading' of manufacturing employment, we find a polarisation in the service sector with rapid expansion in relatively well paying 'business services' sectors but often equally or more rapid expansion in poorly paying personal services and retail employment. Unfortunately the services data do not provide information on nationality of ownership of the firms in question. Overall, however, we see both an expansion and an upgrading of industry in Ireland in the 1990s – alongside the continued growth of 'entrepôt' operations which are largely based on tax avoidance (Honohan, Maître and Conroy, 1998; O'Hearn, 1998).

How then, did this remarkable turnaround occur? Certainly there were fortuitous external circumstances which Ireland was well placed to take advantage of – succeeding early and often in securing certain critical investments by US high technology firms seeking to invest in Europe prior to unification (Barry, Bradley and O'Malley, 1999: 62; Krugman, 1997; O'Hearn, 1998). However, this cannot explain the broad upgrading we have seen above across a range of sectors and firm nationalities. In fact, the state played a central role in upgrading industry and deepening Ireland's production and innovation capabilities in the 1990s.

The state had already played a central part in transforming the education system – an institutional transformation that was now paying off in terms of a plentiful supply of skilled labour. Furthermore, a reserve of emigrant professionals waited for opportunities to return, doing so in large numbers from the mid-1990s. However, in the years around and after the Telesis report, the state began to pursue a wider range of industrial development strategies. New sectors had been added to the list of target sectors – most important of which were software and financial services. The state acted to support emerging indigenous industry and to upgrade the national system of innovation in three major ways (Ó Riain, 2000a).

Firstly, it acted to define the types of involvement in the international economy that would be supported. IDA executives began to work more closely with the managers of transnational subsidiaries in Ireland to try to build up the local operations. The IDA provided valuable investment and other support in particular sub-supply sectors, such as software manual printing (Jacobson and O'Sullivan, 1994) and electronics. In industries such as software design, the state development agencies focused grant aid almost completely on companies producing software products for export – attempting to steer companies away from the 'easy' profits of labour contracting. The state acted in important ways therefore to define the character of Irish industry, without attempting to define the specific strategies to be followed by firms.

However, the state has also made more direct contributions. Its second contribution was to 'making winners'. Private capital was not a major factor in the growth of Irish industry and it is only since 1998 that private investment capital, from both domestic and foreign sources, has become abundant even in leading sectors such as software. Grant-giving became more selective, as recommended by the Culliton Report (Industrial Policy Review Group, 1992), and state agencies 'seeded' venture capital funds. The state agencies therefore promote a general company development programme through their grant-giving practices in a variety of areas including marketing, management development, training and R&D. The precise form this takes can be quite flexible depending on the company itself but the state agencies require that such efforts at company development take place. Some IDA executives had even been involved in company development in the 1980s before the policy shift had found its way into official policy.

Thirdly, the state played a critical role in the creation of a network of industry and trade associations, universities, innovation and technology centres and other fora and groups which provide an associational infrastructure for information-sharing, co-operation and innovation. While these bodies are outside the state or semi-autonomous from it, in most cases they have been founded through state initiatives and underwritten by state guarantees and funding. Nonetheless they form a distinct layer of institutional spaces and social networks between the state agencies and the companies in the industry. A diffuse state influence throughout the industry is built into the organisational structure of the institutions. These institutions are typically located within the universities; staffed by academics and industry people; usually have advisory boards containing industry, academic and state representatives; and have extensive ties to industry through consulting, information days and other activities undertaken at least partly for funding purposes. In many ways these associations and networks perform some of the integrative functions carried out within the corporation in vertically integrated, large firms.

Perhaps the earliest such institutions of relevance were founded in 1980, a time when a great deal of policy interest was focused on the impact of microelectronics on Irish industry. The National Microelectronics Research

Centre (NMRC) was founded in Cork in 1980. Its focus is on research into microelectronic technology and it works successfully with some of the more prominent electronics TNCs. The National Microelectronics Application Centre (MAC) was also founded at that time and was charged with bringing electronics to Irish industry. Based in the University of Limerick, it provides technical advice and houses up-to-date equipment for industry use. It succeeded relatively early in building connections to innovative local firms although in its early years these connections were apparently closer to the larger TNC operations (Sklair, 1988). The late 1980s were a time of institutional innovation. Most of these innovations took place under the banner of the Programmes in Advanced Technology (PATs), funded by EU Structural Funds under the Operational Programme for Industry, 1989-1993. Eolas, the agency dealing with science and technology, had made a series of proposals regarding programmes to support leading and potentially strategic technologies, including software which proved to be the most successful. During the late 1980s and early 1990s a number of institutions and programmes were founded which have received largely positive evaluations from national and international evaluators. These include Teltec Ireland, the Technology Centres, the National Software Directorate and Software PAT, the Applied Research Programme, Bio-Research Ireland and the Mentorship Program.

By defining the character of industrial strategies, implementing company development through grant aid and creating an associational infrastructure for innovation, the state has been able to contribute handsomely in the 1990s to the development of indigenous industry and the upgrading of the national system of innovation more generally. The final question that remains then is how this shift in state policy could take place. In fact, the crisis of the 1980s bore the seeds of the boom of the 1990s in that it opened up space alongside the FDI agenda for alternative industrial development strategies. The crisis stimulated a series of institutional changes that took on their own momentum as they yielded some success.

The IDA itself reorganised internally in 1988 to create two divisions that would look after foreign-owned and indigenous industry respectively. There was however a series of other state bodies which concerned themselves largely with the 'science, technology and innovation' agenda and which were mostly oriented towards indigenous industry, although their success in raising R&D spending levels for example was quite limited until the late 1980s (O'Malley, 1980: 62-63; STIAC, 1995).These included the National Science Council, founded in the late 1960s, and its successor the National Board for Science and Technology founded in 1977. In the mid-1980s science and technology policies were reorganised significantly with a new Office of Science and Technology being formed under a Minister of State (junior cabinet minister) in the Department of Industry and

Commerce. The NBST was merged with the Institute for Industrial Research and Standards in 1987 to form Eolas, a new science and technology agency. Around the same time various agencies were consolidated into one agency to deal with active labour market policy (FÁS) and into another to deal with export marketing (An Bord Tráchtála). In 1994 Forbairt, an agency focused solely on indigenous industry, was created incorporating most of the staff and functions of Eolas and the Irish Industry section of the IDA. In 1998, An Bord Tráchtála was merged into Forbairt, although under some protest from local firms which feared a loss of marketing assistance. Finally these various agencies were folded into Enterprise Ireland, which consolidated these agencies under one institutional roof. We can see therefore that there was an increasingly sustainable and autonomous institutional space available within which the indigenous development agenda could be pursued and the task of building a national system of innovation undertaken.

The new state institutions relied heavily on European Union funds for their activities. Many of the programmes undertaken in the science and technology arena were funded in large part by European Structural Funds. These funds were designated for Ireland as part of an effort to develop the peripheral regions of the EU in the face of the upcoming Single European Market in 1992. Many commentators have commented on the impact of the influx of this capital from the EU, attributing Ireland's growth to these funds. However, the Irish state had put together significant amounts of capital before without being able to develop the economy around them. What was significant about the Structural Funds was that they were the means by which a variety of new, sometimes experimental, measures could be taken without having to fight the rest of the state agencies for funding. The new development regime could develop alongside the old and did not have to challenge the old development model directly for funds and priority, except in rare cases. Furthermore, the EU funds came with significant requirements in terms of performance and outcome evaluation and accounting. While sometimes creating administrative nightmares this also helped to foster a climate where regular evaluation of policies became the norm and where clientelism was mitigated. It was not only the financial impact of the EU funds which was crucial therefore but the institutional space it facilitated for new initiatives. In this case, international funds were used to promote an indigenous development agenda.

The state, through its heavy investment in education, had meanwhile created a new class basis for an indigenous technology promotion and business expansion agenda. The state had effectively pushed the population away from the historically popular professions, using its unusual capacity to shape labour supply to disproportionately expand the number of vacancies in engineering, computer science and other technical fields through the 1980s and 1990s. The danger here was of course a massive brain drain which did indeed take place (Wickham, 1989; NESC, 1991). However, of those who stayed a number started their own companies and combined with a trickle of people from the foreign-owned sector and other organisations to form a constituency which could support the new agenda. The educational investment associated with the FDI model therefore threw up a new technical middle class which could not rely on government patronage in markets and were largely excluded from the existing professions by their education. An unintended consequence of the FDI model was therefore the creation of a social group which would ultimately come to be the foundation of an alternative model of development. Ultimately it was this new class, combining entrepreneurs and technical professionals in a new class compromise which would emerge as the socio-political force at the heart of the Irish boom in the 1990s. Their increasing profits and wages would create rising inequality even as they became firmly embedded at the heart of the Irish economy and polity.

16.4 The distributive state

The evolution of the welfare state represents another example of delayed development. The legacy at the time of political independence in 1922 combined an underdeveloped economy, full adult male suffrage, which was immediately extended to women, and a minimalist state. The inheritance included an attenuated version of British welfare institutions, including the poor relief system, an embryonic social insurance system providing unemployment and sickness compensation to manual employees, limited health and housing services, and subsidised education. Given the under-developed state of the economy, this legacy represented a comparatively precocious set of social citizenship rights relative to the low levels of national income and the tax base (O'Connell and Rottman, 1992). There were few welfare innovations in the first decade of independence under the political leadership of the conservative Cumann na nGaedheal government. The electoral success of the Fianna Fáil party, appealing to less-well-off members of society, including small farmers and business people as well as manual workers, ushered in an era of reforms. Both the coverage and adequacy of unemployment benefits were increased, new income maintenance schemes introduced, and an ambitious public housing programme implemented to clear the urban slums, particularly in Dublin.

The welfare state did expand after World War Two, following, but lagging behind, developments elsewhere in Europe. A unified Department of Social Welfare was established in 1947, taking over responsibility for the majority of social welfare schemes, and the Social Welfare Act 1952 made universal the various existing schemes of income maintenance and introduced a new maternity allowance. Equal rates of unemployment benefit between single men and women were introduced, although married women still received lower rates. The coverage of the system remained restricted, however, and middle-class employees, the self-employed and civil servants were neither covered nor liable to pay contributions. Cousins (1995) comments that these exclusions from the system were consistent with class interests: civil servants, middle class employees in the private sector and the better-off among the self employed had lower exposure to insurable risks, while poorer members of the self-employed received social assistance from an exchequer to which they contributed little. He argues that the Irish system emerging in the 1950s remained fragmented with little commitment to interclass-solidarity, unlike the relative universalism of the system in the UK, or indeed in the Scandinavian countries. During the 1950s also, eligibility for public hospital services, formerly restricted to low-income groups, was extended to those covered by the social insurance system, as well as others on low income, although provision of a broader range of health services fell far short of universal coverage (Maguire, 1987).

In the health area, attempts at reform were discouraged by opposition from private medical practitioners and the Roman Catholic Church to an expansion of state involvement. In the 'Mother and Child Scheme' incident in 1951 the church blocked a major expansion of public health care to provide free ante- and post-natal care to mothers and free medical care to children without a means test, forcing a political crisis and the resignation of the then Minister for Health, Noel Browne. The educational system remained predominantly private, and for most of the population access to education was restricted to primary level, which was subsidised by the state.

Despite these reforms, social rights in Ireland still lagged far behind the innovations in other European countries in the post-war period. Total social expenditure actually fell from 16 per cent of GNP in 1951 to 14 per cent in 1959, a decade of economic stagnation and declining employment (O'Connell and Rottman, 1992).

The quality of social citizenship in Ireland expanded markedly during the 1960s and 1970s as services were improved and coverage of income maintenance expanded. In the income maintenance system, contributory pensions were introduced in 1961, occupational injuries benefits in 1967, retirement and invalidity pensions in 1970 (Cousins, 1995). The 1970s also saw the introduction of deserted wives allowances and benefits, lone-parents allowance, supplementary welfare allowances and the reduction of the pension age from 70 to 65. Coverage of the social insurance system was extended to all employees in 1974 and pay-related benefits were introduced.

In 1967 free second level education was announced, means-tested grants for third level education were introduced in 1968, and there was considerable expansion of third-level institutions from the 1970s onwards. Improved access to second-level education and increased provision at third level resulted in a dramatic increase in educational participation over the following three decades. These initiatives would later contribute a skilled work force to stimulate economic growth in the 1990s, although participation in third-level education has remained strongly related to social class origins. In the field of housing, a major public building programme was initiated in 1965 and output of public housing rose rapidly to the mid-1970s. Reforms in health included a reorganisation of general practitioner services in 1970 which allowed low-income individuals to attend a private practitioner of their choice, and, in 1979, the extension of eligibility for free hospital services to the entire population.

By the end of the 1970s the basic structure of today's welfare state had been established. Much of the period since then has been characterised by efforts to restrain public expenditures. Before examining recent trends in the welfare state it is useful to consider the quality of social citizenship as it expanded since the 1960s. The expansion in social rights that took place during the 1960s and 1970s related to the range of contingencies against which state provision is made available, as well as the public services to which citizens are entitled as of right. The Irish experience of welfare state expansion stands in stark contrast to the Scandinavian pattern in which the expansion of social citizenship took place along two dimensions: (1) universalistic entitlements created solidarity among and between social classes; and (2) a commitment to reduction of inequalities pervaded all areas of policy, thus reinforcing the solidaristic quality of the welfare state (Myles, 1989). In Ireland the principal commitment has been to achieving solidarity, through the expansion of the coverage of the social insurance system, and through the provision of basic levels of service, but the commitment to reducing inequalities has been slight. The Irish welfare state can thus be characterised as a 'pay-related' welfare state which provides a basic minimal level of security and service on near-universal grounds to all resident citizens, but one which mixes public and private components in a manner that allows those with advantages generated in the market to supplement their social citizenship rights with their own resources (O'Connell and Rottman, 1992).

The pay-related nature of the welfare state is particularly obvious in the case of pensions. In 1960 the pension system was expanded from a means-tested provision to an insurance-based system available to manual workers and other paid employees. Insurance coverage was extended to all employees in 1974, and the self-employed incorporated in the system in 1988. The expansion of the coverage of the pension system reflects a solidaristic impetus. However, its three-tiered structure reflects its 'pay related' nature. Entitlement to non-contributory old-age pensions is subject to a means test and provides for those with a history of intermittent or marginal labour force participation. The more generous contributory pensions form a second tier, available to all employees in the private sector as well as to the self-employed, who have a record of contributions. A third tier is formed by the combination of contributory state pensions with private and occupational pensions. Public servants, with a separate state pension system, also fall into this third tier. All three tiers benefited from increases in the real value of state pensions since the 1960s (O'Connell and Rottman, 1992), and Callan and Nolan (this volume) show that the real value of pensions continued to increase over the past two decades, by almost 58 per cent in the case of the personal rate of non-contributory pension, 53 in the case of contributory pension.

In the year 2000, the personal rate of the contributory pension, available to those with a record of contributions, exceeds that of the non-contributory pension by 12 per cent. The contributory pension forms a floor for middle-class employees, who can combine a social insurance pension with occupational pension entitlements, private pensions and savings, all subsidised through tax expenditures, to achieve a more comfortable standard of living in old age. Occupational pensions tend to be earnings related; state pensions are set at a flat rate. Those covered by occupational pensions are more likely to be in white collar rather than manual employment, to be males rather than females, and to work in large rather than small organisations. Thus, retired middle-class employees, former public servants, and middle and high income self-employed enjoy considerably enhanced incomes compared to retirees from other social classes (O'Connell and Rottman, 1992).

This pattern, whereby a universal entitlement at basic level of provision can be supplemented by private resources in a manner that reinforces market-based inequalities, can also be found in other areas of welfare state provision. In health, free hospital care, until changes in 1991, underwrote part of the cost of a stay in a private hospital ward, with the patient paying the difference between the subsidy and the actual cost. Currently, while the state provides a basic level of free hospital care to all, those with private health insurance, subsidised through tax expenditures, can avoid lengthy waiting lists for treatment. In education, a universal entitlement forms a foundation upon which parents can build by adding their own resources to obtain private education. The elimination of fees at third level, introduced in 1994, increased universalism of provision in a formal sense, but as Smyth and Hannan (this volume) show, social class inequalities in access to third-level education are pervasive and persistent over time.

Table 16.1: Social insurance coverage, 1953-97

	Number Insured (1,000s)	per cent of Labour Force with full coverage
1953	724	51.7
1961	713	56.8
1971	808	65.5
1981	944	74.2
1991	966	72.0
1997	1,476	95.9

Source: 1953-1981: Maguire, 1987, 1991 and 1997: Department of Social Welfare, various years

Table 16.1 shows the expansion of the social insurance system from 1953 to 1997. The proportion of the labour force with full coverage expanded markedly over the 1960s and 1970s as increasing numbers of employees were included. Near universal coverage was achieved by the late 1990s, following the inclusion of the self employed in 1988 and new public servants from 1995. This reflects the strategy of inclusiveness to entitlement of basic levels of service.

Figure 16.1: The share of current government expenditure in GNP, by function, 1965-1995

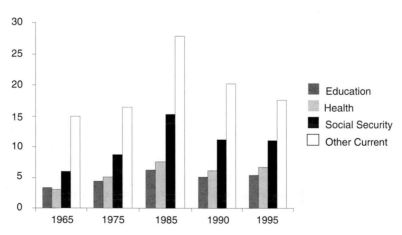

Source: Central Statistics Office, various years, *National Income and Expenditure*

Figure 16.1 shows the evolution of current spending on the largest elements of social expenditure – income maintenance, health, and education – as well as other current expenditure, expressed as a proportion of GNP over the period 1965-95. There was a marked increase in total government spending from 27 per cent of GNP in 1965 to 35 per cent in 1975, followed by accelerated growth, to 57 per cent in 1985. This expansion was mirrored in each of the main areas of welfare state spending in the graph. The most rapid growth took place in social welfare payments, which increased from 6 per cent of GNP in 1965 to 9 per cent in 1975 and to 15 per cent in 1985. The growth from the mid-1970s to the mid-1980s reflected the dramatic increase in unemployment, from 85,000 in 1975 to 226,000 in 1985, peaking at 233,000 in 1987. But demands for improved services in health, and the increase in educational participation, led to marked increases in those areas also.

The dramatic growth in public spending was not matched by increases in revenue, with the result that in the mid-1980s the public finances were out of control, with high budget deficits and a burgeoning public debt. Public sector borrowing increased to 14 per cent of GNP in 1986, and fiscal imbalance has been blamed as one of the main causes of the recessionary period in the early to mid-1980s. Restoring order to the public finances was achieved by severe cutbacks in public expenditure in 1987-90. Total current spending fell by over 10 percentage points in real terms between 1987 and 1989. Total current spending fell from 57 per cent of GNP in 1985 to 42 per cent in 1990 and to just under 41 per cent in 1995.

Figure 16.2a: Welfare state expenditures in real terms (Constant 1989 values)

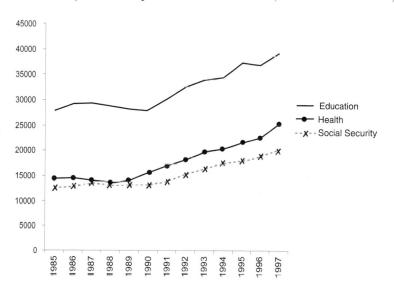

Figure 16.2b: Welfare state expenditures as a percent of GDP

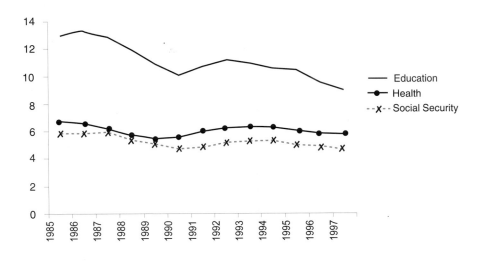

Source: Central Statistics Office, various years, *National Income and Expenditure*

Figures 16.2a and 16.2b show total expenditures on education, health and social security in constant (1989) prices and as a percentage of GDP from 1985 to 1997. These figures allow us to trace the impact of the austerity measures introduced to recover control over the public finances in 1987 and their longer-run impact on welfare state spending. In real terms, total current expenditures fell by about 10 percentage points between 1987 and 1990. The real value of total spending on social security fell by 4 percentage points over this period. This was consistent with the commitment given to the social partners to maintain the value of income maintenance payments, and it also coincided with a brief increase in employment which resulted in lower unemployment (O'Connell, this volume).

Real spending on education fell by about 2.5 percentage points between 1987-1990, and health expenditures fell only marginally during this period. By 1991, the real value of spending in each of these areas had been restored, and real expenditure levels in health were almost 20 per cent above the level in 1987. Over the course of the 1990s, real expenditures have increased gradually in each of the main areas, with the result that in 1997 spending on health was 78 per cent greater than in 1987, spending on education was about 50 per cent greater, and social security transfers had increased by one-third in real terms over the decade. An exception to this general rule is the area of housing, where a dramatic cut-back in the public building programme took place after 1987, and where public expenditure fell from about 5 per cent of total public expenditure in 1987 to 2.5 per cent in 1990. This has led to a dramatic decline in the share of social housing in new house construction, and together with the large-scale privatisation of the existing local authority stock has resulted in the residualisation of local authority housing, which is now mainly targeted at the poor and unemployed (Fahey and Williams, this volume).

Viewed over a longer time-horizon, the austerity measures introduced in 1987 appear as an adjustment in a longer period of rising real expenditure, and it is clear that the bulk of the cuts fell in areas outside of health, education and income maintenance schemes, and that these areas of expenditure accounted for a larger share of total spending during the period of austerity. Over the decade as a whole, welfare spending increased substantially in real terms. But this was also a decade of very rapid growth in the economy. One useful way to view the amount of 'welfare effort' exerted by a society is to measure its welfare spending against its economic output, Gross Domestic Product. When measured against GDP, the decline in welfare effort in Ireland is apparent (Figure 16.2a). Social security spending fell sharply from 13 per cent of GDP in 1987 to 10 per cent in 1990 and then more gradually to 9 per cent in 1997, with a brief increase to 11 per cent in 1993 when unemployment levels increased. Spending on education fell from 6 per cent of GDP in 1987 to 4.7 per cent in 1990, increased to over 5 per cent in the mid-1990s, before declining to a level of about 4.6 per cent in 1997. Expenditure on health fell from 6 per cent in 1987 to 5.6 per cent in 1990 and has subsequently fluctuated around 6 per cent of GDP. In summary, over the past decade, as Ireland became a more prosperous society, it has spent more on the welfare state, but it has made less welfare effort.

In this regard Ireland has diverged from the European pattern of increasing welfare effort. Figure 16.3a shows social security transfers as a percentage of GDP in various countries over the period from 1960-1996. From 1960 to 1987 Irish expenditures followed a trajectory that was similar to other core European countries, although until 1987, the ratio of social security spending to GDP in Ireland lagged behind the European average. After 1987, while the ratio of social security spending to GDP was maintained or increased in most European countries, they fell markedly in Ireland, from 17 per cent in 1987 to 13 per cent in 1996. By 1996, the ratio of social security spending in Ireland had converged with that in the US, 7 percentage points lower than the European average.

Figure 16.3a: Social security spending as a percent of GDP1960-96, selected countries

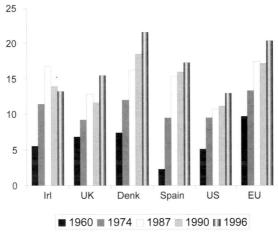

Source: OECD, 1999, Historical Statistics 1960-1997

Figure 16.3b: Total current government spending as a percent of GDP 1960-96, selected countries

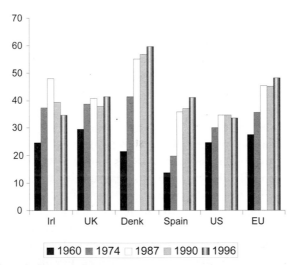

Source: OECD, 1999, Historical Statistics 1960-1997

Figure 16.3b, which presents the ratio of total current government spending to GDP for the same countries over the same time period, shows a very similar pattern in which Irish expenditures increase strongly over the 1960-1987 period, to the extent that the total spending ratio in Ireland exceeded the European average by 1987. This was followed by a marked decline in Ireland, but by near-stability, or increased expenditure levels in the other countries. By 1997, Irish government spending had fallen to 35 per cent of GDP, marginally higher than in the US, and 13 percentage points below the European average.

The recent history of the Irish welfare state is thus a distinctive one in which the welfare effort of the society has declined during a period of rapid economic growth and in a context of centrally-negotiated social partnership. The distinctive Irish pattern features increases in the real value of social security payments, and increases in spending on social services alongside a decline in the welfare effort of society. Underlying this apparent paradox is a continuity of the structural characteristics of the Irish welfare state established by the end of the 1970s. The 'pay-related' or two-tiered welfare state has continued to preserve social solidarity by maintaining a basic level of social citizenship rights on near-universal grounds, but allowed a mixture of public and private provision to ensure that the basic minimum of provision can be supplemented by resources generated in the market. A floor of citizenship rights has been maintained that ensure that those classes disadvantaged in the market are taken care of at a basic level of provision, and middle and higher income groups have been free to supplement that basic level of provision, by relying on their own resources and by drawing on tax expenditures.

The major changes in the social insurance system since 1987 have been, first, the incorporation of self-employed groups in the social insurance system, and new public servants in 1995, an inclusive strategy which broadens the political coalition for the welfare state, and second, the elimination of pay-related social insurance compensation in 1994, a change which emphasises the minimalist elements of universal coverage.

With regard to its response to unemployment, the Irish welfare state has departed in two important respects from a standard 'residual' or liberal welfare regime. First there has been the solidaristic commitment to maintaining and even increasing the real value of unemployment benefit and assistance payments since 1987. This is driven by the terms of the social partnership accord, and is also consistent with the catch-all nature of party politics, but it differs markedly from the radical scaling-back of welfare entitlements that has occurred in other more liberal regimes, such as Britain.

A second departure from liberalism can be found in employment policy. Liberal and conservative social policies tend to favour a passive approach to employment and to eschew active intervention to promote labour market re-entry of the unemployed (Esping-Andersen, 1999). In contrast, the Irish state has been particularly innovative over the past decade or so in bringing about a shift in the balance from passive income support to active labour market policies with temporary employment and training programmes, and in reducing unemployment/ poverty traps. Ireland is a comparatively big spender on such active labour market programmes, which cover a very substantial proportion of the unemployed. In 1996, such spending accounted for about 1.7 per cent of GDP, comparable to expenditure levels in the more interventionist Scandinavian social democratic welfare states (O'Connell, 1998). In Ireland this labour market activation approach is much less a welfare-backlash type welfare-to-work strategy, and much more a social inclusion strategy to increase employability adopted under the tutelage of the EU mainstream. Punitive elements in the activation strategies have been very muted, and attempts to eliminate unemployment traps to returning to work have been more likely to pay people to go back to work rather than withdraw support if they don't (for example the sizeable Back-to-Work Allowance scheme, which provides continuation of up to 75 per cent of social welfare income after long-term unemployed people go back to work).

The evolution of the Irish welfare state can be described as a case of delayed and interrupted development. Ireland lagged behind the development of welfare states elsewhere in Europe in the aftermath of World War Two. Social rights expanded considerably over the 1960s and 1970s, and welfare expenditures climbed sharply through the early- to mid-1980s, but against a background of severe economic problems. The fiscal crisis of the state halted the growth in Irish welfare effort and the nature of social rights then in place became frozen in time. During the more recent period of very rapid economic growth, social welfare spending has increased in real terms but has fallen as a proportion of GDP. Arguably, social partnership preserved the floor of protection during the austerity period, but it has not mobilised support for an expansion of welfare effort during the economic boom. Thus, the institutions of social partnership have preserved the inequalities inherent in the welfare state of the 1980s.

16.5 Vicious and virtuous circles?

The Irish economy may not have shaken off the fundamental features that make it particularly open to the vicissitudes of the global economy. Nonetheless, Ireland has managed in the past ten years to stake out a more rewarding form of participation within that economy. However, the commitment to welfare effort, which had grown during the initial period of growth and during the crisis years of the 1980s, has been diminished; welfare effort has decreased even as national wealth has increased. This is not however a story of neo-liberal globalisation. The state has been central to each stage of the development, and under-development, of the economy and of the welfare state. This involvement has had concrete effects – both on the upgrading of local production and innovation capabilities and on the maintenance of a relatively non-punitive floor to the social welfare system. To understand the recent Irish experience of growth with inequality within an institutional framework of social partnership it is necessary to trace how the developmental and distributive roles of the state have interacted across the past four decades. It will also be necessary to analyse the particular character of the Irish state – both its embeddedness in society through a particular form of catch-all politics and its flexible and adaptive character which has enabled it to diffuse the conflict inherent in the contradictions of the development strategy.

Table 16.2 shows the institutional developments and trends within the Irish political economy across three critical periods – the period of growth from 1960-1973, the period of crisis and contraction from 1973-1987, the period of recovery and boom from 1987-2000. It indicates the emergence of the dominant features of the Irish economy in the 1960s. A development strategy based on economic openness and particularly attracting FDI has been dominant since that period as have the populist, catch-all politics which underpinned the welfare state expansion of that era.

The 1970s saw the consolidation of each of these strategies as each became institutionalised within the state through the emergence of the IDA as the centre of industrial policy-making and the increasing significance of organised political interests in pushing for state spending. The crisis of the 1980s presented challenges to these institutions but did not necessarily destroy them. Instead a certain amount of political space emerged for the consideration of alternative and supplementary roles for the state in the economy.

Table 16.2: Institutional change in the Irish political economy

Period		Development		Distribution
1960-1973	I	Move to attracting FDI	I	Welfare state expansion
	II	Integration into international economy		
1973-1987	III	Consolidation of FDI policy	II	Welfare state consolidation
	IV	Consideration of supplementary strategies in face of industrial contraction	III	Rapid expenditure growth
1987-2000	V	Increased focus on indigenous industry and 'deepening'	IV	Structural adjustment with social partnership
	VI	Definition of key sectors and activities		
	VII	Business development role of state agencies		
	VIII	Creating an associational infrastructure for innovation		

Into these spaces a number of new institutions emerged. Chief among these were the increasingly significant set of industrial development agencies focused on indigenous industry and on business and technological upgrading, and the social partnership institutions put in place in 1987 which set about taking on the macroeconomic and fiscal problems of the state without dismantling existing social protections.

What then was the impact of these shifting institutions? How did the institutional changes in both the developmental and distributional realms of the state interact to shape economic outcomes? Table 16.3 presents some of the major indicators of economic performance and welfare state effort across each of these periods – indicating clearly the pattern of growth, bust and boom in the Irish economy. Although marked throughout by a pragmatic, catch-all politics and a commitment to international integration the road to the current position of the Irish economy has indeed been long and winding.

Table 16.3: Economic performance and welfare effort

Period	Development		Distribution	
	Average annual GDP growth	*Average annual employment growth*	*Social security spending as per cent of GDP*	*Change in all state spending as per cent of GDP*
			Average over period / *Annual per cent change*	*Average over period* / *Annual per cent change*
1960-1973	4.4	0.3	7.0 / +7.1	29.3 / +3.4
1973-1987	3.0	0.1	14.0 / +3.3	45.1 / +2.0
1988-1998	6.5	3.4	14.4 / -2.1	39.5 / -2.7

Growth

The 1960s was a period of growth and relative prosperity in Ireland, after the disaster of the 1950s. An inflow of foreign investment, first from Britain and later from the US, stimulated economic growth – even as free trade eroded the domestic industrial base. The welfare state greatly increased the pace of the expansion it had been undergoing in previous decades. During this period, the developmental and distributive roles of the state evolved relatively separately – although growth certainly helped to pay for welfare expansion and the expansion of the education system in particular would be crucial to improving the country's ability to attract foreign investment. Both the developmental and distributive strategies had their roots in the catch-all politics through which the state was embedded in society. The state was unable or unwilling to challenge domestic capital to promote domestic industrial development or more egalitarian welfare state structures. Neither was it willing to strategically hold the global economy at bay, as the 'Asian Tigers' did. In this context, the state adapted itself to supporting the foreign investment and free trade agenda which was emerging in the Marshall Aid led post-war reconstruction in Europe. FDI filled the vacuum at the heart of Irish industrial policy and by the end of the 1960s had become institutionalised as the dominant industrial development model. Political support for the Fianna Fáil government that ruled from 1959-73 was sustained in large part by welfare state expansion. The weakness of the industrial working class and its political support for Fianna Fáil meant that this took the form of a two-tiered welfare state structure which often reinforced rather than dampened market inequalities.

Bust

This combination of developmental and distributive roles was institutionalised within the Irish state by the early 1970s but when international conditions became less favourable the underlying structural weaknesses in the Irish model were exposed. State intervention had failed to generate a momentum towards the development of an indigenous industrial capacity and a genuine 'national economy' (Mjøset, 1992). The foreign investment led model of industrial development was conspicuously failing to generate significant spin-off development effects, although quite successful in its own terms. When protectionism was finally dismantled in the late 1970s, in the context of a poor international environment, domestic industry collapsed. Furthermore, the strategy of relying on foreign investment had required tax changes that had reduced the percentage of government revenues from taxes on capital and corporations, from 2.3 per cent of GDP in 1965 to 1.2 per cent in 1985. The taxation burden on personal income increased enormously as it went from 4.3 per cent of GDP in 1965 to 11.4 per cent in 1985 (OECD, 1997). These factors combined to create enormous public pressure to increase government spending. Irish catch-all politics combined disastrously with the easy availability of international loans at the time (Stallings, 1992) to create an explosion in public spending and ballooning national debt. Ireland's industrial and trade structure ensured that most of the multiplier effects of this spending exerted themselves outside the national economy. The Irish economy's second social and economic crisis in thirty years was created in the bust of the 1980s by the vicious circle of interactions between developmental and distributive roles of the state. Adaptation in this case proved disastrous, in a situation where breaking the mould of the existing strategies was called for.

Boom

However, it was adaptation in the 1980s which subsequently led to the boom of the 1990s. The crisis of the 1980s created some institutional spaces for experimentation. The strategies of earlier periods had created two social classes which now mobilised to try and reverse the disastrous situation of the 1980s. State investment in education had created a burgeoning professional class, many of whom emigrated but enough of whom stayed behind to form a new industrial development coalition with dissident elements from the IDA and other, more marginal, state agencies. This coalition became the basis of indigenous upgrading and deepening in the 1990s. A second group of unionised workers, many in the public sector, were mobilised through the union movement to enter a series of social partnership agreements which sought to restore macroeconomic and fiscal stability by centrally negotiating wages and other distributional issues. However, these distributional negotiations were clearly cast in 'developmental' terms – focusing on the need to regain competitiveness. These two coalitions between different classes of employees, employers and sections of the state existed throughout the 1980s in an arms-length but complementary relationship. The modified industrial policy finally created the growth that could create a sustainable dynamic of development. The social partnership agreements restored the macroeconomic and fiscal stability necessary for industrial success. As Table 16.3 shows, while social security spending as a percentage of GDP increased by over 3 per cent per annum between 1973 and 1987, it subsequently fell by over 2 per cent per annum over the following decade.[2] While the terms of this accord between the state and the social partners ensured that basic levels of protection were guaranteed to those excluded from national economic recovery, the equality agenda characteristic of more traditional forms of corporatism was less evident.

These two major developmental/distributional coalitions in Ireland have held each other's ambitions in check, assisted by the structure of the Irish state. The neo-liberal impulses of the rising class of internationalised professionals are at least partly held in check in Ireland by the continuing ability of the unions to safeguard the basic social rights guaranteed (at a low level) by the universalistic elements of the Irish welfare state and by the middle class's own self-interest in maintaining the subsidies provided to them by the pay-related welfare state. The social partnership agreements have ensured that integration into the global economy has not decimated social rights. However, the agreements have also presided over a period of rising wage dispersion and weakening welfare effort. This is at least partly due to the increasing lack of voice of unions and other social actors in shaping the lead sectors of the economy. The new classes of technical professionals and self-employed small businesses largely fall outside the institutions of social partnership and have become the basis of spiralling inequality in market incomes in Ireland.

The Irish version of social partnership, which, in essence, has entailed wage moderation in exchange for tax-cuts, has meant that both tax revenues and welfare state expenditures have fallen dramatically in relation to rapidly growing national income. This raises fundamental questions about the development of social citizenship rights in Ireland. While there is growing dissatisfaction with the quality of social services, particularly in health and housing, the state appears committed to further tax cuts, a policy which must entail continued deviation from the European model. Reversing this trend would require a re-negotiation of the terms of social partnership in a manner that would entail a greater share of the fruits of growth being channelled through social rather than market wages: offering improved social services rather than tax cuts in exchange for wage moderation. However, such a shift would also raise very fundamental issues about the trade-offs between wages, taxes and competitiveness.

Clearly, through privatisation and structural adjustment, the direct role of the state in economic activity has given way substantially to the market. However, the state has played a critical role in promoting the successful market participation of the new internationalised professional class – through investment in the education system, through industrial policy that supports greater innovation and through extensive public subsidies which supplement middle class market rewards rather than diminish them. Simultaneously, the rest of Irish society has benefited over the past ten years from the combination of developmental and distributive roles played by the state. Social rights have been maintained and living standards have increased, particularly through increased employment. In the process, the bulk of Irish society has also acquiesced to the increasing gap between themselves and the rising professional and business classes. The intense battles being waged over public sector pay are evidence that those workers in a position to do so are increasingly willing to take action to redress this inequality. What seems doubtful is whether those at the lowest rung of Irish society, caught between a burgeoning service sector of casual employment and a weakening welfare effort, can mobilise the resources to at least keep up with the rest of Irish society. The Irish formula of 'solidarity without equality' may be beginning to face some of its greatest challenges.

NOTES

1 This figure and others in the following discussion are based on unpublished CSO data from the Census of Industrial Production 1991 and 1997. The data is more fully analysed in Ó Riain (2000).

2 The averages for the two periods, 14 per cent over the years 1973 to 1987 and 14.4 per cent over 1987-1997, conceal the fact that social security transfers as a percentage of GDP peaked in 1986-1987 and then declined in the later years.

17

Conclusion: The Irish Experience of Growth and Inequality

BRIAN NOLAN, PHILIP J. O'CONNELL AND CHRISTOPHER T. WHELAN

Introduction

The contributions to this volume have dealt with various aspects of Ireland's recent experience as regards economic growth and inequality. Our aim in this concluding chapter is to bring out important themes running across the different chapters, highlight some key findings, and discuss their implications for the future. For this purpose we focus in turn on economic development, on the state, politics and social partnership, on income inequality and poverty, and on equality of opportunity, before concluding with a discussion of emerging tensions and challenges.

17.1 Economic development

Over the past half-century Ireland has been profoundly transformed. That transformation can be characterised, at least partially, as a shift from a relatively poor, inward-looking agricultural society incapable of sustaining its population, to a prosperous industrial, or even post-industrial, society fully integrated into the international economy attracting immigrants to meet the labour demands of a booming economy.

The pace of that transformation has been uneven. Most of the chapters in this book focus on the experience of the past two decades or so, and thus deal with the most recent transition from the prolonged slump of the 1980s to the boom of the 1990s. But the more recent experience must be viewed in the context of the longer-run process of industrialisation. Many commentators writing at the end of the 1980s were distinctly pessimistic in response to the scale of the crisis confronting Irish society: mass unemployment and emigration, sluggish economic performance and a fiscal crisis of the state. The crisis of the 1980s was then seen by some as reflecting the failure of a highly interventionist state to create the conditions for economic and social progress. Viewed from the perspective of a decade later, these interpretations appear unduly pessimistic, and it is now apparent that the resolution to the crisis was already in train. In fact, as several chapters in this volume show, the foundations of the more recent successes of the Irish economy were laid as far back as the 1960s and pursued consistently since then. These included the promotion of closer integration with the international economy and the investment in increased educational participation.

Small European countries, like regions, have little choice but to adapt to external market forces. A central theme of this volume has been that Ireland's growth experience over the past two decades, and indeed over the twentieth century as a whole, provides a rich case-study with lessons, both positive and negative, for such countries. Ireland began its career as an independent state in the early 1920s with many advantages, and with a standard of living higher than many other countries in Western Europe. Dependence on the British economy proved a major handicap, however, and Ireland became a free rider on Britain's decline. The strong web of dependency between Ireland and the UK only began to weaken after the shift to foreign direct investment and export-led growth in the late 1950s and 1960s. The failure of the inward-looking strategy, especially in the years following World War Two, permeated Irish society. The crucial reorientation in policy from the late 1950s, while overdue, was an enlightened response to changes in the world economy, and can be characterised as a shift from policy appropriate to a dependent peripheral state to that of a region seeking to become fully integrated into a European economy.

The success of this outward orientation has been dramatic in the past decade, though the experience of the late 1970s and early 1980s graphically demonstrated the high cost of inappropriate domestic fiscal policy and failure to adjust rapidly to external shocks. Ireland has had the advantage of the English language, and may be distinctive even among small European countries in the extent to which its labour as well as product and capital markets are very open. The availability of an external pool of skilled migrants ready to return to Ireland when the opportunity arose, and a domestic pool of married women working in the home, was a crucial enabling factor as growth took off. Investment in education – which came later than it might have – has been central in the process of economic growth, particularly as the changing nature of the world economy places even more of a premium on skills. Membership of the European Union has played a vital role as a force for change both economically and more broadly. Ireland's experience also demonstrates the positive role which resources from the European Union's Structural Funds can play in reducing infrastructural deficits.

ever, the development strategy followed consistently over the past 40 or so of attracting foreign direct investment has also clearly been a crucial ingredient. The benefits of critical mass in certain key sectors is now being seen, though it carries with it a certain vulnerability. Like other aspects of Ireland's experience this has lessons for, for example, the Central and Eastern European countries. This strategy depends on the ability of policy makers to make the business and productive climate in their economies sufficiently attractive to capture a significant share of internationally mobile investment – though quite why Ireland has been so spectacularly successful in that regard in the 1990s requires further study. The fact that this strategy may be associated for some time with 'jobless' growth and a dualism in the economy between a high-technology foreign-dominated sector and a more traditional domestic one poses real problems in terms of among other things wage-setting. The role of social partnership-type arrangements in managing these challenges and promoting a long-term focus may then be very important in strictly macroeconomic terms, as well as in other dimensions to which we turn shortly.

Irish living standards in terms of GNP per head began the 1990s at two-thirds of the European Union average, but by the end of the decade most of that gap had been closed. Output per head has been converging on the EU more steadily since the 1970s, though with an acceleration in the 1990s. This brings out the importance of the dramatic decline in the economic dependency ratio in Ireland, from well above the EU average in the 1980s to below that average over the next few years. At a time when this ratio is rising in other European countries, this will make possible a further rapid rise in living standards, holding out the prospect that over the next fifteen years Ireland may achieve a standard of living among the highest within the EU.

17.2 The state, politics and social partnership

The state has played a central role in both Ireland's long-run transformation and the more recent about-turn in Irish fortunes. Responding to the failure of protectionist policies in the 1950s, the Irish state adopted a very active role in seeking to promote economic growth and development by seeking closer integration with the international economy and in attracting foreign direct investment. The adoption of this developmental role was complemented by an expansion of the distributive role of the state, ushering in an era of economic and social progress in the 1960s. However, the international recession in the 1970s revealed structural weaknesses in the Irish economy as traditional indigenous industry contracted in the face of international competition. By the late 1970s there was an explosion of public spending and national indebtedness, so that in the 1980s Irish society experienced economic and fiscal crisis, mass unemployment and renewed emigration.

The interaction between political culture and policy and decision-making means that not all policy options are actually available to a particular state at all times. Market signals are interpreted and internalised through a specific framework in any nation-state. Irish political culture is associated with nationalism, religion, the land, authoritarianism and patriarchy, well established by the time the Irish Free State was established. Subsequently the Constitution provided a template for an agrarian, conservative, catholic, communalist and patriarchal society. In the post World War Two period Ireland diverged significantly from other small democratic European states, in neither integrating into the world economy nor achieving significant growth.

The Irish political culture in place in the 1960s was shaped by the adaptive strategies pursued by Irish nationalism in a predominantly agrarian society. While the Ango-Irish Free Trade Agreement confirmed the formal abandonment of economic nationalism and protection, from the 1960s to the 1980s Irish economic development was generally obstructed by the way in which the political culture was configured, by the distribution of power and resources and by the priorities associated with the national interest. 'Politics without social bases' and the need not to alienate any specific sector of the electorate including the protected domestic sector, the farming community and the trade unions, constrained the policy options available and limited the benefits that could be derived from participation in the European economy. The strategy of trying to avoid distributional conflict by promoting growth through borrowing and spending failed spectacularly in the late 1970s and early 1980s.

In response to the crisis of the 1980s, the adoption of new policies laid the foundations for the boom of the following decade. Central to the new strategy has been the reconstruction of social partnership since 1987, and here Ireland has followed what Rhodes (1998) has called a strategy of 'competitive corporatism' in which the pursuit of international competitiveness, macro-economic stability and employment creation take priority, with less emphasis on the equality agenda of earlier variants of corporatism. The Irish experiment with competitive corporatism, worked out in response to economic and fiscal crisis, was founded on the formation of a consensus between political, trade union and business leaders which recognised both the extent to which domestic economic performance depended upon maintaining national competitiveness, and the need for responsible macro-economic and fiscal management. A feature of the consensus has been agreement not only on the priorities to be pursued in national accords, but agreement also on how the Irish economy works, including the nature of external constraints as well as the inter-relationships among policy instruments and economic outcomes.

In essence, social partnership has involved an exchange of tax-cuts for wage moderation, and entailed a dramatic decline in public spending in relation to national income. Initial success was aided by an upturn in the international economy and a drop in the inflation rate, which allowed a modest pay settlement to be converted into an increase in real disposable income, and paved the way for subsequent agreements. In the 1990s then, a virtuous circle, entailing complementary developmental and distributive roles on the part of the state, and reinforced by corporatist style concertation of incomes and macro-economic policies, provided an environment conducive to rapid growth in output and employment. This is not to argue, however, that competitive corporatism in Ireland has been unproblematic. A series of tensions has emerged as social partnership matured, including sectoral conflicts between and within private and public sectors; difficulties arising from growing earnings dispersion; and problems with the expansion in the scope of partnership. Moreover, social partnership has presided over a period of weakening welfare effort, in terms of the proportion of national income going on social spending.

Social partnership did ensure protection of social rights for the most vulnerable as integration in the global economy proceeded. In particular, real increases in levels of social welfare payments have been achieved. Indeed, the Irish case provides a useful corrective to an over-concentration on institutional typologies of welfare states. While Ireland and the UK have basically similar transfer systems, for example, the Irish system became more effective in reducing poverty among the unemployed in the late 1980s/early 1990s because the safety-net levels of support were increased relatively rapidly in real terms – when the opposite trend was happening in the UK. However, as growth accelerated from 1994 welfare levels have lagged behind. In addition the impact of tax cutting since 1987, central to the Irish social partnership exchange, has been regressive because it has been achieved largely through the reduction of tax rates which has favoured those on higher incomes.

Labour market success and increases in both gross and net earnings can be regarded as the essential *quid pro quo* for the wage moderation negotiated under social partnership. One of the most striking features of Ireland in the 1990s has been the unprecedented growth in employment and the dramatic fall in unemployment – leading to substantial convergence with European employment rates and, particularly in the second half of the 1990s, a peerless performance in cutting unemployment compared to its European neighbours. Nor have these been 'bad jobs': there has been a sustained upgrading in the quality of class positions in the labour market over the past four decades, and the most recent period of very rapid growth has seen a continuation of that trend. The more advantaged positions in the class structure, including professional and skilled occupations, accounted for a disproportionately large share of employment growth. While other less privileged positions also grew in the 1990s this was on a small scale and should not obscure the overall trend towards occupational upgrading. Increased international exposure has also meant that Ireland has participated in the widespread trend towards increased labour market flexibility, and there has been an increase in part-time working and greater use of temporary fixed-term contracts. However, in respect of both these forms of atypical employment, the rate of flexibilisation has been lower in Ireland than the EU average. Moreover, the impact of flexibilisation on the quality of jobs is closely related to the institutional and regulatory context, and in Ireland employment protection legislation was extended in the early 1990s to cover both part-time employees as well those on fixed-term contracts.

While earnings in Ireland have increased in real terms over the past decade or so, substantially more so in net than in gross terms because of the effects of tax cuts, Irish wage levels continue to fall well short of those in the more prosperous European countries. The share of wages versus profits in the Irish economy must be considered in the context of the distinctive role of foreign direct investment. However, there has been a marked fall in the wage share in national income since the mid-1980s, a decline that accelerated after about 1993. This is a trend that sets Ireland apart from both the rest of Europe and the US, where the wage share has generally held up, but it is a trend that reflects the effects of mass unemployment and the impact of migration patterns in Ireland during the 1980s and into the 1990s. While this shift in factor shares has contributed to the competitiveness gain that facilitated the economic boom, its continuation during the more recent period of labour shortages may represent a lagged effect of the adjustment process. The extent to which this trend can now go into reverse is one of the issues to which we return.

17.3 Earnings dispersion, income inequality and poverty

Heightening distributional concerns are far from unique to Ireland. Over the past two decades earnings and income inequality have increased in a considerable number of industrialised countries, in the face of globalisation and technological advance. Increasing earnings dispersion has been pronounced in the United Kingdom and the United States, with returns to education and skill rising sharply. As a small and extremely open economy, external influences are even more important in Ireland, but unlike those two countries the strength of labour market and associated institutions has been increasing rather than declining and the evolution of supply and demand for skilled versus unskilled labour also has some distinctive features. We have seen that over the period from 1987 to 1997 there was in fact a substantial widening in earnings dispersion in Ireland, which already had a relatively high level of earnings inequality compared with other OECD countries. However, rapid increases for those towards the top of the distribution were the dominant force, with no indication that the bottom was falling behind the median, and the increase in dispersion was more pronounced in the 1987-94 period, so rapid economic growth from 1994 on did not lead to an acceleration in the trend.

This was seen to reflect a complex set of influences in the labour market. From the early 1970s the supply of skilled labour in Ireland has been rising rapidly as a consequence of educational expansion, with immigration becoming an important factor in the 1990s. The supply of unskilled labour, on the other hand, fell quite rapidly from the early 1980s as a result of increasing educational participation at second level. Rising demand for skilled labour has been accentuated by the scale of foreign direct investment in the high-technology sector, particularly from the mid-1990s. Estimated earnings functions suggested an increase in returns to third-level education between 1987 and 1994, but this was confined to the middle or older age groups and did not continue from 1994 to 1997 – indeed declining returns for the middle age ranges were then seen. This could be because an increasing supply of skilled workers from education sufficed to offset rising demand for younger skilled workers up to 1994, while from then on immigration of skilled and experienced workers increased.

The pattern found for Ireland brings out the complexity of the links between trends in the earnings distribution and those in overall household income inequality and poverty. In the first place, increasing earnings dispersion does not necessarily mean more low pay. Ireland in the mid-1990s had one of the highest levels of low pay in the OECD, similar to the UK though lower than the USA, but low pay did not increase as earnings dispersion widened. The introduction of a national hourly minimum wage in Ireland in 2000 thus came in a remarkably benign setting, with employment growing rapidly and the market for unskilled labour particularly tight, and is unlikely to have had a significant negative impact on employment.

Recent Irish experience also demonstrates that increasing earnings dispersion is not always associated with a more unequal distribution of income among households. Ireland's household income distribution is among the more unequal in the European Union, similar to the UK, Greece and Spain though less unequal than Portugal. As far as trends over time are concerned, though, that distribution was relatively stable during the 1980s and into the 1990s, certainly with no suggestion of the marked increase in inequality seen in the USA and the UK. From 1994 to 1997, as the pace of economic growth accelerated, the distribution once again was rather stable with little change in summary inequality measures such as the Gini coefficient. When income is adjusted to take the greater needs of larger households into account, there was some tendency for the share of the bottom one-fifth of the distribution to decline. This may reflect a decline in the redistributive impact of social security cash transfers as support rates lagged behind rapidly-increasing incomes from the market.

This was a particularly significant factor underlying trends in poverty in Ireland as the macroeconomy fluctuated throughout the 1980s and 1990s. The overall percentage falling below relative income poverty lines was seen to be fairly stable, if anything trending upwards through 'good times and bad'. This reflected the countervailing influences of unemployment and the level of social security transfers relative to average income: when the economy was performing strongly and unemployment was falling, social welfare transfers tended to lag behind average incomes, and conversely in bad times. As a result there were major changes over time in the composition of the households found below a threshold such as half average income, with the relative position of families disimproving and that of the elderly generally improving during the 1980s, but the opposite trends emerging as growth picked up. Even after that growth was well under way, Ireland was seen to have a high rate of relative income poverty compared with other European Union members, similar to the UK though lower than Portugal.

With relative income poverty lines suggesting little difference between the stagnant 1980s and the booming 1990s, Ireland's experience over the past two decades also illustrates that these measures provide only part of the story in assessing what has been happening to poverty. A complementary poverty measure also incorporating non-monetary indicators of deprivation, incorporated in the global poverty reduction target adopted by Ireland's National Anti-Poverty Strategy, showed a significant decline from 1994 as rapid growth in real incomes and falling unemployment brought deprivation levels down. This decline in deprivation represents a significant improvement in the lives of low-income households, and societal expectations about minimum standards probably lag behind average income when it is increasing so fast. However, these expectations are likely to catch up with average incomes over time when growth slows, so high relative income poverty rates are clearly a structural concern for the longer term which represent a major challenge to social partnership.

There has been much debate internationally about increasing concentration of disadvantage among certain groups and in particular locations. This concern is reflected in the emergence into prominence of the term 'social exclusion' which directs attention to the emergence of multiply deprived groups, trapped in cycles of fatalism, concentrated in the worst housing estates and at risk of transmitting their fate across generations. The evidence for Ireland does not support the more extreme versions of these hypotheses. Sub-sets of cumulatively disadvantaged households experiencing distinctively high rates of poverty can certainly be identified, but they constitute only a small minority of poor households, with poverty being fairly evenly spread across the manual class. As far as spatial concentration is concerned, Irish data for both the 1980s and 1990s show poverty and unemployment to be widely dispersed throughout the country, with little change in the degree of concentration despite the scale of macro-economic change. While clustering is greater in Dublin than elsewhere, overall the clustering effect is relatively modest and does not for the most part involve the emergence of large, sharply delineated 'blackspots'.

What are the consequences of concentrated deprivation where it does exist? In the Irish case this is particularly difficult to assess because public sector housing has become increasingly residualised and more targeted on the poor and unemployed in recent years, as a result of policies promoting tenant purchase, the provision of incentives to exit to the private sector, and a significant contraction in new building. As a consequence local authority tenants constitute an increasingly selected group, with selection likely to have taken place not only on the basis of characteristics such as unemployment, social class and lone-parenthood but also on a range of other characteristics not captured in survey data but likely to be predictive of poverty. In such circumstances it is not surprising that poverty rates for public sector tenants are particularly high. Their socio-demographic profile in terms of measured characteristics was seen to account for much of this disadvantage, but there was an unexplained residual. When factors such as levels of fatalism and perceptions of local employment opportunities and the extent of neighbourhood problems were included in the analysis, the results suggested at most a modest contextual effect. This is entirely consistent with a range of other European studies, which have been unable to establish a substantial independent causal role for neighbourhood.

Irish evidence suggests that this may arise because social segregation and social differentiation in urban areas take more complex forms and are due to a more intricate set of factors than the status and location of housing alone. A study of a range of deprived urban estates revealed significant diversity between and within estates. Core neighbourhood units were often very small, and the emergence of status hierarchies bore no obvious relationship with conventional indicators of disadvantage. The distinctive profile of disadvantage of urban local authority tenants provides a rationale for tailored forms of intervention, which have a particular emphasis on empowerment. However, there is very little evidence that housing environment as such has a substantial independent influence on levels of poverty. Area-based policies which target the 'worst estates', however effective, can have only a limited impact on poverty because most poor people do not live in such estates.

17.4 Increased opportunity and equality of opportunity

The Irish experience of delayed and rapid economic development offers an ideal opportunity to test theories of industrialisation. Such theories hold that economic transformation greatly expands the number of advantaged positions in the class structure, but also that such positions come to be filled on the basis of meritocratic and universalistic principles, rather than social position and family connections. The expansion of professional and managerial positions should bring about an increase in *absolute* mobility, while the exigencies of industrial society for efficiency and rationality should lead to increased meritocracy in selection, generating greater *relative* mobility and equality of opportunity.

Ireland was still in transition from agricultural to industrial society until the 1960s, and life-chances were still hugely influenced by prospects of inheritance. By the 1990s a profound transformation had taken place and Ireland had moved closer than many other European societies to being a post-industrial society. The process of transformation had two distinct phases. The first saw a contraction of the farming sector and an expansion of both white-collar and manual opportunities for employees. The second involved a continued reduction in the agricultural sector but also in manual work. This was accompanied by an increase in white-collar employment and particularly professional and managerial opportunities. Both phases offered substantial opportunities for social mobility but these were greater in the second phase, which was characterised by unprecedented opportunities for mobility into the professional and managerial class and a low-level risk of mobility into the unskilled manual class. Upward mobility reached a new peak even for the working class. The rising tide had indeed lifted all boats.

As a consequence of such changes it was impossible for the professional and managerial class to become a self-recruiting élite and it became an increasingly heterogeneous group in terms of class origins. In addition the degree of self-recruitment among the self-employed declined. So in an important sense the class structure at the top and in the middle became more open. In fact it was at the bottom that a form of social closure emerged as members of the non-skilled working class came to be increasingly drawn from the same class origin. The period from the 1960s also saw a rapid increase in educational opportunities with sustained increases in educational participation, first, beyond compulsory schooling and, later, into third level. These changes constitute significant achievements in absolute terms, as movement up the class structure and progress through the education system became easier. Arguments that economic and social change benefited only a minority or that the outcome was the replacement of one self-perpetuating élite with another are unsustainable.

The Irish experience over the past forty years provides substantial support for the first element of the industrialisation thesis: there has been a marked expansion of advantaged positions in the class structure and an increase in absolute mobility. However, there is little evidence that the expansion of opportunities, leading to increased absolute mobility, has been accompanied by increased equality of opportunity, leading to increased relative mobility, the second element of the thesis.

In industrialised societies education plays a crucial role in the labour market and its impact is therefore central to considerations of trends in meritocratic selection. In Ireland we find little evidence of a reduction in relative educational inequalities. In fact, class disparities in access to third-level education have increased, and post-school education and training is more prevalent among those already educationally advantaged, thus reinforcing, rather than compensating for, earlier inequalities. The persistence of class differentials in education contrasts with the situation relating to gender where a significant reduction of differentials has taken place, a factor which has contributed to the rapid increase in women's labour force participation in recent decades. The rapidity of the overall expansion in participation rates and the erosion of gender differentials make us sceptical of cultural explanations for class differentials in educational attainment.

While there is clearly an important degree of similarity in educational differentials across countries, educational systems can serve to exacerbate or alleviate such inequalities. In Ireland from the late-1960s to the mid-1980s, the main thrust of policy was concerned with the overall expansion of participation levels rather than with reducing class inequalities. The Irish educational system combines a highly centralised system with a significant degree of discretion in policy and practice at school level. The result is a significant degree of competition between schools. The private owners of such schools opposed institutional reform aimed at local communal and regional reorganisation. In the absence of any prospect of radical institutional reform, policy became focused on reducing educational 'disadvantage'. The focus was on those 'failing' or being 'failed' by the educational system and concern was with tackling under-performance by certain groups of children rather than with inequality of opportunity.

When we turn to the relationship between education and occupational and class attainment, and indeed unemployment, we find that educational qualifications have considerable impact. The absolute gap in unemployment rates between those with a Leaving Certificate and without qualifications has increased steadily over time and the relative gap has widened even more dramatically in recent years. Educational qualifications are an increasingly important prerequisite of successful participation in the labour market and strongly influence the type of job obtained. As a consequence education and social class are strongly associated in the adult population. However, no evidence was found that the impact of educational qualifications on class destination had increased over time, and in fact this relationship weakened in the 1980s. In particular the relative advantage conferred by higher levels of education in facilitating access to white collar rather than other classes declined over time.

The weakening effect of education and the independent effect of class origins are directly contrary to the expectation of increasing meritocracy arising from educational expansion and a shift to professional and managerial employment. Given the general nature of the Irish educational system there are fewer linkages than in other countries between type of education and type of occupation achieved. Nevertheless, educational levels and grades do play an important signalling role. It is possible, however, that where increasing numbers of people enjoy high levels of education, employers come to think that such qualifications provide a weaker signal of productivity. High average levels of education, by ensuring an increased number of candidates above particular thresholds, may allow employers to use criteria in addition to education. If the educational system is seen as the main means of discovering talent then the case for increasing merit selection in Ireland is fundamentally undermined, and notwithstanding a substantial expansion of opportunities, meritocracy remains an aspiration.

17.5 The future?

Ireland followed a distinctive path over the course of the second half of the twentieth century. It successfully disengaged from economic dependence on Britain. It fully engaged with the international economy and underwent late and rapid industrialisation. It overcame two momentous economic and social crises, both of which questioned the continued viability of the society as well as the developmental strategies of a highly interventionist state. In the last decade or so of that century it achieved unprecedented growth in both output and employment, leading to convergence with living standards and employment levels in the core European countries. The latter success was achieved in the context of novel social partnership arrangements established in the late 1980s, but was built upon foundations laid over two decades earlier, including active state intervention to promote closer integration with the international economy as well as investment in increased educational participation.

Competitive corporatism has facilitated unprecedented economic growth, a dramatic increase in employment, and a very substantial reduction in unemployment; it has led to a substantial increase in living standards and restored order to the public finances, and it has secured a niche in the international economy. Medium-term prospects for the Irish economy are very favourable, with forecasts of continued growth, albeit at a more modest pace than in the very recent past. Demographic trends, moreover, are favourable, with a young population and a decline in the dependency ratio to an historically low level set to continue for some time to come. This holds out the prospect that within about 15 years Ireland may attain a standard of living in terms of income per head among the highest in the European Union.

Potential problems that might undermine the virtuous circle include vulnerability to international market forces – particularly in specific high-technology sectors, in residual deficiencies in physical infrastructure, and in a growing shortage of labour. The recent period of rapid economic growth and social partnership has also seen a weakening of the distributive role of the state, although this has been balanced by a commitment to maintain a minimum level of social protection. Opportunities and living standards have improved substantially although meritocracy remains an aspiration. Inequality of opportunity in terms of social mobility, educational opportunity and risk of poverty has remained stubbornly high. The political culture appears more comfortable focusing on disadvantage than tackling the deeper structural causes of inequality of opportunity.

Social partnership has been based on a shared consensus on the priorities of economic development and employment growth. Having achieved these goals, and with the emergence of increased wage pressure following from full employment, the institutions of social partnership are likely to come under increasing pressure. This is likely to come from several sources. First, social partnership has not been all-encompassing. The new classes of professionals and entrepreneurs fall outside its institutions and have become the basis of increasing inequality of market incomes. This is mirrored in the state itself, where activities of the developmental agencies have operated beyond the scope of social partnership. Second, tensions over basic distributional issues have emerged between economic sectors, particularly between public and private sector workers, but also between groups within the public sector. Thirdly, the decline in welfare effort relative to national income raises fundamental questions about the quality of social citizenship rights in Ireland into the future.

Experience in other rich countries suggests that the achievement of real equality of opportunity requires a highly interventionist state investing in a substantial upgrading of social services. The scale of economic growth and the demographic dividend over the next decade may make it possible for Ireland to improve those services by increased social spending, while still reducing taxes. Over the longer term, however, a policy which leaves Ireland with a relatively low proportion of national income going on social spending will inevitably lead to a situation where the scope, level and quality of public provision and social protection fail to match higher living standards from the market. Reversing this trend would require a re-negotiation of the terms of social partnership in a manner that would entail a greater share of the fruits of growth being channelled through social rather than market wages.

The period of rapid growth has also been accompanied by a marked decline in the share of wages (versus profits) in national income in Ireland. Slow growth in wages relative to productivity has contributed both to rapid economic growth and to the decline in the wage share, and some reversal in this latter trend appears inevitable: the question is how fast it can happen and how far it can go without derailing the engine of economic growth. Irish society and the institutions of social partnership are now confronted with very fundamental issues about the distribution of the fruits of growth, as well as the appropriate balance between market and social wages. How those issues are tackled will be crucial to the continued sustainability of the distinctive Irish model.

Bibliography

A

Aberge, R., Bjorklund, A., Jantti, M., Pedersen, P., Smith, N. and Wennemo, T. (2000), 'Unemployment Shocks and Income Distribution: How did the Nordic Countries Fare during their Crises?' *Scandinavian Journal of Economics*, 102 (1), 77-99.

Administration (1995), Special issue on 'Strategic Management in the Irish Civil Service', vol. 43, no. 2, Summer.

Allmendinger, J. (1989), 'Educational Systems and Labour Market Outcomes', *European Sociological Review*, vol. 5: 231-250.

Almond, G. A. and Verba, S. (eds) (1963), *The Civic Culture: Political Attitudes and Democracy in Five Nations,* Princeton, NJ: Princeton University Press.

Alter, G. (1992), 'Theories of Fertility Decline: a Non-specialist's Guide to the Current Debate', in J.R. Gillis, L.A.Tilly and D. Levine (eds), *The European Experience of Declining Fertility. A Quiet Revolution 1850-1970,* Oxford: Blackwell Publishers.

Ansell, C. (1999), 'The Networked Polity: Regional Development in Western Europe', mimeo, Berkeley: Department of Political Science, University of California.

Atkinson, A.B. (1971), 'On the Measurement of Economic Inequality', *Journal of Economic Theory*, vol. 2: 244-263.

Atkinson, A.B. (1997), 'Targeting Poverty', *New Economy*, vol. 5, no. 1: 3-7.

Atkinson, A.B., Rainwater, L. and Smeeding, T.M. (1995*), Income Distribution in OECD Countries: Evidence from the Luxembourg Income Study*, Paris: OECD.

Auer, P. (2000), *Employment Revival in Europe: Labour Market Success in Austria, Denmark, Ireland and the Netherlands*, Geneva: ILO.

Aust, A. (1999), 'The "Celtic Tiger" and Its Beneficiaries: "Competitive Corporatism" in Ireland', March, Mannheim: ECPR Joint Sessions.

B

Bannon, M.J, Eustace, J.G. and O'Neill, M. (1981), *Urbanisation: Problems of Growth and Decay in Dublin*, Dublin: National Economic and Social Council, Report no. 55.

Baker, T., Fitz Gerald, J. and Honohan, P. (1996), *Economic Implications for Ireland of EMU.* Policy Research Series No. 28, Dublin: The Economic and Social Research Institute.

Baker, T., Duffy, D., and Shortall, F. (1998), *Quarterly Economic Commentary, April 1998,* Dublin: The Economic and Social Research Institute.

Barrett, A. and Trace, F. (1998), 'Who is Coming Back? The Educational Profile of Returning Migrants in the 1990s', *Irish Banking Review*, Summer.

Barrett, A., Callan, T. and Nolan, B. (1999), 'Rising Wage Inequality, Returns to Education and Labour Market Institutions: Evidence from Ireland', *British Journal of Industrial Relations*, vol. 37, no. 1: 77-100.

Barrett, A., Callan, T. (ed.), Doris, A., O'Neill, D., Russell, H., Sweetman, O. and MacBride, J. (2000), *How Unequal: Man and Women in the Irish Labour Market*, Dublin: Oak Tree Press, in association with ESRI.

Barrett, A., Fitz Gerald, J. and Nolan, B. (2000), *Earnings Inequality, Returns to Education and Emigration into Ireland*, Discussion Paper No. 2493, London: CEPR.

Barrett, A. and O'Connell, P. (2000), *Is There a Wage Premium for Returning Irish Migrants?*, London: Centre for Economic Policy Research, Working Paper No. 2408.

Barro, R. and Sala-i-Martin, X. (1995), *Economic Growth*, New York: McGraw Hill.

Barry, F. (ed.) (1999), *Understanding Ireland's Economic Growth*, Basingstoke: Macmillan Press.

Barry, F. (1999), 'Irish Growth in Historical and Theoretical Perspective', in F. Barry, (ed.), *Understanding Ireland's Economic Growth*, Basingstoke: Macmillan Press Ltd.

Barry, F. and Bradley, J. (1997), 'FDI and Trade: The Irish Host-Country Experience', *The Economic Journal*, vol. 107, no. 441, November.

Barry, F., Bradley, J., Hannan, A., McCartan, J. and Sosvilla-Rivera, S. (1997), *Single Market Review 1996: Aggregate and Regional Aspects: the Cases of Greece, Ireland, Portugal and Spain*, London: Kogan Page in association with the Office for Official Publications of the European Communities, Luxembourg.

Barry, F. and Bradley, J. (1999), *The Comparative Study of Transition and Cohesion*, ACE-Phare Project P96-6242-R, Working Paper WP04, 26 March.

Barry, F., Bradley, J., and O'Malley, F. (1999), 'Indigenous and Foreign Industry: Characteristics and Performance', in F. Barry (ed.), *Understanding Ireland's Economic Growth*, Basingstoke: Macmillan Press Ltd.

Barry, F., Hannan, A. and Strobl, E.A. (1999), 'The Real Convergence of the Irish Economy and the Sectoral Distribution of Employment Growth', in F. Barry (ed.), *Understanding Ireland's Economic Growth*, Basingstoke: Macmillan Press.

Bartley, B. (1998), 'Exclusion, Invisibility and the Neighbourhood in West Dublin', in A. Madanipour, G. Cars and J. Allen (eds), *Social Exclusion in European Cities. Processes, Experiences and Responses*, London: Jessica Kingsley Publishers.

Barton, B. and Roche, P.J. (eds) (1994), *The Northern Ireland Question:* Perspectives and Policies, Aldershot: Avebury.

Bax, E.H. (1990), *Modernization and Cleavage in Dutch Society*, Aldershot: Gower.

Becker, G.S. (1981), *A Treatise on the Family*, Cambridge, Mass.: Harvard University Press.

Beechey, V. (1987), 'Women's Employment in France and Britain: Some Problems of Comparison', *Work, Employment and Society*, vol. 3, no. 3: 369-378.

Berger, P.L. (1987), *The Capitalist Revolution: Fifty Propositions about Prosperity, Equality and Liberty*, Aldershot: Wildwood House.

Bettio, F. and Villa, P. (1998), 'A Mediterranean Perspective on the Breakdown of the Relationship between Participation and Fertility', *Cambridge Journal of Economics,* vol. 22: 137-171.

Bielenberg, A. and O'Mahony, P. (1998), 'An Expenditure Estimate of Irish National Income in 1907', *The Economic and Social Review,* vol. 29, no. 2: 107-132.

Biever, B.F. (1976), *Religion, Culture and Values: A Cross-Cultural Analysis of Motivational Factors in Native Irish and American Irish Catholicism,* New York: Arno Press.

Blanchard, O. (1997), *The Economics of Post-Communist Transition,* Oxford: Clarendon Press.

Blau, F.D. (1998), 'Trends in the Well-being of American Women, 1970-1995', *Journal of Economic Literature,* vol. 36, no. 1.

Blau, F. and Kahn, L. (1996), 'International Differences in Male Wage Inequality: Institutions Versus Market Forces', *Journal of Political Economy,* vol. 104, no. 4: 791-837.

Blau, P.M. and Duncan, O.D. (1967), *The American Occupational Structure,* New York: Wiley.

Boh, K. (1989), 'European Family Life Patterns – a Reappraisal', in K. Boh et al (eds), *Changing Patterns of European Family Life: A Comparative Analysis of 14 European Countries,* London: Routledge.

Böll, H. (1967), *Irish Journal,* New York: McGraw-Hill, translated from the 1957 German edition.

Borjas, G. and Ramey, V. (1994), 'Time-Series Evidence on the Sources of Trends in Wage Inequality', *American Economic Review,* Papers and Proceedings, vol. 84: 10-116.

Borjas, G., Freeman, R. and Katz, L. (1997), 'How Much Do Immigration and Trade Affect Labour Market Outcomes?', *Brookings Papers on Economic Activity,* vol.1: 1-67.

Boudon, R. (1974), *Opportunity and Social Inequality,* New York: Wiley.

Bound, J. and Johnson, G. (1992), 'Changes in the Structure of Wages During the 1980s: An Evaluation of Alternative Explanations', *American Economic Review,* vol. 82: 371-92.

Bowling, A. (1991), *Measuring Health. A Review of Quality of Life Measurement Scales,* Milton Keynes: Open University Press.

Bradley, H. (1989), *Men's Work, Women's Work,* Cambridge: Polity Press.

Bradley, J. and Fitz Gerald, J. (1988), 'Industrial Output and Factor Input Determination in an Econometric Model of a Small Open Economy', *European Economic Review,* vol. 32: 1227-1241.

Bradley, J., Fitz Gerald, J. and McCoy, D. (1991), *Medium-Term Review: 1991-1996.* Dublin: The Economic and Social Research Institute.

Bradley, J., Fitz Gerald, J. and Kearney, I. (1992), *The Role of the Structural Funds: Analysis of Consequences for Ireland in the Context of 1992,* Policy Research Series No. 13, Dublin: The Economic and Social Research Institute.

Bradley, J., Fitz Gerald, J. and Kearney, I. (1993), 'Modelling Supply in an Open Economy Using a Restricted Cost Function', *Economic Modelling*, vol. 10, no. 1: 11-21.

Bradley J., Herce, J-A. and Modesto, L. (1995), 'Modelling in the EU periphery, The HERMIN Project', *Economic Modelling*, Special Edition, vol. 12, no. 3.

Bradley, J., Fitz Gerald, J., Honohan, P. and Kearney, I. (1997), 'Interpreting the Recent Irish Growth Experience', *Medium Term Review: 1997-2003*, Dublin: The Economic and Social Research Institute, April.

Bradley, J., Morgenroth, E. and Untiedt, G. (2000), *HGE4: A HERMIN Model of East Germany*, Report prepared for European Commission, DG XVI, February.

Bradshaw, J. (ed.) (1993), *Budget Standards for the United Kingdom*, Averbury: Alderhsot.

Bradshaw, J., Gordon, D., Levitas, R., Pantazis, C., Payne, S. and Townsend, P. (1998), *Perceptions of Poverty and Social Exclusion (1998)*, Report on Preparatory Research, Bristol Statistical Monitoring Unit, Bristol: University of Bristol.

Brady, J. and Parker, A. J. (1975), 'The Factorial Ecology of Dublin: a Preliminary Investigation', *The Economic and Social Review*, vol. 7, no. 1: 35-54.

Breathnach, A. (1976), 'Towards the Identification of Educational Priority Areas in Dublin', *The Economic and Social Review*, vol. 7, no 4: 367-382.

Breathnach, M. (2000), *R & D and Innovation in Industry: Update on Indicators of Performance*, Dublin: Forfás.

Breen, R. (1984), 'Fitting Nonhierarchial and Association Log-Linear Models Using GLIM', *Sociological Methods and Research*, vol. 13, no. 1: 77-107.

Breen, R. (1985), 'A Framework for Comparative Analysis of Social Mobility', *Sociology*, vol. 19: 93-107.

Breen, R. (1991), *Education, Employment and Training in the Youth Labour Market*, Dublin: The Economic and Social Research Institute.

Breen, R., Hannan, D.F., Rottman, D.B. and Whelan, C.T. (1990), *Understanding Contemporary Ireland: State, Class and Development in the Republic of Ireland*. London: Macmillan.

Breen, R. and Shortall, S. (1992), 'The Exchequer Costs of Unemployment Among Unqualified Labour Market Participants', in J. Bradley, J. Fitz Gerald and I. Kearney (eds), *The Role of the Structural Funds: Analysis of Consequences for Ireland in the Context of 1992*, Policy Research Series No. 13, Dublin: The Economic and Social Research Institute.

Breen, R. and Whelan, C.T. (1992), 'Explaining the Irish Pattern of Social Fluidity: The Role of the Political', in J.H. Goldthorpe and C.T. Whelan (eds), *The Development of Industrial Society in Ireland*, Proceedings of the British Academy 79, Oxford: Oxford University Press.

Breen, R. and Whelan, C.T. (1993), 'From Ascription to Achievement? Origins, Education and Entry to the Labour Force in the Republic of Ireland during the Twentieth Century', *Acta Sociologica*, vol. 36, no.1: 1 86.

Breen, R. and Whelan, C.T. (1994), 'Modelling Trends in Social Fluidity: The Core Model and a Measured-Variable Approach Compared', *European Sociological Review*, vol. 10, no.3: 25-72.

Breen, R., Hannan, D.F. and O'Leary, R. (1995), 'Returns to Education: Taking Account of Employers' Perceptions and Use of Educational Credentials', *European Sociological Review,* vol. 11, no. 1: 59-73.

Breen R. and Whelan C.T. (1995): 'Gender and Class Mobility: Evidence from the Republic of Ireland', *Sociology*, vol. 29, no.1: 1-22.

Breen, R. and Whelan, C.T. (1996), *Social Mobility and Social Class in Ireland,* Dublin: Gill and Macmillan.

Breen, R. and Goldthorpe, J.H. (1997), 'Explaining Educational Differential: Towards a Formal Rational Theory', *Rationality and Society*, vol. 9, no. 3: 275-305.

Breen, R. and Goldthorpe, J.H. (1999), 'Class Inequality and Meritocracy: A Critique of Saunders and an Alternative Analysis', *British Journal of Sociology,* vol. 50: 1-27.

Breen, R., Heath, A.F. and Whelan, C.T. (1999), 'Educational Inequality in Ireland, North and South', in A.F. Heath, R. Breen and C.T. Whelan (1999), *Ireland North and South: Perspectives from Social Science.*

Breen, R. and Goldthorpe, J.H. (forthcoming), 'Class Mobility and Merit: The Experience of Two British Cohorts, *European Sociological Review.*

Brenner, N. (1998), 'Global Cities, Global States: Global City Formation and State Territorial Restructuring in Contemporary Europe', *Review of International Political Economy*, vol. 5, no.1:1-37.

Brenner, N. (1999), 'Beyond State-centrism? Space, Territoriality and Geographical Scale in Globalization Studies', *Theory and Society*, vol. 28.

Brooks-Gunn, J., Duncan, G. and Aber, J.L. (1997), *Neighbourhood Poverty: Volume 1: Context and Consequences for Children*, New York: Russell Sage Foundation.

Buchanan, C. and Partners (1968), *Regional Studies in Ireland*, Report Commissioned by the United Nations on behalf of the Irish Government, Dublin: An Foras Forbartha.

Buhman, B., Rainwater, L., Schmaus, G. and Smeeding,T. (1988), 'Equivalence Scales, Well-being, Inequality and Poverty: Sensitivity Estimates Across Ten Countries Using the Luxembourg Income Study Database', *Review of Income and Wealth*, Series 34: 115-142.

Bumpass, L. (1990), 'What's Happening to the Family? Interactions between Demographic and Institutional Change', *Demography,* vol. 27, no. 4: 483-498.

Burke, E. (1968), *Reflections on the Revolution in France,* Edited by Conor Cruise O'Brien, Harmondsworth: Penguin.

Burtless, G. (1995), 'International Trade and the Rise in Earnings Inequality', *Journal of Economic Literature*, vol. 33, no. 2: 800-816.

C

Cahill, N. and O'Toole, F. (1998), 'Taxation Policy', in Seán Healy and Brigid Reynolds (eds), *Social Policy in Ireland*, Dublin, Oak Tree Press.

Calhoun, C.A. (1994), 'The Impact of Children on the Labour Supply of Married Women: Comparative Estimates from European and US Data', *European Journal of Population* vol. 10.

Callan, T. (1991), 'Income Tax and Welfare Reforms: Microsimulation Modelling and Analysis', *GRS*, no. 154, The Economic and Social Research Institute.

Callan, T. and Farrell, B. (1991), *Women's Participation in the Irish Labour Market*, NESC Report No. 91, Dublin: National Economic and Social Council.

Callan, T. (1993), 'Returns to Educational Investment in Ireland: New Evidence for Ireland', in John Fitz Gerald and Owen Keegan (eds), *The Community Support Framework 1989-93: Evaluation and Recommendations for the 1994-97 Framework*. Dublin: Stationery Office.

Callan, T., Nolan, B. and Whelan, B.J., Hannan, D.F. with Creighton, S. (1989), *Poverty, Income and Welfare in Ireland*, General Research Series No. 146, Dublin: The Economic and Social Research Institute.

Callan, T. and Nolan, B. (1991), 'Concepts of Poverty and the Poverty Line: A Critical Survey of Approaches to Measuring Poverty', *Journal of Economic Surveys*, vol. 5, no. 3: 243-62.

Callan, T. and Nolan, B. (1992), 'Income Distribution and Redistribution: Ireland in Comparative Perspective', in J.H. Goldthorpe and C.T. Whelan (eds), *The Development of Industrial Society in Ireland*, Oxford: Oxford University Press.

Callan, T., Nolan, B., and Whelan, C.T. (1993), 'Resources, Deprivation and the Measurement of Poverty', *Journal of Social Policy*, vol. 22, no. 2:141-172.

Callan, T. and Wren, A. (1994), *Male-Female Wage Differentials: Analysis and Policy Issues*, General Research Series Paper No. 163, Dublin: The Economic and Social Research Institute.

Callan, T., Nolan, B. and O'Donoghue, C. (1996), 'What Has Happened to Replacement Rates?', *The Economic and Social Review*, vol. 27: 439-456.

Callan, T., Nolan, B. and Whelan, C.T. (1996), *A Review of the Commission on Social Welfare's Minimum Adequate Income,* Policy Research Series No. 29, Dublin: The Economic and Social Research Institute.

Callan, T., Nolan, B., Whelan, B.J., Whelan C.T. and Williams, J. (1996), *Poverty in the 1990s: Evidence from the Living in Ireland Survey,* General Research Series Paper 170, Dublin: Oak Tree Press.

Callan, T. and Harmon, C. (1997), *The Economic Return to Schooling in Ireland*, UCD Centre for Economic Research WP 92/23, Dublin: UCD Department of Economics.

Callan, T. and Nolan, B. (1997), 'Income Inequality and Poverty in Ireland in the 1970s and 1980s', in P. Gottschalk, B. Gustafsson and E. Palmer (eds), *Changing Patterns in the Distribution of Economic Welfare: An International Perspective,* Cambridge: Cambridge University Press.

Callan, T. and Sutherland, H. (1997), 'Income Supports in Ireland and the UK', in T. Callan (ed.), *Income Support and Work Incentives: Ireland and the UK*, Policy Research Series Paper No. 30, Dublin: The Economic and Social Research Institute.

Callan, T., Nolan, B., O'Neill, D. and Sweetman, O. (1998), *Female Labour Force Participation and Household Income Inequality in Ireland*, Paper for Irish Economics Association Annual Conference, April.

Callan, T., Nolan, B., Walsh, J. and Nestor, R. (1999), 'Income Tax and Social Welfare Policies', in *Budget Perspectives*, ESRI Conference, 27 September.

Callan, T. and Nolan, B. (1999), 'Income Inequality in Ireland in the 1980s and 1990s', in F. Barry (ed.), *Understanding Ireland's Economic Growth*, Basingstoke: Macmillan Press.

Callan, T., Layte, R., Nolan, B., Watson, D., Whelan, C.T., Williams, J. and Maître, B. (1999), *Monitoring Poverty Trends: Data from the 1997 Living in Ireland Survey*, Dublin: Stationery Office/Combat Poverty Agency.

Calmfors, L. and Driffill, J. (1988), 'Bargaining Structure, Corporatism and Macroeconomic Performance', *Economic Policy,* vol. 3:13-61.

Cantillon, S. and Nolan, B. (1998), 'Are Married Women More Deprived than Their Husbands?', *Journal of Social Policy,* vol. 27, no. 2:151-171.

Card, D. and Krueger, A. (1995), *Myth and Measurement: The New Economics of the Minimum Wage,* Princeton: Princeton University Press.

Castells, M. (1997), *The Rise of the Network Society,* Oxford: Blackwell.

Cecchini, P. (1988), *The European Challenge 1992, The Benefits of a Single Market*, London: Wildwood House.

Cerny, P. (1995), 'Globalization amd the Changing Logic of Collective Action', *International Organization,* vol. 49:595-625.

Central Statistics Office (1997a), *Census 96: Principal Demographic Results,* Dublin: Stationery Office.

Central Statistics Office (1997b), *Labour Force Survey, 1997,* Dublin: Stationery Office.

Central Statistics Office (1998), *Census 96: Principal Socio-economic Results,* Dublin: Stationery Office.

Central Statistics Office (various years), *Annual Services Inquiry*, Dublin: CSO.

Chubb, B. (1982), *The Government and Politics of Ireland*, Oxford: Oxford University Press.

Chubb, B. and Lynch, P. (eds), (1969), *Economic Development and Planning,* Dublin: IPA.

Ciupagea, C. and Lacramioara Manda, A. (1999), *HR4: The HERMIN model of Romania*, ACE-Phare Project P96-6242-R Working Paper WP02, 26 March.

Clancy, P. (1995*), Access to College: Patterns of Continuity and Change*, Dublin: Higher Education Authority.

Clark, C. (1957), *The Conditions of Economic Progress*, London: Macmillan.

Coakley, J. (1993), 'Society and Political Culture' in J. Coakley and M. Gallagher (eds), *Politics in the Republic of Ireland*, Dublin: Folens.

Coakley, J. and Gallagher, M. (eds) (1993), *Politics in the Republic of Ireland,* Dublin: Folens/PSAI Press.

Coale, A.J. and Watkins, S.C. (1986), *The Decline of Fertility in Europe*, Princeton: Princeton University Press.

Coleman, D. (1992), 'The Demographic Transition in Ireland in International Context', in J.H. Goldthorpe and C. T. Whelan (eds), *The Development of Industrial Society in Ireland*, Oxford: Oxford University Press.

Collingwood, R.G. (1940), *An Essay on Metaphysics*, Oxford: Oxford University Press.

Commission on the Status of Women (1972), *Report*, Dublin: Government Publications Office.

Committee on Industrial Organisation (1965), *Final Report*, Dublin: Stationery Office.

Committee on Industrial Progress (1973), *General Report*, Dublin: Stationery Office.

Community Platform (1997), *Achieving Social Partnership: the Strategy and Proposals of The Community Platform at the Partnership 2000 Negotiations*, Dublin: Community Platform and Combat Poverty Agency.

Connell, R.W. (1987), *Gender and Power. Society, the Person and Sexual Politics.* Cambridge: Polity Press.

Coolahan, J. (1981), *Irish Education: History and Structure*, Dublin: Institute of Public Administration.

Corcoran, T., Sexton, J.J. and O'Donoghue, D. (1992), *A Review of Trends in the Occupational Pattern of Employment in Ireland 1971-1990*, Report No. 2, Manpower Forecasting Studies, Dublin; Fás/ESRI.

Corcoran, M.P. and Fahey, T. (1999), 'Methodology and Overview of Estates', in T. Fahey (ed.), *Social Housing in Ireland. A Study of Success, Failures and Lessons Learned*, Dublin: Oak Tree Press in association with the Katherine Howard Foundation and the Combat Poverty Agency.

Corcoran, T., Hughes, G. and Sexton, J.J. (1993), *Occupational Employment Forecasts, 1996*, Report No 3, Manpower Forecasting Studies, Dublin: FÁS/ESRI.

Coulter, F., Cowell, F. and Jenkins, S.P. (1992), 'Equivalence Scale Relativities and the Extent of Inequality and Poverty', *Economic Journal*, vol. 102: 1067-1082.

Council of Europe (1998), *Recent Demographic Developments in Europe 1998*, Strasbourg: Council of Europe Publishing.

Cousins, M. (1995), *The Irish Social Welfare System: Law and Social Policy*, Dublin: Roundhall Press.

Cowell, F. (1995), *Measuring Inequality*, LSE Handbooks on Economics, Hemel Hempstead: Prentice Hall/Harvester Wheatsheaf.

Cox, R. (1993), 'Gramsci, Hegemony and International Relations: An Essay in Method', in S. Gill (ed.), *Gramsci, Historical Materialism and International Relations*, Cambridge: Cambridge University Press.

Crompton, R. and Sanderson, K. (1990), *Gendered Jobs and Social Change*, London: Unwin Hyman.

Crouch, C. (1994), 'Incomes Policies, Institutions and Markets: an Overview of Recent Developments', in Dore et al. (eds), *The Return to Incomes Policy*, London: Pinter.

Curtin, C., Haase, T. and Tovey, H. (eds) (1996), *Poverty in Rural Ireland. A Political Economy Perspective*, Dublin: Oak Tree Press.

D

Daly, M.E. (1981), 'Women in the Irish Workforce from Pre-industrial to Modern Times', *Saothar*, vol. 7: 47-82.

Daly, M.E. (1984), *Dublin: the Deposed Capital*, Cork: Cork University Press.

Daly, M.E. (1997), *Women and Work in Ireland*, Dundalk: Economic History Society of Ireland.

Daune-Richard, A.M. (1998), 'How Does the Societal Effect Shape the Use of Part-time Work in France, the UK and Sweden?' in J. O'Reilly, and C. Fagan (eds), *Part-time Prospects*, London: Routledge.

Davis, E.E., Grube, J.W and Morgan, M. (1984), *Attitudes Towards Poverty and Related Social Issues in Ireland*, Dublin: The Economic and Social Research Institute.

Deleeck, H., Van den Bosch, K. and De Lathouwer, L. (1992), *Poverty and the Adequacy of Social Security in the EC*, Aldershot: Avebury.

Department of Education (1995), *Charting our Education Future*, White Paper on Education, Dublin: Stationery Office.

Department of Education (1966), *Investment in Education*, Dublin: Stationery Office.

Department of Education and Science (1999), *Statistical Report 1996/7*, Dublin: Stationery Office.

Department of Social, Community and Family Affairs (1999), *Statistical Information on Social Welfare Services, 1998*, Dublin: Stationery Office.

Department of Social Welfare (1994), *Statistical Information on Social Welfare Services, 1993*, Dublin: Stationery Office.

Deven, F. et al (1997), *State of the Art Review on the Reconciliation of Work and Family Life for Men and Women and the Quality of Care Services*, Dublin: Dept. for Education and Employment, Research Report No. 44.

Devine, T. (1999), *The Scottish Nation: 1700-2000*, London: Allen Lane.

Dex, S. (1992), 'Women's Part-time Work in Britain and the United States', in B. Warme et al (eds), *Working Part-time: Risks and Opportunities*, New York: Praeger.

Dex, S. (1998), 'Appropriate Indicators of Demand for Labour Markets Segmented by Gender', *Cambridge Journal of Economics*, vol. 22:19-38.

DiNardo, J., Fortin, N. and Lemieux, T. (1996), 'Labor Market Institutions and the Distribution of Wages, 1973-1992: A Semiparametric Approach', *Econometrica*, vol. 64 no. 5:1001-1044.

DiNardo, J. and Lemieux, T. (1997), 'Diverging Male Wage Inequality in the United States and Canada, 1981-1988: Do Institutions Explain the Difference?', *Industrial and Labor Relations Review*, vol. 50, no. 4:629-651.

Dooney, S. and O'Toole, J. (1992), *Irish Government Today*, Dublin: Gill and Macmillan.

Dore, R. (1994), 'Introduction: Incomes Policy: Why Now?, in Ronald Dore et al (eds), *The Return to Incomes Policy*, London: Pinter.

Dore, R., Boyer, R., Mars, Z. (eds) (1994), *The Return to Incomes Policy*, London: Pinter.

Dowding, K.M. and Kimber, R. (1983), 'The Meaning and Use of "Political Stability"', *European Journal of Political Research*, vol. 11, no. 3:229-243.

Drudy, P.J. and MacLaran, A. (eds) (1996), Dublin: *Economic and Social Trends,* vol. 2, Dublin: Centre for Urban and Regional Studies, Trinity College.

Duerloo, M. and Musterd, S. (1998), 'Ethnic Clusters in Amsterdam, 1994-96: a micro-level analysis', *Urban Studies* 35, 3.

Duffy, D. (1999), 'Budget 2000: a Macroeconomic Perspective', in *Budget Perspectives*, ESRI Conference, 27 September.

Duffy, D., Fitz Gerald, J., Kearney, I. and Shortall, F. (eds) (1997), *Medium-Term Review: 1997-2003*, Dublin: The Economic and Social Research Institute.

Duffy, D., Fitz Gerald, J., Kearney, I. and Smyth, D., (1999), *Medium-Term Review: 1999-2005*, No. 7, Dublin: The Economic and Social Research Institute.

Duggan, D., Hughes, G., and Sexton, J.J. (1997), *Occupational Employment Forecasts 2003.* FÁS/ESRI Manpower Forecasting Studies, No. 6. Dublin: The Economic and Social Research Institute.

Durkan, J. (1999), 'The Role of Budgetary Policy in Social Consensus', in *Budget Perspectives*, ESRI Conference, 27 September.

Durkan, J., Fitzgerald, D. and Harmon, C. (1999), 'Education and Growth in the Irish Economy', in F. Barry (ed.), *Understanding Ireland's Economic Growth*, Basingstoke: Macmillan Press Ltd.

E

Eatwell, R. (1997), *European Political Culture*, London: Routledge.

EC Childcare Network (1992), *Annual Report: Employment, Equality and Caring for Children.*

EC Childcare Network (1997), *A Decade of Achievements 1986-1996*, Brussels: European Commission.

Economic and Social Development, 1976-1980 (1976), Dublin: Stationery Office.

Erikson, R. (1996), 'Explaining Change in Educational Inequality – Economic Security and School Reforms', in R. Erikson and J.O. Jonson (eds), *Can Education Be Equalized? The Swedish Case in Comparative Perspective,* Boulder: Westview Press.

Erikson, R., Goldthorpe, J.H., and Portocarero, L. (1979), 'Intergenerational Class Mobility in Three Western European Societies', *British Journal of Sociology,* vol. 30, no. 3:1-34.

Erikson, R. and Goldthorpe, J.H. (1987), 'Commonality and Variation in Social Fluidity in Industrial Nations, Part I: A Model for Evaluating the FJH Hypothesis', *European Sociological Review*, vol. 3:54-77.

Erikson, R. and Goldthorpe, J.H. (1992), *The Constant Flux: A Study of Class Mobility in Industrial Societies,* Oxford: Oxford University Press.

Erikson, R. and Jonsson, J.O. (1996), 'Explaining Class Inequality in Education: the Swedish Test Case', in R. Erikson and J.O. Jonson (eds), *Can Education Be Equalized? The Swedish Case in Comparative Perspective,* Boulder: Westview Press.

Ernst, D. and O'Connor, D. (1992), *Competing in the Electronics Industry: the Experience of Newly Industrialising Economies,* Paris: OECD.

ESF Programme Evaluation Unit (1997), *Preventive Actions in Education*, Dublin: ESF Evaluation Unit.

Esping-Andersen, G. (1990), *The Three Worlds of Welfare Capitalism,* Princeton: Princeton University Press.

Esping-Andersen, G. (1999), *Social Foundations of Postindustrial Economies,* Oxford: Oxford University Press.

European Commission (1999), *Employment in Europe 1998*, Luxembourg: EC.

European Commission (2000), *Employment in Europe 1999,* Luxembourg: EC.

Evans, G. (1992): 'Testing the validity of the Goldthorpe Class Schema', *European Sociological Review*, vol. 8, no. 3:211-32.

Evans, P. (1995), *Embedded Autonomy*, Princeton: Princeton University Press.

Evans, P. (1996), 'Government Action, Social Capital and Development: Creating Synergy across the Public-Private Divide', Special Section *World Development*, vol. 24, no. 6:1033-1131.

Evans, P.B. and Rauch, J.(1999), 'Bureaucracy and Growth: A Cross-National Analysis of the Effects of "Weberian" States Structures on Economic Growth', *American Sociological Review,* vol. 64:748-765.

Expert Working Group on Childcare (1999), *National Childcare Strategy*, Dublin: Stationery Office.

F

Fahey, T. (1990), 'Measuring the Female Labour Supply: Conceptual and Procedural Problems in Irish Official Statistics', *The Economic and Social Review*, vol. 21, no. 2: 163-191.

Fahey, T. (1993), 'Review article', *The Economic and Social Review,* vol. 24, no. 2: 199-209.

Fahey, T. (1999a), 'Social Housing in Ireland: the Need for an Expanded Role?'*Irish Banking Review,* Autumn.

Fahey, T. (1999b), 'Population Ageing in Reverse – the Case of Ireland'. Paper to the Annual Conference of the British Society for Population Studies, September, Dublin.

Fahey, T. (ed.) (1999), *Social Housing in Ireland: A Study of Success, Failure and Lessons Learned*, Dublin: Oak Tree Press.

Fahey, T. and Watson, D. (1995), *An Analysis of Social Housing Need,* Dublin: The Economic and Social Research Institute.

Fahey, T. and Fitz Gerald, J. (1997), 'The Educational Revolution and Demographic Change', in D. Duffy, J. Fitz Gerald, I. Kearney, and F. Shortall (eds), *Medium Term Review: 1997-2003,* Dublin: The Economic and Social Research Institute.

Fahey, T. and Fitz Gerald, J. (1997), *Welfare Implications of Demographic Trends*, Dublin: Combat Poverty Agency.

Fahey, T., Fitz Gerald, J. and Maître, B. (1998), 'The Economic and Social Implications of Population Change', *Journal of the Statistical and Social Inquiry Society of Ireland* 1997/1998.

Fahey, T. and McLaughlin, E. (1999), 'Family and State', in A.F. Heath, R. Breen and C.T. Whelan (eds), *Ireland North and South,* Oxford: Oxford University Press.

Fanning, R., (1978), *The Irish Department of Finance 1922-1958,* Dublin: The Institute of Public Administration.

Farrell, B. (1987), 'The Context of Three Elections', in H.R. Penniman and B. Farrell (eds), *Ireland at the Polls 1981, 1982, and 1987,* Durham, NC: Duke University Press.

Fernie, S. and Metcalf, D. (1996), *Low Pay and Minimum Wages: The British Evidence,* Centre for Economic Performance, LSE.

Fianna Fáil (1977), *Action Plan for National Reconstruction,* Dublin: Fianna Fáil.

Finnegan, B. (1985), *The Democratisation of Higher Education and the Participation of University Women in the Labour Force, 1920-50.* M.A. Thesis, University College Dublin.

Finneran, C. and Punch, A. (1999), 'The Demographic and Socio-economic Characteristics of Migrants, 1986-1996', *Journal of the Statistical and Social Inquiry Society of Ireland* 1998/1999.

FitzGerald, G. (1991a), *The Impact of European Community Membership on Public Opinion in Ireland and Britain,* Dublin: CEEPA.

FitzGerald, G. (1991b), *All in a Life,* Dublin: Gill and Macmillan.

Fitz Gerald, J. (1998), 'An Irish Perspective on the Structural Funds', *European Planning Studies,* vol. 6.677-695.

Fitz Gerald, J. (1999), 'Wage Formation in the Irish Labour Market', in F. Barry (ed.), *Understanding Ireland's Economic Growth,* Basingstoke: Macmillan Press Ltd.

Fitz Gerald, J. and Keegan, O. (eds) (1993), *The Community Support Framework 1989-93: Evaluation and Recommendations for the 1994-97 Framework,* Dublin: Stationery Office.

Fitz Gerald, J., Kearney, I., Morgenroth, E. and Smyth, D. (1999), *National Investment Priorities for the Period 2000-2006,* Policy Research Series No. 33, Dublin: The Economic and Social Research Institute.

Fitzgerald, R. (2000), 'Ireland and European Integration, 1985-1998', in R. Steininger and M. Gehler (eds), *Die Neutralen und die europäischen Integration 1945-1998,* Wein: Böhlau.

Fitzgerald, R. and Michie, R. (1997), 'The Evolution of the Structural Funds', in J. Bachtler, and I. Turok, *The Coherence of European Union Regional Policy,* Jessica Kingsley Publisher and *Regional Studies Association* 1997:14-29.

Fitzpatrick, D. (1984), *Irish Emigration 1801-1921,* Dublin: The Economic and Social History Society of Ireland.

Flatley, J. and McIntosh, S. (2000), *Social Inequality and Spatial Segregation in Seven European Cities.* Stage A Report of TSER Research Project: Between Integration and Exclusion. A comparative study in local dynamics of precarity and resistance to exclusion in urban contexts, London: London Research Centre.

Foster, J., Greer, J. and Thorbecke, E. (1984), 'A Class of Decomposable Poverty Measures', *Econometrica,* vol. 52, no. 3: 761-766.

Frayman, H., Mack, J., Langley, S., Gordon, D. and Hills, J. (1991), *Breadline Britain 1970s: The Findings of the Television Series,* London: London Weekend Television.

Freeman, R. (1993), 'How Much has De-unionization Contributed to the Rise in Male Earnings Inequality?', in S. Danziger, and P. Gottschalk (eds), *Uneven Tides: Rising Inequality in America*, New York: Russell Sage Foundation.

Freeman, R. and Katz, L. (1995), *Differences and Changes in Wage Structures*, Chicago: University of Chicago Press.

Friedrichs, J. (1998), 'Do Poor Neighbourhoods Make their Residents Poorer? Context Effects of Poverty Neighbourhoods on Residents' in H-J Andreß (ed.), *Empirical Poverty Research in Comparative Perspective*, Aldershot: Ashgate.

Fujita, M., Krugman, P. and Venables, A. (1999), *The Spatial Economy: Cities, Regions, and International Trade*, Massachusetts: The MIT Press.

Fukuyama, F. (1992), *The End of History and the Last Man*, London: Penguin.

Furstenberg, F.F. and Hughes, M.E. (1997), 'The Influence of Neighbourhood on Children's Development: a Theoretical Perspective and a Research Agenda', in R.M. Hauser, B.V. Brown and W.R. Prosser (eds), *Indicators of Children's Well-being*, New York: Russell Sage Foundation.

G

Gallagher, M. (1981), 'Societal Change and Party Adaptation in the Republic of Ireland, 1960-1981', *European Journal of Political Research* 9: 269-285.

Gallagher, M. (1990), 'The Election Results and the New Dáil' in M. Gallagher and R. Sinnott (eds), *How Ireland Voted 1989*, Galway: PSAI Press.

Gallagher, M and Sinnott, R. (eds) (1990), *How Ireland voted 1989*, Galway: PSAI Press.

Galligan, Y. (1993), 'Women in Irish Politics', in J. Coakley and M. Gallagher (eds), *Politics in the Republic of Ireland*, Dublin: Folens.

Garry, J. and Mansergh, L. (1999), 'Party Manifestos', in M. Marsh and P. Mitchell (eds), *How Ireland Voted 1997*, Boulder Colorado: Westview.

Garvin, T. (1991), 'Democracy in Ireland: Collective Somnambulance and Public Policy', *Administration*, vol. 39, no. 1: 42-54.

Geary, J. (1999), *Multinationals and Human Resource Practices in Ireland*. Dublin: University College, Centre for Employment Relations and Organizational Performance.

Gellner, E. (1983), *Nations and Nationalism*, Oxford: Basil Blackwell.

Gellner, E. (1987), *Culture, Identity and Politics*, Cambridge: Cambridge University Press.

Gellner, E. (1988), *Plough, Sword and Book: The Structure of Human History*, London: Paladin.

Gereffi, G. (1994), 'The International Economy', in N. Smelser and R. Swedberg (eds), *The Handbook of Economic Sociology*, Princeton: Princeton University Press/Russell Sage Foundation.

Giavazzi, F. and Pagano, M. (1990), *Can Severe Fiscal Contractions be Expansionary? Tales of Two Small Countries*, London: The Centre for Economic Policy Research.

Gibbins, J. (1989), *Beyond the Land: A Survey of the Structure of the Agricultural Policy Process in the Irish State,* Manchester: Manchester Polytechnic Occasional Papers in Social Science.

Gillis, J.R., Tilly, L.A. and Levine, D. (eds) (1992), *The European Experience of Declining Fertility. A Quiet Revolution 1850-1970,* Oxford: Blackwell Publishers.

Girvin, B. (1984), 'Industrialisation and the Irish Working Class since 1922', *Saothar* vol.10:31-42.

Girvin, B. (1986), 'Social Change and Moral Politics: The Irish Constitutional Referendum 1983', *Political Studies,* vol. 34:61-89.

Girvin, B. (1987), 'The Campaign', in M. Laver, P. Mair and R. Sinnott (eds), *How Ireland Voted,* Dublin: Poolbeg.

Girvin, B. (1989a), *Between Two Worlds: Politics and Economy in Independent Ireland,* Dublin: Gill and Macmillan.

Girvin, B. (1989b), 'Change and Continuity in Liberal Democratic Political Culture', in J.R. Gibbins (ed.), *Contemporary Political Culture: Politics in a Postmodern Age* London: Sage.

Girvin, B. (1990), 'The Campaign', in M. Gallagher and R. Sinnott (eds.), *How Ireland Voted 1989,* Galway: PSAI Press.

Girvin, B. (1994a), *The Right in the Twentieth Century: Conservatism and Democracy,* London: Pinter.

Girvin, B. (1994b), 'Constitutional Nationalism and Northern Ireland', in B. Barton and P.J. Roche (eds), *The Northern Ireland Question: Perspectives and Policies,* Aldershot: Avebury.

Girvin, D. (1996a), 'Ireland and The European Union: The Impact of Integration and Social Change on Abortion Policy', in Githens and McBride-Stetson (eds), *Abortion Politics: Public Policy in Cross-Cultural Perspective,* New York and London: Routledge.

Girvin, B. (1996b), 'Irish Economic Development and the Politics of EEC Entry', in Griffiths and Ward (eds), *Courting the Common Market: The First Attempt to Enlarge the European Community 1961-1963,* London: Lothian Press.

Girvin, B. (1996c), 'Church, State and the Irish Constitution: The Secularisation of Irish Politics?' *Parliamentary Affairs,* vol. 49, no. 4:599-615.

Girvin, B. (1997a), 'Ireland' in R. Eatwell (ed.), *European Political Cultures: Conflict or Convergence?* London: Routledge.

Girvin, B. (1997b), 'Political Culture, Political Independence and Economic Success in Ireland', *Irish Political Studies,* vol. 12: 48-77.

Girvin, B. (1999a), 'Political Competition, 1992-1997' in M. Marsh and P. Mitchell (eds), *How Ireland Voted 1997,* Boulder Colorado: Westview.

Girvin, B. (1999b), 'Nationalism and the Continuation of Political Conflict in Ireland', in A. Heath, R. Breen and C.T. Whelan (eds), *Ireland North and South,* Oxford: Oxford University Press.

Girvin, B. (2000), 'Politics in Wartime: Governing, Neutrality and Elections', in Girvin and Roberts (eds), *Ireland and the Second World War: Politics, Society and Remembrance,* Dublin: Four Courts.

Githens, M. and McBride-Stetson, D. (eds) (1996), *Abortion Politics: Public Policy in Cross-Cultural Perspective*, New York and London: Routledge.

Glennester, H., Lupton, R., Noden, P. and Power, A. (1999), *Poverty, Social Exclusion and Neighbourhood: Studying the Area Bases of Social Exclusion*, CASE paper 22, London: Centre for the Analysis of Social Exclusion, London School of Economics.

Goldberg, D. and Williams, P. (1988), *A User's Guide to the General Health Questionnaire*, Windsor: NFER-Nelson.

Goldberger, A.S and Manski, C.F. (1995), 'Review Article: *The Bell Curve* by Herrenstein and Murray', *Journal of Economic Literature*, XXIII, June:762-776.

Goldthorpe, J.H. (1980/1987), *Social Mobility and Class Structure in Modern Britain*, Second Edition, Oxford: Oxford University Press.

Goldthorpe, J.H. (1985), 'On Economic Development and Social Mobility', *British Journal of Sociology*, vol. 36: 549-573.

Goldthorpe, J.H. (1996), 'Problems of "Meritocracy"', in R. Erikson and J.O. Jonsson (eds), *Can Education be Equalized?: The Swedish Case in Comparative Perspective*, Colorado: Westview Press.

Goldthorpe, J.H. (1996), 'Class Analysis and the Reorientation of Class Theory: The Case of Persisting Differentials in Educational Attainment', *British Journal of Sociology*, vol. 47, no. 3:481-512.

Goldthorpe, J.H. (2000), *On Sociology: Numbers, Narratives and the Integration of Research and Theory*, Oxford: Oxford University Press.

Goldthorpe, J.H. and Whelan, C.T. (eds) (1992), *The Development of Industrial Society in Ireland*, Oxford: Oxford University Press.

Goode, W.E. (1963), *World Revolution and Family Patterns*, New York: Free Press.

Goodman, A., Johnson, P. and Webb, S. (1997), *Inequality in the UK*, Oxford: Oxford University Press.

Goodman, L.A. (1979), 'Simple Models for the Analysis of Occupational Mobility Tables and Other Kinds of Cross-Classification Having Ordered Categories', *Journal of the American Statistical Association*, vol. 74:537-552.

Gordon, D., Pantazis, C., Townsend, P., Bramley, G., Bradshaw, J., Holmes, H. and Halleröd, B. (1995), *Breadline Britain in the 1990s*: A Report to the Joseph Rowntree Foundation, Department of Social Policy and Planning, Bristol: University of Bristol.

Gordon, D., Pantazis, C. (1999), 'Inequalities in Income and Living Standards', in D. Gordon and C. Pantazis (eds), *Tackling Inequalities: Where Are We Now and What Can Be Done?* Bristol: Policy Press.

Gornick, J., Meyers, M. and Ross, K. (1997), 'Supporting the Employment of Mothers: Policy Variation across Fourteen Welfare States', *Journal of European Social Policy*, vol. 7, no. 1: 45-70.

Gosling, A., Machin, S. and Meghir, C. (1994), 'What Has Happened to Men's Wages Since the Mid-1960s?', *Fiscal Studies*, vol. 15, no. 4: 63-87.

Gosling, A. and Machin, S. (1995), 'Trade Unions and the Dispersion of Earnings in British Establishments', *Oxford Bulletin of Economics and Statistics*, vol. 57:167-184.

Gottschalk, P. and Joyce, M. (1997), *Cross-National Differences in the Rise in Earnings Inequality: Market and Institutional Factors*, LIS Working Paper No. 160, Luxembourg: CEPS/INSTEAD.

Greaney, V. and Kellaghan T. (1994), *Equality of Opportunity in Irish Schools*, Dublin: The Educational Company.

Greaney, V. and Kellaghan T. (1995*)*, 'Factors Related to Educational Attainment in Ireland', *The Economic and Social Review,* vol. 16, no. 2:141-156.

Green Paper on Abortion (1999), Dublin: Stationery Office.

Gros, D. and Steinherr, A. (1995), *Winds of Change: Economic Transition in Central and Eastern Europe*, London: Longman.

Griffiths, R.T. (1990), 'The Stranglehold of Bilateralism', in Griffiths (ed.), *The Netherlands and the Integration of Europe 1945-1957,* Amsterdam: NEHA.

Griffiths, R.T. (ed.) (1990), *The Netherlands and the Integration of Europe 1945-1957,* Amsterdam: NEHA.

Griffiths, R.T. and Ward, S. (eds) (1996), *Courting the Common Market: The First Attempt to Enlarge the European Community 1961-1963,* London: Lothian Press.

Gunnigle, P. and Roche, W. K. (1995), 'Competition and the New Industrial Relations Agenda', in P. Gunnigle and W.K. Roche (eds), *New Challenges to Industrial Relations*, Dublin: Oak Tree Press.

H

Hagenaars, A., de Vos, K. and Zaidi, M.A. (1994), *Poverty Statistics in the Late 1980s: Research Based on Micro-data,* Luxembourg: Office for Official Publications of the European Communities.

Halleröd, B. (1995), 'The Truly Poor: Direct and Indirect Consensual Measurement of Poverty in Sweden', *Journal of European Social Policy*, vol. 5, no. 2:11-29.

Halpin, B. (1992), 'Change in Intragenerational Mobility in the Republic of Ireland', in J.H. Goldthorpe and C.T. Whelan (eds), *The Development of Industrial Society in Ireland*, Oxford: Clarendon Press.

Hannan, D.F. (1996), *Adapt/Emploi Report on Youthstart in Ireland*, Dublin: The Economic and Social Research Institute.

Hannan, D.F., Sexton, J.J. and Walsh, B. (1991), *The Economic and Social Implications of Emigration*, Dublin: National Economic and Social Council.

Hannan, D.F. and Commins, P. (1992), 'The Significance of Small-scale Landholders in Ireland's Socio-economic Transformation', in J. H. Goldthorpe and C.T. Whelan (eds), *The Development of Industrial Society in Ireland*, Oxford: Oxford University Press

Hannan, D.F. and Ó Riain, S. (1993), *Pathways to Adulthood in Ireland: Causes and Consequences of Success and Failure in Transitions Amongst Irish Youth*, General Research Series No. 161, Dublin: The Economic and Social Research Institute.

Hannan, D.F., Raffe, D. and Smyth, E. (1996), *Cross-National Research on School to Work Transitions: An Analytical Framework*, Background Paper to OECD.

Hannan, D.F., Smyth, E., McCullagh, J., O'Leary, R., McMahon, D. (1996), *Coeducation and Gender Equality: Exam Performance, Stress and Personal Development,*General Research Series No. 169, Dublin: ESRI/in association with Oak Tree Press.

Hannan, D.F., Smyth, E. and McCabe, B. (1997), *Educational Achievement and Labour Market Exclusion in Ireland*, Transitions in Youth Network Working Paper.

Hannan, D.F., McCabe, B. and McCoy, S. (1998), *Trading Qualifications for Jobs: Overeducation and the Irish Youth labour Market*, Dublin: Oak Tree Press.

Hannan, D.F., Smyth, E. et al (1999), 'A Comparative Analysis of Transitions from Education to Work in Europe (CATEWE)', Dublin: ESRI Working Paper no. 118.

Hannan, D.F. and Doyle, A. (2000), 'Changing School to Work Transitions: Three Cohorts', ESRI Seminar paper.

Hardiman, N. (1988), *Pay, Politics and Economic Policy in Ireland 1970-1987*, Oxford: Clarendon Press.

Hardiman, N. (1992), 'The State and Economic Interests', in J.H. Goldthorpe and C.T. Whelan (eds), *The Development of Industrial Society in Ireland*, Oxford: Clarendon Press.

Hardiman, N. (Forthcoming, 2000), 'Taxing the Poor', *Policy Studies Journal*.

Harkness, D., (1969), *The Restless Dominion: The Irish Free State and the British Commonwealth of Nations*, London: Macmillan Press.

Harding, S., Phillips D. with Fogarty M. (1986), *Contrasting Values in Western Europe,* Basingstoke: Macmillan Press.

Harloe, M.T. (1995), *The People's Home: Social Rented Housing in Europe and America,* Oxford: Basil Blackwell.

Harrison, L.E. (1992), *Who Prospers? How Cultural Values Shape Economic and Political Success*, New York: Basic Books.

Heath, A.F., Breen, R. and Whelan, C.T. (eds) (1999), *Ireland North and South,* Oxford: Oxford University Press.

Heckman, J. (1995), 'Lessons from the Bell Curve', *Journal of Political Economy*, vol. 103, no. 5:1091-1119.

Heckman, J. and Borjas, G. (1980), 'Does Unemployment Cause Future Unemployment? Definitions, Questions and Answers from a Continuous Time Model of Heterogeneity and State Dependence', *Economica,* vol. 47, no. 187: 247-283.

Helpman, E. and Krugman, P. (1985), *Market Structure and Foreign Trade: Increasing Returns, Imperfect Competition and the International Economy*, Cambridge: Massachusetts: MIT Press.

Herrenstein, R. and Murray, C. (1994), *The Bell Curve*, New York: Free Press.

Hesketh, T. (1990), *The Second Partitioning of Ireland? The Abortion Referendum of 1983,* Dún Laoghaire, Co. Dublin: Brandsma Books.

Higgins, M.D. (1982), 'The Limits of Clientelism: Towards an Assessment of Irish Politics', in C. Clapham (ed.), *Private Patronage and Public Power,* London: Frances Pinter.

Higher Education Authority (various years), *First Destination of Award Recipients in Higher Education*, Dublin: Higher Education Authority.

Hirschman, A.O. (1991), *The Rhetoric of Reaction: Perversity, Futility, Jeopardy*, Cambridge, Mass: Harvard University Press.

Hirschman, C. (1994), 'Why Fertility Changes', *Annual Review of Sociology*, vol. 20: 203-233.

Hirst, P. and Thompson, G. (1996), *Globalisation in Question: The International Economy and the Possibilities of Governance*, Cambridge: Polity Press.

Hochschild, A.R. (1983), *The Managed Heart: Comercialisation of Human Feeling*, Berkeley: University of California Press.

Honohan, P. (1999), 'Fiscal Adjustment and Disinflation in Ireland: Setting the Macro Basis of Economic Recovery and Expansion', in F. Barry (ed.), *Understanding Ireland's Economic Growth*, Basingstoke: Macmillan Press.

Honohan, P., Maître, B. and Conroy, C. (1998), 'Invisible Entrepôt Activity in Irish Manufacturing', *Irish Banking Review*, Summer.

Horgan, J. (1997), *Seán Lemass: The Enigmatic Patriot*, Dublin: Gill and Macmillan.

Hout, M. (1981), *Mobility Tables*, London: Sage.

Hout, M. (1989), *Following in Father's Footsteps*, Cambridge, MA: Harvard University Press.

Hug, C. (1999), *The Politics of Sexual Morality in Ireland*, London: Macmillan Press.

Hughes, G., McCormick, B., Sexton, J.J. (2000), *Occupational Employment Forecast 2005*, FÁS/ESRI Manpower Forecasting Studies, Report No. 8.

Humphries, J. (1976), 'Women: Scapegoats and Safety Valves in the Great Depression', *Review of Radical Political Economics*, vol. 8:98-121.

Humphries, J. and Rubery, J. (1984), 'The Reconstitution of the Supply Side of the Labour Market: the Relative Autonomy of Social Reproduction', *Cambridge Journal of Economics*, vol. 8:331-346.

I

Iacovou, M. (1998), *Young People in Europe: Two Models of Household Formation*, Working Paper, Institute for Social and Economic Research, University of Essex.

Industrial Policy Review Group (1992), *A Time for Change (Culliton Report)*, Dublin: Stationery Office.

Industrial Development Act (1969), Dublin: Stationery Office.

Inglis, T. (1998), *Moral Monopoly: The Rise and Fall of the Catholic Church in Modern Ireland*, Dublin: University College Dublin Press.

Institute of Social Studies Advisory Service (ISSAS) (1991), *Poverty in Figures: Europe in the Early 1980s*, Luxembourg: Eurostat.

International Monetary Fund (2000), *World Economic Outlook: A Survey by the Staff of the IMF*, Washington D.C: International Monetary Fund.

Irish Marketing Surveys (1977a), *Omnibus: February 1977*, Dublin: IMS.

Irish Marketing Surveys (1977b), *Omnibus: June 1977*, Dublin: IMS.

Irish Marketing Surveys (1997), *Irish Independent/IMS Poll: Election 1997 Poll No. 1,* Dublin: IMS.

Irish Political Studies (1986), 'Data Section', Galway: PSAI Press.

Irish Political Studies (1987), 'Data Section', Galway: PSAI Press.

Irish Political Studies (1988), 'Data Section', Galway: PSAI Press.

Irish Political Studies (1992), 'Irish Political Data, 1991', Galway: PSAI Press.

Irish Political Studies (1994), 'Irish Political Data, 1993', Limerick: PSAI Press.

Irish Political Studies (1995), 'Irish Political Data, 1994', Belfast: PSAI Press.

Irish Political Studies (1996), 'Irish Political Data, 1995', Belfast: PSAI Press.

Irish Political Studies (1998), 'Irish Political Data, 1997', Galway: PSAI Press.

Irish Times, 10 February 1983.

Irish Times, 7 February 1985.

Iversen, T. (1998), 'Power, Flexibility and the Breakdown of Centralized Bargaining', *Comparative Politics,* vol. 28:399-436.

Iversen, T. (1999), *Contested Economic Institutions: the Politics of Macroeconomics and Wage Bargaining in Advanced Democracies,* Cambridge: Cambridge University Press.

Ivory, G. (1999), 'Revisions in Nationalist Discourse among Irish Political Parties', *Irish Political Studies,* vol. 14:84-103.

J

Jackson, J.A. and Hasse, T. (1996), 'Democracy and the Distribution of Deprivation in Rural Ireland', in C. Curtin, T. Hasse and H. Tovey (eds), *Poverty in Rural Ireland,* Dublin: Oak Tree Press in association with the Combat Poverty Agency.

Jacobson, D. (1989), 'Theorizing Irish Industrialization: The Case of the Motor Industry', *Science and Society,* vol.2:165-191.

Jacobson, D. and O'Sullivan, D. (1994), 'Analysing an Industry in Change: the Irish Software Manual Printing Industry', *New Technology, Work and Employment,* vol. 9: 103-114.

Jacobsen, J. K. (1994), *Chasing Progress in the Irish Republic,* Cambridge: Cambridge University Press.

Jargowsky, P.A. (1996), *Poverty and Place: Ghettos, Barrios and the American City,* New York: Russell Sage Foundation.

Jenkins, S. (1991), 'The Measurement of Income Inequality', in L. Osberg (ed.), *Economic Inequality and Poverty: An International Perspective,* New York: M.E. Sharpe.

Jessop, B. (1993), 'Towards a Schumpeterian Workfare State? Preliminary Remarks on Post-Fordist Political Economy', *Studies in Political Economy,* vol. 40:7-39.

Jessop, B. (1994), 'Post-Fordism and the State', in A. Amin (ed.), *Post-Fordism: A Reader,* Oxford: Blackwell.

Johnson, C. (1982), *MITI and the Japanese Miracle,* Stanford: Stanford University Press.

Johnson, D.S. (1991), 'The Economic Performance of the Independent Irish State', *Irish Economic and Social History*, vol. 18: 48-53.

Johnson, D. and Kennedy, L. (forthcoming), 'The Two Irish Economies since 1920, *A New History of Ireland* , vol. 7, Oxford: Oxford University Press.

Johnston, H. and O'Brien, T. (2000), *Planning for a More Inclusive Society: An Initial Assessment of the National Anti-Poverty Strategy*, Dublin: Combat Poverty Agency.

Jonsson, J.O. (1993), 'Education, Social Mobility and Social Reproduction in Sweden: Patterns and Changes', in F.J. Hansen, S. Ringen, H. Uusitalo and R. Erikson (eds), *Welfare Trends in Scandinavian Countries*, New York: M.E. Sharp Armonk.

Jonung, C. and Persson, I. (1993), 'Women and Market Work: the Misleading Tale of Participation Rates in International Comparisons', *Work, Employment and Society*, vol. 7, no. 2:258-274.

Juhn, C., Murphy, K. and Pierce, B. (1992), 'Wage Inequality and the Rise in Returns to Skill', *Journal of Political Economy*, vol. 101, no. 3: 410-442.

Just, F. and Olesen, T.B. (1995), 'Danish Agriculture and the European Market Schism, 1945-1960', in T. Olesen (ed.), *Interdependence Versus Integration: Denmark, Scandinavia and Western Europe 1945-1960*, Odense: Odense University Press.

K

Katz, L. and Murphy, K. (1992), 'Changes in Relative Wages, 1963-1987: Supply and Demand Factors', *Quarterly Journal of Economics*, vol. 107, no. 1:35-78.

Katzenstein, P. (1984), *Corporatism and Change*, Ithaca: Cornell University Press.

Katzenstein, P. (1985), *Small States in World Markets*, Ithaca: Cornell University Press.

Kaufman, J. (1998), 'Chicago: Segregation and the New Urban Poverty', in S. Musterd and W. Ostendorf (eds), *Urban Segregation and the Welfare State: Inequality and Exclusion in Western Cities*, London: Routledge.

Kearney, H. (1989), *The British Isles: A History of Four Nations,* Cambridge: Cambridge University Press.

Kearney, I. (1998a), 'Estimating the Demand for Skilled Labour, Unskilled Labour and Clerical Workers: A Dynamic Framework', Working Paper No. 91, Dublin: The Economic and Social Research Institute.

Kearney, I. (1998b), 'Is there a Stable Migration Equation for Ireland?', Working Paper No. 98, Dublin: The Economic and Social Research Institute.

Keatinge, P. and Laffan, B. (1993), 'The Management of EC Policy in Ireland', in J. Coakley and M. Gallagher (eds), *Politics in the Republic of Ireland*, Dublin: Folens.

Kejak, M. and Vavra, D. (1999), *HC4: The HERMIN Model of the Czech Republic*, ACE-Phare Project P96-6242-R Working Paper WP01, 31 March.

Kelleher, P. (1987), 'Familism in Irish Capitalism in the 1950s', *The Economic and Social Review*, vol. 18, no. 2, 75-94.

Kennedy, K.A. (ed.) (1986), *Ireland in Transition: Economic and Social Change Since 1960*, Cork: Mercier Press.

Kennedy, K.A. (1992), 'The Context of Economic Development' in J. H. Goldthorpe and C.T. Whelan (eds), *The Development of Industrial Society in Ireland*, Oxford: Oxford University Press.

Kennedy, K., Giblin, T. and McHugh, D. (1988), *The Economic Development of Ireland in the Twentieth Century*, London: Routledge.

Keogh, D. (1988), 'The Constitutional Revolution: An Analysis of the Making of the Constitution', *Administration*, vol. 35, no. 4: 4-84.

Keogh, D. (1994), *Twentieth-Century Ireland: Nation and State*, Dublin: Gill and Macmillan.

Kiernan, K. (1999a), 'Cohabitation in Western Europe' *Population Trends* 96.

Kiernan, K. (1999b), 'Childbearing outside marriage in Western Europe' *Population Trends* 98:11-20.

Kitschelt, H., Lange, P., Marks, G. and Stephens, J.D. (1999), *Continuity and Change in Contemporary Capitalism*, Cambridge: CUP.

Kleinman, M.(1998), *Include Me Out? The New Politics of Place and Poverty*, Centre for the Analysis of Social Exclusion, CASE paper 11, London: London School of Economics.

Koman, R. and Marin, D. (1997), 'Human Capital and Macroeconomic Growth: Austria and Germany, 1960-92', London: Centre for Economic Policy Research, Discussion Paper No.1551.

König, W., Lüttinger, P. and Müller, W. (1988), 'A Comparative Analysis of the Development and Structure of Educational Systems', Mannheim: Institut für Sozialwissenschaften, Universität, Mannheim. CASMIN working Papers.

Kronauer, M. (1998), '"Social Exclusion" and "Underclass" – New Concepts for the Analysis of Poverty' in H-J Andreß (ed.), *Empirical Poverty Research in Comparative Perspective*, Aldershot: Ashgate.

Krugman, P. (1987), 'Economic Integration in Europe: Some Conceptual Issues', in T. Padoa-Schioppa (ed.), *Efficiency, Stability and Equity*, Oxford: Oxford University Press.

Krugman, P. (1995), *Development, Geography, and Economic Theory*, Cambridge: Massachusetts: The MIT Press.

Krugman, P. (1997), 'Good News from Ireland: A Geographical Perspective', in A. Gray (ed.), *International Perspectives on the Irish Economy*, Dublin: Indecon Economic Consultants.

Kuijsten, A.C. (1996), 'Changing Family Patterns in Europe: A Case of Divergence?' *European Journal of Population*, vol. 12:115-143.

L

Lane, C. (1993), 'Gender and the Labour Market in Europe: Britain, Germany and France Compared', *Sociological Review*, vol. 42, No. 2: 274-301.

Lane, P. (1998), 'Profits and Wages in Ireland, 1987-1996', Trinity Economic Papers, Techincal Paper No. 14, Dublin: Trinity College.

Landes, D. (1998), *The Wealth and Poverty of Nations*, London: Little, Brown.

Lange, P., Wallerstein, M. and Golden, M. (1995), 'The End of Corporatism? Wage Setting in the Nordic and Germanic Countries', in S. Jacoby (ed.), *The Workers of Nations: Industrial Relations in a Global Economy*, New York: OUP.

Laver, M. (1987), 'Issues, Attitudes and Party Policy', in M. Laver, P. Mair and R. Sinnott (eds.), *How Ireland Voted,* Dublin: Poolbeg.

Laver, M., Mair, P. and Sinnott, R. (eds) (1987), *How Ireland Voted: The Irish General Election 1987,* Dublin: Poolbeg.

Layte, R. (1999), *Divided Time: Gender, Paid Employment and Domestic Labour,* Aldershot: Avebury.

Layte., R., Maître, B., Nolan R. and Whelan, C.T. (1999), 'Persistent and Consistent Poverty in the 1994 and 1995 Waves of the European Community Household Panel', European Panel Analysis Group, Working Paper.

Layte, R., Nolan, B. and Whelan, C. T. (2000), 'Targeting Poverty: Lessons from Monitoring Ireland's National Anti-Poverty Strategy', *Journal of Social Policy,* vol. 29, no. 4.

Leddin, A. and Walsh, B. (1997), 'Economic Stabilisation, Recovery, and Growth, Ireland 1979-96', *Irish Banking Review,* Summer.

Lee, J.J. (1989), *Ireland: 1912-1985. Politics and Society,* Cambridge: Cambridge University Press.

Leslie, D. and Pu, Y. (1996), 'What Caused Rising Wage Inequality in Britain? Evidence from Time Series 1970-93', *British Journal of Industrial Relations*, vol. 34:111-113.

Levy, F. and Murnane, R. (1992), 'US Earnings Levels and Earnings Inequality: A Review of Recent Trends and Proposed Explanations', *Journal of Economic Literature*, vol. 30, no. 3:1333-1381.

Lipset, S.M. (1996), *American Exceptionalism: A Double-Edged Sword,* New York: W.W. Norton.

Lipset, S.M. and Bendix, R. (1959), *Social Mobility in Industrial Society,* Berkeley: University of California Press.

Locke, Richard M. and Thelen, K. (1995), 'Apples and Oranges Revisited: Contextualized Comparisons and the Study of Comparative Labor Politics', *Politics and Society*, vol. 23, no. 3.

Lundberg, S., Pollak, R.A. and Wales, T.J. (1997), 'Do Husbands and Wives Pool Their Resources?', *Journal of Human Resources*, vol. 32, no. 3: 463-480.

Lyne, T. (1987), 'The Progressive Democrats', *Irish Political Studies,* vol. 2:107-114.

M

McAleese, D. (1975), 'Ireland in the Enlarged EEC: Economic Consequences and Prospects', in John Vaizey (ed.), *Economic Sovereignty and Regional Policy,* Dublin: Gill and Macmillan.

McCarthy, D. (1999), 'Building a Partnership', Dublin: Dept. of the Taoiseach.

McCoy, S., Doyle, A. and Williams, J. (1999), *1998 Annual School Leavers' Survey of 1996/97 Leavers*, Dublin: Dept. of Education/ Enterprise, Trade and Employment.

MacDonald, F. (1985), *The Destruction of Dublin*, Dublin: Gill and Macmillan.

Mac Gréil, M. (1973), *Educational Opportunity in Dublin*, Dublin: Research and Development Unit.

Mac Gréil, M. (1977), *Prejudice and Tolerance in Ireland,* Dublin: College of Industrial Relations.

McKeown, K. (1991), *The North Inner City of Dublin: an Overview*, Dublin: Daughters of Charity.

MacLaran, A. (1993), *Dublin: the Shaping of a Capital*, London and New York: Belhaven Press.

MacLaran, A. (1996), 'Private Sector Residential Development in Central Dublin', in P.J. Drudy and A. MacLaran (eds) (1996), *Dublin: Economic and Social Trends,* vol 2, Dublin: Centre for Urban and Regional Studies, Trinity College.

McRae, S. (1990), 'Women and Class Analysis', in C. Modgill and S. Modgill (eds), *John H. Goldthorpe: Consensus and Controversy*, London: The Falmer Press.

Machin, S. (1997), 'The Decline of Labour Market Institutions and the Rise in Wage Inequality in Britain', *European Economic Review*, vol. 41: 647-657.

Mack, J. and Lansley, G. (1985), *Poor Britain,* London: Allen & Unwin.

Maguire, M. (1986), 'Ireland' in P. Flora (ed.), *Growth to Limits: The Western European Welfare States Since World War II: Vol. 2, Germany, United Kingdom, Ireland, Italy*, Berlin: Walter de Gruyter.

Maguire, M. (1987), 'Ireland' in P. Flora (ed.), *Growth to Limits: The Western European Welfare States Since World War II: Volume 4, Appendix,* Berlin: Walter de Gruyter.

Mair, P. (1987), 'Policy Competition' in M. Laver, P. Mair and R. Sinnott (eds), *How Ireland Voted,* Dublin: Poolbeg.

Manning, M. (1979), 'The Farmers' in J.J. Lee (ed.), *Ireland 1945-70,* Dublin: Gill and Macmillan.

Marsh, M. and Mitchell, P. (eds) (1999), *How Ireland Voted 1997,* Boulder Colorado: Westview.

Marsh, M. and Sinnott, R. (1999), 'The Behaviour of the Irish Voter', in M. Marsh and P. Mitchell (eds), *How Ireland Voted 1997*, Boulder Colorado: Westview.

Marshall, G., Swift, A. and Roberts, S. (1997), *Against the Odds: Social Class and Social Justice in Industrial Societies*, Oxford: Oxford University Press.

Maurice, M., Sellier, F. and Silvestre, J.J. (1986), *The Social Foundations of Industrial Power*. Cambridge, Mass.: MIT Press.

Maxfield, S., Schneider, B. (eds) (1997), *Business and the State in Developing Countries,* Ithaca, New York: Cornell University Press.

Mayers, S. and Jencks, C. (1988), 'Poverty and the Distribution of Material Hardship', *Journal of Human Resources*, vol. 24, no. 1: 88-114.

Milkman, R.(1976), 'Women's Work and Economic Crisis: Some Lessons from the Great Depression', *Review of Radical Political Economics*.

Miller, D. (1992), 'Distributive Justice: What the People Think', *Ethics*, vol. 102.

Mills, E.S. and Lubuele, L.S. (1997), 'Inner Cities', *Journal of Economic Literature*, xxxv (June).

Milward, A.S. (1984), *The Reconstruction of Western Europe, 1945-51* London: Methuen.

Milward, A.S. et al (1993), *The Frontiers of National Sovereignty: History and Theory 1945-1992,* London: Routledge.

Mjøset, L. (1992), *The Irish Economy in a Comparative Institutional Perspective,* Dublin: National Economic and Social Council.

Monti, M. (1996), *The Single Market and Tomorrow's Europe: a Progress Report from the European Commission,* London: Kogan Page.

Moore, B. (1966), *Social Origins of Dictatorship and Democracy,* Harmondsworth: Penguin.

Morgan, P. (1995), *Farewell to the Family? Public Policy and Family Breakdown in Britain and the USA,* Institute of Economic Affairs.

MRBI (1983), *Irish Times/MRBI Poll,* February 1983, Dublin: MRBI.

MRBI (1995), *Irish Times/MRBI Poll,* 18 November 1995, Dublin: MRBI.

MRBI (1996a), *Irish Times/MRBI Poll,* (MRBI/4440/96, December 1996) Dublin: MRBI.

MRBI (1997), *Irish Times/MRBI Poll,* (MRBI/4620/97, December 1997) Dublin: MRBI.

MRBI (1983), *21st Anniversary Poll,* Dublin: MRBI.

MRBI (1997), *Irish Times/MRBI Poll,* January 1997, Dublin: MRBI.

MRBI (1999), *Irish Times/MRBI Poll* 2 and 3 November, 1999, Dublin: MRBI.

MRBI (2000a), *Irish Times/MRBI Poll,* 17 and 18 January 2000, Dublin: MRBI.

MRBI (2000b), *Irish Times/MRBI Poll,* 17 and 18 April 2000, Dublin: MRBI.

Muffels, R. (1993), 'Deprivation Standards and Style of Living Standards', in J. Berghman and B. Cantillon (eds), *The European face of Social Security,* Aldershot: Averbury.

Muffels, R. and Vrien, M. (1991), *The Comparison of Definition of Consumption Deprivation and Income Deprivation,* Mimeo, Tilburg University.

Müller, W. and Wolberg, M. (1999), 'Educational Attainment of Young People Over Time in the European Union', in W. Müller et al, *A Comparative Analysis of Transitions from Education to Work in Europe – Based on the European Community Labour Force Survey,* Report of the European Commission.

Murphy, D. (1984), 'The Impact of State Taxes and Benefits on Irish Household Incomes', *Journal of the Statistical and Social Inquiry Society of Ireland,* vol. XXV: 55-120.

Murphy, D. (1985), 'Calculation of Gini and Theil Inequality Coefficients for Irish Household Incomes in 1973 and 1980', *The Economic and Social Review,* vol. 16: 225-249.

Murphy, G. (1996), 'The Politics of Economic Realignment, Ireland 1948-1964', PhD Thesis, Dublin. Dublin City University.

Murphy, G. (1997), 'Government, Interest Groups and the Irish Move to Europe: 1957-63', *Irish Studies in International Affairs,* vol. 8:57-68.

Musterd, S., Priemus, H. and van Kempen, R. (1999), 'Undivided Cities in the Netherlands: Present Situation and Political Rhetoric', *Housing Studies* 14, 5.

Myles, J. (1989), *Old Age in the Welfare State: the Political Economy of Pensions*, Lawrence, Kansas: University Press of Kansas.

N

National Archives of Ireland (1962), Department of the Taoiseach S. 16877X/62 T.K. Whitaker to Minister for Finance 5 January 1962.

National Center for Health Statistics (2000), *National Vital Statistics Report*, vol. 48, no. 3 (March), Hyatsville, MD: National Center for Health Statistics.

National Industrial Economic Council (1967), *Report on Full Employment*, Dublin: Stationery Office.

NESC (1986), *A Strategy for Recovery 1986-1990*, Report No. 83, Dublin: National Economic and Social Council.

NESC (1989), *Ireland in the European Community: Performance, Prospects and Strategy*, Dublin: National Economic and Social Council.

NESC (1991), *Economic and Social Implications of Emigration*, Dublin: NESC.

NESC (1990), *A Strategy for the Nineties: Economic Stability and Structural Change*, Report No. 89, Dublin: NESC.

NESC (1993), *A Strategy for Competitiveness, Growth, and Employment*, Report No. 96, Dublin: NESC.

NESC (1996), *Strategy Into the 21st Century*, Report No. 99. Dublin: NESC.

NESC (1999*), Opportunities, Challenges, and Capacities for Choice*, Report No. 105, Dublin.

NESF (1994), *Ending Long-term Unemployment*, NESF Report No. 4, Dublin: NESF.

NESF (2000), *Enhancing the Effectiveness of the Local Employment Service*, Forum Report No.17, Dublin: National Economic and Social Forum.

Nickell, S. and Bell, B. (1995), 'The Collapse in Demand for the Unskilled and Unemployment Across the OECD', *Oxford Review of Economic Policy*, vol. 11, no. 1: 40-62.

Nolan, B. (1978), 'The Personal Distribution of Income in the Republic of Ireland', *Journal of the Statistical and Social Inquiry Society of Ireland*, vol. XXIII:91-139.

Nolan, B. (1987), *Income Distribution and the Macroeconomy*, Cambridge University Press: Cambridge.

Nolan, B. (1998), *Low Pay in Ireland. Vol. 2, Report of the National Minimum Wage Commission*, Dublin: Department of Enterprise, Trade and Employment.

Nolan, B. and Whelan, C.T. (1996), *Resources, Deprivation and Poverty*, Oxford: Clarendon Press.

Nolan, B., Whelan, C.T. and Williams, J. (1998), *Where are Poor Households? The Spatial Distribution of Poverty in Ireland*, Dublin: Oak Tree Press in association with Combat Poverty Agency.

Nolan, B., Boyle, G., Callan, T., Doris, A., Kearney, I., Fitz Gerald, J., Machin, S., O'Neill, D., Walsh, J., Williams, J., McCormick, B. and Smyth, D. (1999), 'The Impact of the Minimum Wage in Ireland', in *Report of the Inter-Departmental*

Group on the Implementation of a National Minimum Wage, Dublin: Stationery Office.

Nolan, B., Hauser, R. and Zoyem, J.-C. (2000), 'The Changing Effects of Social Protection on Poverty', in D. Gallie and S. Paugam (eds), *Welfare Regimes and the Experience of Unemployment in Europe*, Oxford: Oxford University Press.

Nolan, B. and Whelan, C.T. (1999), *Loading the Dice: A Study of Cumulative Disadvantage*, Dublin: Oak Tree Press in association with Combat Poverty Agency.

Nolan, B. and McCormick, B. (1999), 'The Numbers Affected by the Minimum Wage', in B. Nolan et al, 'The Impact of the Minimum Wage in Ireland', in *Final Report of the Inter-Departmental Group on Implementation of a National Minimum Wage*, Dublin: Stationery Office.

Nolan B. and Whelan, C.T. (2000), '"Urban Housing" and the Role of "Underclass" Processes: the Case of Ireland', *Journal of European Social Policy*, vol. 10, no. 1: 5-21.

O

O'Brien, G. (1921), *The Economic History of Ireland from the Union to the Famine*, London: Longmans, Green.

Ó Buachalla, S. (1988), *Education Policy in Twentieth Century Ireland*, Dublin: Wolfhound Press.

O'Carroll, J.P. (1991), 'Bishops, Knights – and Pawns? Traditional Thought and the Irish Abortion Debate of 1983', *Irish Political Studies*, vol. 6.53-72.

Ó Cinnéide, S. (1998), 'Democracy and the Constitution', *Administration*, vol. 46, no.4: 41-58.

O'Clery, C. (1986), *Phrases Make History Here*, Dublin: O'Brien Press.

O'Connell, C. and Fahey, T. (1999), 'Local Authority Housing in Ireland', in T. Fahey (ed.), *Social Housing in Ireland. A Study of Success, Failures and Lessons Learned*, Dublin: Oak Tree Press in association with the Katherine Howard Foundation and the Combat Poverty Agency.

O'Connell, P.J. (1998), 'Spending Priorities in Labour Market Policies for the Unemployed', *Budget Perspectives*, Dublin: The Economic and Social Research Institute.

O'Connell, P.J. (1999a), 'Sick Man or Tigress: The Labour Market in the Republic of Ireland', in R. Breen, A. Heath and C.T. Whelan (eds), *Ireland, North and South*, Oxford: The British Academy and Oxford University Press.

O'Connell, P.J. (1999b), 'Astonishing Success: Economic Growth and the Labour Market in Ireland,' ILO Employment and Training Papers No. 44, Geneva: ILO.

O'Connell, P.J. (1999c), 'Are they Working? Market Orientation and the Effectiveness of Active Labour Market Programmes in Ireland', ESRI Working Paper No. 105, Dublin: The Economic and Social Research Institute.

O'Connell, P. and Rottman, D. (1992), 'The Irish Welfare State in Comparative Perspective', in J. Goldthorpe and C. Whelan (eds), *The Development of Industrial Society in Ireland*, London: The British Academy and Oxford University Press.

O'Connell, P. and Sexton, J.J. (1994), 'Labour Market Developments in Ireland, 1971-1993', in J. Cantillon, J. Curtis and J. Fitz Gerald (eds), *Economic Perspectives for the Medium Term*, Dublin: The Economic and Social Research Institute.

O'Connell, P.J. and McGinnity, F. (1997a), 'What Works, Who Works? The Employment and Earnings Effects of Active Labour Market Programmes Among Young People in Ireland', *Work, Employment and Society*, vol. 11, no. 4:639-661.

O'Connell, P.J. and McGinnity, F. (1997b), *Working Schemes? Active Labour Market Policy in Ireland*, Aldershot: Ashgate.

O'Connor, P. (1995), *The Barriers to Women's Promotion in the Midland and Mid-Western Health Board*, Limerick: Mid-Western Health Board.

O'Connor, P. (1998), *Emergent Voices: Women in Contemporary Irish Society*, Dublin: Institute of Public Administration .

O'Connor, P. (2000), 'Ireland: A Man's World?', *The Economic and Social Review*, vol. 31, no.1: 81-102.

O'Connor, P., and Shortall, S, (1999), *Does the Border Make a Difference? Variations in Women's Paid Employment, North and South*, in R. Breen, A. Heath and C.T. Whelan (eds.), *Ireland North and South*. Oxford: The British Academy and Oxford University Press.

O'Donnell, R. (1999), 'Ireland's Economic Transformation: Industrial Policy, European Integration and Social Partnership', Center for West European Studies, University of Pittsburgh, Working Paper No.2.

O'Donnell, R. and Thomas, D. (1998), 'Partnership and Policy-making', in S. Healy and B. Reynolds (eds), *Social Policy in Ireland*, Dublin: Oak Tree Press.

O'Donnell, R. and Thomas, D. (forthcoming), 'Social Partnership in Ireland 1987-1997', in H. Compston and J. Berger (eds), *Social Partnership in Western Europe: a Historical and Comparative Analysis.*

O'Dowd, L. (1987) 'Church, State and Women: the Aftermath of Partition', in C. Curtin, P. Jackson, and B. O'Connor (eds), *Gender in Irish Society*, Galway: Galway University Press.

OECD (1993), *Employment Outlook*, Paris: OECD.

OECD (1996a), *Employment Outlook*, Paris: OECD.

OECD (1996b), *Strategies for Housing and Social Integration in Cities*, Paris: OECD.

OECD (1997), *Economic Outlook: Ireland*, Paris: OECD.

OECD (1998a), *Economic Outlook*, Paris: OECD.

OECD (1988b), *Education at a Glance*, Paris: OECD.

OECD (1999), *Economic Outlook: Ireland*, Paris: OECD.

Ó Gráda, C. (1994), *Ireland: A New Economic History 1780-1939*, Oxford: Clarendon Press.

Ó Gráda, C. (1997), *A Rocky Road: The Irish Economy since the 1920s*, Manchester: Manchester University Press.

O'Hearn, D. (1990), 'The Road from Import-Substituting to Export-Led Industrialization in Ireland', *Politics and Society*, vol. 18:1-30.

O'Hearn, D. (1998), *Inside the Celtic Tiger: The Irish Economy and the Asian Model*, London: Pluto Press.

O'Hearn, D. (2000), 'Globalization, "New Tigers", and the End of the Developmental State? The Case of the Celtic Tiger', *Politics and Society,* vol. 28, no. 1: 67-92.

O'Higgins, M. and Jenkins, S.P. (1990), 'Poverty in the EC: Estimates for 1975, 1980 and 1985', in R. Teekens and B. Van Praag (eds), *Analysing Poverty in the European Community*, Luxembourg: Eurostat.

Ohmae, K. (1995), 'Putting Global Logic First', in K. Ohmae (ed.), *The Evolving Global Economy*, Harvard: Harvard Business Review Books.

Olson, M. (1982), *The Rise and Decline of Nations,* New Haven: Yale University Press.

O'Malley, E. (1980), *Industrial Policy and Development: a Survey of Literature from the Early 1960s to the Present*, Dublin: NESC.

O'Malley, E. (1981), 'The Decline of Irish Industry in the Nineteenth Century', *The Economic and Social Review,* vol. 13, no. 1:21-42.

O'Malley, E. (1989), *Industry and Economic Development: The Challenge for the Latecomer*, Dublin: Gill and Macmillan.

O'Malley, E. (1992a), 'Industrial Structure and Economies of Scale in the Context of 1992', in J. Bradley et al (eds), *The Role of the Structural Funds*, Policy Research Series No. 13, Dublin: The Economic and Social Research Institute.

O'Malley, E. (1992b), 'Developments in Irish Industrial Policy since the Mid-1980s', Paper presented to Political Studies Association of Ireland Special Conference, *The State of the Irish Political System,* Cork, 28-30 May.

O'Malley, E. (1992c), 'Problems of Industrialisation in Ireland', in J. H. Goldthorpe and C.T. Whelan (eds), *The Development of Industrial Society in Ireland,* Oxford: Oxford University Press.

O'Malley, E. (1998), 'The Revival of Irish Indigenous Industry 1987-1997', ESRI Seminar paper, 26 February, Dublin: The Economic and Social Research Institute.

O'Malley, E., Kennedy, K.A. and O'Donnell, R. (1992), *Report to the Industrial Policy Review Group on the Impact of the Industrial Development Agencies,* Dublin: Stationery Office.

O'Malley, J. (1987), 'Campaigns, Manifestoes, and Party Finances' in H. R. Penniman and B. Farrell (eds), *Ireland at the Polls 1981, 1982, and 1987,* Durham, NC: Duke University Press.

O'Neill, D. and Sweetman, O. (1998), 'Poverty and Inequality in Ireland 1987-1994: A Comparison Using Measures of Income and Consumption', mimeo, Department of Economics, Maynooth: National University of Ireland.

O'Reilly, J. (1996), 'Theoretical Considerations in Cross-national Employment Research', *Sociological Research Online,* vol. 1, no. 1.

Ó Riain, S. (1999), 'The Flexible Developmental State: Globalization, Information Technology and the "Celtic Tiger"', unpublished MS Thesis. Dept. of Sociology, University of California, Davis.

Ó Riain, S. (2000a), 'The Flexible Development State, Globalization, Information Technology and the "Celtic Tiger"', *Politics and Society,* vol. 28, no. 3:3-37.

Ó Riain, S. (2000b), 'Local Innovation and Global Governance: Irish Business in the 1990s', mimeo, Department of Sociology, University of California, Davis.

O'Rourke, K. and Williamson, J. (1995), 'Around the European Periphery 1870-1913: Globalization, Schooling and Growth', University College Dublin Working Paper WP95/17.

O'Toole, F. (1993), 'Tax Reform since the Commission on Taxation', *Journal of the Statistical and Social Inquiry Society of Ireland*.

O'Toole, F. (1995), *Meanwhile Back on the Ranch: The Politics of Irish Beef*, London: Vintage.

P

Paugam, S. (1991), *La Disqualification Sociale: Essai Nouvelle sur La Pauverté*, Paris: PUF.

Paugam, S. (1996), 'Poverty and Social Disqualification: A Comparative Analysis of Cumulative Serial Disadvantage in Europe', *Journal of European Social Policy*, vol. 6, no. 4: 287-303.

Paugam, S. (ed.) (1996), *L'Exclusion l'etat des Savoirs*, Paris: La Découverte.

Peck, J. (1994), *Work-Place*, London: Guilford.

Penniman, R. (ed.) (1978), *Ireland at the Polls: The Dáil Elections of 1977*, Washington DC: American Enterprise Institute.

Penniman, H.R. and Farrell, B. (eds), (1987), *Ireland at the Polls 1981, 1982, and 1987*, Durham, NC: Duke University Press.

Pérez, S. (1999), 'The Resurgence of National Social Bargaining in Europe: Explaining the Italian and Spanish Experiences', Working Paper 1999/130, Madrid: Juan March Institute.

Petersen, P.E. (1991), 'The Urban Underclass and the Poverty Paradox', in C. Jencks and P.E. Petersen (eds), *The Urban Underclass*, Washington: Brookings Institution.

Pfau-Effinger, B. (1998), 'Culture or Structure as Explanations for Differences in Part-time Work in Germany, Finland and the Netherlands', in J. O'Reilly and C. Fagan (eds), *Part-Time Prospects*, London: Routledge.

Pierson, C. (1998), *Beyond the Welfare State: The New Political Economy of Welfare*, Cambridge: Polity Press.

Pontusson, J. (1996), 'Labor Markets, Production Strategies and Wage-bargaining Institutions: the Swedish Employer Offensive in Comparative Perspective', *Comparative Political Studies*, vol. 29, no. 2:223-250.

Porter, M. (1990), *The Competitive Advantage of Nations*, London: Macmillan Press.

Porter, M. (1998), *On Competition*, Massachusetts: Harvard Business Review Book Series.

Portes, A. (2000), 'The Hidden Abode: Sociology as Analysis of the Unexpected', *American Sociological Review*, vol. 65:1-18.

Post, H. (1989), *Pillarization: An Analysis of Dutch and Belgian Society*, Aldershot: Gower.

Programme for National Recovery (1987), Dublin: Stationery Office.

Prondzynski, F. von. (2nd edn. 1997), 'Ireland: Corporatism Revived', in A. Ferner and R. Hyman (eds), *Changing Industrial Relations in Europe*, Oxford: Blackwell.

Pye, L.W. and Verba, S. (1965), *Political Culture and Political Development,* Princeton NJ: Princeton University Press.

Pyle, J.L. (1990), *The State and Women in the Economy. Lessons from Sex Discrimination in the Republic of Ireland,* Albany, NY: State University of New York.

R

Raftery, A.E. and Hout, M. (1993), ' Maximally Maintained Inequality: Expansion, Reform and Opportunity in Irish Education, 1921-75', *Sociology of Education,* vol. 66: 41-62.

Readers Digest (1964), *Atlas of the British Isles,* London: Readers Digest.

Redmond, G., Sutherland, H. and Wilson, M. (1999), *The Arithmetic of Tax and Social Security Reform,* Department of Applied Economics, Occasional Paper 64, Cambridge: Cambridge University Press.

Regini, M. (1995), *Uncertain Boundaries: the Social and Political Construction of European Economies,* Cambridge: CUP.

Regini, M. (1999), 'Between De-Regulation and Social Pacts. The Responses of European Economies to Globalization', Madrid: Juan March Institute, Working Paper 1999/133.

Reich, R. (1993), *The Work of Nations: A Blueprint for the Future,* London: Simon and Schuster.

Rhodes, R.M. (1986), 'Women in the Family in Post-Famine Ireland: Status and Opportunity in a Patriarchal Society', PhD Thesis, University of Illinois.

Rhodes, M. (1998), 'Globalization, Labour Markets and Welfare States: a Future of "Competitive Corporatism"?', in M. Rhodes and Y. Mény (eds), *The Future of European Welfare: A New Social Contract?* London: Sage.

Ringen, S. (1987), *The Possibility of Politics,* Oxford: Clarendon Press.

Ringen, S. (1988), 'Direct and Indirect Measurement of Poverty', *Journal of Social Policy,* vol. 17, no. 3:351-365.

Roche, J. (1984), *Poverty and Income Maintenance Policies in Ireland,* Dublin: Institute of Public Administration.

Roche, W. K. (2nd edn, 1997), 'Pay Determination and the Politics of Industrial Relations', in T. Murphy and W.K. Roche (eds), *Irish Industrial Relations in Practice,* Dublin: Oak Tree Press.

Roche, W. K. (1998), 'Public Service Reform and Human Resource Management', *Administration,* vol. 46, no. 2:3-24.

Roche, W. K. and Geary, J. (1998), ' Collaborative Production and the Irish Boom: Work Organization, Partnership and Direct Involvement in Irish Workplaces', Dublin: UCD, Graduate School of Business, Working Paper No. 26.

Rodrik, D. (1999), *The New Global Economy and Developing Countries: Making Openness Work,* Washington: Overseas Development Council.

Rose, R. (ed.) (1973), *Electoral Behavior: A Comparative Handbook,* New York: Free Press.

Rottman, D.B., Hannan, D.F., Hardiman, N. and Wiley, M. (1982), *The Distribution of Income in the Republic of Ireland: A Study in Social Class and Family-Cycle Inequalities*, General Research Series Paper 109, Dublin: The Economic and Social Research Institute.

Rottman, D. and Reidy, M. (1988), *Redistribution Through State Social Expenditure in the Republic of Ireland 1973-1980*, NESC Report No. 85, Dublin: National Economic and Social Council.

Ruane, F.P. and O'Toole, F. (1995), 'Taxation Measures and Policy', in J.W. O'Hagan (ed.), *The Economy of Ireland*, Dublin: Gill and Macmillan.

Ruane, F. and Görg, H. (1997), 'The Impact of foreign Direct Investment on Sectoral Adjustment in the Irish Economy', *National Institute Economic Review*, No. 160, April.

Ruane, F.P. and Sutherland, J.M. (1999), *Women in the Labour Force*, Dublin: Employment Equality Agency.

Rubery, J. and Fagan, C. (1995), 'Gender Segregation in Societal Context', *Work, Employment and Society*, vol. 9, no. 2:213-240.

Rubery, J., Smith, M. and Fagan, C. (1999), *Women's Employment in Europe: Trends and Prospects*, London: Routledge.

Ruggie, J. G. (1982), 'International Regimes, Transactions and Change: Embedded Liberalism in the Postwar Economic Order', *International Organization,* vol. 36: 379-415.

S

Sachs, J. (1994), Finlay Lecture, Dublin: University College.

SAHRU (1997), *A National Deprivation Index for Health and Health Services Research*, Dublin: Small Area Health Research Unit, Department of Community Health and General Practice, Trinity College, Technical Report No. 2.

Sandford, C. (1993), *Successful Tax Reform*, Bath: Fiscal Publications.

Sassen, S. (1996), *Losing Control? Sovereignty in an Age of Globalization,* New York: Columbia University Press.

Scannell, Y. (1988), 'The Constitution and the Role of Women,' in B. Farrell (ed.), *De Valera's Constitution and Ours*, Dublin: Gill and Macmillan.

Schmitt, J. (1995). 'The Changing Structure of Male Earnings in Britain, 1974-88', in R. Freeman, and L. Katz (eds), *Differences and Changes in Wage Structures*, Chicago: University of Chicago Press.

Seers, D. (1983), *The Political Economy of Nationalism,* Oxford: Oxford University Press.

Sen, A. (1976), 'Poverty: An Ordinal Approach to Measurement', *Econometrica,* vol. 44: 219-31.

Sexton, J., Canny, A. and Hughes, G. (1996), *Changing Profiles in Occupations and Educational Attainment*, FÁS/ESRI Manpower Forecasting Studies, Report No. 5.

Sexton, J.J. and O'Connell, P.J. (eds) (1996), *Labour Market Studies: Ireland,* Luxembourg: European Commission.

Sexton, J.J., Frost, D. and Hughes, G. (1998), *Aspects of Occupational Change in the Irish Economy: Recent Trends and Future Prospects*, FÁS/ESRI Manpower Forecasting Studies Report No. 7, Dublin: FÁS/ESRI.

Sexton, J.J., Nolan, B., and McCormick, B. (1999), 'A Review of Earnings Trends in the Irish Economy since 1987', *Quarterly Economic Commentary,* December, Dublin: The Economic and Social Research Institute.

Sharing in Progress: National Anti-Poverty Strategy, (1997), Government Publications, Dublin.

Shavit, Y. and Blossfeld, H.P. (eds) (1993), *Persistent Inequality: Changing Educational Attainment in Thirteen Countries*, Boulder: Westview Press.

Sheehan, B. (1996), Crisis, Strategic Revaluation and the Re-emergence of Tripartism in Ireland, Dublin: UCD Graduate Business School. Unpublished Thesis.

Shorrocks, A.F. (1980), 'The Class of Additively Decomposable Inequality Measures', *Econometrica*, vol. 48: 613-625.

Shorrocks, A.F. (1982), 'Inequality Decomposition by Factor Components', *Econometrica,* vol. 50:193-211.

Shorrocks, A.F. (1983), 'Ranking Income Distributions', *Economica*, vol. 50:3-17.

Shorrocks, A.F. (1984), 'Inequality Decomposition by Population Sub-Groups', *Econometrica,* vol. 52:1369-1385.

Simoncic, M., Kuzmin, F., Ptajtar, L. and Potocnik, J. (1999), *HSL4: The HERMIN Model of Slovenia*, ACE-Phare Project P96-6242-R Working Paper WP03, March.

Sinnott, R. (1978), 'The Electorate' in H.R. Penniman (ed.), *Ireland at the Polls: The Dáil Elections of 1977,* Washington DC: American Enterprise Institute.

Sinnott, R. (1987), 'The Voters, the Issues, and the Party System', in H. R. Penniman and B. Farrell (eds), *Ireland at the Polls 1981, 1982, and 1987,* Durham, NC: Duke University Press

Sklair, L. (1988), 'Foreign Investment and Irish Development: A Study of the International Division of Labour in the Midwest Region of Ireland', *Progress in Planning,* vol. 29:147-216.

Smith, A.D. (1991), *National Identity,* London: Penguin.

Smith, M., Fagan, C. and Rubery, J. (1998), 'Where and Why Is Part-time Work Growing in Europe?', in J. O'Reilly, and C. Fagan (eds), *Part-time Prospects*, London: Routledge.

Smyth, E. (1993), Labour Market Structures and Women's Employment in Ireland, PhD Thesis, Dublin: University College.

Smyth, E. (1999a), 'Educational Inequalities Among School Leavers in Ireland 1979-1994', *The Economic and Social Review*, vol. 30, no. 3:267-284.

Smyth, E. (1999b), *Do Schools Differ? Academic and Personal Development Among Pupils in the Second-level Sector*, Dublin: Oak Tree Press/ESRI.

Smyth, E. (2000), 'Gender Differentiation in Educational and Transition Outcomes', CATEWE Working Paper.

Smyth, E. and Hannan, D.F. (1995), *1985/86 School Leavers: A Follow-Up Study in 1992*, Dublin: ESRI Working Paper No. 65.

Smyth, E., and McCabe, B. (1997), *Educational Policy for Socially Excluded Children and Young People: Ireland*, Report under the Socrates Project.

Sørensen, V. (1993), 'Between Interdependence and Integration: Denmark's Shifting Strategies', in A.S. Milward et al, *The Frontiers of National Sovereignty: History and Theory 1945-1992*, London: Routledge.

Soskice, D. (1990), 'Wage Determination: the Changing Role of Institutions in Advanced Industrial Countries', *Oxford Review of Economic Policy*, vol. 6:36-61.

Soskice, D. (1999), 'Divergent Production Regimes: Coordinated and Uncoordinated Market Economies in the 1980s and 1990s', in H. Kitschelt et al (eds), *Continuity and Change in Contemporary Capitalism*, Cambridge: CUP.

SSISI (1975/6), 'A Symposium on Increasing Employment in Ireland', *Journal of the Statistical and Social Inquiry Society of Ireland*, vol. 23, no. 3:37-77.

SSISI (1982/3), 'Symposium on Industrial Policy in Ireland', *Journal of the Statistical and Social Inquiry Society of Ireland*, vol. 24, no. 5:33-72.

Stallings, Barbara (1992), 'International Influence on Economic Policy: Debt, Stabilization, and Structural Reform', in S. Haggard and R.R. Kaufman (eds), *The Politics of Economic Adjustment*, Princeton: Princeton University Press.

Steinmo, S. (1993), *Taxation and Democracy*, New Haven, CT: Yale UP.

STIAC – Science Technology and Innovation Advisory Council (1995), *Making Knowledge Work for Us: A Strategic View of Science Technology and Innovation in Ireland*, Dublin: Stationery Office.

Streeck, W. (1994), 'Pay Restraint without Incomes Policy: Institutionalized Monetarism and Industrial Unionism in Germany', in Ronald Dore et al (eds), *The Return to Incomes Policy*, London: Pinter.

Survey of Grant Aided Industry (1967), Dublin: Stationery Office.

Sweeney, P. (1997), *The Celtic Tiger: Ireland's Economic Miracle Explained*, Dublin: Oak Tree Press.

Swenson, P. (1989), *Fair Shares: Unions, Pay and Politics in Sweden and West Germany*, Ithaca, NY: Cornell UP.

T

Tansey, P. (1998), *Ireland at Work: Economic Growth and the Labour Market, 1987-1997*, Dublin: Oak Tree Press.

Task Force on the Travelling Community (1995), *Report of the Task Force on the Travelling Community*, Dublin: Stationery Office.

Taylor, G. (1996), 'Labour Market Rigidities, Institutional Impediments and Managerial Constraints: Some Reflections on the Recent Experience of Macro-political Bargaining in Ireland', *The Economic and Social Review*, vol. 27, no. 3: 253-277.

Teague, P. (1995), 'Pay Determinination in the Republic of Ireland: Towards Social Corporatism?', *British Journal of Industrial Relations*, vol. 33, no. 2:253-273.

Teahon, P. (1997), 'The Irish Political and Policy-making System and the Current Programme of Change', *Administration*, vol. 45, no. 4:49-58.

Technical Working Group (1998), *Second-Level Funding: Report of the Technical Working Group*, Dublin: Brunswick Press.

Telesis, (1982), *A Review of Industrial Policy,* NESC Report No. 64, Dublin: National Economic and Social Council.

Thelen, K. (1993), 'West European Labor in Transition: Sweden and Germany Compared', *World Politics,* vol. 46, no. 1:23-49.

Thomsen, S. and Woolcock, S. (1993), *Direct Investment and European Integration*, London: Pinter Publishers.

Thorsten, B.O. (ed.) (1995), *Interdependence Versus Integration: Denmark, Scandinavia and Western Europe 1945-1960,* Odense: Odense University Press.

Tilly, L.A. and Scott, J.W. (1978), *Women, Work and Family*, New York: Holt, Rinehart and Winston.

Townsend, P. (1979), *Poverty in the United Kingdom*, Harmondsworth: Penguin.

Townsend, P. and Gordon, D. (1989), 'Memorandum submitted to Social Services Committee of the House of Commons', in *Minimum Income: Memoranda laid before the Committee, Session 1988-89*, London: HMSO.

Traxler, F. (1995), 'Farewell to Labour Market Associations? Organized Versus Disorganized Decentralization as a Map for Industrial Relations', in C. Crouch and F. Traxler (eds), *Organized Industrial Relations in Europe: What Future?* Aldershot: Avebury.

U

UN (1997), *Fertility Trends in Low Fertility Countries,* New York: United Nations.

UN (2000), *Replacement Migration: Is it a Solution to Declining and Ageing Populations?* New York: United Nations.

United Nations Economic Commission for Europe (1949), *Economic Survey of Europe in 1948,* Geneva: United Nations.

V

Van Baselaer, A., Lemaitre, G. and Marianna, P. (1997), 'The Definition of Part-time Work for the Purpose of International Comparisons', Labour Market and Social Policy Occasional Papers No. 22, Paris: OECD.

Van Oorschot, W. and Halman, L. (2000), 'Blame or Fate, Individual or Social? An International Comparison of Popular Explanations of Poverty', *European Societies*, vol. 2: 1-28.

Visser, J., and Hemerijck, A. (1997), *A Dutch Miracle: Job Growth, Welfare Reform and Coporatism in the Netherlands,* Amsterdam: Amsterdam University Press.

Verba, S. (1965), 'Conclusion: Comparative Political Culture', in L. W. Pye and S. Verba (eds), Political Culture and Political Development, Princeton: Princeton University Press.

W

Wacquant, L.M. (1993), 'Urban Outcasts: Stigma and Division in the Black American Ghetto and the French Urban Periphery', *International Journal of Urban and Regional Research*, vol. 17: 266-283.

Walsh, B.M. (1993), 'Labour Force Participation and the Growth of Women's Employment, Ireland 1971-1991', *The Economic and Social Review*, vol. 24, no. 4.

Watkins, S.C. (1992), 'Demographic Nationalism in Western Europe, 1870-1960', in J. R. Gillis, L.A. Tilly and D. Levine (eds), *The European Experience of Fertility Decline, 1850-1970*, Oxford: Blackwell Publishers.

Weiss, L. (1997), 'Globalization and the Myth of the Powerless State', *New Left Review*, 225:3-27.

Weiss, L. (1998), *The Myth of the Powerless State*, Ithaca: Cornell University Press.

Whitaker, T.K. (1969), 'Capital Formation, Saving and Economic Progress' in B.Chubb and P. Lynch (eds), *Economic Development and Planning,* Dublin: IPA.

Whitaker, T.K. (1986), 'Economic Development 1958-1985' in K.A. Kennedy (ed.), *Ireland in Transition: Economic and Social Change Since 1960,* Cork: Mercier Press.

Whelan, K. (1991), 'The Irish Consumption Function and Ricardian Equivalence: The Evidence Re-examined', *The Economic and Social Review*, vol.22, no.3: 229-238.

Whelan, C.T. (1992), 'The Role of Income, Life-style Deprivation and Financial Strain in Mediating the Impact of Unemployment on Psychological Distress', *Journal of Occupational and Organisational Psychology*, 65: 331-341.

Whelan, C.T. (1994), 'Social Class, Unemployment and Psychological Distress', *European Sociological Review*, 12: 1-49.

Whelan, C.T. (1996), 'Marginalization, Deprivation and Fatalism in the Republic of Ireland', *European Sociological Review*, vol. 12, no. 1: 33-51.

Whelan, C.T., Breen, R. and Whelan, B.J. (1992), 'Industrialisation, Class Formation and Social Mobility in Ireland', in J.H. Goldthorpe and C.T. Whelan (eds), *The Development of Industrial Society in Ireland*, Oxford: Oxford University Press.

Whelan, C.T., Layte, R., Maître, B. and Nolan, B., 'Poverty Dynamics: An Analysis of the 1994 and 1995 Waves of the European Community Household Panel Survey', *European Societies*, vol. 2, no. 3.

Whelan, C.T. and Hannan, D.F. (1999), 'Class Inequalities in Educational Attainment Among the Adult Population in the Republic of Ireland', *The Economic and Social Review*, vol. 30, no. 3:285-307.

Whelan, C.T., Layte R., Maître, B. and Nolan, B. (2000), 'Income Deprivation and Economic Strain: An Analysis of the European Community Household Panel', European Panel Analysis Group, Working Paper.

Whyte, J. (1973), 'Ireland: Politics without Social Bases', in R. Rose (ed.), *Electoral Behavior: A Comparative Handbook,* New York: Free Press.

Whyte, J.H. (1971), *Church and State in Modern Ireland: 1923-1970,* Dublin: Gill and Macmillan.

Wickham, J. (1989), 'The Over-Educated Engineer? The Work, Education and Careers of Irish Electronics Engineers', *IBAR: Journal of Irish Business and Administrative Research,* 10: 19-33.

Wijkman, P. (1990), 'Patterns of Production and Trade', in W. Wallace (ed.), *The Dynamics of European Integration,* London: Pinter Publishers.

Wilkinson, F. (1983), 'Productive Systems', *Cambridge Journal of Economics,* vol. 7: 413-429.

Williams, J. and Hughes, G. (1999), *National Survey of Vacancies in the Private Non-Agricultural Sector, 1998,* Dublin: ESRI.

Wilson, J. (1987), *The Truly Disadvantaged: The Inner City, the Underclass and Public Policy,* Chicago: University of Chicago Press.

Wilson, J. (1991), 'Studying Inner-City Dislocations', *American Sociological Review,* vol. 56, no. 1:1-14.

Wood, A., (1994), *North-South Trade, Employment and Inequality: Changing Fortunes in a Skill-driven World,* Oxford: Clarendon Press.

Woshinsky, O.H. (1995), *Culture and Politics,* Englewood Cliffs, New Jersey: Prentice-Hall.